5.00

Don Gresswell Ltd., London, N.21   Cat. No. 1208   DG 02242/71

Environmental Marketing Management

Meeting the green challenge

Environmental Marketing Management

Meeting the green challenge

Ken Peattie

Senior Lecturer in Strategic Management
Cardiff Business School

To my wife Sue, and our sons Alexander
and (doubly since he missed out last time) Mathew

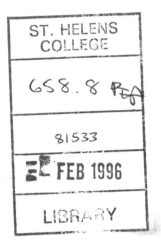
PITMAN PUBLISHING
128 Long Acre, London WC2E 9AN

A Division of Pearson Professional Limited

First published in Great Britain in 1995

© K Peattie 1995

ISBN 0 273 60279 9

British Library Cataloguing in Publication Data
A CIP catalogue record for this book can be obtained from the British Library

10 9 8 7 6 5 4 3 2 1

Typeset by Pantek Arts, Maidstone, Kent
Printed and bound in Great Britain

The Publishers' policy is to use paper manufactured from sustainable forests.

CONTENTS

...d? •
...challeng...
...ge for marketi...
...al Enterprises

Preface

greening of the organ...

Introduction • The corporate respons...
organisational dimensions of greening • ...
Quality Environmental Management • The
evolution of the green organisation • Marketing
within the green organisation • A new vision of
the organisation • *Case study: Volvo's drive to
be green*

environment

Introduction • A complex and changing interrelationship • Business in society • Society and
business in the environment • The physical
environment's impact on business and society •
Balancing the relationship – by market forces or
command and control?

Introduction • The new microenvironment –
same actors, different script? • Macroenviron-
mental forces • Responding to the marketing
environment • The future for environmental
marketing • *Case study: The hole in the sky*

Introduction • Strategy and holism •
Appropriateness • Competitiveness • Effective
decision making • Implementation • Success
factors for environmental marketing planning •
*Case study: Varta batteries – green
power in action*

PREFACE

Concern about the impact that commerce and consumption has on the natural environment upon which we all depend is not a new development. The Ancient Greeks philosophised about it; Elizabethan courtiers worried about it; Victorian industrialists with a paternalistic streak tried to do something to reduce it, or at least compensate for it; and Marxists mulled over the idea that if social unrest didn't undo capitalists first, then environmental degradation would get them in the end. The wave of environmental concern which has been lapping at the heels of those who practise or preach the gospels of management and marketing since the late 1980s is part of this long tradition of environmental concern, but is also different from it. This time the talk is not simply of how business activity should not damage the environment, increasingly it is about how environmental degradation is setting the agenda for the future of business. New environmental legislation, consumer demand for greener products or competitors seizing competitive advantage by improving their environmental performance can all force companies to confront the challenge of 'going green'. For some companies it has become unavoidable, for others it has been adopted as a moral and ethical issue and for others their response to the green challenge is rooted in pragmatic and forward-thinking self-interest. The reason for going green which is perhaps the most compelling, and yet is often overlooked, is that consumers all over the world consistently speak of their desire to purchase credible green products from demonstrably greener companies. If companies are not pursuing improved eco-performance as fast as constraints of technology, cost, competitiveness and consumer understanding allow, then any talk about being marketing-orientated is simply so much rhetoric.

Going green is, like any other significant strategic change, much easier to talk about than to actually do. A variety of problems confront the prospective green marketer, not least the constraints mentioned above. A new problem is the challenge of keeping track of the ever-increasing avalanche of new ideas, opinions and information relating to the environment (for those looking for signposts among the foothills of the growing mountain of green information I can recommend Wehrmeyer's 'Environmental References in Business' published by Greenleaf). Also a problem is that until recently a socio-environmental perspective on marketing and management lacked the theoretical and educational foundations which the dominant techno-economic approach to business enjoys. Courses and books on social and environmental issues exist within our business schools, but are often tucked away as options on the timetable or in obscure corners of the library. This book seeks to address these problems by pulling together many of the best threads of green management thinking from other writers, and attempting to weave them together to present a new perspective on marketing theory and practice. In this respect it is a complementary marketing book; in other words it seeks to present the socio-environmental perspectives on marketing which are not covered adequately by conventional marketing books (although it also presents some 'alternative' ideas to conventional marketing theory). This book will therefore not tell the prospective green marketer everything they need to know about marketing; instead it tells them the things that they are less likely to find in other books. In writing this book, for my own reference I have used Phillip Kotler's 'Marketing Management: Analysis, Planning, Implementation and Control' (which displays a truly biblical breadth of coverage) together with Michael Baker's 'Marketing Strategy and Management' (which I admire for the thoughtful depth of its discussion and sheer readability). I would recommend anyone who needs to understand conventional marketing more fully before examining it from a green perspective to begin with these two books.

Although the environmental crisis is not gaining the media coverage it did during the late 1980s in the wake of the discovery of the hole in the ozone layer or the Exxon Valdez disaster, it is never very far from the headlines, and the news is mostly disturbing. At the time of writing the Berlin climate conference is about to begin, and news that an ozone hole is now appearing over the Arctic or that ocean temperature rises in the Indian Ocean are causing massive coral reef dieback, or that melting glaciers in Greenland now threaten to disrupt the Gulfstream, are once again highlighting the fact that the costs as well as the benefits of our existing way of doing business and developing must be addressed. As a parent of small children I find that it is the potential damage to our children's health, freedom and prospects which is the most urgent reason for trying to reorientate our industrial systems into greater harmony with the environment. I was struck last summer by a news story from Germany that schoolchildren in Cologne had been banned from outdoor activities while low-level ozone concentrations were at a dangerous level. It seems ironic that, in a country which has made such social, economic and technical progress in the last few decades, a failure to develop in harmony with the environment meant that it was no longer safe for children to play outside.

The principle of sustainability is now seen as the 'answer' to these problems and it has been widely endorsed by the majority of the world's governments and most of its largest companies. Operationalising this principle is the greatest challenge facing politicians and managers as we move towards a new century and a new era. The quest for sustainability will be an arduous one, and achieving sustainability may not be enough; some authors are already arguing that we need to move beyond sustaining the environment and its ability to support human development, and look to begin restoring the environment back to some notion of 'full health'. This book does not deal with how to achieve sustainability, but how to move away from the current techno-economic paradigm and towards sustainability. It will hopefully contribute to the debate about moving the path of human commercial and social development away from its current unsustainable or 'terminal' path and towards a more environmentally-orientated approach to business, from which a truly sustainable and 'ecological' approach to business can develop. It is only a small contribution to what will become a massive reorientation of society, but small contributions are important. I was reminded of this fact recently at the theatre by the following speech:

> 'Well, I would consent to cutting wood when people really need it, but why destroy the forests? The Russian forests are literally groaning under the axe, millions of trees are being destroyed, the homes of animals and birds are being laid waste, the rivers are getting shallow and drying up, wonderful scenery is disappearing forever – and all because people are too lazy and stupid to stoop down and pick up fuel off the ground ...Anyone who can burn up all that beauty is a ..., who can destroy something that we cannot create, must be a barbarian incapable of reason. Man is endowed with reason and creative power so that he can increase what has been given him, but up to the present he's been destroying and not creating. There are fewer and fewer forests, the rivers are drying up, the wild creatures are almost exterminated, the climate is being ruined, and the land is getting poorer and more hideous every day ... (but) when I go walking by the woods that I saved from being cut down, or when I hear the rustling of the young trees I planted with my own hands, I'm conscious of the fact that the climate is to some extent in my power too, and that if mankind is happy in a thousand years' time, I'll be responsible for it even though only to very minute extent.'

These words could scarcely be more topical, and yet they were written some hundred years ago. They come from the play, Uncle Vania, written by Anton Chekhov, first published in 1897, which was an adaptation of his 'The Wood Demon' written in 1889. The speaker is Astrov, a doctor like Chekhov himself, and the character in the play who most reflects Chekhov's own mixture of idealistic optimism for the future and loathing of the selfishness and of the obsession with triviality of contemporary society.

Astrov's speech contains all the essential ingredients of the green challenge that confronts society today:

- an environment in crisis as a result of human activity;
- alternative, and less environmentally damaging, ways of living which are being neglected;
- a need to apply our powers of reason and creativity to find more sustainable ways of living;
- a recognition that the physical environment is, to some extent, in our control;
- a focus on the long term when considering the consequences of our actions;
- a belief that we can each play a small part in securing the future of mankind tomorrow.

This book is part of my own small attempt to develop reasonable and creative ideas for doing business in a way that will not destroy the planet. i have written it because, like Astrov, I want to believe that 'if mankind is happy in a thousand year's time, I'll be responsible for it even though only to a very minute extent'.

Ken Peattie
April 1995

ACKNOWLEDGEMENTS

I owe a number of people a large 'thank you' in relation to this project. To Sue, thank you for putting up with me doing this at a very illogical stage in our life together; thank you to my colleagues Pierre McDonagh and Andrea Prothero for their generosity with their ideas and information and also to Peter Wells for the ideas which were the foundation for table 1.3; to Karen and Sally for handling the bits of typing which were beyond my amateur touch-typing; to John Elkington and Julia Hailes at SustainAbility for providing me with access to so much valuable information; to the various companies that have provided me with information and with permissions to reproduce text and diagrams; to others who have provided me with useful information, particularly Moira Ratnayaka, and to my co-researchers and past and present students who have shown an interest in my work, and to the various people within Pitman who have helped the whole project along.

PART 1

An introduction to environmental marketing

CHAPTER 1

It's a small world

'Crises have both positive and negative characteristics. They can represent a threat to the status quo but at the same time can be seen as a symptom that something is wrong. They thus represent an opportunity to correct an imbalance and move on to a new level of organization.'
(Norman Myers, *The Gaia Atlas of Planet Management*)

INTRODUCTION – THE EARTH, A PLANET IN CRISIS?

In his book, *Market Led Strategic Change,* in typically thought-provoking fashion, Nigel Piercy poses the question 'What is there left to say about marketing?' Since it would be reasonably easy to sink a battleship simply by loading it up with every currently available marketing text, this is a very good question. This book explores marketing from an important, but often overlooked, perspective by examining the relationship of marketing to the environmental and social crisis that confronts mankind. Crisis might seem to be a strong and emotive word to use, but that does not make it inappropriate. Although there is much debate about the precise causes, extent and potential consequences of virtually every issue which concerns environmentalists, there is little doubt that the environment is in crisis. The environmental causes for concern include the following:

● Each spring a hole appears in the Antarctic ozone layer. It is now some 18 million square kilometres in size, or wide enough to swallow up all of Europe. This hole then dissipates, reducing ozone density around the globe. Ozone density over Europe during March 1994 was 10–20% below normal. Scientists estimate that each 1 per cent drop in ozone will increase the incidence of human skin cancer by between 3 and 6 per cent

(Jones 1987). At current rates of incidence two out of three Australians will develop some form of skin cancer during their lifetime. America's Environmental Protection Agency (EPA) predicts ozone depletion over northern mid-latitudes to peak at around 10 per cent, but more pessimistic predictions of between 18 and 30 per cent have been made.

● Levels of atmospheric carbon dioxide and other 'greenhouse' gases are increasing as a result of human activity and are predicted to create an increase in mean global temperature of between 1.5 and 4.5°C during the next century. The greenhouse effect is very difficult to prove due to the sheer complexity of global climate systems. The twelve years between 1980 and 1991, however, included the eight years with the highest global average temperatures recorded in the last century. The projected consequences could be catastrophic; one study estimates that, if current warming trends continue, by 2060 the disruption to agricultural systems would leave some 360 million people starving (Lean and Hinrichsen 1992).

● Out of an estimated 30 million species on earth, only about 1.5 million have been identified and catalogued, but only a few hundred thousand now exist in sufficient quantities to avoid being qualified as 'at risk'. Species loss is estimated at between 10 to over 100 every day, which makes the impact of human activity on earth unparalleled in terms of eliminating other species since the events that eliminated the dinosaurs some 65 million years ago (Meadows *et al* 1992).

● The margins of the oceans, on whose shores 70 per cent of the world's population live, and which provide around 50 per cent of the fish harvest, are becoming increasingly polluted. In the USA dead bottlenosed dolphins, so contaminated with chemicals such as PCBs (polychlorinated biphenyls) that they meet the government's criteria for a 'toxic waste hazard', have been washed up on beaches. The deaths of over 1000 dolphins, washed up on the shores of the Mediterranean between 1990 and 1993, have been linked to contamination from PCBs, industrial heavy metals, and the equivalent of 17 Exxon Valdez oil spills each year (World Resources Institute 1993).

● The limit of cultivable land is close to being reached. According to 1990 UN figures an estimated 6 to 7 million hectares of land are being lost annually due to soil erosion, while waterlogging, salinisation and alkalinisation damage accounts for another 1.5 million hectares each year (United Nations Population Fund 1990).

● Despite the global abundance of water, it is becoming increasingly scarce in many regions and increasingly difficult to use in many others because of pollution. While oil was the economic resource that occupied the thoughts of environmentalists and policy makers in the 1970s, it is water that is growing sufficiently short in many parts of the world to be viewed as the ultimate constraint on population and economic growth (Pearce 1990). In 1990 11 nations had water supplies per person below the level accepted as the bare minimum to allow economic growth (World Resources Institute 1992).

● Rainforests are a vital component in the world ecosystem and contain more than half of the earth's species, but half of these have already been destroyed. If the 1990 depletion rate of tropical rainforest is maintained, there will be none left before a child born in that year reaches 50. Pressure to continue rainforest liquidation is high since 60 per cent of the remaining forests are located in five of the world's most indebted countries. Pollution is causing damage to the trees that the logger's axe does not deplete. Western Europe

has long since lost virtually all of its primary forests, but the existing forests are mostly sustainably managed. Pollution damage to trees costs Europe at least $30 billion (14 billion ECUs) each year, which is three times the cost of the air pollution measures needed to protect them (Meadows *et al* 1992).

● The land which we inhabit is itself becoming increasingly polluted. Norway has discovered some 7000 sites contaminated by hazardous chemicals and metals. Government estimates for the cost of cleaning these up are between 2.25 and 4.5 billion ECUs (£3 billion and £6 billion) according to figures published in *Nordic Environment* in 1991.

THE EVOLUTION OF THE GREEN CHALLENGE

Concern about the impact of economic activity on the environment has been an issue of varying importance on society's agenda over many centuries. Taking Britain as an example, Lowe and Goyder (1983) identify four earlier high-water marks in environmental concern: the 1880s, the 1920s, the late 1950s and the early 1970s. These episodes can be viewed individually or seen as part of a gradual process of deepening environmental concern. Downes (1972) presented this process in the form of a cyclical model (*see* Fig. 1.1). The shortening intervals between the high-water marks suggest that this cycle is actually a tightening spiral of concern. Each high-water mark coincides with the end of a period of sustained economic growth. At such times the environmental consequences of growth will be most obvious, and the tendency to react against materialist values will be at its strongest. The first of these periods – the depression of the 1880s – was the first time the benefits of industrialisation were seriously challenged. As McCormick (1989) explains:

'The depression outlined the growing belief that industry was not necessarily the "Great Provider"; the source of the nation's economic and political power was now portrayed as destructive of the moral and social order, human health, traditional values, the physical environment, and natural beauty.'

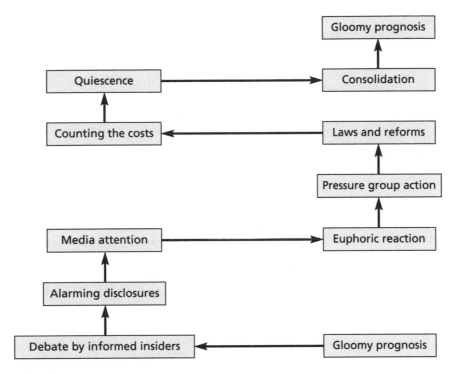

Fig. 1.1 The cycle of environmental concern
(adapted from Downes (1972))

The discipline of marketing is one of many that has had to come to terms with mounting environmental concern, first in the early 1970s and more recently in the late 1980s/early 1990s. The environmental high-water mark of the late 1950s coincided with the emergence of marketing as an explicit management philosophy and discipline. Both phenomena were by-products of 1950s' economic growth. Concern about the environment was a reaction to the unintended outcomes of rapid economic growth, while marketing was adopted by companies in an attempt to sustain the levels of growth that they had enjoyed. This lends a certain irony to the dramatic coming together of marketing and environmentalism that was to occur some 30 years later.

The early 1970s – the first environmental marketing challenge

The 'counterculture' of the late 1960s and early 1970s challenged many of the underlying values and assumptions within industrialised society. It was also a time when many of the effects of decades of environmental neglect began to manifest themselves; most dramatically in the form of rivers so polluted with toxins that they could be set alight. Predictions of an impending environmental crisis were widely debated and addressed as a significant item on the business agenda for the first time. This was largely prompted by the publication of books such as Paul Ehrlich's *The Population Bomb* in 1969 and the Club of Rome's *Limits to Growth* in 1971. These drew attention to the fact that we live in a finite world in which continuous and uncontrolled economic growth and population expansion would eventually exhaust the natural resources and systems upon which we all depend. The reaction of companies, governments and academics to such gloomy environmental prophecies varied widely. While one major oil company responded to *Limits To Growth* by attacking it publicly in a series of advertisements, another funded an annual sponsorship scheme for the best project which furthered the *Limits to Growth* work.

It is perhaps ironic that it was oil which dampened down the growing flames of environmental concern that *Limits to Growth* had sparked into life. Gloomy environmental predictions were generally forgotten in the economic chaos that followed the oil crises of 1973 and 1978, and the *Limits to Growth* predictions appeared to be discredited. Rising oil prices brought a whole new range of oil reserves into being. Previously these had not been counted as reserves because they were uneconomic to extract. Seeing a resource, whose supply was said to be limited, being almost magically expanded by the simple mechanism of rising prices produced a comforting illusion that the power of economics could overcome the physical constraints of the planet.

The mid-1980s – when greed was good

The oil crises had some other side-effects which conspired to make the *Limits to Growth* projections seem overly pessimistic. Rising oil prices slowed economic growth and forced businesses and homes to become more energy efficient. This in turn reduced pollution. The path of global economic development moved further away from the exponential and energy-intensive path which formed the most pessimistic (and therefore most widely publicised) projection of the *Limits to Growth* research. As we entered the euphoric economic growth of the mid-1980s, the predictions of the Club of Rome and the concept of the environment as a constraint seemed less and less relevant. The belief in free markets, and the freer the better, became widespread. In the 'go-for-growth' attitude of the mid-1980s all forms of regulation of business were vigorously attacked, particularly in the USA and the UK, in the name of liberating free enterprise. Environmental regulation, like all others, was attacked as a hindrance to economic development. This logic was reflected in UK Government publications with titles like the 1985 Department of the Environment White Paper, *Building Businesses Not Barriers*, and the 1986 Department of Employ-

ment White Paper, *Lifting The Burden*. Thankfully the majority of environmental legislation and energy-saving measures, which were the legacy of 1970s' environmental concern, remained in place. This ensured that the 1980s' growth in industrialised economies was not accompanied by a proportional rise in energy consumption and pollution.

The end of the 1980s – a new environmental marketing revolution

As the 1980s progressed, it became increasingly clear that, although the starkest predictions of resource depletion and population explosion had failed to materialise, all was far from well with the planet. A number of published analyses of the environment appeared during the late 1980s and early 1990s including the Worldwatch Institute's *State of the World* reports, the World Resources Institute's *World Resources* reports and *Environmental Almanacs*, the Organization for Economic Co-operation and Development's (OECD) *State of The Environment* report and the *Second Report of the United Nations Environment Programme*. These showed that according to a wide range of indicators, the environment was coming under increasing stress. Scientific evidence and environmentalist concern about ozone depletion, climatic instability linked to global warming, and satellite evidence of rapid rainforest destruction all drew the attention of the media. Concern among consumers and the electorate began to mount, with the inevitable consequence being that environmental issues moved from the fringes to the centre of the business and political agenda.

Concern about the environment increased steadily among the population of the industrialised world during the 1980s, to become the primary concern among 85 per cent of people according to the findings of Carson and Moulden (1991). This concern was not limited to industrialised nations. A 1988 Harris poll of 14 countries, which included nine less industrialised nations, found high levels of concern about environmental issues such as the pollution of drinking water and land. A majority of those interviewed in every country expected pollution levels to

Table 1.1 Environmental protection or economic growth?

Country	Percentage of people wishing their country to emphasise protecting the environment ahead of economic growth
India	43
Philippines	59
Turkey	43
Chile	63
Poland	58
Mexico	72
Brazil	71
Hungary	53
Uruguay	64
Russia	56
Republic of Korea	63
Ireland	65
Great Britain	56
Netherlands	58
Canada	68
West Germany	73
Denmark	77
USA	59
Finland	72
Norway	72
Japan	58
Switzerland	62

Source: Gallup (1992)

worsen and believed that deterioration of the environment would be detrimental to public health. Table 1.1 shows that the desire to emphasise environmental protection rather than economic growth was also strong among less industrialised countries.

For those in government or managing businesses it is tempting to view this phenomenon as 1970s' environmental concern revisited, and therefore something transitory. However, there are some significant differences between 1970s' environmentalism and what can be termed the green movement which emerged in the late 1980s. Many of these are summarised in Table 1.2 (Peattie and Charter 1994). One interesting difference is that the concern generated by *Limits To Growth* concentrated on the issue of shortages of economically important resource inputs. This was only one part of the *Limits to Growth* agenda, but it was the one that hit the headlines. It was

also the one which businesses and governments could debate most confidently on their 'home ground' of economics. The problems that emerged during the 1980s were not concerned with inputs, but dealt more with the other half of the *Limits to Growth* agenda – the effect on the environment of the outputs of indiscriminate economic growth. Global warming, ozone layer depletion, the effects of pollution on health and the loss of biodiversity are all output related. America faces no immediate shortage of key mineral resources, but it is rapidly running out of suitable places to put its waste (the USA is not short of space, but there are few sites for which a landfill is a socially acceptable, technically feasible and an economically attractive use of land). Between 1978 and 1988 the number of operating landfills declined from 14 000 to 5500 and is forecast to drop below 2000 by the year 2000. Another key difference is that the economic recession of the early 1990s did not dispel the environmental concern among consumers and the electorate, although it did reduce its rate of growth (Lynn 1991).

WHAT'S GONE WRONG AND WHAT'S IT GOT TO DO WITH MARKETING?

An effective response to any crisis requires an understanding of its causes. There are a wide range of organisations and individuals being blamed for environmental degradation. Marketing and marketers have been popular candidates along with capitalism, economics, industry, accountants, politicians, consumers, business schools, the Catholic Church and governments. A search for culprits and the allocation of blame are understandable, but ultimately meaningless and fruitless activities, as Joe Cappo explained in *Advertising Age*:

'Thanks to all of us the planet is in trouble. From the factory owner who spills poison into our drinking water, to the teenager who swills soda from a disposable bottle, to the primitive hunter who kills rhinoceroses (*sic*), we are all guilty of contributing to the world's growing environmental problems. But something new has been added in recent years to this striving for a better life. What we used to call progress

Table 1.2 The evolution of environmental concern

Factor	1970s' environmentalism	1990s' Green
Emphasis	On 'environmental' problems	On the underlying problems with our social, economic, technical or legal systems
Geographic focus	On local problems (e.g. pollution)	On global issues (e.g. global warming)
Identity	Closely linked to other anti-establishment causes	A separate movement embraced by many elements of 'the establishment'
Source of support	An intellectual élite, and those at the fringes of society	A broad base
Basis of campaigns	Used forecasts of exponential growth to predict future environmental problems (e.g. *Limits to Growth*)	Uses evidence of current environmental degradation (e.g. the hole in the ozone layer)
Attitude to businesses	Business is the problem. Generally adversarial	Businesses seen as part of the solution. More partnerships formed
Attitude to growth	Desire for zero growth	Desire for sustainable growth
View of environment/business interaction	Focused on negative effects of business activity on the environment	Focuses on the dynamic interrelationship between business society and the environment

is being interrupted by a worldwide revolution. In this case, the revolutionaries are consumers, and their battle cry is for products and services that will preserve a cleaner, healthier, richer environment for themselves and their children.'

The dominance of economics and technology

Society, in its present form and on its current trajectory of development, cannot be sustained indefinitely. The physical environment has limited resources and a limited capacity to absorb pollution and waste. The underlying cause of society's current unsustainability relates to the way in which economics and technology have come to dominate our thinking about business and the environment. To quote for a moment from the Green Party:

'Relentless pursuit of GNP is leading to catastrophic and perhaps permanent deterioration of our environment . . . Political decisions should reflect a far deeper awareness of our need to live in harmony with the environment than industrial nations have yet allowed . . . It is the lack of this perspective that has permitted industrial nations to measure their success or failure in terms of increasing material consumption alone, even though the pursuit of such consumption is now steadily choking the planet. It has also led us increasingly to regard domestic social problems in merely technical terms – a process which has stimulated social alienation and decay . . . Other values – personal, social, and even religious – have been forced to yield before an overwhelmingly economic and technical view of things.'

Conventional marketing within industry is very much a product of this predominantly techno-economic perspective. This has created what Johnson (1991) characterises as a 'grey' culture

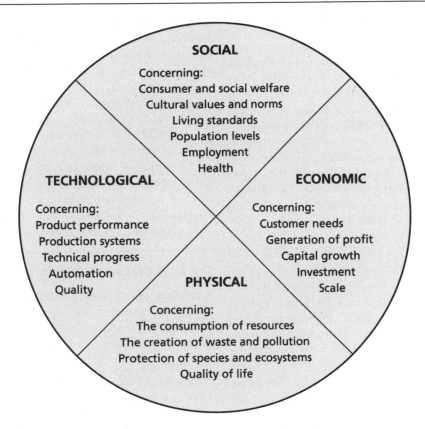

Fig. 1.2 The STEP Framework – a balanced view of the business agenda

which is not sustainable and is therefore 'terminal'. To transform this into a 'green', sustainable culture, there is a need to balance consideration of the economic and technical impacts and aspects of businesses with understanding of their social and physical implications. The STEP Framework presented in Fig. 1.2 presents an approach to marketing in which the conventional techno-economic paradigm is complemented by the addition of a socio-environmental perspective. In the 1970s concern about the physical environment and about the social impacts of business gave rise to both 'ecological marketing' and 'societal marketing'. The oil crises of the 1970s took some of the momentum out of the societal marketing movement, but it did not prevent it from maturing into a sub-discipline of marketing represented by a substantial body of theory and backed up by a range of tools, techniques and practical examples to aid the marketer wishing to tackle the social quadrant of the STEP Framework. Ecological marketing fared less well and has yet to develop into a discipline with the depth to enable marketing practitioners and academics to help steer businesses towards a more environmentally sustainable future. This book is part of the movement to fill in the missing environmental quadrant in the STEP Framework. Although social issues are just as important as environmental issues in the greening of business, to prevent the wheel of societal marketing from being 'reinvented' it will not be a major focus of this book. However, since environmental and social issues are essentially indivisible, social issues will make regular appearances.

The neglected importance of the physical environment

The environment's role in business is profoundly obvious, but easy to overlook. It provides every business with its inputs, and a destination for all its outputs. It also provides a business with the physical space within which its operations occur. For businesses dealing directly with environmental resources, such as agriculture, tourism or oil (three of the world's largest industries) the importance of the physical environment has always been apparent. Among others, when the physical environment was discussed, it was usually in geographic terms regarding the relative locations of customers, producers and material inputs or in economic terms with 'land' as a factor of production. Until recently, for many businesses the environment merely formed a backdrop against which the story of economic, technological and social progress unfolded. The green challenge involves taking a fresh and physical view of the world; it is about businesses recognising that the world does not simply consist of the bland economic concept of 'land', but is made up of many ecosystems, bioregions and of a diverse range of flora and fauna which are important whether or not a market exists for them.

A green perspective also involves viewing people as physical, as well as social and economic, entities. One of the reasons that humankind's management of the planet has gone so badly astray is that we tend to deny or forget that we are, among other things, one species of mammal. Humankind is subject to the forces of evolution, just as much as any other species. Virtually all of our physical and psychological traits can be explained in terms of the environment and the survival needs of our ancestors. This has been studied for many years in the fields of anthropology and human ecology, and popularised through books such as Desmond Morris's *The Human Animal*. For some 99 per cent of humankind's existence, 99 per cent of people lived a relatively 'natural' existence as hunter–gatherers or primary growers and pastoralists. What could be termed the 'modern western' lifestyle of industrialised countries offers us many wonderful things and leaves us free from the threat of many diseases or environmental threats which would have blighted the lives of our ancestors. It is not a life that our minds or bodies are naturally suited to, however, since evolutionary change cannot respond that rapidly. Many people follow a sedentary lifestyle which impairs their health, eat a diet which is too refined and rich in fats and sugars, and endure levels of stress which affect their mental health and happiness. Twentieth-century life has freed many people from what could be termed the 'cruelty' of nature, but in losing touch with nature, society has also abandoned a range of 'real' values and sources of satisfaction.

The facts that economics forgot

A reliance on an economic approach to managing businesses, societies and the planet would be less of a problem if we had perfected economic theory. Woods (1991) labels neo-classical economics:

'an "IF" doctrine: IF there are no costs of production not reflected in price . . . IF competition is perfectly free . . . IF information is full, accurate and readily available . . . IF there are no political exigencies such as legal guarantees of state control over certain aspects of institutional life . . . IF there are no unresolved concerns for human rights or social justice . . . IF, IF, IF.'

Conventional economics certainly demonstrates some worrying shortcomings in relation to the physical environment.

● It assumes that the physical environment imposes no limit on economic activity.

● It treats environmental and social damage caused by business activity as 'externalities' which do not directly affect the operation of the market and the decision makers within it.

● It places no value on anything for which a market does not exist. Therefore stratospheric ozone is economically worthless, despite the fact that the majority of life on earth depends on it as a shield from harmful ultraviolet radiation.

● It undervalues land (which includes all natural resources in economics) compared to human labour and financial capital. Many less industrialised countries are liquidising their environmental capital in exchange for financial capital from industrialised countries in a way which appears beneficial because the only cost attached to obtaining the resources is the cost of extraction.

● As Schumacher (1973) points out, prior to industrialisation humankind lived on the income from nature, but industrialisation led humankind to live by 'cashing in' nature's capital. Conventional economics encourages the destruction of the environment because it fails to distinguish between resource capital and income.

● For a science that is supposed to encompass 'the everyday business of life' for humankind,

economics ignores a great many things. Gray (1990) points out that 'the vast majority of the biosphere is . . . not covered by price (air, water, common land, habitat, species, ozone layers, etc.).' Without a price these factors exist outside of economics, and since progress is measured in economic terms, their use and degradation have been invisible to businesses, companies and consumers even though they may have been very evident to environmentalists and people as citizens. Henderson's (1991) concept of an informal non-monetary 'love economy' which underpins (and heavily subsidises) the formal monetary economy is detailed in Fig. 1.3.

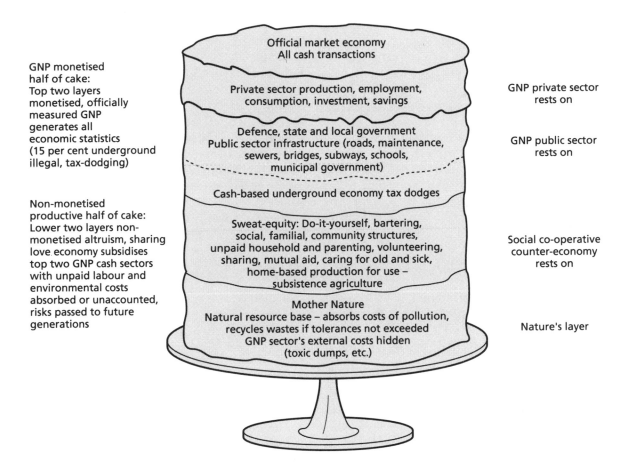

Fig. 1.3 The whole economic cake
(Source: Henderson (1991))

Wrong goalposts, wrong yardstick?

The economically dominated approach to management and government emphasises growth (an increase in things) rather than development (an improvement in things). The assumption which underpins the management of companies and economies is that growth should be maximised. Economic growth has been pursued relentlessly over recent decades because of the assumption that it will help to solve society's problems. As Senge (1990) notes:

'For most American business people the best rate of growth is fast, faster, fastest. Yet virtually all natural systems, from ecosystems to animals to organizations, have intrinsically optimal rates of growth. The optimal rate is far less than the fastest possible growth.'

The assumption that economic growth will lead to an improvement in other aspects of society, such as the elimination of poverty and an improvement in health indicators like child mortality is an ill founded one. During the 1980s there was considerable economic growth, but poverty (measured as relative to median income levels) in North America and much of Europe actually increased (McFate 1991). America represents many people's idea of the success of free markets in creating wealth, but according to figures from the US Census Bureau the mean income of the poorest 20 per cent of families fell during the 1970s and 1980s, and by 1990 20.6 per cent of all American children were living in poverty. The benefits of 'trickle-down economics' barely even reached a trickle for many people. In terms of child mortality, no correlation exists between mortality rates and economic living standards, but a very strong correlation exists between mortality rates and rates of female literacy and use of contraception (WRI 1992).

Since 1929, the method of measuring the economic growth which all societies aspire to create, has been Gross National Product (GNP). GNP is used as a surrogate measure for a society's affluence and welfare. It is a measure of total economic activity and because of this it makes no distinction between activities which benefit society (development) and those which do not (the costs of renewal). Therefore a company which creates pollution and then pays to have it cleaned up is boosting GNP. By contrast a company which invents a new process which removes that pollution and also saves energy would reduce GNP making everyone economically 'worse off'. GNP as a measure creates some strange situations whereby countries are economically better off in the short term by declaring war upon a neighbour, and where oil spills such as the Exxon Valdez provide an enormous 'boost' to the economy. An economic system in which every fire, flood, pollution disaster, theft and murder makes a contribution to society's principal objective would not appear to be operating in the best interest of society or the environment.

Soft curves, hard realities

One of the comforting things about economics is that there always appears to be room for mistakes to be corrected. Cairncross (1991) among others suggests that market mechanisms will cause prices of finite materials to rise if their supply runs short, which will reduce demand and slow consumption. This idea works better in theory than in practice. It assumes that the market is a free one in which prices are free to rise in relation to supply as well as demand. Furthermore, economic theory does not recognise ecological distinctions between resources. If one poor country's main resource is wood, in the shape of a certain species of tree, the last specimen of that species will not be priceless in the face of a massive global timber supply. If readers are tempted to think that rarity value will ensure the survival of the tree because it will become of interest to collectors, it is worth remembering that rarity value did not save the dodo (an ecological celebrity of its day) and hundreds of thousands of other species. Since the majority of species have no name, they are unlikely to have any form of price tag despite their rarity value.

Alternatively, the reader might query the harm of losing one species of tree with nothing sufficiently special about it to make it economic to either protect or grow commercially. The Pacific Yew (Taxus brevifolia) was just such a tree. It was usually cut down by loggers in the forests of

North Western America who sought to get at more valuable trees such as the Douglas Fir. The discarded yews were then burnt because it was not even economic to haul the wood away. The loggers who reduced it down to only a few clumps nicknamed it the 'trash tree'. Then, in 1991, as the species teetered on the brink of extinction, completed trials of Taxol, a new drug derived from chemicals in the tree's bark, showed it capable of attacking cancers which had proved otherwise drug resistant. Taxol entered the US market in 1992 and has since treated thousands of women with ovarian cancer, a disease which kills over 4000 women each year in the UK alone. Taxol has been described by scientists as the most important discovery in 15 years in the fight against cancer, but it almost never happened because one species of tree had no apparent economic value.

A final point about the idea that people simply switch resources as they become scarce is that it assumes that people are willing to change their behaviour. Consider fishermen in pursuit of the blue fin tuna in the South Pacific: as tuna stocks became depleted, and the costs of catching fish rose, did they simply trade in their fishing boats and become economists? No, they travelled further in their fishing trips using longer nets with smaller mesh sizes. All over the world consumers are offered a range of other food products to choose from and will not accept ever-increasing fish prices, and since farmed fish also help to keep the price down, the fisherman has little choice but to put ever-increasing effort into exploiting a dwindling natural resource.

Intuitively one would expect an industry to manage its resources sustainably to ensure its own survival. This intuition assumes a long-term perspective that is often missing in the business world of short-term pressures. It also assumes that those who own an industry are concerned about its long-term survival. Meadows *et al* (1992) relate the following anecdote:

'Ecologist Paul Ehrlich once expressed surprise to a Japanese journalist that the Japanese whaling industry would exterminate the very source of its wealth. The journalist replied "You are thinking of the whaling industry as an organization that is interested in maintaining whales; actually it is better viewed as a huge quantity of (financial) capital attempting to earn the highest possible return. If it can exterminate whales in ten years and make a 15 per cent profit, but it could only make 10 per cent with a sustainable harvest, then it will exterminate them in ten years. After that, the money will be moved to exterminating some other resource."'

The smooth-curve, continuous functions which symbolise economic theory make every action appear reversible. Ecological systems, unlike market economics, operate on a threshold principle (although it is worth noting that there is some debate about this among environmental systems theorists). The system will flex and self-correct in the face of any external pressure for as long as possible in an effort to maintain system stability. Eventually a point will be reached where the system can no longer cope, a threshold is crossed and the system collapses, sometimes irrevocably. In the case of rainforest land, once the shading and water-retaining properties of the trees are removed, desertification processes set in rapidly. This makes lost areas of rainforest virtually impossible to restore after a short period. An ecosystem is like a ten-pound note. If you tear it in half, you do not have anything in either hand worth five pounds. Instead you have an urgent need for sticky tape.

A selfish science

Individualism is central to economic theory and also to marketing. In economics, the 'invisible hand' of self-interest supposedly guides the market towards the most efficient and effective allocation of resources. Goldsmith (1993) attacks the market mechanism as one that 'is totally blind to all biological, social, ecological, aesthetic and moral considerations of any sort, and that only responds to the shortest-term economic considerations'. Stead and Stead (1992) in commenting on the effects of the extreme individualism which dominates economic theory quote Herman Daly's assertion that such individualism actually represents 'the invisible foot that kicks the heck out of the common good'. Economic man is said to be motivated primarily by self-interest, and yet evidence exists all around us of people behaving in an altruistic manner. At the time of writing, the crisis in Rwanda is centre stage in world news coverage. The details emerging of the atrocities that have occurred to destroy the country from within, the heroism of aid organisations such as Médecin Sans Frontières, and the volume of aid donated by ordinary citizens around the world make the economic assumption that self-interest governs the everyday business of humankind appear bizarre.

It is curious that the individualism which underpins economic theory is often presented as 'natural' and supported by rather misapplied Darwinian notions of 'the survival of the fittest'. Altruism and co-operation by contrast are viewed as something unnatural and a product of 'civilisation'. In fact, the reverse may be true. The altruism which many people exhibit is perhaps less a function of civilisation and more deeply connected to our natural instincts. Other species of mammal, and primates in particular, demonstrate altruistic instincts, for example by putting themselves in danger to defend the offspring of other adults. Such behaviour is connected to a deeper drive to ensure the continuance of the social group and even the species, rather than the selfish need for self-protection and the continuance of the individual's genes. It is the transformation of a tribal species into a global community in which individualism and individual freedom is prized above the common good which is perhaps unnatural.

As a result of the obvious problems that conventional economics and accountancy practices have had in coping with the realities of the physical environment, new economic perspectives are now emerging to challenge conventional theory. Organisations such as The Other Economic Summit and the London Environmental Economics Centre are working to develop new economic concepts and models which integrate the environment into economic thinking. In Germany a ten-year project has been established to devise a new economic measure to replace GNP – Gross Ecological Product (GEP). This mirrors traditional economics and accounting approaches but in a way that incorporates environmental criteria.

Delocalisation – industrialisation and physical separation

In traditional, pre-industrial societies, production and consumption were mostly a local affair. Goods and services were tailored to meet the needs of local customers, often on an individual basis. Any surpluses were used for trade. With industrialisation the source of production and the consumer became increasingly distanced from one another. Techniques of mass production replaced traditional craftsmanship, and individual consumers merged into new and unfamiliar mass markets. This became one of the driving forces behind the emergence of marketing, a formal management discipline which aimed to restore producers back to a situation where they were 'close to the customer', psychologically if not physically. Industrial society created consumers who were ignorant about how products were produced, whereas in village life the consequences of production were obvious. It also allowed those responsible for production to live away from the site of production so that it was no longer in their 'back yard'. In the northern towns of Victorian Britain, the mansions of the factory owners were built above the 'smoke line'. The consequences of the twentieth century's environmental degradation, such as the thinning ozone layer and the presence of pesticides in our food, cannot be so easily avoided.

Reductionalism

Reductionalism has become a central pillar of academic research and of management practice. The scientific method which dominates modern academic theory in a wide range of disciplines is highly reductionalist in its approach. Schumacher (1973), in explaining why economic activity has become so environmentally hostile, listed as one of six underlying misconceived ideas the principle that 'valid knowledge can be attained only through the methods of the natural sciences'.

In management practice Duck (1993) suggests that companies facing challenges tend to cope by using a reductionalist approach which breaks complex problems down into simpler components. This works well for dealing with algebraic problems, but less well within organisations with their own complex internal 'ecology'. Duck suggests that such a reductionalist approach is tempting for the following reasons.

● It appears to resolve much of the complexity and ambiguity that accompanies organisational change.

● It allows managers to spread responsibility for dealing with problems around.

● It creates a checklist of things to do in each component area. Many of these checklist tasks, when implemented, will create reassuringly real and measurable improvements.

Compartmentalisation

A related concept to reductionalism is compartmentalisation, the tendency to erect artificial barriers between the elements of holistic systems defined through reductionalism. Companies are compartmentalised through the definition of organisational structure, and the distribution of resources through budgets assigned to individual tasks or functions. These budgets are fiercely defended by each budget holder in the face of potential reductions or transfers, regardless of the overall costs and benefits of the changes.

The same effect applies at the level of the economy or society as a whole. Compartmentalisation allows the actions of one company to be considered without regard to the whole economy. For example, in *Liberation Management* Tom Peters extols the virtues of ABB's restructuring programme which maintained levels of customer service and profitability while drastically cutting the number of corporate staff from 4000 to 200. The implication is that every company could and should follow suit. But what if they did? The mass unemployment involved would tip the entire economy into a massive recession and damage the interests of the new-look ABB as much as everybody else.

At a societal level, many proposed traffic-calming schemes in the UK have been rejected or shelved on the basis of costs and limited budgets. This is despite the fact that the sums involved will be a fraction of the costs in health care and loss of earnings of those individuals who will be involved

in accidents because of the lack of traffic-calming measures. Pollution prevention measures are also rejected as too expensive, even though the much greater costs to the forestry industry in terms of tree damage must be met. It is a curious truth that the costs of prevention are usually seen as optional and therefore avoidable or postponable, while the costs of repairing any damage are seen as a necessity.

An understanding of the environment and environmental problems has also been hampered by the reductionalist and fragmented approach. As Avernous (1991) states:

'Exposure to pollutants has, indeed, been studied and treated in a compartmentalised manner. Yet there is growing evidence that multiple exposure to a variety of contaminants through the simple actions of eating, drinking water and breathing may also produce unsuspected health difficulties. The traditional approach for dealing with problems in only one medium at a time, such as air or water . . ., (may) have unwanted effects – the transfer of pollution from one medium to another, for instance.'

Scale

Economics has traditionally promoted a 'big is beautiful' mentality within business thinking because of the perceived advantages provided by economies of scale. One underlying assumption in grey growth is that technological advances and increasing economies of scale will make products more affordable for people. Davis (1991) challenged this by contrasting 1957 prices with 1987 prices (adjusted for inflation) for a range of goods from houses to bananas. Although household goods such as washing machines and televisions had experienced a significant reduction in real prices, the reverse trend was true for houses and many foodstuffs – two of the most important of all household expenditures. Davis speculates that the gains in productivity that scale efficiencies and technology have brought, have been offset by the complexities of distribution and the overheads associated with the increasing scale of business enterprises.

The increasing scale of businesses has wider implications beyond the unit costs of goods.

Etzioni (1988) points out that economic exchanges rarely take place among equals and that one party usually has a power advantage over another which can distort the operation of the market. As the size of companies increases, so their ability to influence consumers, communities and governments increases. Such power can be abused and business history is littered with examples of large companies using their economic power for ends which benefit neither the consumer, the community or the environment. An interesting example comes from the 1930s when the General Motors' salesforce was having difficulties selling its new line of petrol-engined buses. The company's response was systematically to buy up and close down as many electric tram and bus companies as it could. The strategy worked, although GM was later fined a token $5000 for criminal conspiracy, and its treasurer was fined a token $1 for his part in dismantling Los Angeles' $100 million streetcar system (Carvioner 1977). The purchasing power of large companies can be such that it forces suppliers to accept business at below their target level of profitability. To reach their profit targets, suppliers must arrange their pricing structures in ways which allow the high volume/low margin business from big companies to be subsidised by low volume/high margin business from small companies. As Davis (1991) notes, this trend disguises the real internal operating efficiency of large and small enterprises. Legislative limits on volume discounts would be necessary to 'level the playing field' between large and small companies.

The pursuit of economies of scale has been important in the growth and structuring of organisations during the industrial era. For the technical aspects of a production system, the principle of economies of scale appears to hold true. It is more cost effective to operate one big furnace, or to use one large truck than to operate two small ones. In the social, environmental and strategic dimensions of a business, however, there can be considerable diseconomies of scale. Strategically, a single truck or furnace may be economic to operate, but by placing 'all its eggs in one basket' it can make the company vulnerable to breakdowns and problems of inflexibility. There is no good having one huge truck if two consignments need to go in different directions at the same time. Socially, as organisations become larger they tend to ossify and become bureaucratic and conservative. Although increasing size is meant to produce economies in terms of shared overheads between Strategic Business Units (SBUs), in practice it tends to produce alienation, internal competition and cost-cutting through administrative amalgamations.

Macho-management – too much testosterone?

Another view of the reasons behind the destruction of the environment is that the worlds of politics and business are still very much male-dominated, and that male values and behaviour are intrinsically environmentally hostile. Hofstede (1983) defined cultures that have highly 'masculine' values as stressing performance, making money, achieving visible results and a 'big is beautiful' philosophy. Since many of these are typically achieved at the expense of the environment, masculine cultures (which prevail in most companies) would seem 'inherently unfriendly to the environment' (McIntyre et al 1992). According to Dossi (1992):

'Our world – the world of rational decisions, technical progress, labour division and industrial production – is a world shaped by male values and visions. It has favoured rational knowledge over intuitive wisdom, science over religion, competition over co-operation. Its social and political structures are based on abstraction and quantification.'

She goes on to outline an emerging 'feminine' style of management based on flexibility, consensus, caring, co-operation, the sharing of information and the nurturing of relationships. These qualities, she further notes, were scorned by the traditional 'male' approach until they proved to be key factors in the success of Japanese companies. However, the fact that these Japanese companies developed these qualities without significantly greater female management input suggests that the labelling of such characteristics as either masculine or feminine is somewhat misleading.

Making generalisations on the basis of gender are always flawed, and to some extent run contrary to the spirit of the green movement and its emphasis on individuality. However, women managers are demonstrably more concerned about environmental issues (Charter 1990a) and their progression beyond the 'glass ceiling' should accelerate the greening process. The Body Shop's status as one among relatively few large companies run by a woman and also a pioneer in terms of green excellence, certainly bolsters the intuitive logic in the idea that women would make better stewards of our world than men.

Misplaced techno-optimism

Our technical ability to change the environment has outstripped our intellectual and philosophical ability to understand and appreciate the systems of which it consists. The technological focus within society has led to an optimistic belief that more and better technology will always overcome environmental problems. This was reflected in the conviction of Kahn *et al* (1976) that humankind's ingenuity will overcome problems of resource scarcity.

The scientific tradition is firmly steeped in a view of mankind fighting against nature, with technology forming mankind's weaponry (the male generalisation is used here because, as Midgely (1992) points out, this particular war is usually symbolised by a masculine science and technology in conflict with a capricious feminine natural world). Early civilisations tended to revere nature. The western scientific tradition that emerged during the eighteenth century viewed nature as something which needed to be overcome and enslaved. Thus Boyle wrote:

'Nature . . . is represented as a kind of goddess, whose power may be a little less than boundless . . . the veneration wherewith men are imbued for what they call nature, has been a discouraging impediment to the empire of man over the inferior creatures of God.'

Bacon called upon

'the true sons of knowledge to overcome Nature in action . . . to conquer and subdue nature, to shake her to her foundations.'

This earliest of world wars has been continuing ever since, and should humankind emerge as the eventual victor, it will also join a growing range of other species on the casualty list.

Many serious ecologists reject the concept of environmental salvation through technological advances. Instead they place an emphasis on changing our lifestyles and in many cases returning to more traditional, smaller scale and less environmentally hostile technologies. However, it would seem a missed opportunity to insist that technology should roll back to the best of traditional technologies when it may also be able to move forward to claim the benefits of new technologies which innovate in harmony with the environment. As Midgely (1992) puts it:

'Most of us have begun to see that the party is over. The planet is in deep trouble; we had better concentrate on bailing it out . . . we need all the help we can get from our scientists in reaching a more realistic attitude to the physical world we live in.'

The idea that science will overcome all environmental problems has increasingly been challenged in recent years, not just by environmentalists, but by the scientific community itself. Even the relatively conservative and technologically optimistic Royal Society of London and the US National Academy of Sciences announced in a joint statement:

'If current predictions of population growth prove accurate and patterns of human activity on the planet remain unchanged, science and technology may not be able to prevent either irreversible degradation of the environment or continued poverty for much of the world . . . The future of the planet is in the balance.'

CRISIS, WHAT CRISIS?

Inevitably there are those who are sceptical about the environmental crisis and caution against overreaction. Any attack on the dominant techno-economic paradigm is unlikely to succeed without a fight, when many vested interests and reputations are at stake. The view that technology and economics will prevail is still strongly endorsed by many people. Popoff (1990) stresses that our perception of environmental problems has increased because our ability to detect them has increased, with measurement techniques capable of detecting contamination at concentrations as low as one part per quadrillion (the equivalent of finding a postage stamp in an area the size of Texas). He also suggests that environmentalists have emphasised the negative effects of technology while overlooking its many benefits and the many risks posed by the natural world. It is ironic that he cites the control of malaria through DDT as a success story of technology overcoming a threat from nature. In fact in 1990 there were 107 million clinical cases of malaria with around one million deaths. In sub-Saharan Africa 50 per cent of the population is infected, and 40 per cent of the world's population is classified as at risk from the disease (WRI 1992). More worryingly, the mosquitos that carry the disease are becoming increasingly resistant to the pesticides used to combat them, and the disease itself has evolved to resist a succession of drugs.

Singer (1992) stresses:

'a major achievement of technology has been the development of natural resources, essential for economic growth and increased standard of living. Individual resources may become depleted but substitutes have always become available . . . the real price of every commodity has been falling, measured in terms of average wage (which) totally destroys the Malthusian mirage.'

It is interesting that falling commodity prices are promoted here as a virtue, when they have done so much to depress standards of living and hamper development in less industrialised countries. It is also unclear how technology will find a substitute for non-market resources such as soil, rainforests, stratospheric ozone or genetic diversity.

Singer also attacks the idea that there is a scientific consensus about global warming, describing the scientific evidence as inconclusive and the computer models that predict rising sea levels as inadequate. The rational scientific approach to the environment tends to rely on 'proof' of any phenomenon before taking remedial or preventative action. Baden (1992) reinforces this view by attacking the 'do-no-harm' principle proposed by

environmentalists, insisting that the burden of proof should remain in favour of business who should not have to prove that products are safe. According to the *Brundtland Report* (World Commission on Environment and Development 1987), some 65 000 industrial chemicals are in regular use, while toxicity data is available on less than 1 per cent of these. Over 1000 new chemicals are introduced each year, 80 per cent of which are not tested for toxicity. By not requiring businesses to prove that these are safe, society is involved in a game of environmental 'Russian Roulette'. A reliance on scientific proof has often provided an excuse for procrastination and inaction among businesses and governments. Schmidheiny (1992), in describing the first meeting of the 50 business leaders who comprise the Business Council for Sustainable Development, talks of their initial problems saying:

'We focused on the great uncertainties associated with climate change, ozone depletion, deforestation, loss of genetic diversity, effects of toxic chemicals, rapidly growing populations and the like. If the nature of the problem is so imprecise, how could a group of business people formulate a precise response? One member suggested we issue a call for more research and be done with it.'

Singer's requirements for proof would also require many years of research and the further refinement of scientific theories and computer models before decisions or actions could be taken. Meanwhile the circumstantial evidence pointing to a warming planet continues to mount. The 1980s contained six out of seven hottest years since records began. A five year moving average of global temperature shows that over the last 100 years, global mean temperature has risen by almost 1°C. 1994 witnessed freak hot weather conditions across much of the Northern Hemisphere. These facts may not prove that global warming is occuring, however, they would suggest that it would be prudent to take precautions against global warming until we have proof that it is not.

The case of CFCs and the ozone layer is instructive when considering the lack of conclusive proof about global warming, and the problems of allowing the burden of proof to rely on those concerned with the environment to prove that products are harmful. The damage being caused to stratospheric ozone by CFC-borne chlorine released into the atmosphere was predicted in 1974, yet it was not until 1984 that the ozone hole was detected. It took a further three years to gather sufficient 'proof' of CFCs' guilt to prompt concerted international action to tackle the problem. Since CFCs take 15 years to make their way from the earth's surface to the stratosphere, the improvements made once the case was proven will not be felt until beyond the year 2000. The fact that CFC levels are currently falling reflects the fact that the USA banned CFC-driven aerosols in 1978 (long before any case was proven) triggering a 25 per cent drop in global CFC manufacture.

There are several other arguments used to counter the emphasis on the environmental crisis.

● *How many lives will be saved?* Baden (1992) ridicules the Environmental Protection Agency's listing of wood preservatives as hazardous waste as expecting to cost $5.7 trillion (2.7 trillion ECUs) per life saved. Environmental protection is based on many things other than protecting the quantity of human life. Many pollutants damage ecosystems in the long term or reduce the quality of human life through low-level poisoning, as is the case with lead. The use of loss of human life to judge the significance of environmental degradation can be likened to jumping off a skyscraper and mentally pausing half-way down to think, 'Well, no harm done yet'. If business law was organised on the 'lives saved per ECU' principle, companies would find the business environment becoming a great deal less stable.

● *Economic growth must come before environmental protection.* Baden suggests that major environmental problems in terms of immediate threats to economic and human health, rank far below other problems. He argues that poverty exacerbated by population expansion is the problem and that 'with economic progress nations have the money and the technology, and develop the preferences, to allocate resources to environmental protection'. This assumes that economic and human health are not linked to the state of the environment, and overlooks the fact that some 40 years of concentration on economic growth has not eradicated the poverty which apparently prevents environmental protection. How many more years of economic growth would be needed? Another 40?

● *Environmentalists do not represent the public interest.* Baden (1992) characterises environmentalists as a special interest group who seek costly and inefficient public regulations by lobbying, capitalising on photo opportunities of environmental destruction and acting as 'crisis entrepreneurs' in stoking public fears for the benefit of their own coffers rather than as 'selfless seekers of the environment'. These are interesting arguments. On the costs of environmental legislation, Baden criticises the 'waste' of the transaction costs and lawyers' fees associated with US Superfund projects. Environmentally speaking this is a waste, yet employing lawyers contributes to exactly the form of economic growth which he earlier argued was so important as a precondition for environmental protection. It is also caused by companies using the legal process to fight against meeting their responsibilities for cleaning up environmental damage. The point about environmental groups not representing the public interest prompts the question, 'Who does?' The actions of governments are usually dominated by electoral time-frames and outcomes more than any concept of long-term societal good. While companies, for all their rhetoric about social respon- sibility, are unlikely to sacrifice the interests of their managers, shareholders or customers in the name of society's best interest. Environmental groups typically represent more people in terms of paying members than political parties, trade unions or other representative groups. In the UK, the National Trust and the Royal Society for the Protection of Birds each have more paid up members than any political party (McIntosh 1990).

● *What about the less industrialised countries?* Another argument against increasing environmental protection is that much of the environment that needs to be protected is in less industrialised countries who are rich in environmental capital but need to exploit it to develop economically. As

Baden puts it, 'Worrying about global warming is a luxury that many developing nations feel they cannot afford'. It is curious to see politicians, economists and industrialists vigorously opposing environmental protection on this basis when they have been quite happy to preside over decades of trade terms which have proved disadvantageous to these countries. The assumption that the less industrialised countries were benefiting from the grey economic approach is not borne out by the facts. During the 1980s, a decade famous for its economic growth, the 40 poorest countries (which contain one sixth of the world's population) experienced reductions in per capita income (Brown 1992). It is also somewhat presumptuous of those in industrialised countries to prescribe particular patterns of economic development for less industrialised countries. Consumers and citizens in less industrialised countries have also been shown to favour environmental protection of the environment over economic development (whose benefits rarely seem to accrue to the masses). Since a greater proportion of people in less industrialised countries make a living directly from the environment, environmental protection would appear to be a more important priority than economic growth modelled on western technologies and economic theories.

A TURNING POINT

Environmental problems, and the reasons behind them, tend to make depressing reading, and people's reaction to them varies. Pessimists and fatalists may conclude that there is little left to do but to enjoy what is left, before it is gone for ever. Optimists may prefer to concentrate on the many vast and unspoilt areas of the natural world, and the apparent robustness of natural systems (which anyone who has tried to prevent weeds from emerging within a paved area can testify to) and to conclude that nature, perhaps aided by technological innovations, will prevail and that the planet will recover. The problems that result from adopting either of these positions is neatly illustrated by an anecdote from *Die Zeit* used to introduce Koechlin and Müller's book, *Green*

Business Opportunities: The Profit Potential (1993). When the German physicist and philosopher Carl Friedrich von Weizsacker was asked whether he was optimistic or pessimistic about the prospects for achieving sustainability, he replied:

'I like to respond to that question with the story of the three frogs that fell into the milk: an optimist, a pessimist and a realist. The optimist and the pessimist both drowned, the first because he didn't do anything, thinking everything would turn out for the best anyway, the latter because he thought the situation was hopeless. The realist said: "All a frog can do is thrash about." So he did. And suddenly there was butter under his feet and he climbed out.'

If humankind is going to 'thrash about' productively, a range of new perspectives, ideas and approaches are going to be required. Already 'alternative' blueprints for economics, businesses and society which allow the environment to be managed sustainably are emerging. Perhaps the most significant of these is the 1987 *Brundtland Report, Our Common Future* (WCED 1987), which concluded:

'The time has come to break out of past patterns. Attempts to maintain social and ecological stability through old approaches to development and environmental protection will increase instability.'

Commoner (1990) calls for a paradigm shift in business thinking to reconcile business and the environment. Yaranella and Levine (1992) outline three alternative paradigms on which societies, industries or companies can base their philosophy and progress. The dominant business paradigm of today is identified by Yaranella and Levine as a 'mass industry' mentality. This 'grey' paradigm is Newtonian in the sense that it attempts to understand the world in mechanistic and reductionist terms. It is also *technocentric* in its emphasis on the ability of technology to control and harness nature, *econocentric* in its insistence on using monetary values as the basis of decisions and *anthropocentric* in seeing the environment as something which exists to support humankind's activities. The initial response to the green challenge has been to develop new, clean technologies; to begin to assign monetary values to natural

Table 1.3 Alternative paradigms for the business – society – environment relationship

Issue	Era			
	Pre-industrial	*Industrial*	*Environmental*	*Ecological*
Nature	Goddess and guide, abundant but threatening	For exploitation and to be subdued	For efficient use and conservation	The Earth as Gaia
Environment	Local, intrinsic to people's lifestyle, sustained	An infinite free good, and an 'externality', gradually liquidated	A finite resource to be managed and shared, a man-made threat	Emphasis on the biosphere
Technology	Traditional, small and simple, low energy	High capital and energy, large scale and complex	High-tech, clean-tech, often quick-fix	Small scale low energy
Economics	Based on environment, social relationships, and survival	Growth and profit, belief in 'trickledown', emphasis on ownership	Sustainable growth, new measures, concern for 'The Commons'	Sustainability, steady-state, post-Keynesian
Society	Traditional, feudal, religious, local	Class structure focus, more nationalistic, shaped by marketing	New Age, professional and middle-class values more international	Decentralised, democratic and global
Social Perspective	People as subjects, and social group members, belief in divine will and nature's power	People as workers, consumers and individuals; belief in human power & industry	Liberal, post-consumer, humanist, people as citizens, belief in innovation/intervention	Eco-centric, post-humanist' return to socio-eco-symbiosis
Business	Trading of surpluses, craftsmanship	Mass production, free enterprise, a social role model	A target for reform and constraint, also partners in eco-reforms	Closed loop, humane, value-driven
Marketing	Informal, face-to-face, constrained by church and society	Mass product marketing, increasingly formalised and widespread	Fragmented markets, responding to green consumerism	Constrained by society?, emphasis on needs

resources and to try and correct market mechanisms to protect environmental resources. Such steps aim to integrate the environment into the grey paradigm, but they are more geared to preserving the status quo than the environment. Although such changes can be viewed as positive, the environmental lobby often criticises them as damaging in their role of postponing more significant change. Averting the looming socio-environmental crisis will involve a move to a new paradigm, rather than the re-tinting of the existing one. Table 1.3 adapts some of the ideas of Yaranella and Levine to chart the potential evolution of the dominant socio-economic paradigm in reference to the environment.

Shifting paradigms is always disconcerting. The arrival of the Newtonian paradigm caused chaos as it replaced the dogmatic certainties of the entrenched ecclesiastically based scholastic paradigm. In moving towards sustainability, the challenge that faces society is similar to a spacecraft approaching re-entry into the earth's atmosphere. If the change of course does not create a sufficient 'angle of attack' into the atmosphere, the craft will simply skim off the earth's magnetic field and, having failed to establish an orbit, it will become lost in the vastness of space. Conversely, by changing course too suddenly, the angle of attack into the atmosphere becomes too steep, and the craft will quickly burn up during re-entry. The progress of society needs to get back 'down to earth' and back in step with nature, but it is only likely to work if the change is significant but introduced gradually. For this reason, this book aims at the important first paradigm shift towards environmentalism. There are other books which concentrate on practical but minimal adjustments to the existing order, and there are also more visionary books which explore what a truly sustainable society and company will need to be like (Stead and Stead 1992, Davis 1991). This book focuses on the role of marketing in the context of a shift of the business paradigm to the intermediate environmentalist position. This will only be a transitory phase in the journey towards sustainability, but every journey begins with a first step, and the quicker this journey begins, the better.

REASONS TO BE CHEERFUL

There is, at least, reason to be cautiously optimistic. There are many aspects of human life on earth that are moving in a positive direction. Life expectancy, health care provision and income levels in most countries have improved significantly in the last 20 years. Food output has continued to rise ahead of population growth. If wastage could be reduced and patterns of distribution made more equitable, the world's existing population could all be adequately fed. Child mortality rates have fallen dramatically, partly as a result of greatly improved rates of immunisation (although the bottom-line figures still make relatively depressing reading with some 12.9 million children dying in 1990 from preventable diseases according to the World Resources Institute and

1960	1962	Publication of Rachel Carson's *Silent Spring* Global problems with insecticides
1970	1972	US National Environmental Protection Act; formation of National Environmental Protection Agency
	1972	First Earth Day
	1972	First Earth Summit; formation of United Nations Environmental Agency
	1974	First energy crisis
	1975	OECD establishes principle of 'polluter pays'
	1974–5	Energy conservation becomes major international political issue for first time
	1975	US federal law requires environmental assessment of federal projects
	1976	Clood of trichlorphenol vapour speads through Seveso area of Italy
1980	1980	Publication of World Conservation Strategy and Brandt Commission Report
	early 1980s on	Environmental audit carried out by many large companies
	1983	Further dioxin release at Seveso, Italy
	1983	Greenpeace and Friend of the Earth develop public confrontaion and symbolic confrontation strategies to capture public awareness in, e.g. whale conservation issues
	1984	Bhopal India, major escape of toxic fumes kills 4,000, injures tens of thousands
	1985	European Commission agrees first environmental assessment regulation

1985	Ozone hole findings published
1985	Environmental audit becomes part of acquisition and disposal procedure in North America
1986	Chernobyl nuclear power plant disaster
1987	Single European Act 1986; first American environmental audit regulation
late 1980s on	'Deep green' eco-guerilla movement, western USA
1987	Montreal Protocol plans CFC reductions
1987	Publication of Brundtland Report, entrenching sustainable development as key strategic dimension in environmental policy
1988	Implementation across Europe of Environmental Assessment Directive
1989	Exxon Valdez disaster in Alaska
1990 1990	Principle of integrated pollution control in United Kingdom Environmental Protection Act
1990	London Agreement on ozone depletent phase out
1990	Defeat of California 'big green' environmental legislation; local adoption of many aspects
1991	Proposal for European Environmental Agency
1991	Draft Eco-Audit Directive, Europe
1992	In opposition to local environmental regulation, many California companies in deep recession threaten removal to less regulated states
1992	GATT publishes report on world free trade and environmental issues
1992	Second Earth Summit of UN in Rio de Janerio

Fig. 1.4 Milestones on the green pathway
(adapted from Environmental Assessment Group, Kent County Council; EcoCommunity Programme IMRIC U of Greenwich)

UNICEF figures revealing that one in three children are malnourished).

We also know that although the last 30 years has contained a number of disturbing revelations about the environment, many steps have been taken to protect and improve its quality. Figure 1.4 maps out some of the disasters and the responses that have driven the environmental debate forward since the early 1960s. The response to the 1970s' oil crises proved that we can change our behaviour as consumers and as managers when we need to. Consumers and businesses alike quickly adapted to use less energy, in many cases without significantly compromising their quality of life or their level of output.

The news about environmental resources is not all gloomy, since some are increasing rather than declining. Among industrialised nations the amount of land devoted to forest is increasing (although unfortunately in places at the expense of the more environmentally valuable wetland ecosystems), and barring damage from pollution or climatic change, its future seems assured. International action has also rescued several endangered species such as the Ibex, the Whooping Crane and the African Elephant. A greater proportion of land is now protected (in principle at least) than ever before, and an increasing trend towards co-operation between countries has brought progress on a range of environmental issues. The action taken during the 1970s, the late 1980s and early 1990s are having some positive effects on some of the worst problems. Data from Brazil's space agency shows that the rate of destruction of Amazonian rainforest has lessened recently. Similarly the monitoring of Antarctic ozone suggests that, although ozone levels have hit record lows, the rate of ozone thinning is also decreasing. Slowing down the rate of environmental degradation is a long way from stopping or

reversing it, but it is an important first step. Another encouraging sign is that the early 1990s have seen the volume of writing and research findings which are relatively positive from an environmental viewpoint increasing dramatically in comparison to the number of articles published about looming disaster.

Another reason for cautious optimism is the findings published in *Beyond The Limits* (Meadows *et al* 1992), the follow up to *Limits to Growth*. Re-running an updated version of the World3 computer model of the global economy which formed the basis of *Limits to Growth*, suggested that, although time and the range of options is narrowing rapidly, a path forward exists in which the standard of living of both industrialised and non-industrialised societies is improved while still moving towards sustainability. Given progress on population control and environmental protection there is still the opportunity to stabilise world population at an average standard of living roughly equivalent to that enjoyed in Western Europe at present within a sustainable economy. The bad news contained in *Beyond the Limits* was that only this path, combined with a relatively optimistic set of assumptions about population growth and the contribution of technology, prevents our social system 'overshooting' its environmental limits.

Readers might wonder what the most pessimistic outcomes of the World3 simulation were. This involved an environmental and social 'meltdown' around 2020 after which living standards and life expectancy would decline to reach a level equivalent to the start of this century by around 2060. As to the assumptions fed into the model to create such an economic collapse, they were simply the continuation of existing policies. It is time to say something new about economics, business and marketing, and time to say it quickly.

CHAPTER 2

The principles of environmental marketing

'The world we have created today . . . has problems which cannot be solved by thinking the way we thought when we created them.'
(Albert Einstein)

INTRODUCTION

It is now widely accepted that societies, econ-omies and the businesses within them need to find a more sustainable path for future development. Achieving this will involve saying some very new things about marketing, and perhaps rediscovering some fundamental marketing truths. Since the 1950s the population of the world and the consumption levels within industrialised societies have witnessed explosive growth particularly during the last two decades (*see* Table 2.1). Marketing has contributed to the current environ- mental crisis, because of its central role as a driving force behind the unsustainable growth in consumption (or what could be termed overconsumption). Marketing as it will become, by contrast, will become part of the solution. This will require the marketing of new, more sustainably produced products, new companies, new lifestyles, new values and new ideas.

'GREEN' – THE NEW MARKETING BUZZWORD

Increasing environmental concern manifested itself in many ways during the late 1980s. Green political parties attracted more votes, environmental groups' membership lists grew, investors began to channel money into green and ethical companies and funds, and the media became increasingly preoccupied with environmental issues. However, it was through their purchasing behaviour that most people decided to express their increasing concern about the state (and future) of the environment, as shown in Table 2.2 opposite.

Table 2.1 From *Limits to Growth* to the search for sustainability: population and consumption figures (1970 and 1990)

	1970	1990
Global human population	3.6 billion	5.3 billion
Annual population growth rate (%)	2.1%	1.7%
Annual population increase	76 million	92 million
Urban population	1.3 billion	2.4 billion
Automobiles	250 million	560 million
Annual consumption of:		
Oil	17 billion barrels	24 billion barrels
Natural gas	31 trillion cubic feet	70 trillion cubic feet
Coal	2.3 billion metric tons	5.2 billion metric tons
Fertiliser	32 million metric tons	140 million metric tons
Metals	1.6 billion metric tons	2.5 billion metric tons
Municipal waste generated annually (OECD only)	302 million metric tons	420 million metric tons

In the business world the vocabulary of management was suddenly expanded by the discussion of 'green consumers', 'green markets' and 'green products' and the practice of 'environmental' or 'green' marketing. In many cases this label described marketing activity that sought to create competitive advantage by convincing customers that particular brands were in some way less harmful to the environment than others. Much of what passed for environmental marketing in the initial stages had very little to do with marketing, and even less to do with the environment. It was often opportunistic and based on the generation of tactical advantage rather than the pursuit of strategic change. This opportunism was demonstrated during the launch of America's National Wildlife Federation's Corporate Conservation Council environmental awards for business, when several large companies nominated themselves simply for complying with government regulations. Selling and public relations activities with a green theme were rife, but had little connection to customer needs or to the realities of the environmental impact of the products involved.

Table 2.2 Personal expressions of environmental concern: (Percentage engaging in green behaviour)

Countries	Avoided environmentally harmful products (%)	Active in environment group (%)	Voted/ worked for pro-environment candidate (%)
USA	57	11	19
Canada	77	12	15
Japan	40	4	14
Germany (West)	81	10	18
United Kingdom	75	10	10
Netherlands	68	7	21
Denmark	65	10	18

Source: Gallup Health of the Planet 1992

As public concern about the environment was translated into increasingly stringent environmental legislation, and as pressure groups and the media became increasingly expert in exposing green 'hype', so environmental marketing has begun to focus on more fundamental and significant changes within businesses. To develop further and to make a contribution towards sustainability, environmental marketing will require many things. It will require investment, technological breakthroughs, practical successes and luck. Perhaps more importantly it will require the education of consumers and managers and the creation of a new set of tools and concepts with which to tackle the green challenge. It is to these last two areas that this book will hopefully make some contribution.

WHAT IS ENVIRONMENTAL MARKETING?

The attempts being made to develop a marketing response to the green challenge has caused a great deal of controversy and some confusion. This is perhaps not surprising since key concepts such as 'green', 'environment', 'sustainable' and 'marketing' mean different things to different people.

Environmental defined

McDonagh (1994) examines what 'green' means within the context of advertising, and concludes that for different people 'green' will relate to one or more of the components in Fig. 2.1.

A feature of the green challenge so far is the degree to which it has tended to become bogged down over semantics. Companies and commentators have been uncertain whether they should or should not refer to a product as 'environmentally friendly/responsible/sound/improved/legitimate or safe'. Although the term 'green marketing' has been popular in the UK and some other countries, in the international business environment it does not have a universally consistent meaning. In some countries the word 'green' denotes a style of politics but not an approach to marketing and commerce; in countries such as Germany and the UK green is associated with verdancy and nature but in Spain green is associated with low-cost and low-quality goods.

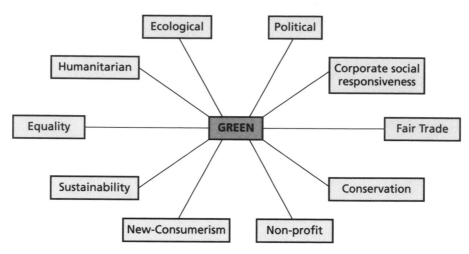

Fig. 2.1 The many meanings of green
(adapted from McDonagh (1994))

Environmental marketing is the label used in other countries such as the USA, but the word 'environmental' also poses problems. For example, there is no direct German translation for the English use of the word 'environment'. Another criticism levelled at the concept of 'environmental' marketing and management is that it suggests something 'out there' rather than something 'right here'. Environmental issues are not something external; they are close at hand. Pollution is not just about clear skies and clean rivers; there is growing environmentalist concern about the exposure to pollution that occurs when we drive our cars, attend our workplaces or drink from our taps. The usage of the word 'environmental' has also changed in recent years. Environmentalism and the social concern which affected companies in the late 1960s and early 1970s were separate strands in a more widespread reappraisal of social values and the role of institutions such as businesses and government. During the 1990s the social and ecological agendas have become so intertwined that to talk about environmental issues without considering social issues, or vice versa, would be virtually meaningless. This merging of social and environmental issues is also reflected in the increasing environmental concern being shown by 'humanitarian' charities such as Oxfam. Large-scale irrigation projects that displace thousands of people, the provision of land for the indigenous peoples of Amazonia, the environmental impact of refugees, the human problems caused by desertification are all issues on which Oxfam is campaigning; putting it very much on a convergence course with environmental organisations (Oxfam 1993).

Trying to separate out the environmental and the social elements of environmental marketing is not particularly helpful. The state of the environment will increasingly influence what society can and will do, while the structure and nature of society in every country will determine how the environment is utilised and the degree to which it is consumed or sustained. It is through meeting the environmental challenge that the welfare of the greatest number of people throughout the globe is likely to be protected and enhanced. Marketing theory has always been dominated by the state of marketing in industrialised countries where 'social issues' mean product safety, consumer choice, fair pricing and protection from misleading or stereotypical advertising. In many less industrialised countries the most pressing social issues are also environmental issues concerning the provision of clean water, food and protection from the elements and disease for the majority of the population. For the purposes of this book, the term 'environmental marketing' will be used, in the sense of relating marketing to the inseparable social and physical (green) environments in which consumers and businesses exist.

The whole concept of green consumers, green products and environmental marketing has been attacked by some environmentalists as invalid. The Environment Council believe that 'there is no absolute definition possible. The only real green product is no product'. It would be interesting to know whether the authors of this statement would consider themselves to be 'green' and, if so, whether they are involved in any form of con-sumption beyond self-sufficiency. Charter (1992) suggests that since 'green' is an unattainable and absolute label, 'greener marketing' should be used.

In principle this avoidance of absolutes is under-standable, unless a product actually involves putting the environment back together again, it can always be viewed as less than totally green. How-ever, in practice, marketing and business have always used a language of absolutes to express rela-tive concepts. We therefore talk about durable products that do not last forever; we talk about expensive products that we can still afford and we talk about global products which are not available in every store on the planet. In management terms companies practice Total Quality Management and still make mistakes (although hopefully fewer of them). To make green products and environmental marketing a special case in which only politically correct and carefully qualified labels can be used seems unrealistic. It also seems unnecessary since research has shown consumers to be singularly unimpressed by vague and general environmental claims such as 'environmentally friendly' (Davis 1993). Perhaps going green should be seen as some-thing absolute, something that companies can aspire to, and something that can inspire the people within them. We might never get there, just as we might never achieve 100 per cent customer satisfac-tion, but it is something worth striving towards.

The 'green movement' which emerged during the late 1980s represents a fusion of many different concerns ranging from people who wish to protect specific species or historic buildings to those con-cerned with issues such as homelessness, poverty or animal welfare. This loose but potentially powerful federation of interests is spoken of as addressing a 'green agenda', which in turn presents a 'green challenge' to society, businesses and governments. Environmental marketing is a response to this change, and is part of the change itself.

Marketing defined

The origins of marketing are pragmatic, and Eng-lish dictionaries still define marketing in terms of goods being taken to a market to be bought and sold. Over time what is meant by 'marketing' has continually evolved. During the 'production era' the typified industrial business until the 1930s, 'marketing' generally related to a set of post-pro-duction activities. During the subsequent 'selling era' these marketing activities grew in importance, and were increasingly supplemented by pre-pro-duction activities such as market research. It was not until the late 1950s that marketing evolved into a distinctive management philosophy and dis-cipline which explicitly linked business success to customer satisfaction and systematically set about achieving them as interdependent goals.

There is a wide range of definitions of market-ing to choose from. The Chartered Institute of Marketing defines it as 'the management process responsible for identifying, anticipating and satis-fying customer requirements profitably'. This is a very pragmatic, but rather narrow view of mar-keting. Kotler (1994) defines marketing more broadly as '... a social and managerial process by which individuals and groups obtain what they need and want through creating and exchanging products and value with others'.

Marketing's origins lie in the industries which manufacture tangible consumer goods. From there, it spread into the markets for industrial goods, service markets and even into not-for-profit markets such as education, health care and charitable services. However, a great deal more than goods and services is marketed to us today. Formal and professional marketing techniques are increasingly being applied to entire industries, companies, political parties, government policies and even ideas. Unsustainable economic policies, technologies, development projects and manage-ment theories have all been sold successfully to society to the detriment of the environment. Mar-keting techniques may have been used to sell grey growth to society for the last 30 years, but it has been a process of selling rather than marketing. Marketing emphasises the needs and wants of the customer rather than the needs of the producer. Grey growth has been based on economics and technology – two sciences which are very product-orientated (with monetarist economics being perhaps the ultimate embodiment of the product concept). The aim of economic growth is meant to be an improvement in the quality of life for the people within society. Economic growth and technological advancement rapidly became ends in themselves, however. Success was measured in terms of output (GNP) as opposed to customer satisfaction in terms of people's quality of life. The work of Schumacher (1973) can be seen as an attempt to make both economics and technology more customer-orientated. The subtitle of *Small is Beautiful* is 'Economics as if people mattered' and one of his key concepts is of 'appropriate technology', particularly in terms of the transfer of technology between industrialised and less industrialised nations.

In the search for a solution, new more sustainable products, services, companies, government policies, laws and ideas will have to be marketed successfully if the environmental crisis is to be turned from a threat into an opportunity.

Environmental marketing can be defined as:

the holistic management process responsible for identifying, anticipating and satisfying the requirements of customers and society, in a profitable and sustainable way.

In its underlying quest to satisfy consumers and in terms of the steps in the marketing process, environmental marketing resembles conventional marketing. The difference between the two lies in a philosophy which tries to balance the techno-economic market perspective with a broader socio-environmental approach.

THE EMERGENCE OF ENVIRONMENTAL MARKETING

The evolution of marketing is composed of a series of responses to major external challenges. Pre-industrial marketing, based around craft production and personal relationships with local customers, was challenged by the urbanisation and mechanisation of the Industrial Revolution. The industrial era created expanding markets which required an emphasis on production, logistics and selling to get the goods to the customer. In the late 1950s the challenge of increasingly saturated and competitive markets led to the birth of an explicit marketing philosophy (Baker 1992). The publication of Rachel Carson's *Silent Spring* and Ralph Nader's *Unsafe at Any Speed* in the early to mid-1960s created concern about the social responsibility of businesses and their impact on the natural environment and the health and welfare of the planet. This concern was heightened during the early 1970s in response to *Limits to Growth* and resulted in the emergence of both the 'societal marketing concept' and the 'ecological marketing concept'. In response to the new green challenge which emerged during the 1980s, these early concepts have amalgamated to create an environmental marketing concept.

Environmental marketing differs from its societal and ecological forbears in its intertwining of ecological and social concerns, in the breadth of the ecological agenda that it tackles and in its potential application across all types and sectors of business. Environmental marketing goes beyond societal marketing in four key ways.

● It is an open-ended rather than a long-term perspective.

● It focuses more strongly on the natural environment.

● It treats the environment as something which has an intrinsic value over and above its usefulness to society.

● It focuses on global concerns rather than those of particular societies.

Environmental marketing also goes beyond the 1970s' ecological marketing concept which was defined by Henion (1976) as:

'concerned with all marketing activities: (a) that have served to help cause environmental problems and (b) that may serve to provide a remedy for environmental problems'.

This approached things rather simplistically by trying to isolate and label particular products, companies or industries as environmentally good or bad. It also used a narrow definition of environmental problems which was restricted to the creation of pollution and the depletion of energy and other resources.

Environmental marketing has outgrown its roots as a minority or 'alternative' subject to become a widespread element of marketing practice in many countries (although there is a separate debate to be conducted over the extent to which the substance as opposed to the trappings of environmental marketing has been adopted as yet). In markets as diverse as cars, detergents, batteries, personal computers, running shoes, investment funds, holidays and ice cream, leading brands have been marketed under a green banner. Some very unlikely candidates have been seen jostling for a share of the green mantle. Nuclear electricity, the British Conservative Party and cars such as BMWs and Volvos are some of the products that have surprised industry commentators and their customers by leaping aboard the green bandwagon, if not embracing the green agenda. The interest in environmental issues among consumers means that marketers should be spearheading the drive towards improved corporate environmental performance. However, many companies have yet to embrace the environment as an issue related to customers and marketing, as well as an issue relating to the environment and production. In Lent and Wells' (1992) study of top US companies, while 77 per cent of top managers saw the environment as strategically important, and 63 per cent of production managers were taking some responsibility for environmental management, only 28 per cent of marketers were getting involved in the environmental management effort.

THE FUNDAMENTALS OF ENVIRONMENTAL MARKETING

Environmental marketing is based on three principles: social responsibility, the pursuit of sustainability and an holistic approach. The emergence of modern social responsibility began in the

1920s when Oliver Sheldon's philosophical vision of management called for a balance between technological efficiency and the welfare of society. Sheldon's theme was picked up by Wallace B. Donham, Dean of the Harvard Business School, in an address delivered at Northwestern University in 1929:

'Business started long centuries before the dawn of history, but business as we now know it is new – new in its broadening scope, new in its social significance. Business has not learned how to handle these changes, nor does it recognise the magnitude of its responsibilities for the future of civilisation.'

Over sixty years later, the increasing evidence of the environmental damage caused by unsustainable economic growth, has given these words a more profound and urgent ring. Buchholz (1991) identifies five common elements among the many definitions of corporate social responsibility.

1 Businesses have responsibilities that go beyond the production of goods and services at a profit.

2 These further responsibilities involve helping to solve important social problems, especially those that businesses helped to create.

3 Businesses are responsible to a broader constituency than their shareholders.

4 Businesses have impacts that go beyond simple market-place transactions.

5 Businesses serve a wider range of human values than can be captured by a sole focus on economic values.

Social responsibillity

The issue of what represents good or bad corporate social performance has been the subject of some confusion. This is mainly caused by a focus on activities rather than outcomes, when it is really the outcomes of activities that define performance (Woods 1991). The original social reporting movement of the 1970s died a swift death in the face of resistance from businesses who viewed it as another 'stick' with which regulators could beat them. In the 1990s increased concern about the social responsibility of business has increased the business community's interest in some form of social reporting as a means of tracking and demonstrating social responsibility.

The evolution from societal marketing to environmental marketing involves the adoption of two deceptively simple sounding concepts. The first is *holism* – the idea that a business should be managed as a total system, and not simply as a collection of functions or business units. The second is *sustainability* – the concept that the activities of businesses to satisfy customers, shareholders and other stakeholders today should not be at the expense of the ability to satisfy them in the future. For marketing managers, the challenge is to find ways to implement these concepts so that our business systems will become environmentally and socially viable, as well as economically and technically viable.

Holism

In 1920 Smuts wrote *Holism and Evolution* which proposed that nature's evolutionary progression towards ever more complex forms and organisations is driven by a tendency to form wholes that are more than the sum of the parts, through the process of ordered groupings. It is only through the appreciation of whole entities and the interactions among them that life can be understood. The problem with holism is that it entirely contradicts the reductionist principles of the western rational scientific tradition. We can observe holistic relationships all around us, but they cannot be subjected to experimentation by the rational scientific method. Holism has therefore been largely rejected by the academic establishment in life and social sciences.

Holism in management is not a new idea, but it is an idea still waiting to happen. Writers such as Drucker and Unterman promoted the ideas of holism in the 1960s and 1970s. Unterman's (1974) study of top management in American financial institutions concluded:

'Few top executives have been trained to integrate and assess a host of many kinds of factor. The top man by experience and background is usually a specialist not a generalist. It takes a most exceptional skill to use what Peter Drucker calls a "holistic approach". Relatively few executives have this ability.'

Even where companies attempted to manage in a holistic manner, Unterman found:

'When profit centres become highly successful there is a tendency to overlook the total plan and the holistic process is not enforced.'

In the intervening 20 years, the trend towards specialism in management training and the emphasis on 'rational scientific' approaches and linear thinking have increased. The increasing scale and complexity of business enterprises have also made the application of holistic management thinking even more difficult. Senge (1990) criticises the reliance on the 'cause and effect' approach of linear thinking in terms of seven 'learning disabilities' it creates within organisations:

- an emphasis on individual roles and jobs instead of the whole organisation;
- a tendency to blame external parties;
- a belief that problems can be solved by taking aggressive action against whichever external party is causing the problem;
- a fixation with sudden specific events;
- a failure to perceive threats which emerge gradually (often referred to rather gruesomely as 'boiled frog syndrome' after a famous experiment conducted by some French schoolchildren);
- a belief that the effects of decisions are virtually immediate;
- a belief that management teams interact across functional boundaries to solve problems, when in fact they often expend much more effort in maintaining boundaries and protecting individual interests.

Holistic management was originally prescribed for companies to tackle the problems of internal control and co-ordination that large and diverse companies face in responding to turbulent environments. In other words, it had an internal, closed-systems, production orientation. Holism for environmental marketing involves taking a more external, open-systems marketing orientation. It involves seeing a company not just as an holistic entity in techno-economic terms, but as

Fig. 2.2 Environmental marketing in its organisational context

part of a socio-environmental ecological system. The principles of ecology can be summarised as follows (Commoner 1972).

1 *Everything is connected to everything else.* Ecology envisages the environment as a 'web of life', in which a change to one strand can have repercussions throughout the whole network. Companies, customers, competitors, shareholders, citizens and ecosystems are all interconnected. This concept is sometimes taken to ridiculous extremes in an attempt to deny its value. A web is a physical system and therefore subject to forces such as inertia and the dissipation of energy. A butterfly flapping its wing in Australia will therefore not spark a hurricane somewhere else. The importance of the analogy lies in the fact that as strands of a web are broken, so the forces acting on the other strands alter, often imperceptibly. If enough strands are severed the web will simply collapse.

2 *Everything goes somewhere.* Physics teaches us that matter and energy cannot be destroyed but always go somewhere. Environmentalists' concerns often revolve around the problems caused by outputs from industrial systems ending up in the wrong place. This could be the effect of CFCs in the ozone layer, the presence of pesticides in food, or the discovery of weapons-grade plutonium in German lock-up garages.

3 *Nature knows best.* The 'balance of nature' present in any ecosystem may have taken millions of years to reach a stable and renewable balance. Attempts to alter the balance of nature for economic gain frequently backfire.

4 *There is no such thing as a 'free lunch'.* Every human intervention in the workings of the environment has some cost. The bill for lunch may arrive decades later, and to a different address, but environmental damage inevitably has to be paid for by someone.

Because environmental marketing is an holistic management process, it extends well beyond the normally recognised boundaries of marketing theory and practice. Environmental marketing essentially amalgamates six relatively well established approaches to management (as shown in Fig. 2.2).

● *Societal marketing.* Prothero (1990) provides a useful summary of how environmental marketing has evolved from the societal marketing concept.

● *Relationship marketing.* Relationship marketing emerged partly as a response to the shortcomings of marketing concepts developed from consumer markets when applied to industrial marketing. Gummesson (1987) suggests that industrial firms depend less on the manipulation of the marketing mix's four Ps, and instead rely on reaching a critical service support level in their relationship with customers, distributors, suppliers so that 'all activities of the firm build, maintain and develop customer relations'. For consumer goods companies, environmental marketing presents a similar relationship-building challenge.

● *Strategic management.* The external focus of environmental marketing to consider socio-environmental issues is closer to that of strategic management than conventional marketing. It also shares with strategic management a longer-term perspective and an internal agenda that encompasses all of a company's operations.

● *Human resource management (HRM).* Environmental marketing looks to move marketing and business away from the mechanistic techno-economic paradigm to become more human and more humane. It shares a concern for the people within the internal environment with the field of human resource management. The greenness of a product will relate to the treatment of people within the company as well as the ecological impacts of products and production processes. It is the exploitation of workers in developing countries that has led environmentalists to campaign against many multinational producers of cash crop products such as tea, coffee and chocolate. Premier Brands, aware of growing concern among staff and the public about the working conditions of the tea-pickers employed by its suppliers, launched a fair trade initiative. Tea plantations are now selected on the basis of eco-performance and social criteria such as employment policies, and boxes of Typhoo Tea now carry a 'Caring for tea and our tea-pickers' logo.

● *Total quality management (TQM).* Environmental marketing shares with TQM a mandate to consider all aspects of the organisation and a need to instil an entirely new philosophy into the whole business. In many cases companies are adapting the concept of eco-performance for inclusion within the concept of quality and speaking in terms of Total Quality Environmental Management (TQEM).

● *Business re-engineering.* Re-engineering is another 1990s' management buzzword which has much in common with environmental marketing. Re-engineering means different things to different people, but it commonly involves 'a fundamental reappraisal of where and how the company creates value for its stakeholders' (Talwar 1993). Re-engineering involves taking a radical redesign approach to the organisation and its current way of doing things. Environmental marketing with its emphasis on clean technology and process redesign shares the 'clean sheet' mentality of re-engineering – an approach which has the potential to bring companies remarkable benefits and extreme pain.

Each of these areas is crucial for environmental marketing to succeed. However, this book will not dwell on any of them, partly because each has a distinct and well established literature devoted to it. Instead this book will concentrate on the core elements of 'environmental marketing', and to those related more to the green environment than the social environment. Given the holistic nature of environmental marketing, this means that the boundaries that will have to be drawn between environmental marketing and these other fields are bound to be arbitrary.

Sustainability

The concept of sustainable development originates from the 1980 World Conservation Strategy in planning the optimum use of renewable resources. It was further crystallised and more widely disseminated as a result of the *Brundtland Report* (WCED 1987).

The concept of sustainability is breathtakingly simple in theory, and yet the process of translating it into action has proved controversial. Sustainability involves 'development that meets the needs of the present without compromising the ability of future generations to meet their own needs' (WCED 1987). This means only consuming resources at a rate which allows them to be replaced, and only producing pollution at a rate that the environment can assimilate. Creating a sustainable world economy will ensure that the standard of living enjoyed by people today will not be at the expense of the generations to follow. Sustainability appears simple enough in relation to a renewable resource like a forest – if you cut one tree down, you plant another. But what about resources like oil and coal which will not be renewed, other than in a geological time-frame? Using a non-renewable resource sustainably involves consuming it at a rate which allows a sustainably managed renewable resource to be substituted for it in the future (Daly 1990).

The controversy over sustainability revolves around whether it aims to sustain the environment, or to sustain economic progress. Ultimately, the two aims are so intertwined that to attempt to separate them becomes meaningless. Without economic progress the poverty that blights the lives of so many countries and people will ensure that much of the environment continues to be exploited unsustainably. Without environmental protection, economic progress will be increasingly hampered by the costs associated with environmental problems such as ozone depletion, global warming and the health effects of pollution.

Sustainability is often criticised as a repeat of the '*Limits to Growth*' arguments. There are important differences between the two, however. *Limits to Growth* stressed the idea that economic expansion would ultimately be limited by the environment and its 'carrying capacity'. The sustainability concept embodies a more reciprocal relationship in which the technological, economic and social development which humanity engages in also determines the limits of the planet's ability to meet our needs. Sustainability is also a less confrontational issue. Talk of zero growth or limits to growth tended to put environmental groups and businesses in very adversarial positions. The concept of sustainable development

provides a common ground on which they can meet to attempt to achieve mutually acceptable progress.

Jacobs (1991) identifies three key components of sustainability, each of which conventional market economics has failed to deliver up until now.

1 *Futurity* – a long-term perspective which gives equal consideration to the needs of future generations and to our own. In marketing terms it translates into a concern to ensure that both the needs of future consumers and those of todays, are satisfied.

2 *Welfare* – a measure of the benefits that individuals accrue from society. This includes conventional economic components such as income, but also quality-of-life issues such as environmental quality.

3 *Equity* – an attempt to balance the distribution of economic costs and benefits between different countries, regions, socio-economic classes, ethnic groups or sexes.

Sustainability is no longer an 'alternative' policy; it is now a generally agreed principle of future economic growth and development. The International Chamber of Commerce's *Charter for Sustainability* has been signed by over 1000 of the world's leading companies, and sustainability is an inherent part of European Union (EU) policy following the publication of the Fifth Environmental Action Plan, *Towards Sustainability*. Individual governments are also attempting to define their own path towards sustainability with initiatives such as Japan's *New Earth 21*, Holland's National Environmental Policy Plan, *To Choose or to Lose* and the UK's 1994 *Sustainable Development: The UK Strategy*.

A number of factors will need to come together to create the conditions under which real progress towards sustainability can be achieved. Table 2.3 demonstrates how a whole range of elements within society can become either inhibitors or promoters of sustainability depending on their nature. Marketing and consumption are only two out of many forces whose interplay will determine the

Table 2.3 Sustainability promoters and inhibitors

Promoters	Inhibitors
Slow population growth	Rapid population growth
Political or social instability (e.g. refugee influxes)	Relative socio-political stability
Globalism	Nationalism, regionalism, racism
Long-term thinking, e.g. consideration of 'inter-generational equity' issues	Short-termism
Equity, justice and protection of human rights	Despotism, repression, violation of human rights
Fair trade	Unfair terms of trade, protectionism
Peace, low levels of military spending	Arms race, high spending
High priority for sustainable development	Low priority for sustainable development
Trust/openness	Suspicion/defensiveness
Corporate commitment, precise objectives	Corporate cynicism, ad hoc approaches
Stable investment climate	Unstable investment climate
Low inflation	High inflation
Government-industry-NGO dialogue	Communications breakdown, long-running disputes
Strong regulatory framework, properly policed	Weak or non-existent regulatory framework; poor policing
Business involvement in early stages of policy and standard formulation	Business consulted late, or not at all
Harmonised standards, a 'level playing field'	Divergent standards, environmental barriers to trade
Incentives and performance-based standards	Uniform, overly-legalistic standards
Clean, energy- and resource-efficient technology	End-of-pipe technology, obsolete 'smokestack' technology exported from North to South (or East)
High educational standards and achievement, investment in education	Poor educational standards and achievements
Strong business ethics	Corruption, backhanders

Source: *SustainAbility*

speed and turbulence of our progress towards sustainability. Changes to consumption, commerce and marketing will only be effective as part of a wider re-engineering of our social, legal, political, economic, administrative and education systems, as detailed in the *Brundtland Report* (WCED 1987). In an age where market mechanisms have an increasing influence well beyond the traditional conception of 'the market-place', however, marketing and consumption will be particularly important forces in the quest for sustainability.

To achieve sustainability in practice, it will need to be translated into some concept of corporate eco-performance. This will reflect the socio-environmental impacts and outcomes of a company's products and the activities involved in the production process and the operation of the company (*see* Fig. 2.3). Although it is easy enough to identify the components of the organisation which will contribute to eco-performance, it is less than straightforward to quantify their impact. This is partly because the concept of what is environmentally good represents a 'moving target'. Environmental concerns vary over time, between different countries and among different stakeholders within the business environment. It is ironic to note that DDT, for example, was originally promoted as a solution to environmental

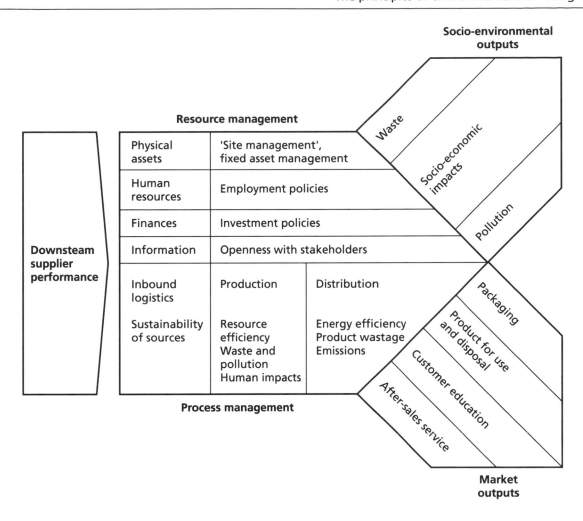

Fig. 2.3 Components of corporate eco-performance
(Source: Peattie and Charter (1994))

pest problems that was safe enough to eat, and CFCs were marketed as 'exceptionally environmentally inert'. More recently fuels such as premium unleaded petrol and diesel, heavily promoted as green fuels, have come under attack for unacceptable emissions of benzene and particulates respectively.

Hocking and Power (1993) illustrate the problems of interpreting claims about eco-performance.

'Suppose a company has reported that it has reduced its emissions by 10 per cent over the last year. As a statement of fact, this would appear to show an improvement. If, however, the level of business activity responsible for those environmental emissions has fallen by 20 per cent over the last year, then the apparent improvement is seen to be a deterioration in environmental performance.'

On the other hand, if a company calculates its emissions on a per-unit-of-output basis, then assuming that there are some eco-efficiencies of scale, the faster it grows the better its environmental performance would appear to be, even though the environmental damage it is causing is increasing.

THE IMPLICATIONS OF ENVIRONMENTAL MARKETING

The challenge of greening the philosophy and practice of marketing will require a re-evaluation of some of its most fundamental elements. Detailed consideration of many of the issues is provided in later chapters, but some of the basics are worth summarising here.

A new approach to consumers

The pioneering management theorist, Henri Fayol, once quipped about sending out for workers, but human beings turning up instead. Similarly, environmental marketers need to reconsider their approach to consumers. The word 'consumer' epitomises a view of customers, not as people, but as a means of consumption. Consumer is an abstract term which perhaps suits the academic context, but for companies, talking about consumers tends to make the people who buy their products seem somehow distant, abstract and dehumanised. Talking about 'our customers' rather than 'the consumers' can help to ensure that companies keep the relationship with them personal, human and responsible. Environmental marketers need to view consumers as customers, as citizens of society and also as physical human beings (or this could be stretched to 'corporeal beings' to create three Cs).

Marketing theory tends to focus on one customer want or need at a time. However, people have a variety of wants, some of which may conflict. Consumers might want personal mobility, and also want a safe and clean urban environment in which to raise their children. While purchasing a car might satisfy the first need, it would contribute to the dissatisfaction of the second. Just as a product is more accurately analysed as a 'bundle of benefits', a customer should be considered as possessing a 'bundle of wants and needs'. In the face of conflicting desires to consume and conserve, customers may increasingly seek satisfaction through non-purchase decisions, such as repairs. In reducing environmental degradation, green consumer behaviour addresses an inherent human need for a viable environment, which may sometimes be at the expense of more explicit material wants. One of the consequences of the green challenge is that consumers are becoming aware of the trade-offs involved in meeting their material wants and in meeting their socio-environmental needs. Recent years have witnessed an increasing range of conservation-orientated behaviour among consumers, from the recycling of cans and bottles to the boom in returning consumer durables to the supply chain through small ads or car boot sales.

A new concept of customer satisfaction

In the past, customer satisfaction has been judged in terms of the performance of the product at the moment (or during the period) of consumption. An environmentally concerned consumer may reject a product because they are made aware of the social or environmental harm that it causes in production or disposal. They may also avoid a product because of the activities of a producer, its suppliers or investors. The UK Green Party recently advised its members to avoid Ecover detergent products, despite their environmental excellence, following alleged violence by staff from the parent company, Group 4, against green protesters at Twyford Down.

An extended time horizon

Environmental marketing requires a longer time perspective than grey marketing. The marketer's time horizon must now go beyond the economic lifetime of the product to consider the environmental impact of its disposal and the long-term effects of product use. In the case of a waste product such as plutonium 239, this means considering a waste product that will still be hazardous to people (assuming humankind exists that long) as far removed from us, as we are from prehistoric cave dwellers. The ozone layer saga is a perfect example of the need for a longer time horizon because it involves the following elements.

● *A considerable time period before the environmental problem manifested itself.* CFC use began in the 1920s, and predictions that they may be damaging the ozone layer emerged in 1974. Only ten years later were the predictions shown to be correct.

● *A time lag between product use and environmental impact*. It takes 15 years for released CFCs to reach the stratosphere.

● *A long-term effect*. Each chlorine molecule will continue destroying ozone molecules until it collides and reacts with atmospheric methane to form hydrochloric acid and returns to earth as acid rain.

● *An open-ended problem*. A great deal of CFCs are stored within foam insulation and refrigeration units. Estimates put the global total of CFC-filled refrigerators at over one billion, containing some 22 000 tonnes of CFCs which will need to be disposed of safely.

A widened horizon

Geographically the green challenge forces companies to think internationally and globally to understand the socio-environmental impact of their products, production processes and sourcing policies. Economically it also forces them to think across industry boundaries. It cannot be understood or tackled from a nationalistic or a single industry standpoint. The fact that the issues cut across all industries, from those in the environmental 'front line' to businesses with no obvious environmental implications, was demonstrated when British Telecom won the 1993 British Environmental Reporting Award. In his acceptance speech, Deputy Chairman Mike Bett (the Director responsible for environmental issues) said:

> 'In the increasingly competitive world of international telecommunications I think it would be true to say that environmental issues are unlikely to be a major factor in determining BT's future prosperity. But the environment concerns us all, and a healthy and prosperous community is a fundamental necessity for the successful future of all UK industry and commerce.'

An open mind

The green challenge may also require marketers to abandon many of their preconceptions about their customers, their products and the nature of their market. The green challenge is emphasising the socio-environmental costs of products when marketers are used to focusing on the techno-economic benefits and their role in solving, rather than causing, problems for customers. The problem about what to do with discarded products, which used to be the consumer's problem, is now a challenge for the marketer. In some cases marketers are actively helping consumers to use less of their products – a very novel concept for marketing. Einsmann (1992) explains how when product managers championed the concept of a refill pack for Procter and Gamble's Lenor fabric softener:

> 'they had to overcome the conventional wisdom in the company: that the inconvenience of the refill packs would be unacceptable to consumers. Research closed the argument. Once refills were market tested, it was quickly apparent that the inconvenience of refilling ... was more than offset by consumers' satisfaction at reducing the amount of plastic waste that had to be put in the rubbish bag.'

An expanded product concept

If green consumer satisfaction depends upon the production process and on all the activities of the producer, we are approaching the situation where the company itself is becoming the product consumed. Drucker's (1974) famous concept that 'Marketing is the whole business seen from its final result, that is from the customers' point of view', seems set to become an enforced reality for many businesses, because the green movement means that customers (or those who influence them) are now actively looking at all aspects of their company. With surveys revealing that at least 60 per cent of consumers say they would withdraw their custom from companies which are exposed as polluters (Clifton and Buss 1992) the concept of defining the product in terms of what the customer consumes looks to be increasingly dangerous.

An opportunity focus

In the past the environment has been viewed in terms of legal responsibilities and cost burdens by businesses. However, environmental marketing should be a positive approach; it is as much about new opportunities as about new threats and restrictions. One interesting example is the mountain bike. Bikes are a potentially important piece in the green jigsaw. They can provide cheap and convenient personal mobility (often more effectively than cars within increasingly gridlocked urban areas) without contributing to airborne pollution, combined with healthy exercise. However, the success of the mountain bike has not been achieved by marketing its worthiness, but by marketing it as a fun and fashion item. As a colleague, Dr Peter Wells, observed, the success of mountain bikes has not come from marketing them as an alternative to cars, but as an alternative to surfboards.

The annual market for environmentally based goods and services is now expanding rapidly. Total European Union (EU) expenditure on tackling 12 key environmental problems between 1991 and 2000 is estimated by the Centre for Exploitation of Science and Technology at £860 billion (645 billion ECUs). The OECD puts the market in OECD countries alone at over $200 billion (93 billion ECUs) and expanding at 5.5 per cent annually. The OECD's figure uses a relatively narrow definition of green goods and services, and a broader definition used by Banque Paribas puts the existing market at over $700 billion (327 billion ECUs). According to Management Information Services for 1992, spending on environmental protection by US firms accounted for $169.8 billion (80 billion ECUs) and created four million jobs. The green challenge also provides a firm with a chance to reassess what business it is in and to rethink its strategic positioning. During 1991 *the Economist* pronounced:

'For far-sighted companies, the environment may turn out to be the biggest opportunity for enterprise and invention the industrial world has ever seen.'

A need for demarketing

One unavoidable conclusion of environmental marketing logic is that, where a product is being consumed and produced in an unsustainable way,

it may have to be demarketed (either voluntarily or forcibly) to reduce consumption. This may sound unlikely, but within tourism destinations such as Cyprus have developed a successful policy of attracting fewer but wealthier tourists in an effort to conserve the quality of the destination itself (Clements 1989). Taxation increases on fossil fuels have also been justified by governments as a 'conservation measure'.

Marketing grows up

Environmental marketing should not be confused with attempts to exploit consumers' environmental concern to promote companies or sell products. Ottman (1992a) makes the point that environmental marketing issues are 'real' issues. Instead of talking about consumer 'needs' such as whether clothes are 'whiter than white', environmental marketing means tackling issues which affect the fundamentals of people's quality of life, and which may even prove life threatening. A good example of the collision between the real and the trivial that environmental marketing involves is the story of CFC-115. It was less popular as a refrigerant or as an aerosol propellant than some of its CFC siblings, but it found a niche use in stabilising whipped toppings. Asked whether they want stable whipped toppings for their desserts, consumers would probably answer 'yes'. Asked whether they would prefer stable whipped toppings or a stable ozone layer, consumers would have little difficulty in choosing. Baker (1991) suggests that 'real marketing' has four essential features:

1 starting with the customer;
2 a long-run perspective;
3 full use of all the company's resources;
4 innovation.

If the third point were amended to become 'full and efficient use of all the company's resources', then there is a strong argument that environmental marketing is 'real marketing'. In view of the almost universal concern about the environment being shown by consumers all around the world and their desire to purchase greener products from greener companies, environmental marketing could be viewed as the only 'real' marketing.

Mitchell and Levy (1989) anthropomorphise marketing by characterising it as being 'barely out of its pram'. Perhaps marketing in the 1980s was enjoying a childhood in which it grew and learnt. It certainly showed a lot of childish characteristics in not worrying too much about the future or about the consequences of its actions on others. As the challenge of achieving sustainability grows, so the time has come for marketing to 'grow up' and play a full role in the creation of a society that can be enjoyed by all, today and tomorrow.

The consequences of failing to integrate the physical environment into marketing are significant. This places a whole new burden on the discipline. Until now, the worst consequences of poor marketing were generally unsatisfied customers and poorly rewarded shareholders. Getting marketing wrong in relation to the environment will have implications beyond the customers and shareholders of companies to affect the quality of life for future generations the world over. Governments and companies everywhere are relying on market mechanisms to play a major part in reducing and correcting environmental damage. For such market mechanisms to work, consumers and companies must be properly informed and willing and able to purchase products with an improved eco-performance. If marketing responds with more green hype rather than substantial changes, the consequences are potentially serious and were summarised by the American Ten-States Attorney Generals' Task Force into two key dangers expressed in their *Green Report*.

1 If consumers begin to feel that their genuine interest in the environment is being exploited, and in response rebel, they would no longer seek out or demand products that are in fact less damaging to the environment. If this were to occur, the environmental improvements that could have been achieved would be lost.

2 The tone, content and number of environmental claims might lead the public to believe that specific environmental problems have been adequately addressed and solved. This, in turn, could actually impede finding real solutions to identified problems by causing consumers to set aside their environmental concerns, making the assumption that these concerns had been addressed.

THE KEY ELEMENTS OF ENVIRONMENTAL MARKETING

The key characteristics of environmental marketing can therefore be summarised as:

1 a balanced approach to the social, technological, economic and physical aspects of businesses and societies that allows companies to STEP forward;

2 an emphasis on long-term sustainable qualitative development rather than short-term unsustainable quantitative growth;

3 an holistic approach aimed at reversing the reductionalist and fragmented approach of previous business theory and practice;

4 a consideration of consumers as real human beings rather than as hypothetical 'rational economic' entities;

5 an emphasis on meeting the genuine needs of consumers, rather than on stimulating superficial desires;

6 a recognition that consumers and society have multiple and sometimes conflicting wants and needs;

7 a view of the company and all its activities as part of the 'product' that is consumed;

8 a recognition that the large-scale, long-distance nature of the current economy is not sustainable, and that in the future small and local will be beautiful;

9 embracing the concept of eco-performance which incorporates the non-market outputs of the company, the performance of the product during and after use and the environmental impact of companies which contribute to the creation and marketing of the product elsewhere in the supply chain;

10 the pursuit of added socio-environmental virtue as well as added techno-economic value.

CHAPTER 3

The environmental marketing context – business, society and the environment

'Towards what ultimate point is society tending by its industrial progress?
When the progress ceases, in what condition are we to expect that it will
leave mankind?'
(John Stuart Mill 1857)

INTRODUCTION

Those involved in business have always been faced with the challenge of integrating their activities into society as a whole. In Mesopotamia around 1700 BC, King Hammurabi introduced a code whereby death sentences were handed out to any builders whose negligence led to the death of citizens, or to innkeepers who kept a rowdy establishment that disturbed local residents. This probably struck the business community of the day as a little on the draconian side, but it must have driven home the point that businesses needed to take account of their impact beyond generating customer satisfaction and wealth. The green challenge requires marketers and marketing to balance the material needs of individual consumers against the best interests of consumers and society, and to balance the short-term pressure for profit against the longer-term requirement to create sustainable growth. The result is a broadening of the marketing agenda beyond the conventional 'magic triangle' involving the three Cs of Company, Customer and Competitors. This agenda must now encompass the relationship of the company and its competitors to society and the environment, and embrace the long-term future of all concerned (see Fig. 3.1).

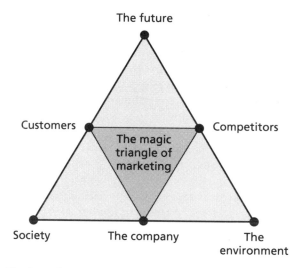

Fig. 3.1 **The expanded environmental marketing agenda**

A COMPLEX AND CHANGING INTERRELATIONSHIP

In the 1970s, environmentalist concern centred on the effect of business on the environment, and pressure for social responsibility was linked to the effect of business on society. The evolution of the new green agenda has increasingly revealed that the relationship between business, society and the

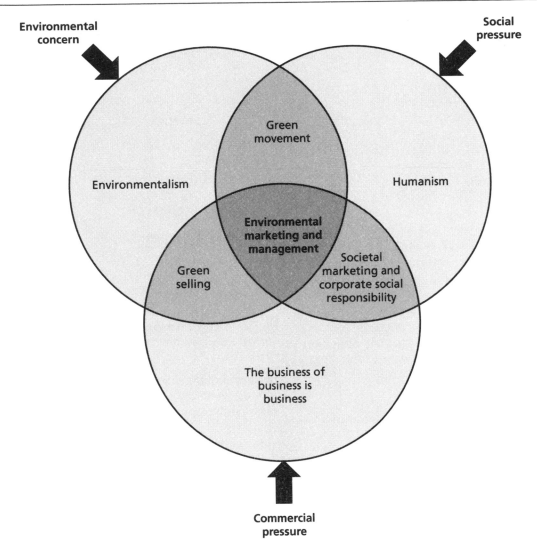

Fig. 3.2 The conventional approach to the business–society–environment interrelationship

environment is not a pair of 'one-way streets', but a set of complex interdependencies. Up until the Industrial Revolution, life was closely related to the environment and largely regulated by its seasons and processes. Individuals' needs were mostly met within the context of their family and local community, often through non-commercial exchanges based on reciprocity or redistribution of wealth (Goldsmith 1993). The technology that emerged from the Industrial Revolution allowed nature to be harnessed and then altered and to some extent controlled. The management of soil fertility, fuel, food and water supplies, waste disposal, housing, flood prevention and law and order moved away from a local, community basis to become managed by centralised social or business institutions. The economic paradigm gradually switched from one which followed nature, to one which exploited nature for economic development. With the current environmental crisis, another shift is taking place. Instead of economic trends shaping the physical environment, the reverse is happening as environmental trends once again begin to shape the economy.

The management perception of the relationship between business, society and the environment is presented in Fig. 3.2. As concern for the customer, society and the environment increases, so each of the three 'balloons' expands. This produces a range of possible management responses to any issue. As concern about the future and about social and environmental issues increases, so the three circles are pushed together enlarging the central area of environmental marketing. Conversely, a reduction in socio-environmental pressure will cause these balloons to deflate and retract.

The move to a genuinely sustainable society is unlikely to be achieved while our perception of business, society and the environment is one of separate but occasionally overlapping worlds. A greener perspective is provided by the concentric circles model shown in Fig. 3.3. This implies that all of the activities of a business take place within the context of society, and that all of society's activities take place in the context of the physical environment.

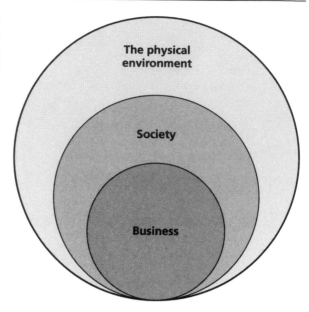

Fig. 3.3 A green perspective on the business–society–environment interrelationship

BUSINESS IN SOCIETY

The role of businesses in society

Industrialisation, the capitalist system that has overseen it, and the businesses within that system, have brought the citizens of industrialised countries a wide range of technical and economic improvements that few of us would be keen to sacrifice. However, there is a growing realisation that these have come at a socio-environmental price. This is not a new idea: the philosophers of Ancient Greece and Rome frequently bewailed the effects of increasing commercialisation. More recently, much of Marx's writings identified the potential environmental, as well as social, consequences of capitalism, encapsulated in his remark in *Das Kapital* that 'Capitalism simultaneously exhausts the two sources of riches: the earth and the worker.' Marx also foresaw that with the increasing reliance on monetary exchanges, there would be increasing divisions between people into buyers and sellers, and the transformation of

more and more elements of society into 'the commodity form'. Where once we might have relied on ourselves or our friends and family for the baking of bread or the making of music, now it is purchased impersonally through the market.

This process has created a population almost totally dependent on businesses. In pre-industrialised society, food, water, clothing, shelter, warmth, light and activities to pursue were provided directly from the environment through the efforts of individuals and the social groups to which they belonged. Today the vast majority of us depend on businesses to fulfil all of these and many other needs. Our need for money to buy goods and services, and to some extent our social needs for 'belonging' and status are fulfilled by working for other businesses. If we manage to earn more than we spend, the excess is invested in yet more businesses whose success will (hopefully) bring a worthwhile return on the investment. The public services that we depend upon are also largely funded by tax revenues from businesses and their employees. Both directly and indirectly, the material standard of living that we all experience (which is perhaps a more appropriate term than the conventional concept of automatically 'enjoying' a material standard of living) is largely a product of the total efforts of the business community within society.

This dependency gives businesses enormous power to influence individuals, communities and society as a whole. Through marketing communications, lobbying, political donations and the way in which they organise their corporate resources, businesses can influence the laws, government, values and economic development of a country. This power is compounded by the increasing size and international scope of large companies. Businesses also have an enormous power to do good, evidenced all over the world by examples of community housing initiatives, environmental improvements and programmes for training, education and health care. In meeting the green challenge, to quote Peter Bright of Shell International Petroleum Co. Ltd.:

'Business is often seen as the enemy of the environment, the polluter. There is, however, a tide of change and it is now increasingly being seen as the essential partner, as part of the solution and not the problem.' (Burke and Hill 1990)

Bernstein (1992) views such pronouncements as premature, and businesses certainly have along way to go before they are genuinely repositioned as more a part of the solution than a part of the problem. However, the concept of partnership is an important one, because it is more likely to create socio-environmental progress than an adversarial power struggle between business and society.

Businesses also have a less obvious but equally powerful influence on many of the beliefs and values held within society. The two core values of the traditional business paradigm are also central to marketing: a belief in individualism and a belief in 'the market'. Both of these principles have been so powerfully promoted and defended by businesses that an attack on business on the basis of their socio-environmental impact is often rebutted as an attack on individual liberty and freedom. The focus of consumer sovereignty is very much on individual liberty, and that 'the only grounds on which consumer sovereignty may

be attacked is by a refutation of our conception of liberty' (Hutt 1936). Environmental protection is presented as only achievable at the expense of individual freedoms to drive our cars where we want, when we want, carrying as many people as we want, with as large an engine as we want. Individual liberty is an important principle, but the green challenge has shifted the basis of the discussion about freedom and consumption. Freedom is often discussed in terms of the liberty to consume, as opposed to the right to freedom from the consequences of others' consumption. This is beginning to change, for example with the emphasis on the right to be free from the dangers of passive smoking instead of on the right of the individual to smoke. There is also growing concern about the cumulative consequences of individual consumption decisions. If everyone exercises their freedom to drive at the same time, the result is not the freedom of the open road, but an unpleasant stay in a traffic jam. Marketing cannot address the consumption decisions of the individual without considering their cumulative effect. For any individual consumer a decision to have cosmetic surgery might provide significant benefits of increased self-confidence and feelings of self-worth. However, the societal consequences of a growing market in what could be termed 'optional' cosmetic surgery in countries like the USA is altering perceptions about what constitutes a 'normal' nose, or what the 'normal' appearance of a 50-year-old person is. This may impact negatively on the quality of life of consumers who cannot afford, or who do not wish to endure, surgery, but find perceptions about appearance (including their own) being changed by the consumption decisions of others. To defend current patterns of consumption on the basis of liberty and freedom, as business has tended to do, involves making some very simplistic assumptions about the nature of freedom and the consequences of individuality expressed through consumption.

One of the most powerful influences on societal values is the mass media, and the advertisers and advertising which funds and influences it. A detailed discussion of the social impact of advertising comes from Goldman (1992) who paints a picture of advertising as an insidious force which manipulates our image of ourselves and our relationship with society and the environment. The result of this, according to the US Centre for the Study of Commercialism, is the creation of a new generation of consumers who will 'buy till they die' to the detriment of their own health, the environment and society. They blame the role of the mass media in failing to encourage social concern and involvement, or to show the positive side of lifestyles involving moderation or simplicity.

Some media are now explicitly recognising the importance of their role and the potential socio-environmental impact of commercial advertising. The following advertising policy comes from *Green* magazine.

'We believe advertising is a persuasive and powerful force within modern society and *Green* believes that advertisers should be aware of the reponsibilities which this creates.

Over the last few years consumers have become more cynical about green advertisements, following many abuses which have made it harder for environmentally responsible companies to present their case.

Green is committed to reversing this trend. In the future business will have to be ethical in order to survive and profit. This will become a key issue for advertisers in the nineties. Business has the right to promote the benefits of products to readers. And readers have the right to view advertisements that do not abuse their trust. All advertising is expected to be legal, decent and honest. But we believe in something more.

We believe that advertising should not patronise or exaggerate. We believe that advertising should not hijack irrelevant emotions as a smokescreen for an absence of real benefits. We believe that advertisers should be aware of their responsibilities with regard to sex, race, class and age stereotypes.

We believe that advertising should stand up to the closest scrutiny in terms of claims made, and always be an informative, practical and stimulating medium. We oppose subliminal advertising techniques.

Green will refuse to run advertising which flagrantly ignores these principles, even if it means a loss of revenue.'

Successful companies, and the practices and entrepreneurs behind them, are also increasingly used as role models on which other aspects of society such as education, health care and government are being remodelled. Proponents of this trend point to the need to eradicate the waste and inefficiency which is often prevalent in non- commercial sectors. Critics point to the inappropriateness of market-based approaches to areas such as education and health which results in competition between institutions instead of more socially beneficial co-operation.

Can society trust its businesses?

The trust in capitalism, business and the 'captains of industry' that was a common feature of much of the twentieth century has weakened significantly in recent decades. Alan Gerstenberg, General Motors' Chairman during the 1970s, reacting to Harris Poll figures, commented:

'... one public opinion poll after another tells us the average American does not understand how free enterprise works. Business is ... not regaining the confidence of the public it once enjoyed ... Back in 1965, 55 per cent of American households said they had "great confidence" in (business) leadership ... in 1972, only 27 per cent said they felt the same way. To me, this is most disturbing.'

After another 16 years during which the business community had the opportunity to improve the public's understanding, Harris Poll figures in 1988 showed only 19 per cent of respondents expressed confidence in major companies. Similarly, a study by the Institute of Business Ethics found that only 17 per cent of the UK population rated the honesty of top businessmen as 'high' (IBE 1988). Although confidence in all forms of institutions fell markedly over this period, businesses experienced the sharpest drop. This loss of trust is reflected in the call of Frank Popoff, Chairman of Dow Corning, when speaking on environmental issues: 'Don't trust us, track us'.

Society has also learnt to be distrustful of the 'official' reassurances that are routinely provided in response to environmental concern. According to MORI research among British consumers, less than half placed even a 'fair amount' of trust in what scientists working for industry or for the government say about environmental issues. When Dutch consumers were asked 'Whom do you believe about the environmental compatibility of products?' only 5 per cent described the manufacturer as 'believable'. This compares with 89 per cent who named leading green groups such as Greenpeace (Einsmann 1992). In September 1993 a Gallup Poll of UK consumers showed that five out of six consumers would not accept more pesticides in drinking water if they were told that the levels did not pose a threat to human health and that water bills would be lower as a result.

Such mistrust may not be misplaced. Oil companies responded to environmentalist concern about the possibility of a significant oil spill in Prince William Sound by saying that the chances of such an accident were 'one in a million'. In fact the ill-fated Exxon Valdez was only the 8549th oil tanker to negotiate those waters (Buchok 1992). Similarly, before incidents such as Chernobyl and Three Mile Island the risk of a serious nuclear accident was estimated as being as low as one in a billion years of reactor operation. In fact Chernobyl happened after only 4000 reactor years world-wide.

Societal influences on business

Although the power of businesses continues to grow, businesses still depend on society for their custom, work-force, investment and the regulation of the business environment (which protects businesses as well as customers, investors and society). The influence of society on business is a mixture of the intended and the unintended. Consumers can influence businesses intentionally through the courts or through the consumer movement, or unintentionally through aggregate changes to their lifestyles and purchasing patterns. Other players within the business environment including insurers, banks and suppliers can intervene to influence a particular company's relationship with society. Legislation provides a powerful influence on business and its effects stem from both regulations specifically aimed at controlling business activity and other measures which will have implications for partic-

ular businesses. Within society, three of the most important forces acting to shape the activities of companies are customers (dealt with in detail in Chapter 4), shareholders and regulations.

Shareholders

Shareholders, because they own companies, are obviously an important influence on them. This influence does not amount to control in the majority of large business enterprises due to the fragmentation of ownership. Shareholders' expectations play an important part in determining corporate priorities. The greater the pressure for short-term returns from investors, the more difficult it will be for any company to plot a path towards sustainability. Institutional shareholders such as pension funds have the potential to influence corporate policy relatively directly. According to Elizabeth Holtzman, New York City Comptroller:

'As the emerging owners of corporate America, with a financial and future stake in corporate activity, pension funds have an obligation to speak up. Poor management decisions, sloppy stewardship of natural resources, inattention to the consequences of wasteful and hazardous production practices can shrink the present return on our investments, and – a more sobering prospect – diminish our world.'

For individual shareholders the opportunity to exercise an influence may be limited to selling shares or exercising voting rights at shareholders' meetings. Such meetings are increasingly being used as an opportunity for shareholders to publicly scrutinise corporate social and environmental performance. Friends of the Earth have adopted a tactic of using small shareholdings within front-line companies to lobby for environmental improvement. The voting rights of shareholders have also become an important weapon for environmentalists. In 1979, a group of Swiss environmentalists called M-Frühling was established with the aim of gaining control of the Migros co-operative, Switzerland's largest retailer. By 1987, the group's 16 000 members had received 20 per cent of the voting rights from the 1.3 million members.

Regulation

Although the 'invisible hand' of the market will guide many companies towards greater social and environmental responsibility, it will not touch or motivate all companies. One of the key problems with regulation is that it is inevitably reactive, since the vested interests who oppose change always seem to be stronger than those who lobby for proactive legislation. This often results in little more than the bolting of the empty stable's door or the shuffling of a problem from one arena to another. Both these principles were demonstrated by the UK's Clean Air Act. It was only introduced after London smog killed some 4000 people in December 1952. The resulting regulations mainly caused companies to simply build taller chimneys and spread their pollution about rather more evenly. Other criticisms levelled at regulations as a method of making companies more socially and environmentally responsible include the following.

● *Problems with enforcement.* Where a compliance-orientated approach to the conduct of business is followed, it can only be effective in maintaining business standards if there is rigorous enforcement. This means both the effective detection and prosecution of business that break the rules. For example there were 16 500 water pollution incidents reported in England 1984–5, but only around 200 of the most serious incidents resulted in any form of prosecution. The polluter only pays if it is made to pay. In countries like Brazil and in parts of America such as New York State, a new breed of specialised 'green-cops' have been created to enforce environmental law. In countries such as the USA, Holland, France and Brazil individual citizens can take companies that violate environmental standards to court, along with any government agencies who fail to enforce environmental standards.

● *Punishments which fail to act as a deterrent.* The provisions of the UK's Contaminated Land (Remediation) Bill allow maximum fines of up to £20 000 (15 000 ECUs) even though the cost of cleaning up a polluted site could run into millions. Public relations costs aside, this creates a situation where it still pays to pollute, despite legislation.

● *An emphasis on minimum standards which companies must meet, but which provide no incentive for companies to exceed.*

● *The prescriptive nature of regulations fails to harness the creative ability of managers to solve problems.*

● *The creation of pollution havens.* While many countries will go to great expense to improve the global environment, other countries may benefit economically from offering manufacturers a low-cost 'pollution haven' while simultaneously benefiting from the improved global environment created by the actions of others. Elkington *et al* (1991) suggests that such 'free riders' could be dealt with using a similar approach to that embodied in the Convention on Narcotic Drugs. This obliges signatories to take action, in the form of a trade embargo for example, against states who transgress whether or not they are signatories. Stevens (1993) points out that 'a range of empirical studies has failed to confirm claims that there are widespread "pollution havens" ... environmental costs are simply not high enough to outweigh other factors in investment decisions.' She also cautions, however, that for some specific basic industries such as the refining of oil and metals, cement, pulp and paper and commodity chemicals a gradual migration of specific whole 'dirty' industries from industrialised to less industrialised countries may be underway.

Other important societal influences on business include the following.

1 *Financial incentives.* Governments can encourage greening among companies through economic instruments such as taxation and subsidies. Taxes are a very effective method of influencing businesses, but in many resource-rich countries such as Canada, the tax structure within the economy has previously been organised to encourage extractive industries such as mining, logging and oil extraction. With increasing environmental concern, tax systems are now being used to reduce pollution and protect the environment. One effective approach is taxing pollution. In Holland pollution charges led to a drop in emis-

sions within the top 14 polluting industries of 50 per cent between 1969 and 1975, a further 20 per cent cut by 1980 followed by a further 10 per cent by 1986 (Opschoor and Vos 1989). Other tax initiatives have been levelled against specific environmentally harmful inputs. In Sweden and Norway, where acid rain is a major concern, fuels are taxed according to their sulphur content. Taxes can also be levelled according to how a product is used, for example against non-returnable containers. Subsidies are also being provided to encourage environmentally orientated behaviour among businesses and their customers. Examples include the setting aside of agricultural land to allow it to regenerate, the provision of grants for domestic insulation and the donation of free compost bins to households in some UK local councils.

2 *Societal culture and values.* In some of the more radical ecological thinking, the fact that those who manage companies are people too appears to be overlooked. The values that managers bring with them into a business are a product of the wider cultural environment (although this is in turn influenced by business). As environmental concern and awareness have grown in society, they are increasingly reflected in managers' own attitudes. A survey of 200 UK senior business people was conducted by MORI in May 1989. The survey produced some interesting findings. Compared to the general public, business people were:

● 50 per cent more likely to choose a product because of green packaging or advertising, or to have donated to an environmental charity;
● twice as likely to have campaigned about an environmental issue or joined an environmental group or charity;
● almost four times as likely to have switched to lead-free fuel.

When asked to estimate the general public's tendency to buy green products or give money to environmental charities, the managers' average estimate was 40 to 50 per cent too low. This underestimation of the public's green concern suggests that business people may be out of touch with the strength of green feeling within the population. Similarly, the common perception among

the public that business people don't care about the environment appears to be misplaced, although there may be differences in the way that managers behave as managers and the way that they behave as consumers and citizens.

3 *Codes of conduct.* Codes of conduct relating to issues including the environment, social responsibility and business ethics are becoming increasingly common. Many companies produce their own codes or adopt codes for their industry, such as the chemical industry's 'Responsible Care' programme. Externally generated codes are another means by which society can attempt to influence businesses. In the USA the Coalition for Environmentally Responsible Economics (CERES) released the Valdez Principles in September 1989 in the wake of the Exxon Valdez disaster during March of that year. CERES then adopted a policy of negotiating with companies, and then using the proxy votes of socially aware institutional investors (such as churches) and using 'shareholder proposals' at annual general meetings to encourage companies to adopt the principles. It is ironic that Exxon was one of the first companies where a shareholder ballot to include the principles was fought off. Exxon attacked the proposal to ballot shareholders on the basis that issues of environmental quality were matters of 'ordinary business operations' which should not involve shareholder input (Barnard 1990). This must have seemed ironic to the company's three quarters of a million shareholders who had had to watch some $3 billion (1.4 billion ECUs) of their assets being swallowed up by the aftermath of the Exxon Valdez disaster.

4 *Social and family pressures.* In a survey of British company directors conducted by *Director* magazine, one of the most powerful sources of pressure perceived by managers as pushing them towards improved environmental performance was their own circle of family and friends (Nash 1990). In Japan the concept of 'correctness' is an important cultural influence on business. There is a growing concern among Japanese managers to avoid the social disgrace which is now attached to managers of companies which behave in a socially or environmentally irresponsible way.

Balancing social and economic responsibilities

The combined social influences on business create pressure for companies to fulfil certain responsibilities beyond the key marketing objectives of satisfying customers and creating a profit. Hay and Gray's model (Fig. 3.4) shows the business community as a whole evolving towards increasing social responsibility over time. An alternative approach is to consider the different components that make up the responsibilities of a business. Caroll lists four types of responsibility that firms can pursue:

1 economic responsibilities
2 legal responsibilities
3 ethical responsibilities
4 discretionary responsibilities.

The implications of the model are that there is a two-way split between the basic, mandatory responsibilities to make a profit and stay within the law, and the more optional responsibilities of meeting and exceeding society's expectations for behaviour. Different industries and companies are moving through the stages of the model at vastly different paces. The evidence from scandals such as those involving Guinness, BCCI and Bofors show that the degree of social responsibility varies among companies. A typical pattern is that where ethical and discretionary responsibilities are not fulfilled (as has frequently been the case in relation to the environment) then market pressure will force the company to respond in pursuit of its economic responsibilities, and new legislation will turn a discretionary responsibility into a mandatory legal one.

SOCIETY AND BUSINESS IN THE ENVIRONMENT

Environmental impact

The physical environment within which we exist is a miraculous balance of ecological systems which took some 4.5 billion years to evolve. Although people have been altering their environment since they learned to use simple tools, it is only during the last 250 years of industrialisation that resource exploitation and waste production have reached unsustainable levels. In that time we have created an environment that is largely man-made.

The environmental impact of business is so much an integral part of the world in which we live that it would be impossible to catalogue all the ways in which our world has been shaped by

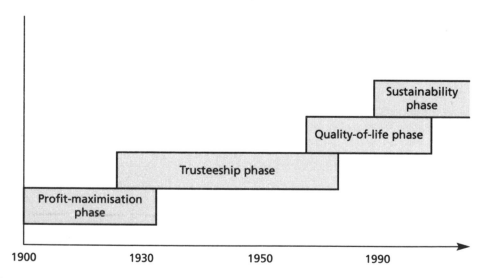

Fig. 3.4 The evolution of corporate responsibilities
(adapted from Hay and Gray (1974))

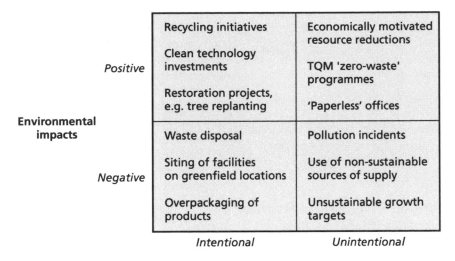

	Intentional	Unintentional
Positive	Recycling initiatives Clean technology investments Restoration projects, e.g. tree replanting	Economically motivated resource reductions TQM 'zero-waste' programmes 'Paperless' offices
Negative	Waste disposal Siting of facilities on greenfield locations Overpackaging of products	Pollution incidents Use of non-sustainable sources of supply Unsustainable growth targets

Environmental impacts (vertical axis) / **Corporate environmental strategy** (horizontal axis)

Fig. 3.5 The environmental impact grid

business. An important distinction can be drawn between *intentional* impacts on the environment in the form of mineral extraction, farming, forestry and construction with those that are *unintentional* such as oil spills or the accidental transfer of unsuitable species between ecosystems. We can also differentiate between *negative* and *positive* impacts on the environment as represented by deforestation and (appropriate) reforestation respectively. Figure 3.5 contrasts these two dimensions to produce a simple environmental impact grid. The challenge facing companies is to shift their position away from the undesirable to the desirable and to do this will require greater intent.

The combined impact of humankind's activities in the social, technological and economic quadrants of the STEP Framework (*see* page 9) on the physical quadrant can be expressed through Ehrlich and Ehrlich's (1990) IPAT Formula:

Impact = Population x Affluence x Technology

Business activities including marketing have relatively little direct influence on the population component of the equation (although marketers involved in the manufacture of condoms or the operation of dating agencies might see things differently). Marketing does influence both the level of affluence of society and the technology which creates it, however. Affluence equates to the demand for goods and services, and its environmental impact equates to the combined resources needed to support each person's lifestyle. Technology represents the means by which the demand for goods and services is satisfied. This produces four ways to reduce our environmental impact.

1 *Reducing the rate of population growth.* In industrialised countries most populations have become relatively stable and in many cases are declining. Globally the birth rate has dropped from 2.1 per cent in 1971 to 1.7 per cent in 1991. The absolute numbers added to the population each year continues to grow, however. In 1971 the global population grew by 76 million; in 1992 it grew by 92 million. Should 1993 birth and death rates remain constant, by the year 2150 the global population would have increased by more than 120 fold to reach the impossible total of 694 billion (WRI 1992). Birth control has become a major industry, which will face new opportunities as less industrialised countries seek to restrict their population growth. It is also a major marketing challenge since in many of these countries the value system is strongly influenced by Islam or the Catholic Church.

2 *Adopting less affluent lifestyles.* The 'time is money' culture that has become widespread among western industrialised countries is another cause of environmental degradation. Fast-paced living has a number of effects:

● It demands convenient pre-packaged, disposable products.
● It leads companies to pursue fast and effective strategies rather than resource-efficient strategies.
● It has led to a massive increase in stress-related illnesses which affect our quality of life and drain our health care resources.
● It discriminates against products which are slower to use or to produce. Everything from cars to computers are marketed on the basis of speed. Printing on recycled paper is seen as more expensive than using virgin paper, partly because it requires more frequent cleaning of the printing machinery, and therefore an additional delay.

3 *Supporting our lifestyles with a more efficient use of resources.* There is considerable opportunity to experience the same level of benefits from goods and services while consuming fewer resources. The majority of products are inefficiently produced or inefficient in use. A report by the American Environmental Protection Agency (EPA) (quoted in Morris 1991) revealed that:

● 87 per cent of goods and materials are thrown away after one use;
● only about 15 per cent of the fuel burned by cars is converted into motion;
● 75 per cent of the energy within the fuel consumed in US power plants is wasted in production or distribution;
● up to 50 per cent of corn grown for food is wasted in harvesting and processing.

In many cases the existing technology simply needs to be managed better. Lovins (1990) relates the story of two young engineers who, armed with an $800 (374 ECUs) computer and some enthusiasm, created changes in a Georgia power company plant which saved $20 million (9.3 million ECUs) in fuel costs over five years.

4 *Developing new, 'clean' technologies which support our lifestyle with less environmental damage.* (*See* Chapter 11.)

Each of these changes involves a significant marketing challenge. Reducing population growth may reduce the potential for market growth among companies operating in less industrialised countries. If those in industrialised countries also begin to adopt less resource-hungry lifestyles this will also present challenges to marketers more used to constant expansion in the desire to consume and more used to appealing to people's desire for Veblen's 'conspicuous consumption' than any concept of 'conspicuous frugality'. To use resources more efficiently will need considerable customer education and new green technologies will all have to fight for their share of the market often against entrenched and cheaper grey alternatives.

Perceptions of the environment

Society's perception of the environment has changed over time. For our ancestors the environment was something local that could either support or destroy their existence, and was therefore to be feared or worshipped. Industrialisation and the advance of technology allowed the environment to be 'conquered' and exploited. The consumer society then provided a range of goods and services which acted to insulate individuals from the environment. Central heating, air conditioning, refrigerators, cars, sunglasses and personal stereos all helped to keep the environment at bay, so that it could be either largely ignored or enjoyed in the context of leisure. Today the environment is something global, urgent, personally relevant to all and something to worry about. Einsmann (1992) refers to Procter and Gamble's research into consumer perceptions. When German consumers were asked to describe their fears and worries the environment was a greater worry to people than illness, unemployment or inflation. When groups of US consumers were asked to draw their cities in ten years' time, instead of drawing gleaming high-tech developments, the majority of people 'drew pictures of smog, overcrowding and overspilling garbage'. Warnings about the dangers of exposure to sunlight, smog reports on the weather bulletins and even the implications of many environmental marketing campaigns provide constant reminders that the environment that we depend upon now increasingly threatens our welfare. On the dimensions of personal relevance and urgency, environmental problems and their consequences are perceived as much closer in both time and space.

Another dimension of our perception of environmental problems is that it is dominated by infrequent, large-scale events such as the disasters at Chernobyl or Bhopal, while most of the environmental damage is caused by many small events. Oil pollution is a serious environmental problem and one that most people tend to associate with oil tanker disasters such as the Amoco Cadiz or the Exxon Valdez. However, tanker spills only account for about 12 per cent of the oil which enters the sea each year. The other 88 per cent involves losses from the 'normal' activities of production and consumption including leakages during tanker loading/offloading and the washing out of ships' tanks at sea. It is a sobering thought that 20 times as much oil as was lost from the ill-fated Exxon Valdez is poured down drains annually by American car owners doing their own oil changes – lost oil which would make ideal catalytic cracker feedstock and which could help preserve oil reserves. Such figures demonstrate that although lobbying for double-hulled oil tankers is one way to reduce oil pollution, practical and significant contributions can also be made by changing industrial working practices and our individual patterns of consumption and product usage.

Another important influence on our environmental perception is the balance of costs and benefits associated with any environmental issue. Hopfenbeck (1993) notes:

'In spite of the knowledge that, worldwide, almost 1500 people die in traffic accidents every day, we continue to break new records for the number of licences issued!'

In addition to deaths are injuries from traffic accidents which affect around two million people each year in Europe alone. Vehicles account for 75 per cent of all carbon monoxide emissions and more than 40 per cent of all atmospheric nitrogen oxides and hydrocarbons. This means that approximately half of the health costs associated with illness caused by air pollution (estimated at 19 billion ECUs in the USA alone) relates to vehicles. Any disease, any form of pollution, or the activities of any army that caused this level of suffering would cause an immediate global outcry. In the face of the perceived benefits that the 400 million cars around the world bring, the death toll on the roads and the general level of socio-environmental 'car sickness' barely registers in the news headlines.

THE PHYSICAL ENVIRONMENT'S IMPACT ON BUSINESS AND SOCIETY

Every society is strongly influenced by the nature of the physical environment within which it exists. The British obsession with the weather, the Mediterranean siesta and the increased incidence of depression during the Scandinavian winter are all examples of this influence. Humankind is no different from any other species in having to adapt to the demands of the environment in order to survive. Like many other species, in the process of surviving and thriving, humankind has learnt to shape the environment. This could be viewed as a 'natural' process and the current state of the planet as a natural consequence of the evolutionary process. What sets humankind apart from other species is the scale of environmental change which we are capable of creating, and the fact that we can consciously both comprehend the extent of the consequences of our activities and choose the path of our own evolution. While all other species evolve in a physical sense, humankind is also subject to economic, social and technical evolution.

To say that we are dependent on the environment is to state the deeply obvious. For much of the twentieth century, however, there has been a thread of optimism running through society that the application of technology would replace dependence on our environment with mastery of it. This optimism was reflected in a vision of the colonisation and exploitation of space. The implication of this being that ruining the earth would not necessarily be the end of humankind's story if, in the meantime, we could successfully reach for the stars. The fate of the American 'Star Wars' programme has shown the limitations of the idea of colonising space and retrieving extraterrestrial resources. If it proved economically and technically impossible to place relatively well understood weapons technologies in space, how likely could it be that we could use space as either an escape hatch or an extraterrestrial supermarket?

The environment provides the physical framework within which businesses, their customers and other stakeholders exist. However, as Capra (1983) observes, the mechanistic, economic models which have dominated the last century of our development dismiss the ecological contexts in which economic activity occurs. One of the most fundamental assumptions which underpins the corporate and marketing strategies of companies is that this physical framework will remain stable. In truth, no element of the physical environment can be taken for granted. Scotland is famous for many things including the beauty of its scenery, the warmth of its hospitality and its plentiful supply of rainfall; but in 1993 the Fort William region, normally one of the wettest in Britain, suffered its worst drought in 30 years. British Alcan's aluminium smelting plants at Fort William and Kinlochleven, which use some 30 million tonnes of water daily, were forced to cut output by 25 per cent while they waited for the local climate to return to normal. An issue like global warming and the potential for rising sea levels may seem remote from the majority of businesses, that is until you realise that 40 per cent of British industry is located on the coast or alongside estuaries. Predictions about the climatic effects of global warming mean that over the next 30 to 40 years such businesses could be subject to floods every three to five years, of a magnitude only previously experienced once a century.

Environmental limits to growth

The concept of limits to growth, and the question of what will happen when particular resources grow scarce or become exhausted has preoccupied philosophers, monarchs, economists, environmen-

talists and scientists throughout the ages. In 1972 The Club of Rome's *Limits to Growth* project attempted to develop a comprehensive computer model of the world's economy and its interaction with the physical environment. Projections on population levels and economic development rates were fed into the model, and the model then computed the levels of economic growth and population that the world will be able to sustain in the future. The main conclusions were:

1 If the present (1972) growth trends in world population, industrialisation, pollution, food production and resource depletion continue unchanged, the limits to growth on this planet will be reached sometime in the next 100 years. The most probable result will be a rather sudden and uncon- trollable decline in both population and industrial capacity.

2 It is possible to alter these growth trends and to establish a condition of ecological and economic stability that is sustainable far into the future. The state of global equilibrium could be designed so that the basic material needs of each person on earth are satisfied and each person has an equal opportunity to realise his or her individual human potential.

3 If the world's people decide to strive for this second outcome rather than the first, the sooner they begin working to attain it, the greater will be their chances of success.

This was followed up twenty years later by *Beyond the Limits*, a 1990s' rerun of the World3 model (Meadows *et al* 1992), which concluded that:

'Many crucial (re)sources are declining and degrading and many sinks (for waste and pollution) are overflowing. The throughput flows that maintain the human economy cannot be maintained at their current rates indefinitely, or even for very much longer.'

The impact on society

Health

Environmentalism in the 1970s did not attract more widespread support because it was seen as an attack on society and its values in a way which sought to protect nature at the expense of the welfare of people. One reason that environmental issues are attracting more interest in the 1990s is the increasing evidence that societal welfare is being directly affected through the issue of health. The figures behind a number of environmentally linked illnesses makes alarming reading.

● In the UK environmentalist group reports suggest that one in seven children now suffers from asthma, with one in three suffering in some urban areas. This is considerably more than the number of clinically recorded cases, but even these have been increasing at an annual rate of around 5 per cent for the last decade.

● The incidence of brain tumours has grown by 30 per cent over the past 40 years.

● A study quoted in the *British Medical Journal* showed that over the last 50 years the sperm count of men has halved, while their quantity of semen has decreased by a quarter. The only plausible explanation is that something in the environment is responsible. The next step is to identify what that something is. The chief suspects are oestrogen-like compounds such as PCBs.

The very basic necessities of life are being polluted, or are perceived as being polluted, in ways which threaten to impair human health. Even air is a concern for consumers living in urban areas, with pollution-conscious commuters in Tokyo now able to buy a personal supply of bottled air from local department stores. Environmentally related health concerns are strongest in North America where:

● 60 per cent of American and almost 80 per cent of Canadian consumers believe that agricultural chemicals and preservatives used in food production can impair their health, according to research by the Angus Reid Group;

● 69 per cent of US consumers believe that environmental problems are triggering an escalation in health problems (Ottman 1992a);

● the US National Wildlife Federation's Environmental Quality Index showed that nearly 40 per cent of Americans experience significant health problems related to drinking water.

The human costs of environmental degradation are even more obvious in countries where environmental protection has received a lower priority. In Bulgaria democratisation led to the release of previously classified public health research data (Friedman 1990). This showed that people living near heavy industrial complexes, in comparison to the rest of the population, were:

● nine times more likely to suffer from asthma;

● seven times more likely to suffer from skin diseases;

● four times more likely to suffer liver disease; and

● three times more likely to suffer from nervous system disorders.

Safety

A 1986 report by the UNEP suggested that the increase in the number of people being killed by 'natural' disasters was rising at a rate out of step with population growth. This meant that, unless people for some reason were choosing to live in more unstable areas, human intervention was creating a more unstable and threatening natural environment. The report pointed to factors such as:

● increased tropical storm activity and intensity resulting from increasing atmospheric carbon dioxide levels, partly resulting from man-made emissions;

● flooding caused by deforestation, dams and atmospheric warming;

● dams implicated in triggering major earthquakes in several countries including China, India and Greece;

● desertification caused by rainforest clearance and the cultivation of cash crops on unsuitable land;

● avalanches and landslides linked to deforestation, ski-run creation and building projects.

Although there is a tendency for such disasters to be thought of as 'natural' or as 'Acts of God', therefore, there is growing evidence that human activity is an important contributory factor.

Employment

As societies move towards protecting the environment, some people working in environmentally sensitive sectors will lose their jobs. Sadly this is inevitable. It is not, however, a good reason for resisting the need to protect the environment. It would be rather like arguing against peace on the basis that jobs in the defence industry will be threatened.

The employment argument against increased environmental protection is based on the assumption that a maximum economic growth approach will create the most jobs. There is growing evidence that maximising economic growth does not necessarily bring about increasing employment. According to Goldsmith (1993) such grey growth is achieved by replacing people in the production process with capital (in the form of dependable and cost-effective technology). He cites the example of the US steel industry which increased its productivity during the 1960s by 45 per cent while reducing its work-force by 75 per cent. A country such as France was expected to increase its unemployment level from 10 per cent in 1993 to 12.6 per cent in the year 2000, even with average annual economic growth of 2.4 per cent. For the EU as a whole 25 million new jobs will need to be created by 2010 to meet the employment needs of the EU's growing work-force.

The increasing size of companies, particularly through the massive wave of acquisitions and mergers of the mid-1980s and the 'restructuring' they inevitably involve, has contributed to a decrease in employment in companies whose economic output is increasing. In the past job losses were mostly associated with unprofitable companies cutting costs to regain competitiveness. Today job losses in profitable and growing companies are becoming increasingly common, suggesting that economic growth is no guarantee of increasing employment. In many sectors, numerous small companies are being replaced by larger more economically efficient companies, with an accompanying reduction in employment. Douthwaite (1992) points out that the groceries provided by Britain's 292 Sainsbury's stores would in the 1950s' economy have been provided by some 37 000 assorted small retailers. These would have provided 130 000 full-time and 24 000 part-time jobs as opposed to the 38 089 full-time and 61 912 part-time jobs existing within Sainsbury's as of 1990.

The service sector has traditionally been the answer to creating jobs in response to the employment decline in the manufacturing sector. However, technology is now beginning to reduce employment in service industries. A *New York Times* article from February 1993 pointed out that the US postal service planned to reduce the number of postal workers by 47 000 as a new computer system for reading and sorting letters was introduced, and that AT&T was planning to replace 6000 operators by robots which can recognise key words of speech. The conclusion was that 'most American workers are employed in tasks that can be done by computers, automated machinery and robots'. Within the UK banks have been reporting record years for growth and profit while making significant reductions in their work-force.

These arguments are not intended to be either anti-technology or anti-big business. They simply demonstrate that to argue against green growth on the basis of fears about unemployment is to make the questionable assumption that grey growth creates or protects employment. A move towards a greener economy could have a beneficial effect on employment. If greening means reducing our usage of raw materials, a move towards more labour-intensive and more service-orientated business would be desirable. A greener economy may mean different jobs for people, but not necessarily fewer jobs for people. Fields such as pollution control equipment, nature-orientated tourism, natural and urban environment clean-up projects, energy conservation, environmental education and publishing are all likely to grow as providers of jobs. A 1983 report by the UK Association for the Conservation of Energy and Environmental Resources suggested that a ten-year programme of domestic insulation costing between £10 million and £24.5 million (7.5–18.4 million ECUs) would create between 50 000 and 128 000 jobs and save between £1.4 billion and £2.8 billion (1–2 billion ECUs) per year. In the USA, although the EPA found that 33 000 jobs were lost as a result of 155 pollution-related factory closures from 1971 to 1983, some 167 000 jobs had been created in the pollution abatement industry by 1985.

The economic impact

Whenever environmental protection is discussed, the economic consequences are always emphasised by the vested interests in the industries involved. There is a common pattern when any product or process comes under attack on the basis of environmental concern. First, the industries that produce and/or use the offending technology defend against criticism by arguing that it is important for the technical and economic performance of a product, process or industry. Phasing it out, they claim, will lead to consumers suffering from poorer quality products and will lead to the loss of jobs and growth within the economy. After a delay and the watering-down of proposed legislation against the technology in question, the relevant industries unveil an alternative technology. The suffering of consumers and losses of jobs which are actually related to the new legislation (as opposed to downsizing, recession or mismanagement) rarely appear. This has been the story with the removal of CFCs as an aerosol propellant (where their banning was heralded as an economic disaster in the 1970s in the USA), textile finishing chemicals such as alkylated phenol ethoxylates and lead in petrol. Technical and economic barriers to the change from grey technologies to alternative green ones seem relatively low compared to the 'softer' barriers of managerial conservatism.

The result of the anti-green lobbying by industries under environmental pressure has been to build up an expectation that increased environmental protection must go hand-in-hand with a reduction in economic growth and business activity. This does not have to be the case. If companies manufacture products designed to last longer than existing models, they will reduce the turnover available from new unit sales, but instead could look to servicing, upgrades, accessory sales and reconditioning to gain increased turnover from existing units. There is also a growing environmental industry which is contributing both to environmental protection and improvement as well as economic growth. The OECD estimates that the 'environment industry' including companies involved in waste management, pollution control equipment and environmental services, includes 30 000 companies in the USA, 20 000 in Europe and 9000 in Japan (Stevens 1992).

Although it is often the economic costs of increasing environmental protection that are emphasised, the costs of poor environmental performance should not be underestimated. A range of incidents have demonstrated the economic wisdom of investment to guard against environmental disaster.

● Acid rain costs in (former West) Germany are estimated at 140 million ECUs annually in terms of forestry damage, and 470 million ECUs for property according to German Ministry of the Interior estimates.

● In the 12 years after the partial core melt-down in the nuclear reactor at Three Mile Island, clean up costs had reached over $1 billion (470 million ECUs) and compensation claims had reached over $300 million (140 million ECUs).

● The escape of toxic methyl isocyanate at the Union Carbide plant in Bhopal in 1984 left an estimated 50 000 people seriously injured and a death toll put as high as 5000 according to official estimates. It led to a $470 million (220 million ECUs) out-of-court settlement with the Indian Government.

BALANCING THE RELATIONSHIP – BY MARKET FORCES OR COMMAND AND CONTROL?

Discussions about the need to protect the environment inevitably involve questions about whose responsibility it should be, who should pay the costs involved, and whether the market mechanisms that have so successfully degraded the environment can be turned around to protect it. The debate as to whether environmental protection should be driven by regulation and funded by taxation, or whether it should be left to the private sector and market forces is rather a curious one. Nobody expects his or her personal safety to be left to the play of market forces. We all expect our taxes to pay for an army to defend us against external attack and to step in during natural disasters and other emergencies. We also expect our taxes to fund a police force to enforce the laws enacted by our government to protect us from harm from other citizens or organisations. This does not stifle a thriving market for products relating to our personal safety, from burglar alarms to cars with safety cages. By the late 1980s, Americans were actually paying more for burglar alarms and private security devices than they were paying in taxes for public police forces (Reich 1987). Protecting the environment is simply an extension of the logic of our desire for national and personal security because without a healthy environment, our health and our very lives are in danger (which makes it curious that many of the politicians who are most hawkish in their desire to support expenditure on national security, are the most strongly opposed to expenditure on environmental protection; why should soil become so precious when somebody else might want it, and yet be so expendable when we must pay to prevent it from eroding or becoming polluted?).

Individual consumers, however patriotic, cannot and would not make purchasing decisions which will ensure the national security of their country. Similarly consumers, however green, cannot and would not make purchasing decisions which will entirely protect their environment. Green consumption and environmental marketing is only a partial answer to the problem of achieving sustainability. So too is legislation. What is certain, is that unless the powerful forces of marketing and consumption are aligned to the political, legal, educational and social efforts to reach sustainability, the dream of a sustainable society will be replaced by the nightmare of environmental catastrophe.

CHAPTER 4

A new marketing environment

'The successful company is the one which is the first to identify emerging consumer needs, and to offer product improvements which satisfy those needs. The successful marketer spots a new trend early, and then leads it.'
(Edward G. Harness 1982)

INTRODUCTION

The elements of the world beyond the company which are of interest to marketers are referred to collectively as the marketing environment. Kotler (1994) defines it as consisting of:

'the external actors and forces that affect the company's ability to develop and maintain successful transactions and relationships with its target customers.'

From the marketing environment comes the demand for the goods and services that the company produces, the resource inputs it depends upon, and the competitors and constraints that it faces. An important role for the marketing philosophy and function within a company is to make it 'outward looking' so that it confronts and responds to the world beyond the factory gates. This forces the vision of the company to move beyond the familiar and controllable internal environment to focus on a world beyond, which can often seem bewildering, unpredictable and hostile. The actors and forces in the marketing environment are shown in Fig. 4.1.

Keeping informed about the marketing environment, analysing it to understand the implications of the changes taking place within it, and developing effective responses to it are considerable challenges for any company. Faced with accelerating technological change, shortening product life cycles and fragmenting customer needs, it becomes increasingly difficult for companies to monitor and understand changes in their marketing environment. Many of the changes are intertwined in ways that make them difficult to monitor and manage. In the case of the physical environment, environmental degradation is likely to have a knock-on effect in terms of pressure group action, media interest, public opinion and political response which may eventually combine to alter the legal, economic or competitive situation that a company faces.

In spite of its importance as the framework within which businesses operate and as a driving force behind other changes, the physical environment has typically been neglected during analysis of the marketing environment. It was interesting to pick up a 1992 book entitled *The Business and Marketing Environment* (Palmer and Worthington 1992) and note that although the economic, international, political, demographic, socio-cultural, technological and legal environments all merited their own sections, there was little or no mention of the green, physical environment. This is not an indictment of the book, which is excellent when judged on its own terms, but it is an indication of the way in which the grey marketing and management culture takes the physical environment for granted. The emergence of the green challenge has pushed the physical environment on to the agenda for marketers, and added another set of complex, unpredictable and often poorly understood factors for them to deal with.

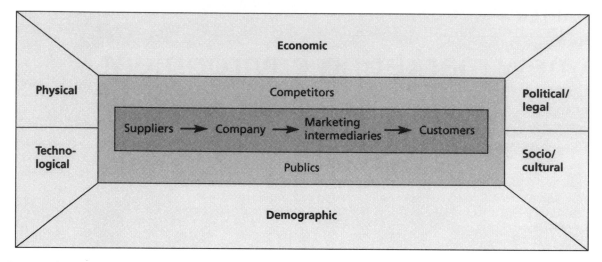

Fig. 4.1 The marketing environment
(Source: Kotler (1988))

The net effect has been to make a difficult task considerably harder. Kiernan (1992) explains the relatively poor response of many senior managers to the green challenge as a reflection of 'strategic overload'.

The effect of the green challenge on companies has been likened to the oil price shocks of the 1970s. However, this holds true in some markets more clearly than others. A manager from a chemical company or a manufacturer of aerosols would have a very different perspective on the significance of the green challenge to another manager working for a computer software firm. As environmental degradation increases, so the effects of the green challenge will be felt more deeply in a wider range of markets.

There are four main ways in which the behaviour of the forces and actors in the marketing environment can affect a company's ability to deliver customer satisfaction at a profit:

1 by affecting the extent or the nature of the demand for the goods or services of a business;

2 by changing the production economics or the production methods available to a business;

3 by altering the ability of a business to satisfy the needs of its customers in comparison to its competitors;

4 by altering the viability of the company as a whole in terms of its social, political and legal acceptability, or its economic health.

True to the spirit of holism, the marketing environment should be thought of as an interconnected whole. In practice, dealing with it is made simpler by subdividing the environment into:

● different parties within the *microenvironment* (those which influence and interact with the company directly and regularly), and

● elements of the *macroenvironment* (the wider social and environmental context whose forces help to shape developments within the microenvironment).

THE NEW MICROENVIRONMENT – SAME ACTORS, DIFFERENT SCRIPT?

Customers

The most important of all the players in the market is the customer, around whose wants and needs all the marketing effort revolves. The eco-performance that a company achieves may be a direct result of customer pressure, or it may be restricted by the customers' willingness to accept green price premiums or alternative green products. During the first phases of environmental marketing, consumer pressure has been important, but still secondary to the impact of legislation as a driving force behind environmental improvement. The influence of the green consumer will grow as environmental awareness among consumers spreads and improvements are made to the environmental information available through ecolabelling schemes, consumer groups and consumer guides. Specialised marketing research services are now being developed to keep marketers up to date on the evolution of consumers' environmental concern. In the USA there are now a number of regular and detailed green market reports available to marketing managers, such as The Roper Organization's *Green Guage* and Environmental Research Associates' *Environmental Report* (Winters 1990). The role of the green consumer is considered in more detail in Chapter 5.

A company's customers can be made up of individual consumers and households, other organisations, retailers or other forms of reseller, or governmental and other public service providers. Organisations as green customers can have considerable impact on their suppliers, and therefore on a number of industries. It is becoming increasingly common for companies who are concerned about environmental performance to use it as an important criterion when selecting suppliers and to insist upon suppliers conducting an environmental audit. A 1989 survey of 2636 businesses in Spain, Sweden, Germany and The Netherlands conducted by 3M found that environmental quality was selected as the most important criterion for selecting suppliers by 20 per cent of companies. Value for money came second as the most important criterion for 17 per cent. In a 1993 survey among US purchasing managers conducted by *Purchasing* magazine, 40 per cent said that they had 'bought green' during the past year, mostly in response to changing legislation, or to suggestions from inside the organisations (*Purchasing* 1993). Governments and other major institutions can represent large

markets which may wish to avoid suppliers with a poor eco-performance in order to appear socially responsible themselves. Kiernan (1992) reports the following anecdote:

'One of the world's largest paper companies commits a minor technical environmental violation in the state of Maine. As a result, in May of 1992, the US federal government imposes a three-year ban on government paper purchases from the company. Cost to the company in lost revenues? Over $100 million.'

Competitors

After legislation and the customer, the competition is the next most important external influence on environmental marketing. Many companies' greening strategies are sparked by competitor initiatives which leave the company at a strategic disadvantage. Varta's introduction of the mercury-free battery into the UK was rapidly matched by Ever Ready's mercury and cadmium-free product. Alternatively a greening strategy may be deferred because of fears of retaliatory price cutting by competitors.

Suppliers

Marketers' concern about suppliers has traditionally been twofold. Strategically, marketers want security from any disruption to supply which would affect the company's ability to serve its customers. Operationally, the cost and quality of supply must ensure that prices and quality standards of finished products can be maintained. Environmental marketing places a much greater emphasis on the relationship with suppliers, since a great deal of the environmental impact of a product will relate to the production of raw materials and energy needed to manufacture products. Environmental performance can become an important issue in supplier choice (*see* Chapter 11 for further details). Marketing departments also act as purchasers for a variety of services to support the marketing effort such as advertising and market research. A move towards a green strategy may require a different approach and a change of marketing services suppliers.

Marketing intermediaries

The majority of manufacturers rely on other companies to distribute and sell the products to the customer. Intermediaries play an important part in representing the manufacturer to the final consumer, in passing information between the consumer and the manufacturer and in facilitating the economic exchanges involved in marketing. The role of intermediaries in the environmental marketing process is considered in more detail in Chapter 14.

Publics

For every business there are groups of people who are not customers or part of the industry, but who have an interest in the business and often a potential influence upon it. These are often referred to as the company's publics, and they can include local communities, government, media organisations, investors, financial institutions, insurance companies, interest groups and the general public.

Local communities

The increasing scale of businesses can lead them to dominate the communities within which they operate. The sheer scale, complexity and delocalisation of business enterprises can lead to them becoming alienated from the communities within which they grew. In the case of Lothian Chemical in Scotland, after more than a decade of complaint by local residents concerning pollution in and around the site, it was forced to quit its site by its landlord, Edinburgh District Council. Among a poll of over 1000 US adults who were asked 'Who is doing their share to help reduce environmental problems?', local businesses were cited by 45 per cent of respondents, compared to the 22 per cent who cited large corporations. Becoming more local is an important aspect of the green agenda, which can produce benefits for customers, employees and the communities within which businesses exist.

Government

Environmental degradation has become a major issue on the agenda for governments all over the world. This concern was reflected in the 1992 Rio Summit which represented the largest intergovernmental conference in history. Governments have to balance the pressure for economic growth to increase living standards and fund public expenditure against the pressure for environmental protection and an improved quality of life. Following the publication of the *Brundtland Report* (WCED 1987), the majority of governments around the world have embraced the principles, if not the practice of sustainability. Although the environment forms only one strand of government policy, its influence on other aspects such as transport and industry is increasing. In some instances it can become a crucial issue. In The Netherlands the national environmental policy plan attempted to achieve sustainable development at a national level. The proposals within the plan to reduce the level of private transport proved so controversial that the Christian Democrat/Liberal coalition government split. In the ensuing elections, the Prime Minister, Ruud Lubbers was returned to power with his environmental plan endorsed by the electorate.

Government policy on the environment tends to contain a mixture of command-and-control style regulations, financial incentives and the promotion of industry self-regulation. These can affect the prices of products, quantitative aspects of eco-performance (such as outputs of emissions) or the nature of the technology used (*see* Table 4.1 over).

Media organisations

The environment has become increasingly visible as a media issue. In newspaper journalism Brookes *et al* (1976) recorded steady but minor coverage of the environment in the pages of *The Times* between 1953 and 1965. This was followed by a threefold increase between 1965 and 1973 in terms of the proportion of space devoted to environmental issues. Between 1985 and 1989 the use of the phrase 'environmentally friendly' in a sample of printed media had leapt from once a month to 30 times a day, and the word 'recycling' was used nine times as often (Mitchell and Levy 1989). 1993 saw a reduction in green news

Table 4.1 Governmental responses to environmental concern

Type of policy	Variables affected		
	Price	Quantity	Technology
Regulation command-and-control		• Emissions standards (USA – Federal/Calif.) • Quotas and bans (USA – CFCs)	• Mandated technical standards (USA, Europe, Japan – Catalytic converters) • Efficiency standards (USA – Fuel efficiency)
Economic incentives	• Effluent charges (Netherlands) • Deposit plans (Bottles – Germany Cars – Norway) • Green taxes (Fuel taxes – Netherlands, Sweden)	• Tradable emissions permits (USA – Sulphur dioxide) • Tradable production permits (USA – Lead trading program)	• Research & Development subsidies (Japan – MITI electric battery program)
Industry self-regulation		• Individual corporate targets (USA – Pollution Prevention Pays, 3M) • Industry collection systems (Germany – DSD France – Eco-emballage)	• Guidelines on cleaner technologies (Japan – Keidanren Environmental Charter)

Adapted from the World Bank's *World Development Report 1992*, by Simon (1992)

coverage among British newspapers, with the majority removing a full-time environment correspondent from their staff. This was despite considerable evidence of continuing concern among their readership. It is also ironic in the face of poll findings from MORI, in which two thirds of editors of key national media felt that businesses were not paying sufficient attention to their social responsibilities.

The more dramatic and therefore newsworthy environmental degradation becomes, the closer the interest that media organisations will take in corporate environmentally related deeds and words. The speed and global coverage of today's media also has profound implications. As Mulhall (1992) notes:

'The massive impact of instant media in accelerating the message of gross environmental incompetence by our leaders can be summarized in three letters – CNN. It means that a company's reputation can be destroyed globally in one day.'

The media have been particularly vociferous in savaging companies whose high profile environmental performance has been exposed as relatively one-dimensional. Procter and Gamble introduced new Ariel washing powder as a green brand on the basis of its concentrated formula and resource saving compact size. When it was revealed that the product had been tested on animals, the company was greeted with front-page headlines in the *Daily Star* announcing that 'Animals Die For Green Soapsuds'.

Two further challenges are presented to companies by the interest being taken by the media. The first is that media organisations are adopting the environment as an issue for advocacy and campaigning as opposed to objective reporting. Charles Alexander, as Science Editor with *Time* magazine, is reported as saying, 'I would freely admit that on the environmental issue we have crossed the boundary from news reporting to advocacy.' Or as Teya Ryna, Vice President of the Society of Environmental Journalists, put it, 'The "balance report" in some cases may no longer be the most informative. Indeed it can be debilitating. Can we afford to wait for our audience to come to its conclusions? I think not.' The second problem is that media coverage of environmental issues has tended to confuse as often as it has enlightened. Bernstein (1992) notes that although there is usually a mainstream scientific consensus on most environmental issues, media coverage highlights the differences of opinion and uncertainties. This has the effect of making the nature of the problems, their causes, effects and potential solutions appear more uncertain than they are. Like managers, most media correspondents have little training in environmental issues. Where an issue goes beyond the columns of the environmental correspondent, the reporting often lapses into misinformation. During the initial response to the discovery of the ozone hole, Britain's *Today* newspaper told its readers that CFCs were released every time they opened their fridge doors.

So far, the media has put greater pressure on companies seeking to capitalise on environmental concern, than on those who are the cause of it. The practice of 'spotlighting' companies making green claims has led to an increasingly cautious approach to greening. Despite its environmental excellence, The Body Shop has been the subject of two different television documentaries seeking to 'expose' the company as hypocritical. A typical marketing manager's response to this might be 'If a company which has made such a wholehearted effort to be green is coming in for this level of media hostility, what hope would a greening strategy for my company have?' In Canada, the supermarket chain Loblaw ran into considerable environmentalist criticism in the media following the launch of its 'Green Line'. This reaction was described by Loblaw's President as:

'a tragedy for the environment. Our ultimate strategy was to force other retailers and manufacturers in the food industry to make the environment their number one priority ... (now) I'm sure that manufacturers will just back away from dealing with issues that have to do with the environment.' (Sutter 1989)

Investors

In a MORI poll, some two thirds of leading institutional investors and business journalists shared the sentiments of leading media editors in viewing companies as not paying enough attention to social responsibility. The relationship between investors and companies varies from country to country. Elkington *et al* (1991) partly ascribes the decline of the USA as a manufacturing power and the rise of Japan and Germany to differing shareholder expectations. US firms are judged on the basis of quarterly results which encourage short-termism. German and Japanese investors play more of a long-term partnership role which provides more opportunity to justify environmental investments.

In a 1990 survey by Touche Ross, only 9 per cent of UK companies responding felt under shareholder pressure to improve eco-performance compared to 20 per cent in The Netherlands and 70 per cent in Denmark. Institutional investment is being affected by increasing awareness of the risks and costs of poor environmental performance in terms of insurance costs, responses to tougher legislation, lost business among green consumers and the dangers of environmentally unsound acquisitions. It is also being driven by the rising interest in green investment and a recognition that a greener strategy can generate competitive advantage and cost reductions through greater resource efficiency (Tennant and Campanale 1991). According to a 1991 survey, conducted by Dewe Rogerson, of 80 senior fund managers from major institutional investors:

- 67 per cent believed that environmental factors had a significant effect on business;
- 58 per cent said that a coherent and effective environmental strategy enhanced their perception of a business;
- 40 per cent said that environmental performance was an important factor in their investment decisions;
- only 11 per cent viewed the environment as unimportant.

In addition to the interest in eco-performance shown by conventional institutional investors, there is a growing market for environmentally and ethically screened investment. In the UK the 18 green investment trusts and three green unit trusts by 1994 accounted for £600 million (450 million ECUs) in funds. Although this may seem insignificant in the face of a market worth over £100 billion (75 billion ECUs), and in comparison to an American green investment market worth over $650 billion (304 billion ECUs), it is impressive considering that the market only began in 1984 with Friends Provident Stewardship Fund (Pridham 1994). Although green funds represent a small minority of total investment, the public relations implication of green investment decisions can be disproportionately large. Following its achievement in being named as Green Retailer of the Year, Tesco was disturbed by the publicity surrounding its de-listing from the Merlin Jupiter Ecology Fund because of its role in out-of-town shopping development and the use of overpackaging.

Financial institutions

Banks large and small play an important part in the financing and control of businesses and development projects. Like retailers they have a role as gatekeepers and influencers. At one end of the scale there are massive, global financial institutions, which are a key force in channelling the direction of economic growth. The World Bank, for example, has recently embraced the importance of sustainable development. This follows considerable criticism of the socio-environmental performance of their development projects and the investment of millions of dollars in projects which have proved to be environmental disasters, such as the settlement of the Amazon Basin, the Brazilian power sector dams, and settlement of Indonesia's outer islands. At the other end of the scale, an important new trend within less industrialised nations is 'village banking' which provides low interest rates for local, human-scale projects instead of aid.

High street financial institutions have also become involved. In 1991 The National Westminster Bank became the first major British bank to launch a campaign to improve both the environmental performance of its own operations and to influence the behaviour of its customers. 1992 witnessed the Co-operative Bank giving strong emphasis to the use of environmental criteria in its lending policy.

Insurance companies

Environmental risk is coming to dominate the thoughts of insurance companies, and is reflected in the insurance bills that a company receives. With the introduction of specific Environmental Impairment Liability (EIL) insurance, insurers are no longer attempting to estimate risks by analysis of paper records, but instead are insisting on technical audits of sites and processes. In the USA the environmental insurance market boomed in the early 1980s. The number of insurers offering EIL rose from 15 in 1982 to 40 in 1983, but the market collapsed in 1984 when claims of over $90 million (42 million ECUs) far outstripped the $35 million (16 million ECUs) collected in premiums. Instead of being one component of general insurance cover, EIL must now be covered by specific policies. Cover is expensive and only available to companies able to demonstrate proactive environmental risk management, pollution control and minimisation systems and tightly controlled waste management systems. Cover is usually limited to sudden accidental pollution incidents, as opposed to environmental damage caused by gradual pollution or normal waste disposal operations.

The UK Centre for the Study of Financial Innovation has developed proposals for a technique which would assess the potential environmental risk for insurers and investors that different companies pose. The index takes a company's potential for exposure to environmental liabilities and contrasts this with the company's ability to deal with such liabilities (in terms of management systems, financial resources and technology) to create an environmental credit rating. Such an index would require considerably more freedom of access to environmental information than currently exists, but if developed and implemented it could revolutionise the environmentally related financial forces acting on a company.

Interest groups

There is a wide range of groups with some form of interest in the environment. While some will be local and linked to a specific issue, others will be global and will span across the full spectrum of green causes. Growth in memberships increased dramatically during the 1980s, as did the resources at groups' disposal. Greenpeace doubled its membership and total budget every two years during the 1980s, ending with over 4 million members world-wide. Groups' effectiveness in terms of political lobbying and their ability to target the consumers of key grey companies and industries also increased substantially. In the USA green groups spent around $500 million (234 million ECUs) on lobbying during 1987 and 1988 (Holcombe 1990). Green interest groups became increasingly competent at using 'offensive' marketing techniques to get their message across and put pressure on grey marketers. As Strid and Cater (1993) observe, green groups' advertising 'has the look and feel of professional advertising, quite simply because it's done by some of the same talent that does a lot of big-name, corporate campaigns.'

Green interest groups vary in terms of the approach that they take towards specific issues and the businesses related to them. There are three basic approaches.

1 *Direct action.* A group such as Greenpeace emphasises direct action, which might come in the form of welding shut a pipe dumping radioactive waste, or using bodies and boats as a shield to prevent the harpooning of whales. Groups vary in the extent to which they will break the law in their fight against practices they see as unethical. In the most extreme cases some businesses have been affected by environmental terrorists who use force to attack grey businesses. An example comes from Canada where some dark greens have taken to spiking mature trees to make them unusable for sawmills.

2 *Campaigning and lobbying.* Other groups emphasise the need to provide information to consumers, citizens and businesses to encourage better eco-performance. Friends of the Earth places a great deal of emphasis on its lobbying and communication activities. Some of the major campaigns in recent years have focused on nuclear power, agrochemicals, farming, construction and car manufacturing.

3 *Partnership.* A very distinctive feature of the 1990s' green movement compared to the 1970s' environmental movement is the degree to which businesses and green groups are willing to work together to tackle environmental problems. For marketers, partnership opportunities exist to tie promotions in to environmental issues or charities. Finnish company Nokia used a tie in with the World Wide Fund for Nature (WWF) and its Panda logo to launch its recycled paper products, and outsold its nearest rival two-to-one, despite a 50 per cent smaller advertising budget.

Although groups will mostly favour one of these three approaches, they can vary between them as circumstances demand. Companies facing pressure from green interest groups have tended to make two fundamental mistakes.

● The first is to react negatively to environmentalist criticism by adopting a strategy from the 'D' list of

Defend
Deny
Discredit
Disprove
Deflect.

Such responses can be counter-productive, since, given conflicting stories from green groups and a company, the company is likely to finish second in the race for credibility (*see* Table 4.2).

● The second mistake is to regard interest groups as something that only exists 'out there' in the external environment. The millions of members of green groups not only exist in the marketing environment, some of them are very likely to exist inside the marketing department. This makes any attempt to create a false impression on eco-performance rather dangerous. In the wake of the Braer oil disaster, an internal BP memo advising managers to 'keep their heads down' cast the company in a reactive and negative light (in contrast to its carefully nurtured image for environmental responsibility) when it was leaked to Greenpeace and appeared on a large *Financial Times* advertisement.

Table 4.2 Sources of credible environmental information

	Percentage of consumers surveyed describing group as a 'very good unbiased source of environmental information'
Environmental groups	37
Consumers groups	24
The news media	19
Retailers	9
Government	7
Product manufacturers	5

Source: Kamena (1991)

General public

Although only a certain proportion of the general public will be a company's customers, it is still important to foster a positive image among society as a whole. In marketing terms it is important for customers to feel that their behaviour as consumers is socially acceptable. For cigarette companies, their major battles are not against one another or even for their consumers (who are mostly product dependent). Instead they fight to survive in the face of public support for tough legislation to restrict their marketing activities and the use of their products and also they must fight to prevent mounting social pressure from undermining their customers' desire for the product.

Since 1982 an EU survey has been tracking the general public's attitudes towards the environment (together with energy), using a representative group of 12 000 adults. The following key trends have emerged.

● A clear majority consider that 'protecting the environment and preserving natural resources are essential to economic development'.

● Concern is increasing about the state of the global and national environment, although most Europeans are relatively satisfied with the quality of their local environment. The key global issues which concern people are ozone depletion, acid rain and the greenhouse effect.

● The state of the environment is seen as a problem in both the short term and the longer term, with the main concerns being chemical pollution, rubbish, overuse of agrochemicals, industrial waste and pollution of lakes, rivers and seas.

● Although a significant number of people linked energy sources to environmental problems (ranging from 43 to 45 per cent identifying coal and oil as a problem to under 20 per cent for nuclear energy), they tended to be confused about the effects of particular fuels. Most expected technology to make energy sources cleaner and allow consumption to continue to grow, and therefore were not actively pursuing energy conservation.

MACROENVIRONMENTAL FORCES

The macroenvironment of a business is difficult to analyse since it contains no clear-cut boundaries. '*PEST analysis*' is a popular and simple framework which subdivides the external world into factors relating to the Political, Economic, Social and Technical environments. This is a 'broadbrush' approach, rooted in a marketing perspective which neglects the physical environment. A more detailed framework which includes the physical factors is *SCEPTICAL analysis*, which examines the external world in terms of a more flexible set of nine environmental dimensions.

● Social
● Cultural
● Economic
● Physical
● Technical and scientific
● International
● Communications and infrastructure
● Administrative and institutional
● Legal and political.

The implication of the sequence of initials being that a marketer should be sceptical of the feasibility of a marketing strategy that has not been checked against each of these factors. During the 1990s and beyond, the physical environment will continue to deteriorate. Given an expanding global population and the continuation of unsustainable economic activity, this is unavoidable and it will have a knock-on effect in all other sectors of the macroenvironment. Key aspects in the physical environment that marketers may need to monitor include loss of specific species or habitats, disruption or destruction of ecosystems including weather systems and the protective ozone layer, and depletion of important resources such as water and fossil fuels.

Social dimensions

Demographic change has always affected consumption patterns and marketing activities, and it looks set to become increasingly important in determining the fate of humankind. Total population numbers are important as a factor in determining the environmental impact of the marketing system (*see* IPAT model on page 49). Conventionally marketers view population growth as a beneficial form of market expansion. However, more people will only produce more custom where new potential customers can afford to purchase. Sadly, much of the forecast population growth will occur in the least industrialised nations and will be associated with deepening poverty and the creation of needs that society and its business systems are unlikely to fulfil.

Population numbers tend to dominate discussions relating to the future of consumption. This makes sense for the very important issues of providing the basics of life such as food and water. For other forms of product, there are other demographic factors which are important beyond total population numbers. Social trends towards later marriages and increasing number of divorces are acting to create an increased number of households in countries where the population is steady or declining. The consumption of many products including consumer durables such as washing machines, televisions, cars and bathroom suites,

together with other products such as newspapers, fuel and mortgages is related to the number of households, rather than to the level of population. In 1981 only 12 per cent of UK households consisted of one person. By 1989 25 per cent of households were single people, forecast to rise to 31 per cent by 2001.

Another demographic shift with implications for the green challenge is identified by Ford (1992a), who suggests that industrialised societies are becoming more child-centred as a result of the 'baby boomers' becoming parents, often at a lifestage where individual ambition has waned and is replaced by concern for their children and the world that future generations will inherit.

Cultural dimensions

Within society, decisions about people's lifestyles, spending, consumption, investment, employment and political activities are all influenced by a range of cultural values and beliefs which are shared generally and among specific groups. The green challenge is a challenge to the very heart of what Johnson (1991) defines as our current 'terminal' (unsustainable) culture. Kotler sees the key cultural values as being expressed through six relationships.

1 *Relationship to yourself.* Self-discovery and self-development are important aspects of green thinking. The 1980s saw people defining themselves by their careers and their possessions. In future as work becomes less widely available for all, and as the social acceptability of conspicuous consumption declines, so people will be more likely to define themselves by their interests and their relationships.

2 *Relationship to others.* The advertising agency HKBD produced a light-hearted set of four 'isms' to describe the last four decades and the central questions which characterised them:

1960s *Me-ism* 'Where am I at (man)?'

1970s *Them-ism* 'What do others think of me?'

1980s *Self-ism* 'What do I think of myself?'

1990s *Us-ism* 'Where are we all going (together)?'

It would be ludicrous to imagine that social eras happen to coincide neatly with calendar decades, or that everyone within society is preoccupied with the same question, but the 1980s did seem to have a character that is very different to the early 1990s.

3 *Relationship to institutions.* There is a gradual decline in people's trust in, and loyalty to, organisations (*see* Chapter 3). This makes it important for companies not only to act responsibly, but also to be seen to be acting responsibly through a policy of openness and the disclosure of information. It also makes companies who are not acting responsibly more prone to leaks and 'whistle blowing'.

4 *Relationship to society.* As environmental problems and their social consequences increase, so the proportion of people wishing to change and challenge society will increase. Also likely to increase will be the number of people who wish to escape from the emerging problems through more sophisticated home entertainment and computer game systems, more exotic holidays and virtual reality experiences.

5 *Relationship to nature.* The desire to conquer and subdue nature has been the dominant trend in our relationship to nature for over 200 years. More recently the realisation has grown that there is a need to protect and cherish our natural systems. A great deal of consumption appears to relate to our need to 'get back to nature'. Gardening and fishing represent the world's most popular pastime and sport respectively, and each could be said to appeal to our natural instincts as hunter/gatherers. A whole range of markets are being successfully attacked by 'natural' products including foods, cosmetics, holidays and fabrics. The improbably named American futurist Faith Popcorn (1992) sums up the nature of the turning point in our relationship with the environment by saying, 'For the first time ever in the history of mankind, the wilderness is safer than "civilisation".'

6 *Relationship to the Universe.* Organised religion has been the framework within which people have conventionally related to the Universe. Although the influence of the Church in industrialised countries has continued to decline in the industrial era, it still remains an important influence. The decline of formal, organised religion in industrialised countries has left something of a spiritual void left to be filled for many people. Humanism and environmentalism are both movements which have fulfilled many of the same needs for people as religious faiths, without the need for faith. The waning general belief in a supernatural architect of the planet also increasingly places the burden for caring for it on to all of us.

As well as values, beliefs are an important element in defining culture. A range of long held beliefs have been challenged by the growing environmental crisis and by green thinking. They may be challenged explicitly through the work of green interest groups or through the writings of green economists, philosophers and politicians. Within popular entertainment, which both reflects and shapes cultural beliefs and values, the environment is becoming an increasingly important theme. Films such as *The Emerald Forest* confronted issues of ecosystem destruction and the displacement of indigenous peoples, while the documentary *Whale Nation* produced a harrowing account of a species under threat from industrial exploitation.

The end of the world is an important cultural concept whose dramatic possibilities have always appealed to authors, musicians, film makers and other artists. In pre-industrial times the end of the world was typically a religious affair. In books and films of the post-war decades, the end of the world was usually threatened by a force outside of society. This could be cold-war opponents, aggressors from another planet, or a megalomaniac with an anti-social disposition and a hefty personal nuclear arsenal tucked away in some undersea hideout. During the late 1980s and early 1990s the theme of society being threatened by an environment turned hostile by economic growth, big business or technology has become popular. On the written page and on the screen tales of impending ecological destruction of the existing order have been told with much drama (for example, Margaret Attwood's *The Handmaid's Tale* or Frank Herbert's *The Green Brain*) and with considerable humour (for example, Ben Elton's *Stark* and *Gridlock*).

Popular music is another important medium which can influence beliefs and values, particularly among younger consumers. The 'Woodstock Generation' might relate to the lyrics of Joni Mitchell's *Big Yellow Taxi*, Cat Stevens' *Where Do The Children Play?* or Crosby, Stills and Nash's *To The Last Whale* which, in the early 1970s, reflected contemporary environmentalist concern about the problems of life on a small, finite and crowded planet. For a newer generation of consumers and managers in the early 1990s the lyrics from REM's *Green*, World Party's *Goodbye Jumbo* or Galliano's *Twyford Down* drive home a message reflecting a planet threatened by the consequences of environmental degradation.

Perhaps the most powerful influence in shaping and expressing contemporary culture is television. The 1980s witnessed an increasing trend towards nature-based television documentary programmes and greater news coverage of issues such as global warming and ozone depletion. In 1967 the BBC devoted 30 programming hours each week to environmental issues; by 1987 this had quadrupled to 120 hours. Documentary series such as *Life on Earth* and *Fragile World* have brought detailed and emotive images and information about the environment and its problems into the homes of millions. Mainstream programmes have also carried an increasing amount of environmental information. Travel programmes, for example, have begun to emphasise the environmental implications of holiday products and the need for sensitive behaviour among consumers. For younger viewers factual nature programmes have been joined by a new generation of environmentally related cartoon characters such as 'The Smoggies' or 'Captain Planet'.

Each of these cultural expressions of environmental concern may appear far removed from the business agenda, but the cumulative effect is to produce a world of consumers who are becoming increasingly sensitive to the idea of a planet in peril. Perhaps the most powerful combination comes when a cultural icon uses the power of popular music, film or television to heighten environmental awareness. The intervention of Brigitte Bardot to prevent the culling of seals, Sting's work to protect the Amazon rainforest or HRH Prince Charles's concern on a range of environmental issues all ensure that the media profile and public consciousness of green issues is raised considerably.

Economic dimensions

The interaction between economic development and environmental degradation will become increasingly clear during the 1990s. In many industries the increasing costs of environmentally related activities such as waste disposal, emission reduction and the cleaning of contaminated sites will limit the opportunities for economic growth. Economic and eco-performance are often spoken of as though there was necessarily a trade-off between the two. The two are fundamentally linked, and poor eco-performance can rapidly destabilise the economic environment of a company. Following the Bhopal tragedy, Union Carbide's share price fell sufficiently to trigger a hostile takeover attempt. To avoid the takeover the company was forced to dispose of important business assets.

Economically the 1990s will bring some major new challenges to the fabric of our environment. The creation of the Single European Market is expected to create economic growth and an increase in infrastructure development and road transport that will be difficult to reconcile with the objectives of the European Union's Fifth Environmental Action Plan, *Towards Sustainability*. Similarly, the economic growth envisaged in the creation of the North American Free Trade Association is forecast by some commentators to have disastrous ecological consequences (Goldsmith 1993), despite the review of the ecological implications of the NAFTA treaty undertaken before its signing in 1993. Elsewhere in the world, there is concern about the environmental implications of economic liberalisation in Eastern Europe (the World Bank puts the cost of cleaning up Eastern Europe at around 93 billion ECUs – £200 billion) and the impact of the dramatic economic growth forecast for South-East Asia and particularly China, dubbed the 'Sleeping Dragon' by Napoleon, the world's most populous country.

Technological dimensions

Technological advances are at the heart of 'cornucopian' optimism that humankind's ingenuity will solve the environmental crisis. Various advanced technologies have been suggested as providing at least partial solutions. The use of water heated above 374°C and pressurised to 218 atmospheres (when it enters a 'supercritical' state) to treat toxic wastes appears to have the potential to break down some of the most feared pollutants, such as PCBs, into basic and harmless molecules. Nuclear fusion advances hold out the promise of clean energy without the dangers of Chernobyl-style nuclear accidents. Biotechnology and genetic engineering provide hope for reductions in some of the most dreaded diseases and the expansion of global food supplies without further increasing our dependence on agrochemicals.

The idea of technology as the way forward for marketing was echoed by McKenna (1990) who predicts a renaissance in business based around a marriage of the traditional 'soft' skills of marketing with the 'hard' advances in technology. The increasing rate of technological change and the amount of money invested in research and development (R&D) by companies would appear to support such optimism. However, the targets for current R&D expenditure do not quite match the eco-cornucopian ideal. Of the five industries spending the most on research and development, three are aircraft and missiles, chemicals and the car industry. This rather prompts the question: 'Are more aircraft, missiles, cars and chemicals what society and the environment it depends upon really need?' The answer to this (with the exception of missiles where it is hard to conceive of a green product) rather depends on whether or not the R&D money is being channelled into producing more fuel-efficient, low-pollution planes and cars and safe and safely produced chemicals.

In recent years environmentally related technologies have only attracted a small share of commercial, government and academic research expenditure. OECD figures for 1989 showing public expenditure in selected European countries are presented in Table 4.3. Although governments throughout the industrialised world are putting aside an average of 2 per cent of their research budgets for environmental research, this is mostly used for research on ecosystems and natural resources. Relatively little of it is used for environmental technologies such as pollution control equipment or clean technology, which would have the potential to create new products and markets (Brown 1992).

Table 4.3 Public expenditure on environmental R&D in selected countries (1989)

	Environmental R&D expenditure ($m)	Share of total government R&D expenditure ($%)
Austria	11	1.4
Denmark	28	3.0
France	95	0.7
Germany	420	3.4
Italy	120	1.9
Netherlands	75	3.8
Switzerland	85	2.0
UK	170	2.3

Investment in green technologies provides no guarantee that they will reach the market. There can also be difficulties in moving innovations in environmental technology out of the research laboratory and into the production systems of companies. Studies completed by the OECD and Ecotech found that efforts to capitalise on the potential benefits of emerging clean and low-waste technologies have stumbled upon a number of barriers including:

● environmental policies which are either too weak to motivate improvement, or which are subject to uncertainty over their enforcement or future direction, leading to a lack of certainty and investment among companies;

● the perception among strategic decision makers that investment in environmental technology is expensive, risky or not really relevant to their everyday business;

● problems with the transfer of technology due to a lack of access to information, particularly among small firms, and a lack of specialist independent advice;

● insufficient internal resources in terms of capital for investment or suitably trained and skilled staff for implementation and operation.

Another factor which may tend to lessen the chances of technological innovation averting the environmental crisis is the trend towards R&D which enhances current technology rather than that which develops new technologies. Emphasis on the marketing concept and a 'market-pull' rather than 'technology-push' approach to product development are combining with spiralling R&D costs to encourage companies to improve what customers already know (which is relatively low-risk) rather than developing something truly innovative.

International dimensions

The marketing environment which companies address is increasingly international in its nature. Green issues frequently need to be considered on an international level since environmental processes do not conform to human geopolitical boundaries. The acidification of lakes is a prime environmental concern within Sweden, for example, but over 70 per cent of the damage is related to sulphur dioxide emissions originating outside Sweden. Pollution is not the only environmental problem to cross European boundaries. Cross-border traffic of hazardous goods and waste has increased dramatically with over 100 000 registered border crossings of hazardous substances per annum within the EU alone (OECD 1991). Even a European company serving a highly localised and distinctive demand within its country will find itself influenced by environmental legislation and regulations that originate from Brussels or from the growing list of international accords and treaties.

A response in terms of environmental legislation or the expansion of environmental marketing

in some countries will count for little if the green challenge is ignored in others. Data from the OECD's 'GREEN' computer model predict that, if all the 24 OECD member countries acted to try and cut greenhouse emissions back to 1990 levels, the OECD would need to cut projected growth in greenhouse emissions by 44 per cent over the next 60 years. However, this would only cut the growth in emissions globally by some 11 per cent, if less industrialised countries continue on the basis of expanding the use of subsidised energy.

The need for a global approach and the problems of countries operating independently were demonstrated by the German Green Dot scheme which produced a sudden cheap glut of recycled materials. This stunted the growth of the emerging recycling industries in several other European countries. The environment is also becoming a factor in international trade agreements, often as a bone of contention where environmental regulations are opposed on the basis that they represent a 'disguised' tariff barrier.

Although the environment is a global concern, the sophisticated marketing techniques of industrialised nations have yet to reach many less industrialised nations and many of those emerging from former communist regimes. The impact of capitalism on the environments, economies and societies of Eastern Europe will be a key issue for the end of the twentieth century. There is some evidence that the 'honeymoon' period of the unquestioning embrace of capitalist solutions may be ending. MORI research in 1991 found that only 24 per cent of Poles objected to foreign inward investment. A year later the figure had jumped to 37 per cent.

Within the international environment, concern is also mounting about the increasing power of multinational companies (MNCs) and their role in the exploitation of environmental capital, particularly in less industrialised countries. Clairmonte and Cavanagh (1992) present a searing indictment of the activities of MNCs in their analysis of the global beverage trade, the majority of which is controlled by five companies. Clairmonte and Cavanagh paint a picture of companies whose power is such that they can level rainforests and crowd out peasant food growers to establish vast plantations. Through commodity price fixing, takeovers and alliances with local politicians they continue to increase the profit outflow while local gains are minimised. In search of opportunities these companies then turn their high-pressure marketing machines on these developing markets. This results in a consumer lifestyle symbolised by Coca-Cola, bottle-fed babies and brand name alcohol consumption superimposed on a society where even the basics of clean drinking water and basic nutrition are lacking.

Communications and infrastructure dimensions

The development of new transport infrastructure has been crucial in creating the high-speed and delocalised marketing and distribution systems that exist today. Changes to the transport infrastructure have also been instrumental in environmental degradation. During the 1970s and 1980s, the length of motorway expanded 150 per cent in Europe and a staggering 500 per cent in Japan. This contributed to a rise in traffic volume of 100 per cent and 300 per cent respectively. Investment in road building in countries like Britain has been at the expense of public transport systems such as rail and bus. Other countries have responded to this challenge with massive investment in public transport, which in The Netherlands outweighs expenditure on road building. An interesting cultural note pointed out by the environmental lobby is that expenditure on roads is spoken of as 'investment' while expenditure on rail is spoken of as 'subsidy'.

Although vehicle manufacturers are working on a range of relatively clean vehicles, one of the main barriers that will face any new rival to the conventional petrol or diesel engine car is that the infrastructure for refuelling them already exists. In France the development of electric vehicles is being accompanied by government investment in a network of recharging points.

A great deal of the environmental impact of transport comes from the need to move people as well as goods. Telecommunications offers opportunities to replace journeys to other companies and countries through work with 'teleconferencing' and journeys to work with 'telecottaging'. The vision of work centred around the home as part of the information society has been widely predicted since Toffler's *Futureshock* (1970). It has only materialised in a small way in industries such as computing as yet. People living within the nuclear family, or a fragment of it, are unlikely to desire to work from home while work is an important form of social contact. Similarly home-working does not fit well with traditional management styles which emphasise the need for supervision, control and reassurance that work is being done.

Administrative and institutional dimensions

There is a vast array of non-government institutions which are becoming increasingly interested in the environment and the environmental impact of companies.

- *Labour organisations*. These include trade unions and the likes of the International Labour Organization.
- *Employers' organisations*. Chambers of commerce at international, national and local level and organisations such as the Confederation of British Industry are increasingly addressing environmental issues and providing green information for their members.
- *Trade associations*. In many industries the need to improve the environmental image of the industry as a whole has led to trade associations taking environmental initiatives. Furthermore, the activities of some companies within an industry can come under pressure from a trade association which reflects the concern of the majority of companies.
- *Industry watchdogs*. Watchdog organisations may be set up to monitor a specific corporate activity, or a range of activities across specific industries. In the UK the Advertising Standards Authority has taken an interest in the green claims being used by advertisers.
- *Economic institutions*. Environmental issues have become increasingly central to the work of

the Organization for Economic Co-operation and Development (OECD) and the World Bank.

● *Educational institutions*. Schools, colleges and universities are increasingly emphasising environmentally based education and research initiatives.

● *Churches*. In the USA churches have begun to integrate environmental concern into their doctrine. The Presbyterian Church in 1991 changed the church canon to make it a sin to 'threaten death to the planet entrusted to our care' (Associated Press 1991). The Catholic Church has also added environmental concern to its new catechism (Woodward and Norland 1992) although many environmentalists would view this as incompatible with their continuing stand against artificial contraception.

Legal and political dimensions

Environmental law and policy instruments are becoming an increasingly important influence on business and trade, particularly with respect to multinational companies. Within Europe, by 1991 over 250 environmentally related European Community directives (and another 200 with some environmental provisions) and regulations relating to the environment had come to dominate the development of environmental law in European member states. The basis of European Union law dates back to the 1952 Treaty of Rome which references the environment under Articles 100A (harmonisation of the internal market) and Article 130S (the environment). The unanimous voting rule which previously hampered progress under Article 130S was modified to allow qualified majority voting by the 1992 Maastricht Treaty.

The relationship between companies and the legal process in relation to the environment has also begun to change. The USA is taking a lead in making pollution a criminal offence in which the offenders are treated like criminals. In the USA, Chief executive officers (CEOs) of polluters such as Pennwalt (who spilled 75 000 gallons of carcinogenic chemicals into a stream) are being required by the courts to plead guilty in person instead of through corporate lawyers (Harrison 1990).

Green political parties have had a major impact on the political scene without actually gaining access to any significant degree of political power. The success of the Greens at the 1987 European elections drove home to the conventional political parties that the importance of environmental issues to the electorate could no longer be judged on the basis of Green Party membership. Mainstream parties hastily bolstered the environmental elements of their manifestos, and generally all shades of political opinion have attempted to present themselves as 'best for the environment'. The effect has been to reduce the environment to a consensus issue (Cairncross 1991) addressed in order not to lose votes, rather than embraced in order to win them.

The environment remains an important issue among voters. A poll taken among American voters just before the 1988 Presidential elections put only drugs and gun control ahead of the environment in terms of the priorities for the new administration. In a Times Mirror survey, 22 per cent of US voters polled said that they had chosen past presidential candidates according to their position on environmental issues (Donaton and Fitzgerald 1992).

RESPONDING TO THE MARKETING ENVIRONMENT

The ability to understand, anticipate and react to trends and changes within the marketing environment is crucial to success in any form of marketing. Responding to the green challenge presents a company with a whole range of new relationships and trends to understand. According to Diffenbach (1983), a company passes through three phases in coming to terms with any significant external change.

1 *Appreciation stage* – in which books, articles, newcomers or unforeseen events encourage a company to take a longer-term and wider-ranging look at the world around them. Developing an appreciation of the physical environment might be sparked by legislative change, customer enquiries or a competitor initiative.

2 *Analysis stage* – which involves finding sources of useful external information, and collating information to discover key trends, relationships, opportunities and threats.

3 *Application phase* – when the new view of the external world is translated into new strategies and action plans.

The majority of businesses claim to have become more aware about the green challenge and will therefore have entered and possibly progressed through the appreciation stage. The analysis stage presents much more of a challenge since it requires companies to gather new information from unfamiliar sources. Both the rise in environmental audits and the increasing circulation of environmental publications such as the *ENDS Bulletins* are symptomatic of more companies entering the analysis phase of meeting the green challenge.

Given the increasing rate and unpredictability of change within the marketing environment, the business of identifying significant trends is both important and difficult. America is furthest advanced in the art of 'futurism', and the trends that emerge there typically make their way across the Atlantic to influence the European business environment before too long. The trends emerging in the American market-place will have particular relevance to the emergence of environmental marketing. Leading futurist Faith Popcorn (1992) in *The Popcorn Report* paints a picture of industrialised society at a turning point in the relationship between people, society and the natural environment. The twelve emerging trends she identifies include the following among others.

● *Cocooning* – a tendency for individuals to become more 'stay at home', partly as a reflection of living in a world which has become more hostile both environmentally and socially.

● *The decency decade* – a return to many traditional values during the 1990s of the home, the family, thrift. This will be reflected in a 'new traditionalism' in consumer behaviour.

● *Cashing out* – people increasingly using the gains they have made from participation in the 'rat race' to escape from it to do something more personally rewarding and involving a slower pace of life.

● *Small indulgences* – consumers making small luxury purchases to reward and sustain themselves in the face of a struggle against a difficult world.

● *Staying alive* – increasing health consciousness, reflecting growing concern about the effect of lifestyle and environment on our health and life expectancy.

● *The vigilante consumer* – a new breed of socially and environmentally aware and active consumers who want companies to become more 'humane'. They will be willing to influence companies through more than their purchasing decisions, by taking actions ranging from simply rearranging supermarket shelves to place green brands at the front, to organising boycott campaigns against irresponsible companies.

● *Save our society* – an increasing concern about the future of society in the face of the decline of the traditional family unit, persistent unemployment and increasing threats from urban violence and drugs. This will be manifested in an emphasis on three critical Es: Environment, Education and Ethics.

The green challenge may also require marketers to review the relationship between the company and its marketing environment. Conventionally marketing concerns itself with the process of responding to the environment, while in fact the practice of marketing also shapes the environment around it. The development of the technological environment is based mainly on the output of commercially sponsored new product development programmes. The socio-cultural environment is deeply affected by the images and values projected throught the medium of advertising (Goldman 1992). The economic environment is highly influenced by the prices set by producers and the physical environment is impacted by the distribution requirements of companies. The green challenge requires marketers not just to scan the marketing environment in the search for opportunities and threats, but also to comprehend

1960s	1970s	1980s	1990s
Coal (mining and air pollution)	Aerosols	Aerosols	Aerosols
Detergents	Airports	Agriculture	Agriculture
Mining and quarrying	Asbestos	Airports	Air conditioning
Pesticides (e.g. DDT)	Automobile fuel efficiency	Animal testing	Airlines & airports
Water (dams)	Biotechnology (accidental release)	Automobiles exhaust emissions (e.g. lead)	Animal testing
	Chemicals (e.g. dioxins, PBBs, PCBs)	Biotechnology (deliberate release)	Armaments
	Coal (mining and air pollution)	Chemicals (e.g. dioxins, PBBs, PCBs)	Automobiles (fuels, cars)
	Deep sea fishing	Coal	Banking
	Detergents	Computers	Biotechnology
	Heavy lorries	Deep sea fishing	Catering
	Metals	Detergents	Chemicals
	Motorways	Fertilisers	Coal
	Nuclear power	Forestry	Computers
	Oil tankers	Incineration	Crematoria
	Packaging (e.g. glass bottles)	Insurance	Deep sea fishing
	Passenger jets	Landfill	Detergents
	Pesticides/herbicides	Motorways	Dry cleaning
	Pulp mills	Nuclear power	Electricity supply
	Tobacco	Oil tankers	Electrical equipment
	Toxic waste	Onshore oil and gas	Fashion
	Transport	Packaging	Fertilisers
	Water	Paints	Fish farming
	Whaling	Pesticides/herbicides	Fishing
		Plastics	Forestry
		Pulp and paper	Incineration
		Refrigeration	Insurance
		Supermarkets	Investment
		Tobacco	Landfill
		Toxic waste	Meat industry
		Tropical hardwoods	Mining
		Tuna fishing	Motorways
		Water	Nuclear power
		Whaling	Office supplies
			Oil tankers
			Onshore oil and gas
			Packaging
			Paints
			Paper
			Pesticides/herbicides
			Plastics
			Property
			Pulp and paper
			Refrigeration
			Schools
			Shipping
			Supermarkets
			Textiles
			Tobacco
			Tourism
			Toxic waste
			Transport
			Tropical harwoods
			Tyres
			Water

Fig. 4.2 The environmental marketing front line
(Source: *SustainAbility*)

and take responsibility for the socio-environmental impacts of the company and its marketing strategy.

THE FUTURE FOR ENVIRONMENTAL MARKETING

Environmental analysis requires companies to take a view about the likely future development of the market, and the actors and forces within it. Few companies are so reactive and responsive that they do not take some view about the most likely future scenario as the basis of their future strategies and plans. During the late 1980s, one common prediction was that recession would dampen down enthusiasm for the physical environment, much as it did in the 1970s. This proved largely incorrect, with concern about the environment holding steady among consumers and voters. The worst effect of the recession was a slowing of the growth in environmental concern. By the end of the decade the green challenge was being acknowledged as a permanent 'fact of life' for marketers and marketing. In a survey of 156 top UK marketers virtually all of them saw the green challenge as a permanent change to the marketing environment as opposed to a passing fad (Mitchell 1989). The key questions about the future of the green challenge relate to the rate at which it will grow, the issues that will become of greatest importance to the different parties in the marketing environment, and which industries will be the next focus of green concern. Figure 4.2 looks back at how the environmental marketing front line has evolved over the last four decades.

The next landmark year for the green challenge, in terms of media coverage and societal concern about environmental degradation, will be 1997. This will coincide with the 10th anniversary of the publication of the *Brundtland Report* and the 25th anniversary of the United Nations Conference on the Human Environment which founded the United Nations Environment Programme and of the publication of *The Limits to Growth*. This will be followed by the end of the millennium which will probably be a signal for a general reassessment of society and the direction in which it is heading.

CASE STUDY

The hole in the sky

No other environmental issue illustrates the interplay of forces within the marketing environment as clearly as the discovery of a hole in the ozone layer. The action of sunshine and lightening on oxygen (O_2) molecules produces ozone (O_3) molecules, which accumulate to form a layer in the stratosphere. Here they absorb most of the incoming UV-B radiation, a form of ultraviolet radiation which is adept at damaging organic matter including human skin and eye tissue, plant crops and the plankton which floats near the surface of the oceans. In 1974 scientific papers in America predicted (a) that chlorine molecules reaching the stratosphere could break up the unstable ozone molecules and (b) that CFCs were reaching the stratosphere and releasing chlorine. In America environmentalists began campaigning against aerosol sprays, and sales of aerosol cans declined by some 60 per cent as a result. By 1976 socially responsive companies led by Johnson and Johnson publicly abandoned the use of CFCs in aerosols, and by 1978 CFCs were outlawed as an aerosol propellant in the USA. Much of the rest of the world failed to follow the American lead, and CFCs continued to be used in aerosols and a range of other products and processes.

In 1984 scientists working with the British Antarctic Survey recorded an unprecedented 40 per cent drop in ozone density, and with the publication of their findings in 1985 the phrase

►

'ozone hole' entered everyday language. The findings should have galvanised industry and governments into action, but there was no proof that CFCs were the culprits and the processes behind the formation of the hole were poorly understood. CFC producers and the countries whose economies benefited from their production opposed any measures aimed at cutting back CFC production. The United Nations Environment Programme (UNEP) was instrumental in motivating governments to sign the Montreal Protocol in October 1987 which aimed to cut production of the five most damaging CFCs by 20 per cent by 1993 and a further 30 per cent by 1998. This was followed by the London Agreement in 1990 which agreed the phase out of all production of CFCs and other key ozone depletants by the year 2000.

Environmentalist pressure on CFCs intensified with the organisation of a global consumer boycott and pressure being placed on retailers to remove CFC-driven aerosols from their shelves. Many companies involved in CFC production continued to respond in a defensive manner. Faced with the anti-CFC campaign organised by Friends of the Earth, The British Aerosol Manufacturers Association, ICI and ISC Chemicals joined forces to complain about Friends of the Earth's campaign to the Advertising Standards Authority. The ASA was already busy, however, dealing with environmental claims relating to the ozone layer which included the claim from Rover that its Metro Surf was 'ozone friendly' because it ran on unleaded petrol (an interesting claim in view of the lack of connection between the two issues).

Other companies were responding more proactively. Du Pont, the world's largest CFC producer, spent over $170 million searching for CFC substitutes, as well as pledging to abandon CFC production. The backlash against CFCs helped to fuel a range of technological innovations. New aerosol propellants, solvents and refrigerants were developed. Systems were developed to capture and recycle CFCs instead of releasing them into the atmosphere when refrigeration units were serviced or decommissioned. While some companies responded by reverting to pump-action technology for their aerosols, others took advantage of the investment by contract aerosol fillers in new equipment to create HCFC-driven aerosols.

PART 2

Environmental marketing: the strategic challenge

CHAPTER 5

Green consumerism – from consumption to conservation

'There are two ways to get enough. One is to continue to accumulate more and more. The other is to desire less.'
(G.K. Chesterton)

INTRODUCTION

Meeting the needs of the consumer is the primary challenge that every marketer faces. The requirement to produce a profit can be temporarily abandoned, but if a company's market offering doesn't meet the needs of the customer then failure is unavoidable. The relative importance of 'demand pull' from green consumers, or 'legislative push' from socio-environmental legislation varies widely between different forms of market. In most markets the final consumer and the buyers within any marketing intermediaries, are an important influence on the greening process. As the environmental crisis deepens and is translated into increasing societal concern and environmental education for consumers, so the influence of green consumer behaviour will grow. This chapter examines the extent and nature of green consumption, while Chapter 9 deals with issues of consumer segmentation, green markets and targetting the green consumer.

CONSUMPTION

The entry in *Chamber's Dictionary* for the word 'consume' is quite thought provoking. It defines it as 'to destroy by wasting, fire, evaporation, etc.: to use up, to devour, to waste or spend, to exhaust'. Dramatic stuff, and the images that it conjures up make the mission of marketers to serve the consumer sound less like a noble enterprise, and more like complicity in a crime. It is perhaps little wonder that the concept of the 'green consumer' is viewed as an oxymoron by Ottman (1992a), since consuming means the use of resources and the creation of waste. This inconsistency may become increasingly difficult for individuals to reconcile, leading to a second phase of greening in which the actual need to purchase any given product is challenged by the consumer. Once this begins to happen, it will mark the transition from a consumer towards a conserver society.

During the late 1980s the term 'green consumer' joined the business vocabulary in recognition of the fact that the actions and decisions of many consumers were increasingly being influenced by environmental issues. The publication of *The Green Consumer Guide* in 1988, and its subsequent adaptation and translation into Chinese, Danish, Dutch, Finnish, German, Italian, Japanese, Norwegian, Spanish and Swedish, has enshrined the label in the consciousness of the public. Since it is becoming something of a global standard, we will stick with the label 'green consumer' even though 'green customer' would be a more accurate reflection of the variety of activities that consumption entails, and less of a contradiction in terms. Similarly green purchasing would be a more appropriate description of their activities than green consumption.

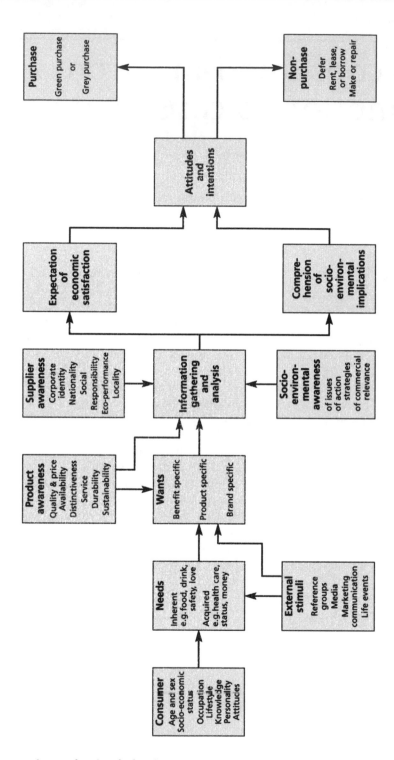

Fig. 5.1 A green perspective on buying behaviour

The role of consumption

Perhaps because we engage in the process of consumption every day, the complexity and profound importance of its role within society tend to be overlooked. Consumption is more complex than it might appear. We tend to think of it as an economic process, but consumption is also 'a social and cultural process involving cultural signs and symbols' (Bocock 1993). Even at a practical level, consumption is not a single activity, but a process which includes several distinct activities including product or service selection, purchase and use (*see* Figs 5.1 and 5.2). Similarly the concept of an individual consumer can be misleading. The process of purchasing and consumption can involve a variety of different people who can initiate, influence or make the purchase decision, make the purchase or use the product.

Marketers and economists view consumption relatively rationally in terms of the satisfaction of wants and needs through the features and technical performance of products. Sociologists tend to view consumption as a symbolic, social process, in which products are not consumed for what they are and do, but for what they symbolise. While marketing is criticised by the sociologists for ignoring the symbolic elements of consumption, marketers could counter by accusing the sociologists of reading meaning into everything. Tomlinson (1990) criticises Michael Baker's use of the Mars Bar as one of several examples of outstanding packaging which use 'simple designs and vivid colours (which) attract the shoppers' attention'. Tomlinson claims that Baker is missing the point because 'outstanding packaging purveys particularised meanings, connotes chosen values ... Mars (means) exotic (other planets) and durable (the God of War) – no wonder it can help you work, rest and play.' This sounds like a plausible analysis, until one considers that the Mars Bar was named after the company's founder.

The process of consumption plays a number of roles in society.

● *It occurs in an attempt to fulfil our needs and wants.* Baudrillard (1988) sees a move from purchases based on desires rather than needs in industrialised countries as important in transforming consumption into a social, as opposed to a purely economic, activity.

● *It drives the economy,* since although supply and demand might exist, unless they are brought together to create, purchase and use, there will be no economic activity. Bocock (1993) goes further and states that the importance of consumption within society has acted to legitimise the entire capitalist economic system.

● *It can provide entertainment.* Daydreaming about possible purchases, studying consumer guides in search of the optimal choice and the actual process of shopping can provide entertainment in itself, particularly in the case of infrequent high-value purchases such as cars, holidays or electrical goods.

● *It helps to define ourselves.* Consumer goods purchases are an important element of the sense of identity that people construct for themselves (Kellner 1992). During (1992) suggests that the words 'consumer' and 'person' are now virtually synonymous.

● *It can make a statement about who individuals are and how they perceive themselves.* In the delocalised urban economy, unlike the village economy, most people are strangers with no understanding of each other's status or personality. The use of products from cars through T-shirts to hairstyles is necessary to express oneself and make a mark in an increasingly large society.

● *It can be a reward,* ironically one that is often administered in order to compensate for the work that must be completed in order to earn the money with which to consume. The theme of 'buy one – you deserve it' is commonly used in advertising. Baudrillard (1988) suggests that it is the idea of purchasing, as much as the act of purchasing itself, which now acts as a motivator.

● *It is used as a proxy measurement of success,* particularly within industrialised economies.

● *It can provide compensation for experiences and forms of satisfaction that are no longer available to consumers.* One of the explanations behind the massive rise in goods being purchased by and for children, is that many of the 'simpler' pleasures of exploring open spaces or playing together in the street are much less available in urban societies where green space is often at a premium, where traffic dominates the streets and where parental fears about their children's safety restrict opportunities for exploration.

● *It gives us power.* By purchasing or not purchasing, a consumer can experience real, if not necessarily significant, power. Consumers may buy locally to support and encourage their local retailers or patronise fair trade suppliers in an attempt to benefit others. Alternatively they may avoid going back to a restaurant where they received poor service or avoid purchasing Nescafé because of concerns over Nestlé's marketing of infant formula milk in less industrialised countries. The basis of the market economy stresses the power of the consumer.

● *It can become a disease.* Although newspaper reports claiming that 15 per cent of the British population are 'shopaholics' are clearly an exaggeration, shopping addiction has become recognised in America as a serious problem for some people. While alcoholism and drug addiction provide an escape from reality through a certain form of consumption, shopping addiction uses the very process of consumption as an escape.

The profound importance of the process of consumption and the role of marketing in stimulating and guiding it are difficult to grasp. This is partly because of the 'commodification' of culture, foreseen by Marx and explored by Goldman (1992), which involves everything from health care, to art, religion and political parties being reduced to the level of a commodity to allow them to be marketed for consumption. In relation to the environment, a combination of a growth in material consumption per person in industrialised countries, combined with population expansion in less industrialised countries, is making the current trajectory of global consumption and conventional assumptions about the benefits of existing patterns of economic growth unsupportable. Durning (1992) explains that the process of consumption is at a turning point because:

'Limiting the (industrialised) consumer lifestyle to those who have already attained it is not politically possible, morally defensible, or ecologically sufficient. And extending that lifestyle to all would simply hasten the ruin of the biosphere. The global environment cannot support 1.1 billion of us living like American consumers, much less 5.5 billion people, or a future population of at least 8 billion.'

Durning predicts that in the future (when we enter into the ecological paradigm) the members of today's consumer society will find themselves living 'a technologically sophisticated version of the lifestyle currently practised further down the economic ladder'. Arriving at this point will require changes to the legal, economic, technical and social environment within which marketing exists. For the commercial environmental marketer, the challenge will be to adapt to meet changes in the pattern of demand (as demand for some unsustainable products drops, and as growth in demand is replaced by a geographical redistribution for others) and to the nature of demand (which will focus more on elements such as sustainability, durability and increasing satisfaction through non-material consumption).

In terms of the social consequences of the consumer society, Tomlinson (1990) views consumption trends as a driving force in the fragmentation of society and the increasing isolation of the individual. Home-based consumption has allowed people to become increasingly 'private' and withdraw from society and its obligations and interactions. Home entertainments, food delivery services, home shopping systems, canned beers, home fitness centres and home banking are part of a growing list of products allowing the private house to become the focus of the consumer's lifestyle and consumption behaviour. Instead of enjoying the communal experience of watching a film in a cinema, by the mid-1980s around 97 per cent of all films in the UK were viewed on the small screen.

Even the household is fragmenting in response to consumption-driven lifestyles. Commenting on a Henley Centre study of leisure trends Tomlinson presents a vision of:

'suitably androgynous figures labouring away at different forms of pleasure: someone typing on the computer keyboard in a study bedroom; someone working out to an exercise tape in a bedroom; ... someone slumped into the sofa watching the television and someone standing over the hob across from the microwave in the kitchen ... In their picture of the cellular household at work and play the Henley Centre pundits picture the connoisseur consumer as recluse, and leisure as a specialist monadic activity.'

He notes that in the UK two major spending priorities were on home entertainment and foreign holidays, both a means of withdrawing from society. Even that other popular form of escapism, TV viewing, has become a less communal affair. The advent of multiple sets in households and the use of video recorders to allow programmes to be viewed at different times has led to increasingly individual viewing habits within households.

DEFINING GREEN CONSUMPTION

In response to the environmental concern of the early 1970s, concepts such as Fisk's (1973) theory of 'responsible consumption' and Mead's (1970) concept of 'responsible simplification' reflected the concern about limits to growth with calls for a decrease in consumption. At the same time, the social pressure on business was reflected in studies of the 'socially conscious consumer' (Anderson and Cunningham 1972). Environmental marketing involves providing consumers with more sustainable and socially acceptable products; therefore green consumption must involve consuming in a more sustainable and socially responsible way.

The role and importance of green consumption and green consumerism have been the subject of some debate. Johnson (1991) commenting on green consumption sees it as 'at best a way of slowing world degradation, a means of buying a little more time'. Christensen (1991) goes further in an article entitled 'Don't Call Me a Green Consumer' by arguing the case that green consumerism is counter-productive because it disguises the real issues and simply buttresses and perpetuates the 'born to shop' attitudes which emerged in the 1980s. Durning (1992) sums up the arguments:

'At its best green consumerism is a potent new tactic for environmental advocates, allowing them to bypass the halls of parliaments and send their message directly to boardrooms. At its worst, green consumerism is a palliative for the conscience of the consumer class, allowing us to continue business as usual while feeling like we are doing our part.'

However, green purchasing and green consumption are each only a facet in the change of lifestyle that is needed among industrialised countries to make our economic growth sustainable. They will have an effect only as part of a wider process of change, but that wider change process will not be able to happen without them.

In *The Green Consumer Guide,* Elkington and Hailes (1988) define green consumption as the process of avoiding products which are likely to:

- endanger the health of consumers or others;
- significantly damage the environment in production, use or disposal;
- consume disproportionately large amounts of resources during production, use or disposal;
- cause unnecessary waste through overpackaging, excess product features or an unduly short lifespan;
- use materials derived from endangered species or environments;
- involve cruelty to, or needless exploitation of, animals;
- adversely affect other countries, particularly developing countries.

Such negative discrimination has already occurred against a number of products including battery-laid eggs, fur coats and CFC-propelled aerosols. Among UK consumers, for example, 67 per cent of a sample of 1000 adults said they had stopped using or buying foods or products they believed to be dangerous or environmentally harmful (Smith 1990). Firms themselves can become targets, a survey of 1000 US consumers by J. Walter Thompson revealed that 64 per cent would boycott products from a 'dirty' company (Levin 1990). Consumers can also turn against entire industries that they see as undesirable. Research

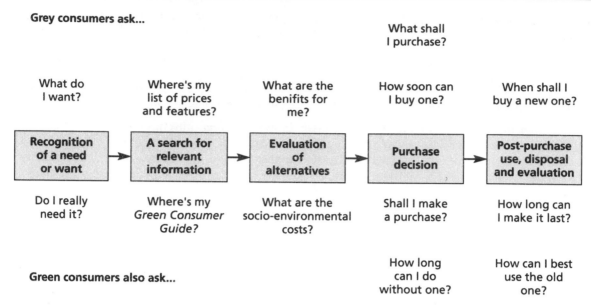

Grey consumers ask...

What shall
I purchase?

What do
I want?

Where's my
list of prices
and features?

What are the
benifits for
me?

How soon can
I buy one?

When shall I
buy a new one?

| Recognition of a need or want | → | A search for relevant information | → | Evaluation of alternatives | → | Purchase decision | → | Post-purchase use, disposal and evaluation |

Do I really
need it?

Where's my
*Green Consumer
Guide?*

What are the
socio-environmental
costs?

Shall I make
a purchase?

How long can
I make it last?

Green consumers also ask...

How long
can I do
without one?

How can I best
use the old
one?

Fig. 5.2 Greening the buying process

by the American Society of Plastics Industries found that 54 per cent of consumers expressed unfavourable attitude towards the plastics industry in   December 1991, compared to 34 per cent in February 1990.

Seeing green consumption in terms of product avoidance only provides a partial picture of the changes that environmental concern is prompting. Other changes include discriminating positively in favour of brands with a good perceived environmental image, or changes in the price that consumers are willing to pay for a product with an improved eco-performance. These changes are already being reflected in the information about consumers being gathered in countries such as the USA. A survey in the USA by J. Walter Thompson described by Levin (1990) revealed that 82 per cent of consumers were willing to pay a 5 per cent premium for greener products. The split between positive and negative product discrimination is exemplified by green investment products. It is possible to invest in a fund such as the Ethical Investment Fund, whose emphasis is on avoiding companies which harm society or the environment, or to invest in a fund such as the Merlin Ecology Fund, in which companies with an outstandingly positive eco-performance are sought out.

Green consumer behaviour cannot be viewed simply in terms of purchasing and the choice between products. Consumers may respond to the green challenge in a wide range of ways other than purchasing involving the way they use, maintain, replace and dispose of products. Green consumer behaviour can also include purchase and consumption avoidance. We can define green consumer behaviour as 'the purchasing and non-purchasing decisions made by consumers, based at least partly on environmental or social criteria'. Figure 5.2 proposes a model of green consumer behaviour.

The green consumer

The use of the label 'green consumer' implies that they are a subset of consumers who are in some way different from conventional consumers. The concept that green consumers are a specific group is worth challenging. Kardash, as early as 1974, suggested that virtually everyone can be classified as an 'ecologically concerned consumer'. This is because, providing that other factors such as price are relatively equal, most people would discriminate in favour of an environmentally superior product.

During the late 1980s environmental concern reached a point where it became a socially accepted norm (Schwepker and Cornwall 1991). This is increasingly reflected in a move from green consumers as a subset of consumers to green concern and consumer behaviour being exhibited throughout the population. A 1990 survey conducted by Warwick, Baher and Fiore Associates found that 96 per cent of consumers claimed to use environmental criteria in their purchase decisions at least occasionally.

In many ways it is misleading to generalise and attempt to categorise the 'green consumer'. Attempts to do so on the basis of socio-demographic and personality variables have generally run into problems (Diamantopoulos *et al* 1994). A person will not be a 'green' consumer in the same (relatively) enduring and definite way that a consumer might be categorised as male, blond, Jewish, Hispanic, teenage, tall or left-handed. One consumer might buy lead-free petrol in a car which is relatively economical, safe, quiet and recyclable. Such a consumer might be categorised as 'green' in relation to car ownership, but perceived as a grey consumer simply for owning a car. The degree of green concern varies among consumers, as does the particular environmental issues which concern them and the types of purchase to which this concern extends. It is perhaps easier to analyse green consumption in terms of green purchase decisions than in terms of green consumers. Green consumption is a behaviour pattern which is fundamental to a minority of consumers, but is superimposed on existing consumption behaviour among the majority of consumers that can be classified as green.

THE BUYING PROCESS

Consumption is not a single activity, but a series of activities that can be described as the buying process. Grey marketing has always focused on the elements of the buying process which lead up to the actual purchase. The needs and motives of consumers have therefore tended to dominate the thinking of practitioners and the research agendas of academics, followed closely by issues of information gathering and purchase choice. Environmental marketing requires a more balanced view of the purchase and consumption

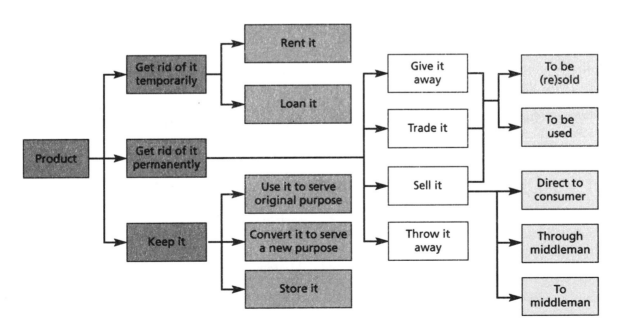

Fig. 5.3 Post-purchase product use and disposal
(Source: Jacoby *et al* (1977))

process, with much more emphasis being placed upon post-purchase issues of product use and disposal (*see* Fig. 5.3).

1 The recognition of a need or want

Needs come from within ourselves, and are fairly broad in scope. They range from the basic necessities of life such as water, food and clothing, to increasingly sophisticated needs for things such as entertainment, status and spiritual fulfilment. Needs are translated into wants, which relate to specific means of satisfying a given need, usually through consumption of a product. While needs are relatively enduring, wants can be extremely transitory. While we all have an enduring need to be entertained and amused, few people today would attempt to meet that need through the purchase of a pet rock.

One of the simplest and most enduring models which attempts to explain how needs and wants motivate our purchasing and other behaviour is Maslow's need hierarchy. The conventional approach to the model is that as a more basic level of need is satisfied, an individual's behaviour will aim to satisfy a higher level of need. Environmental concern during the 1970s was very much an avenue for self-actualisation among an intellectual elite. During the 1980s it became increasingly clear that green issues drove certain needs at all levels of the model.

● *Physiological needs.* Our needs for the basic necessities of life, food, drink, clothing, warmth and shelter are the most fundamental of all needs. These account for a relatively small proportion of all purchases in industrialised economies, but may dominate the thoughts of the majority of consumers in poorer countries.

● *Safety needs.* Well publicised issues of product sabotage, outbreaks of food poisoning, food additives and chemical residues, dangerous toys and unsafe cars have made safety an important issue among consumers. This can lead to a demand for more and more secure packaging, such as tamper-proof containers. It can also lead to a growth in green products with a perceived safety advantage,

such as organic food. Consumers are certainly worried about the environment. A study by the US National Anxiety Center found that five out of the top ten sources of anxiety were environmental – nuclear waste, the ozone layer, air pollution, water pollution and garbage.

● *Social needs.* The need for belonging, love and acceptance. Environmental concern is often related to the potential effects of environmental hazards on our loved ones.

● *Esteem needs.* Much of the conspicuous consumption of the 1980s related to people's need for esteem and individuality.

● *Self-actualisation.* Contributing to the survival of the planet and the security of future generations is an increasingly important area for people to seek fufilment.

Marketing theory usually deals with the creation of one particular want from a particular need. However, consumers have a set of needs, and a single product can address more than one need, and more than one level within Maslow's hierarchy. Buying an old house with one's partner with the aim of turning it into a dream house can be viewed as providing everything from the basics of shelter to the fulfilment of a dream and the starting point of a new hobby. In some cases, the translation of one need into a want can come into conflict with other needs. Romeo and Juliet's mutual attraction may have fulfilled their love needs, but it had disastrous consequences in terms of their social and safety needs.

Heightened awareness about green issues now exists among the population as a whole, often as a result of increased media coverage, advertising or pressure group activity. A demand for green products may reflect a long-standing interest in environmentalism, a concern for future generations; a rejection of the values of the consumer society, or simply a willingness to try something different. This becomes translated into a generic desire to purchase green products from green companies. It can also be channelled into a desire not to make a purchase, either in terms of doing without something or actively boycotting a product or company.

2 The search for relevant information

A key element of green consumption is a desire for more information about the relationship between products and the environment. Procter and Gamble's research indicates that consumers want more environmental information than currently appears on labels and in advertising (Alvord 1991). Green consumers will often actively pursue information; the major household products manufacturers have witnessed an increasing number of environmentally related calls to their consumer hotline services in recent years.

Exposure to green information sources certainly appears to influence consumer purchasing decisions. The Council for Economic Priorities' (CEP) *Shopping for a Better World* has reached nearly a million American consumers. Follow-up research by CEP suggests that 78 per cent of readers have changed brands as a result of reading the guide which ranks over 2400 popular brands against 11 social and environmental criteria. Henion (1972) found that when consumers were presented with information about detergent phosphate content at the point-of-sale, it changed consumers' purchase behaviour consistently in favour of the low-phosphate content products.

Green consumer guides have been one of the most important sources of credible information for green consumers to date. After *The Green Consumer Guide* was launched in late 1988 in the UK, it stayed in the non-fiction top ten bestsellers list for over nine months. Such guides do more than inform consumers; they empower consumers in the face of issues which usually inspire feelings of helplessness. By 1993 there were at least 44 different practical green consumer guides available. Many of these were increasingly specialised and included titles such as:

● *The Organic Consumer Guide*
● *The Green Parents' Guide*
● *The Cruelty Free Shopper*
● *The Ethical Consumer Guide*
● *The Global Consumer*
● *Student Shopping for a Better World.*

Consumer organisations have also become increasingly important in terms of alerting consumers about the environmental dimensions of their purchase decisions. The Consumers' Association in the UK has been very much at the forefront of campaigns for purer drinking water, cleaner beaches and better air quality. They produced their own green guide entitled *You and the Environment: Balanced Advice for Consumers on the Pros and Cons of Going Green* (McBratney 1990). A survey of eight different consumer magazines over a six-month period revealed nearly 150 articles or sections devoted to environmental issues (Davidson 1992).

The early phase of green consumption was characterised by a paucity of useful information for consumers (Charter 1992). Increasing information from green guides, environmental groups, consumer groups, government agencies and businesses should be creating better informed consumers, but this is not necessarily the case. Much of the information is contradictory, and the point is being reached where consumers are reaching information overload (Dwek 1993). A major survey conducted by Friends of the Earth revealed that 63 per cent of people were unsure about what was green and what was not in the market-place. This may reflect wider uncertainty about environmental issues themselves. Research 2000's survey found that nearly two thirds of consumers agree that there is 'too much conflicting scientific evidence about these environmental problems', while Worcester (1993) found that 39 per cent agreed with the statement 'I don't fully understand environmental issues' (although, this is a slightly curious question. It is doubtful whether 60 per cent of environmental scientists would claim to fully understand environmental issues).

3 The evaluation of alternatives

Marketing theory has tended to assume that where a need is translated into a want and is backed up by the power to purchase, then a purchase will result. Any conflicts inherent in purchasing are considered in terms of the opportunity costs of choosing among different potential purchases in the face of limited disposable income. Evaluating alternatives is often reduced to selecting between different products and competing brands in search of a purchase that will yield satisfaction. For green consumption, there are several levels of alternative purchase behaviour.

● *Non-purchase.* For the green consumer, not purchasing will be an important alternative. As Wall (1990) comments, 'The most subverse act in a consumer society is the refusal to consume; it is also one of the safest.' It can also be an economical and satisfying alternative when the consumers can meet their own needs, whether by making food or clothes or repairing their home or car. Another form of green consumer behaviour is to maintain durable goods and resist replacing them until absolutely necessary. Such a 'make-do-and-mend' approach can result in a slowing down of the consumer purchase cycle, an increase in demand for spare parts and a demand for repair and reconditioning services.

● *Borrowing, hiring and leasing.* A green alternative to purchasing and therefore consuming is to borrow, hire or lease a product. By possessing a product only during usage and returning it to the supply chain afterwards, resources are conserved. Like the second-hand market, there are markets with a long tradition of a hire segment including cars, books and specialist clothing. There are also growth segments such as toy libraries, tools and baby equipment. Borrowing is another obvious alternative to consuming for the green consumer, but since it takes place informally it isn't of major concern to environmental marketers.

● *Buying second-hand.* By purchasing a second-hand product a green consumer will be able to satisfy his or her needs without causing the consumption of more natural resources. There are many markets such as houses, cars, books and hi-fi which have a large and long-standing second-hand segment. There are also new growth segments in second-hand goods such as dress agencies.

● *Alternative products.* Environmental concern might encourage some consumers to consider meeting their needs by the purchase of products which are radically different to their conventional purchases. This could involve substituting between physical resource intensive goods and human resource intensive services. So a need for leisure might be translated into a holiday (environmentally sensitive of course), rather than a new hi-fi system. Alternatively green consumers might trade-down technology to meet their needs for transportation to work with bicycles rather than cars, and their needs for cleaning in the kitchen with vinegar or baking soda instead of kitchen cleanser.

● *Alternative brands.* The consumer behaviour that has created the most interest in the early phase of environmental marketing is the switching of consumer purchases to 'alternative' green brands. These can sometimes be from specifically green suppliers, or they can be green brands developed by conventional producers. A 1991 Mintel survey revealed that in the UK 46 per cent of women and 31 per cent of men actively sought out green alternatives when shopping. Mintel also found that 50 per cent of consumers said they would be willing to switch away from their conventional brands to buy products from a company with a green image. Such switching between brands is quite possible given the erosion of conventional brand loyalty. A survey by the Roper Organization showed that in the USA brand loyalty has declined sharply in recent years with only 46 per cent of consumers in 1991 claiming to be brand loyal – a 10 per cent drop compared to three years earlier.

● *Lifespan-based purchasing.* A particular form of brand switching, is a move towards product lifespan-based purchasing. This involves buying high-quality products with a longer potential lifespan, usually at a price premium. This trend is creating a demand in some markets for durable, premium-priced products, usually backed up by a lifetime guarantee.

● *Keep faith with existing brands.* Brand-loyal consumers may go green as and when their usual brand produces a green product variant. This may involve buying refill packs of the usual product such as fabric conditioner, rather than buying a large dispenser each time.

4 The purchase decision

Having evaluated alternative purchases and alternatives to purchase, green consumers will proceed to take action to satisfy their needs. For marketers it is the purchase decision that is crucial. In addition to deciding what to buy in terms of products and brands, consumers will consider the following during purchase decision making.

● *Where to buy.* For some products such as coffee and gift products, alternative channels have been set up which allow customers to patronise socially responsive organisations. Most charities now sell gift products by mail order. Traidcraft supplies coffee which is produced by workers' co-operatives in developing countries. These co-operatives offer better standards of living, reinvestment and greater environmental protection for the producer area than the conventional multinational producers. Issues related to green channels are considered in Chapter 14.

● *How much to buy.* A green consumer may decide to purchase, but at a reduced level. Energy consumers, in both a domestic and commercial context, are tending to continue to use and buy energy; but they actively seek ways in which to consume less.

● *When to buy.* Purchase timing can be affected by a variety of factors. In terms of green purchases, consumers may wait until claims for improved eco-performance are validated by an official green label or an organisation like the Consumers' Association. Alternatively, green consumers may delay the purchase of a product until an environmentally improved alternative is available. Following the discovery of the hole in the ozone layer, and the adverse publicity about CFCs, there was a lull in demand in the market for refrigerators as consumers delayed their purchases in the hope that a greener alternative would be announced.

5 Post-purchase behaviour

Green consumers may behave differently to conventional consumers after a particular purchase has been made.

● *Product use change.* The green consumer may continue to use the same products, but in a different way. A green consumer may follow the advice of environmental groups and drive at between 50 and 60 miles per hour to reduce the petrol consumption and emissions of the car.

● *Reuse of products.* A green consumer may reuse part or all of a product in the context of other needs and wants. The green gardener can usually be found planting out seeds in old yoghurt pots and ice cream tubs, rearing seedlings under cloches made from old PET (polyester thermoplastic) soft drinks bottles and nourishing the soil using composted kitchen and garden waste.

● *Product disposal.* Green consumers will tend to dispose of products safely and, where possible, usefully. Serviceable consumer durables will be passed on to other consumers, possibly through selling them second-hand or donating them to charity. Safe disposal services will be used for environmentally hazardous items such as old fridges and car batteries.

● *Recycling of waste packaging.* Research by the Aluminium Can Recycling Association found that 53 per cent of consumers in 1992 claimed to recycle some of their used packaging compared to 33 per cent in 1989. They also found that 55 per cent said that their purchase decisions are influenced by the nature of the packaging materials used. Post-purchase recycling concerns can have an effect on the purchase decision. Rehak (1993) describes how 20 years of personal loyalty to a soap powder brand was overcome simply because its packaging, unlike some rivals, used a metal grommet to attach the handle to the box which had to be removed before the local recycling centre would accept it.

● *Care and maintenance.* Green consumers may give increased attention to the care and maintenance of consumer durables in an attempt to increase their lifespan and delay the need for replacement. This may in turn feed into their purchase decisions, with products designed for easy care and to facilitate consumer maintenance being favoured.

POST-PURCHASE DISSONANCE

Post-purchase dissonance occurs where the consumers fail to achieve the satisfaction from a purchase that they expected. This could be because the product fails to perform as expected, because the consumer learns new information which makes the purchase less appropriate or because the product was an inappropriate choice to meet the underlying need. Ottman (1992a) suggests that the avoidance of worry, guilt or any other form of post-purchase dissonance is behind the increase in green consumption. Environmental concern leads to environmentally conservative shopping behaviour where the consumer buys smaller, concentrated, less packaged products and tries to avoid associations with toxic emissions or large-scale mass production.

Avoiding post-purchase dissonance is also an important issue for the marketing of green products. A product which fails to measure up to consumers' needs and expectations, however good its eco-performance, will not succeed in the market-place. As Ottman (1992) notes, 'one buys a laundry detergent to get clothes clean, not to save the planet'. The danger of green products that do not compete adequately in terms of primary performance is that they will prejudice consumers against green products in the wake of disappointing experiences. To avoid such post-purchase dissonance from setting in, it is important to ensure that purchasers' pre-purchase expectations are matched by their post-purchase experience. This can be done by managing expectations down (which may be difficult in the face of hyperbolic grey competitor performance claims) or to ensure that the product does not disappoint in use.

Although there have been reports of widespread disappointment with green products, the evidence is inconclusive. A McCann Erickson/ Harris survey of European consumers in 1992 found that 31 per cent of consumers had been disappointed by a green product although over 50 per cent were willing to accept a trade-off between primary performance and environmental performance. The Roper Organization's 1992 survey of US consumers showed that 34 per cent thought green products 'do not work as well as regular brands'. It is difficult to know whether such dissonance reflects real experience of green brands, or an expectation that green brands will work less well.

In large value purchases, consumers are very prone to searching for information to justify their desire to purchase, to create consonance between their self-perception and the product or service in question. Once the money has been handed over, doubts may beset the purchaser when the process of justifying the purchase has ended. At this point the customer is likely to be very interested in further positive reinforcement, but is also very vulnerable to any evidence which creates dissonance and dissatisfaction. For the environmental marketer it is important to create marketing communications which confirm the wisdom of past purchase decisions as well as attempting to create new sales. Creating excellent after-sales services is another important way to minimise the dangers posed by post-purchase dissonance.

INFLUENCES ON PURCHASE AND CONSUMPTION DECISIONS

Economic rationality

Rational economic approaches to consumption are based on concepts of the marginal utility of products and purchasers' attempts to maximise personal benefit at minimum cost. Rational economic models generally assume that buyers act in their own best interests and that sales of a product will be stimulated by factors such as:

- a low price;
- a low price for any complementary products;

- high prices among competitors and substitutes;
- increasing real and disposable incomes;
- high promotional expenditure.

Although there is usually evidence of economic rationality within the behaviour of even the most irrational of consumers, it is an incomplete and often potentially misleading approach to predicting consumer behaviour. In practice consumers are often poorly informed about price, they assume that a higher price indicates higher quality, or they avoid buying low-priced brands because it does not fit in with their self-image. There is an assumption implicit in the marketing literature that decisions based on economic criteria are rational. However, the green consumer may be well aware of the failure of conventional economics to cater for environmental issues and may therefore make a highly rational but economically disadvantageous purchase. For the green consumer the rational economic model is particularly inappropriate because most green consumers have rejected self-interest as the sole influence on the buying process, and because they are generally willing to pay more for a product with an improved environmental performance or from a company with a good environmental record.

Price sensitivity

A key behavioural question is the extent to which customers are willing to pay a price premium for improved eco-performance in products. Companies often quote the problem of passing additional costs on to the customer as an argument against greening. Several studies have addressed this question. Among 2450 Consumers' Association members surveyed, 90 per cent bought green products on some occasions and 81 per cent were willing to pay more for green products. This poll and others by groups like NOP and Mintel suggest that between a quarter and half of all Britons would pay up to 25 per cent extra for (credible) products with improved environmental performance. Consumers vary in the degree to which they are willing and able to meet any premium which choosing a green product variant will involve. The Roper Organization study of US consumers found that up to 40 per cent of consumers stated that their response to the environmental challenge was limited because green products were currently 'too expensive'.

Cultural factors

Consumers in different countries will be influenced by different cultural norms and values relating to the environment and society. This may lead to very different patterns of green consumer behaviour. In Japan, for example, there is a tradition of frugality. This was suppressed during the 1980s, partly as a result of governmental attempts to stimulate consumption. This trend was somewhat reversed during the early 1990s with a move away from conspicuous consumption. For many consumers purchasing in a way that minimises environmental damage is a moral question of right and wrong. Green consumption is part of a desire to redress the balance away from the rather cold and mechanical view of the world which the dominant economic and technical perspectives have created, towards a more value-driven and humane society.

Social factors

Social and psychological approaches to consumption explain purchasing behaviour in terms of the need for social standing, acceptance and prestige. This was originally proposed in relation to 'conspicuous consumption' in which many purchases are not motivated by individuals' personal needs, but by their need to impress others (Veblen 1899). The 1980s were a decade during which conspicuous consumption reached new heights. Concern about the environment has brought about something of a backlash within some social groupings against conspicuous consumption and the profligate use of resources. Where once a fur coat might have been worn by someone seeking to gain approval from their social group, now such a coat might be left at home for exactly the same reason. As green consumption gains momentum, so social peer pressure may motivate increasing numbers of consumers towards environmentally and socially acceptable consumption. Anderson and Cunningham (1972) in looking at socially responsible consumers found that socio-psychological variables were a far better predictor of consumer behaviour than socio-economic variables. They typified the socially conscious consumer as being 'a pre-middle age adult of relatively high occupational status ... typically more cosmopolitan, but less dogmatic, less conservative, less status conscious, less alienated'.

Lifestage

Lifestage is an important influence on consumption. Parents are more likely to be concerned about the environment than adults without children. Ottman (1992a) sees the arrival of the 'baby boomers' at a lifestage where they are well established in their careers and entering parenthood as a key driver behind green consumption. Many parents are motivated towards green consumption for the sake of their children, while others find themselves under direct pressure to buy green brands from their offspring following the environmental education that they receive in school.

In addition to acting as key initiators and influencers in the green buying process within households, children often also have the time and motivation to campaign for environmental improvement in a way that their parents might intend to, but never fulfil. Educational services and the media are providing children with a great deal of environmental information. As environmentally motivated consumers and campaigners, children can be a force to be reckoned with. For example towards the end of 1990, McDonald's received some 3000 letters sent to its headquarters by Kids Against Pollution.

Lifestyle

Consumers vary in terms of whether or not they are willing to alter their lifestyle as well as their purchase behaviour to make a contribution. In 1992 a study of US consumers by the Roper Organization found that around half of consumers didn't do more for the environment because they felt that the onus was on companies

to solve the problems that they create. Around half also stated that they were 'too busy' to make lifestyle changes to help protect the environment. Seymour and Giradet (1987) outline a philosophy for a green lifestyle.

● *Assume responsibility yourself.* Schwartz (1987) suggests that 'industrialised society once promised us a job, but no longer honours that promise' and that 'this broken promise will require individuals to take greater responsibility for their own welfare'.

● Keep things local.
● Avoid specialisation.
● Avoid violence.
● Be moderate.

A range of guides for creating a green lifestyle, in addition to making green purchases, are available to consumers, and *50 Simple Things You Can Do to Save the Earth* has sold over 3.5 million copies in the USA. However, most consumers are more interested in achieving or maintaining a lifestyle, rather than changing their own in favour of the environment. Having fought hard to achieve a lifestyle, they may be reluctant to compromise it in favour of one that is more environmentally sound, even if they are also interested in protecting the environment. Here lies the appeal of green consumerism, which allows consumers to make an environmental contribution through brand or product choice rather than through lifestyle changes. Since green consumerism alone is unlikely to bring sufficient improvement in the environment, lifestyle change will become more important during the second phase of environmental marketing. Labels such as 'low-impact living' have been put forward to describe the type of lifestyle change needed, which involves 'living simply so that others may simply live'.

Convenience

Although cost is often discussed as the main barrier to green consumption, convenience may be a more important influence. One of the earliest attempts to harness the power of the green consumer came from Holliman's (1971) *Consumers' Guide to the Protection of the Environment*. The focus of Holliman's book was more on post-purchase behaviour in the home rather than at the supermarket check-out. The advice was based on reducing consumption by steps such as pressing slivers of soap together or unwinding old woollen garments to reuse the wool. Although the advice was practical and economical, it was not geared to making consumers' lives easier.

In today's industrialised society, where it is common for both partners in a 'conventional' household to work, and where an increasing number of households with children are managed by only one parent, the demand for convenience has never been greater. Products such as microwavable, individually portioned food, or disposable nappies are undeniably convenient and may appeal to consumers whose desire to 'buy green' is outweighed by their need for convenience. Mothers of young children are demonstrably more concerned about the environment than most other groups within society. However, the demands of young children are such that everyday psychological survival may take precedence in their purchasing decisions over a longer-term desire to help protect the environment. If consumers can be presented with a form of green consumer behaviour which is also convenient, the potential for a positive response is considerable. Einsmann (1992) relates an anecdote of Procter and Gamble's attempts to test nappy composting in a German town. Marketing data identified that the town contained 4000 mothers of children in the nappy-wearing age range. Invitations were mailed out asking mothers to place used nappies in their biodegradable waste receptacles. The invitation drew a response from 4200 mothers keen to participate in the scheme.

Psychological factors

An important psychological dimension in green consumption is our desire for control. Grey consumption has always stressed individuality, and the power of the individual through consumption. Green consumption often involves a return to more communal forms of consumption and the reduction of that individual control. One reason why most of us prefer to be the driver of a car rather than a passenger on a bus is that, as the driver, we have control. This need for control can work for or against the environment. Ottman (1992a) views the need for control as a driving factor in green purchase decisions. Faced with an environment that seems increasingly out of control, consumers are seeking to re-establish control through their purchase decisions.

On the other hand, in the case of cars, part of the toll of environmental and human damage caused by driving could be reduced if drivers were willing to devolve more control. Bowen (1993) describes the potential for a vehicle navigation system:

'which links the vehicle into a terrestrial equivalent of an air traffic control system. On main roads the car travels as part of a convoy, keeping a fixed distance from the one in front: vehicles can travel much more closely than would have been safe in the past because a computer reacts faster than the human brain. If there is trouble ahead the convoy will slow down. It would be possible to make the driver redundant in towns and main roads, but so far consumer resistance has blocked this.'

Perceptions

However rationally we think that we are behaving, we each make decisions and take action from our personal and subjective viewpoint. The information which influences our decision-making process reaches us through our senses, and passes through our own unique perception filter. Several different individuals, each given the same information about the environment, and about the environmental implications of various products, would undoubtedly each come to their own individual conclusions about the importance and nature of the green challenge and how it should affect their purchasing decisions. In passing through our perception filters, different items of information will be consciously or instinctively categorised according to their perceived importance, personal relevance and credibility. Environmental marketers cannot afford to assume that simply presenting consumers with 'the facts' is enough, or that the consumer once presented with these facts will react as the marketers would themselves. The perception of an issue may be at odds with the reality. For example, when asked what proportion of solid waste is accounted for by plastics, a sample of American consumers guessed 69 per cent, well out of line with the real figure of 13 per cent.

Learning

Pavlovian learning approaches see purchasing as a response to an external stimulus. So while shoppers might not salivate at the sound of a bell, they can be encouraged to purchase when exposed to a cue such as a point-of-sale display. Attempts to apply such a motivational learning approach to persuading consumers to purchase is very open to the charges of manipulation that were raised against marketers in Vance Packard's (1957) *The Hidden Persuaders*.

Motivation

Psycho-analytical motivational models use Freudian psychology to explain purchasing behaviour in relation to our desire to satisfy our instinctive drives within the constraints imposed by society. The process of evolution has programmed into all of us a desire for our genes to survive, a desire which can be stronger than the desire to survive as an individual. This is translated into a very powerful urge to see our children survive, thrive and live lives that are an improvement upon our own. People naturally want the best for their children, and this is expressed in a strong wish to see them inherit a viable environment. Guilt is another powerful psychological motivator. As consumers become aware of the consequence of their consumer behaviour, they can experience feelings of guilt which motivate them towards greener consumption. A 1985 survey of 289 'housewives' sponsored by Addis revealed that 43 per cent experienced guilt feelings about the amount of rubbish they threw away, 89 per cent thought that local authorities have a strong responsibility to provide recycling

facilities, and 94 per cent expressed a willingness to sort out their household waste to aid recycling.

These different approaches will tend to vary in their relevance when explaining any given form of consumer behaviour. Each of them will help to provide clues as to why and how purchases are made, none of them is likely to provide the entire answer. So while the choice of an investment fund might be entirely dominated by rational economic criteria, the choice of a particular model of car might have more psycho-analytical or sociologically based explanations. A consumer's progress through the purchase process will be very different according to the nature of the product. One would go through the five stages very differently according to whether the product being purchased was a packet of cornflakes or a new house.

RESPONDING TO THE GREEN CONSUMER

The response of a company to the green consumers within its market will depend on a number of factors. Of prime importance is whether the company's eco-performance represents an opportunity or a threat in terms of the likely response of consumers and consumer organisations.

For companies faced with the opportunity of growing demand for green products, Ottman (1992b) recommends anchoring the response around four E factors.

1 *Easy* – make it easy for your customers to be green.

2 *Empower customers* – provide them with solutions.

3 *Enlist the support of the customer.*

4 *Establish credibility* – with all the stakeholders of the business to guard against any form of backlash.

CONSUMERISM

The consumer movement is an important potential influence on the marketing of almost any product.

During the 1980s the consumer movement and the green movement began to overlap in some of their areas of interest. In terms of the eco-efficiency of products, both movements want to see efficiently made, high-value products being offered to consumers. However, consumerism stresses the need to get ever more consumption out of a given amount of money, while the green movement stresses the need to reduce consumption. A 1990 Haney Group survey of 330 consumer group leaders in America revealed that environmental issues accounted for two out of the top three issues that they saw confronting local and national consumer groups in the 1990s. In the UK the Consumers' Association ran a series of investigations into green products, pollution, waste disposal, packaging and the loss of green space. Even the basic principles of consumerism have been amended to accommodate environmental issues. The original declaration of consumer rights by President Kennedy covered four basic principles:

- the right to safety;
- the right to be informed;
- the right to choose;
- the right to be heard.

The International Organization of Consumers' Unions has since supplemented these principles with four more:

- the right of satisfaction of basic needs;
- the right of redress;
- the right to consumer education;
- the right to a healthy environment.

The consumer boycott

Perhaps the most powerful extension of consumerism is the consumer boycott. These vary between a relatively passive refusal to purchase and consume to more active, organised and direct protests against a company. The model for modern consumer boycotts was set by the boycotting of Saran Wrap in the USA during the Vietnam War. This campaign, backed by widespread leaflet distribution, was organised in protest at the involvement of the manufacturers of Saran Wrap, Dow Chemicals, in producing napalm. The effectiveness of consumer action against products was demonstrated by the anti-fur campaigners in 1972 when within a few months of their campaign aimed directly at UK consumers a complete ban on leopard, cheetah and tiger products was introduced.

Consumer boycotts can be related to a social issue, such as the campaign against Nestlé over its marketing of infant formula milk in less industrialised countries, or an environmental issue such as the world-wide boycott of CFC aerosols. Rehak (1993b) notes that in the USA an annual publication entitled *National Boycott News* put forward a conservative estimate of at least 125 active boycotts in force across America by the end of 1992. He also suggests that such formalised boycotts are only the 'tip of the iceberg' since the 71 per cent of American consumers who had switched brands over environmental issues were each involved in their own private boycotts.

Responding to consumer boycotts

A boycott can be highly economically damaging in the short term, and fatal to a company's green image in the longer term. A marketer faced with a consumer boycott can respond in several ways.

- *Ignore the problem.* Keep a low media profile and avoid any actions which could be interpreted as an admission of guilt.
- *Fight.* A company may opt to fight a boycott by trying to discredit or disprove it, to overcome it with promotions or discounts, to press for legal or political intervention or to stress the threats posed to job prospects and prosperity.
- *Explain.* Use PR, an emphasis on the positive aspects of the company's performance (such as conformance to government standards) and a willingness to meet with pressure groups to defuse the situation.
- *Comply.* Work with pressure groups to adopt voluntary self-regulated standards and then lobby for the whole industry to comply with such high standards.

CASE STUDY

Low-tech medicine

The market for herbal and natural remedies has been one of the most spectacular growth stories of the late 1980s and early 1990s. Products that were once thought to be the province of those with an 'alternative' lifestyle have been the focus for a flurry of market research activity, advertising and product launches. Mintel's market research indicates that in the five years after 1988, herbal remedies, which form the largest sector in the alternative medicines market, grew by around 50 per cent in value. Homeopathic products enjoyed a 44 per cent rise, while aromatherapy products grew from a small initial base by 30 per cent between 1992 and 1993. Boots, the high street chemist, followed up with its own independent research and calculated that the market for herbal and homeopathic products had doubled over five years.

So, why in an age of ever more sophisticated medical science and synthetic medicines, were such ancient products making a dramatic market comeback? Part of the answer relates to general trends in more over-the-counter medication, instead of medication on prescription. Moira Patterson, Mintel senior market analyst, commented:

'There has been an increasing trend in self-medication in the UK. This is partly the result of a greater awareness of health, fitness and diet issues in general, but it has also been spurred on by government policy.'

Another reason is a growing mistrust of conventional synthetic medicines. The holistic philosophy behind homeopathic treatments also appeals to consumers. While the approach to using synthetic medicines is a rather impersonal matching up of the symptoms or illness to the relevent chemicals, homeopathy is a more humanist approach which emphasises the need to treat the whole person as an individual. It is not only in the UK that alternative medicines are challenging the mainstream medical market. In Germany the total market is worth over 240 million ECUs (£320 million) and in France the herbal remedy Boiron is the best-selling cough and cold remedy.

The market growth that has been achieved by alternative medicines has largely been achieved without the benefit of major advertising campaigns or particularly effective distribution arrangements. The small size of most producers has limited their marketing communications to trade marketing and customer education leaflets. Distribution arrangements were initially limited to health shops. The signs are that this situation is changing and mass market status is approaching for alternative medicines. In the UK a prime-time TV series dedicated to herbal remedies screened during 1993 gave mass media coverage to the issues and ingredients, if not to the actual products. Market-leading companies such as New Era and Potters have been boosting their advertising coverage in the national and womens' press. Leading products such as Nelsons' 'Pollenna' hay-fever cure were recording summertime sales of some 200 000 units. In distribution terms the products have moved into the pharmacies in recent years to sit alongside their conventional synthetic counterparts, and the major supermarkets are becoming increasingly interested. Major players in the pharmaceutical industry are also beginning to cast an acquisitive eye over the alternative medicine companies. The first major acquisition was made by Scholl who took over Gerard House, second only to Potters in the UK herbal remedy market. Many industry observers predicted this to be the first of many such acquisitions. Others saw it as the beginning of the end. Much of the consumer appeal of these products lay in their 'cottage-industry, back-to-nature' image and the absence of a slick marketing machine behind the products. If the enthusiastic but somewhat naïve marketing of these small companies is replaced by the marketing professionalism of their new parents, will the customer still believe in the product?

Adapted from Murphy, C. (1993) 'Thyme and Potion', *Marketing Week*, 11 June, pp. 30–3.

CHAPTER 6

The green challenge for marketing

'At present our whole society is based on a vicious circle of ever-increasing production and consumption, without questioning whether we are really any happier or healthier for it. By seductive advertising and salesmanship we are constantly brainwashed to consume what the manufacturer wants us to, and not what we really need.'
(Holliman 1971)

INTRODUCTION

The development of marketing has involved many gradual, evolutionary changes. Every now and again the change becomes sufficiently significant for some form of marker to be put down, and a new era to be declared. The biggest watershed for marketing came with the formalisation of the marketing concept during the late 1950s/early 1960s. Since then a range of different approaches to marketing have been developed including relationship marketing, international marketing, internal marketing and micro-marketing. Although none of these has been declared a landmark change, there is a growing sense that formal marketing as it is becoming is in some ways very different to formal marketing as it has been up until now. This is linked to a range of concepts including the emergence of the 'post-consumer society', the 'information age', the 'age of discontinuous change' and the 'post-industrial society'.

Different perspectives on this perceived transition of society and of marketing have gradually been integrated into a proposition that we are moving out of the 'modern' world, and into the realms of 'post-modernism'. Few terms in the world of management theory inspire such extreme reactions as 'post-modernism'. It suffers from being semantically nonsensical, and from acquiring a reputation (often deservedly) encapsulated by the joke which opened Stephen Brown's review of post-modernism in marketing (1993):

'What's the difference between the Mafia and a post-modernist?'
'A post-modernist makes you an offer you can't understand.'

The idea that there was a 'modern' era, and that we have evolved beyond it, somehow sits more comfortably when discussing styles of architecture than the substance of management practice. Since marketing is a relatively young discipline, and since its academic theory and business practice have rarely been at the same stage of development at the same time, the search for a definitive form of 'post-modern' marketing is likely to be difficult. What this search is perhaps symptomatic of is a dawning recognition that there is a discrepancy between marketing as it was supposed to be and marketing as it is having to become. Brown contrasts the modern with the post-modern on a number of organisational dimensions. Among other things post-modern means:

- something chaotic rather than controlled;
- intuition and humanism instead of scientific rationality;
- embracing ambiguity instead of demanding certainty;
- emphasising stasis rather than progress;

- heterogeneity and plurality rather than the homogeneity of mass production and consensus;
- an emphasis on youth and equality instead of age and hierarchy;
- participation instead of contemplation.

These changes can be viewed as a green reaction to decades of unsustainable grey 'modern' marketing. This is not to equate post-modernism with green, because other attributes of post-modernism, such as an emphasis on cynicism, or on superficial style over substance, are clearly not part of the green agenda. However, most of the post-modernist attributes make sense either as symptoms of grey marketing reaching its limits, or as a reaction against it and a desire for a greener alternative. To label these many symptoms of, and reactions to, unsustainable growth as 'post-modernism' gives them a coherence and a sense of 'progress' that they do not deserve. In reality the transition is more one of back-tracking, retracing some steps that led down a blind alley to find a different and ultimately more rewarding path. It is a return to the 'real' marketing of meeting customer needs instead of manipulating customer perceptions. The fact that the characteristics of post-modern marketing are symptomatic of its unsustainability are demonstrated by Brown's assertion that 'the urge to consume is a characteristic symptom, perhaps *the* characteristic symptom, of the post-modern condition.' If this is the case, something else must come after unsustainable consumption, and therefore something else must lie beyond the transitional phase of post-modern marketing.

In pre-industrial times marketing for the artisan and craftsman involved nurturing their relationship with their local customers in order to sustain their business. If the green agenda rolls on with sufficient force to move society into the ecological, as opposed to just the environmental paradigm, then marketing might one day even have to go full circle with a return to an emphasis on craftsmanship, localised production and closer relationships with customers. In the meantime, with the emergence of new-traditionalism and new-realism in consumer behaviour, then perhaps we should be discussing new-traditionalism or new-realism, rather than post-modernism, within marketing.

CHALLENGING THE MARKETING PHILOSOPHY

There are three very distinct dimensions to the green challenge to marketing: a philosophical challenge, a practical challenge and a credibility challenge. The philosophical basis of marketing is the 'marketing concept' which replaced the product and the production-orientated selling concepts. It emerged during the late 1950s and was crystallised within Levitt's (1960) classic article 'Marketing Myopia'. Since then there has been much debate concerning the scope and substance of marketing. The key elements of the marketing concept as it emerged were as follows.

1 *A customer orientation.* Instead of viewing customers as a means to create profit if they could be persuaded to buy, the marketing concept positioned customer needs as the driving force of the business. The concept of consumer sovereignty has become a keystone of the marketing philosophy.

2 *An integrated marketing effort.* Non-marketing orientated companies still engage in marketing activities, but these are mostly post-production orientated and involve supporting the selling effort with research, planning and promotion. For marketing-orientated companies marketing is a guiding principle and an integrating force within the company. Marketers like to view marketing as 'the glue that makes a company stick together'.

3 *Profits through customer satisfaction.* The selling concept pursues profit through sales volume expansion and cost reduction. The marketing concept views customer satisfaction as an objective in itself, which, if achieved, generates profits in turn.

In the face of greater scrutiny of the role of business organisations within society, the marketing concept has been an important argument used to legitimise business activity. The justification that businesses exist to create wealth became insufficient, particularly as the extent to which the discrepancies in the distribution of that wealth became increasingly apparent. The justification that businesses exist to serve customers and to satisfy their wants and needs has a much more egalitarian ring, since a great many more people will use the products of a company than will share in the wealth that it generates.

The inherent logic and apparent worth of the marketing concept make it relatively difficult to attack, an attribute it shares with the concepts of sustainability and social responsibility (not that this has deterred some critics of all three). Perhaps because of this 'motherhood' appeal, the marketing concept has been subject to relatively little theoretical scrutiny (Houston 1986). Articles attacking marketing and the marketing concept have appeared periodically:

- 'The Faltering Marketing Concept' (Bell and Emory 1971);

- 'Is It Not Time to Discard the Marketing Concept?' (Sachs and Benson 1978);

- 'Has Marketing Failed, Or Was It Never Really Tried?' (King 1985).

The key criticisms contained in such challenges can mostly be classified under four headings.

1 The marketing concept is unrealistic.

2 The marketing concept is too passive.

3 The marketing concept is simply impossible.

4 Marketing in practice is poorly directed.

Criticism 1. The marketing concept is unrealistic

The growing consumerism movement has been used as evidence that the marketing concept exists in rhetoric rather than reality. *Business Week* in 1969 suggested that 'In the very broadest sense, consumerism can be defined as the bankruptcy of what the business schools have been calling "the marketing concept".' If the marketing concept was widely held and effectively put into practice, consumers should not need to take legal action,

seek legislative change or mount campaigns against products or companies in order to achieve satisfaction.

The green challenge has posed similar questions over whether the marketing concept is anything more than a socially acceptable justification for business activity. There is ample evidence that consumers want greener products from greener companies. Despite this, experience from a range of industries including cars, construction, agriculture and chemicals has shown that companies are willing to put a great deal of effort into resisting the introduction of tougher environmental standards.

From a social perspective, Tomlinson (1990) explores several concerns about consumer culture and the marketing that drives it.

1 Consumption is increasingly viewed as the means by which freedom and independence is expressed, yet many people on low incomes are effectively 'disenfranchised' from the consumer society.

2 Issues of marketing style have overwhelmed issues of substance so that real performance differences between products are masked. This could be the stylish promotion of unexceptional goods or the emergence of 'personality politics' in place of serious political debate in our choice of government. As Tomlinson notes:

'The ability to stylise anything: toothpaste, clothing, roach spray, food, violence, other cultures around the world, etc., provokes a comprehension of the world which focuses on the easily manipulated surfaces. Most notably, as the evanescent becomes increasingly 'real', reality becomes increasingly evanescent.'

3 Consumption has become the framework within which many social interactions are now controlled. For example, large publics are increasingly only acceptable at 'orchestrated media events such as Live Aid or Sport Aid, but not in the more spontaneously usable spaces of our everyday environments. Consumer culture is not a vibrant or at all spontaneous street culture: it is a culture of the spectacle.' One effect of the UK's 1994 Criminal Justice Act is to make it increasingly difficult for any large group of people to

gather together unless it is for the purpose of consuming – a slightly chilling thought.

4 Consumption patterns are increasingly reinforcing a pattern of society in which individuals are relatively isolated into family units. In the face of this isolation consumption through the mass media increasingly influences our opinions, standards and the knowledge available to us. Where social values were once developed and communicated by social interactions, they are increasingly absorbed from the technology of the media. This makes the concentration of parts of the media into the hands of a relatively small number of companies and entrepreneurs a matter for societal concern.

5 As the marketing emphasis in society increases so we witness 'the transformation of some of our most traditional and innocent and often casual pastimes and pleasures. It is not any inherent character or attraction of an activity that guarantees its buoyancy in everyday life. Rather, it is the marketing strategy of market men and media programmers that determines much of our consumption.'

6 In an age when freedom is dominated by the freedom to consume, how real is this freedom, when so many of the consumption choices that we face are so carefully constructed for us?

A sociological view of marketing and consumption tends to cast the customer in the role of the victim of manipulation by the marketing profession. Marketers and free-market economists tend to paint a picture of the company and its marketers as the humble servants of the all-powerful consumer. As with most such dichotomies, the truth hovers somewhere in the middle.

Criticism 2. The marketing concept is too passive

Organising a business around the needs of customers has been criticised as too passive and reactive (Zeithaml and Zeithaml 1984). Brookes (1988) suggests that 'satisfying customer needs and wants at a profit is the classic marketing dictum ... (but) ... the dictum misses the point. It is passive, at best a sort of anticipatory servanthood, a pursuit of marketing without power.' Brooks suggests that the next development for marketing is leverage marketing in which 'the core purpose of marketing is persuading and influencing and serving some degree of power over both competitors and consumers.' Whether this is a step in a different direction, or merely a return to the selling concept is a moot point. The question that Brooks' ideas prompt is whether marketing-orientated companies do operate along the lines of 'anticipatory servanthood'. The answer to this appears to be that they do when it suits them. If the likely outcome of consumer requirements is threatening to corporate growth, profits or internal power balances, companies will proactively spend a great deal of money on political lobbying and 'customer education'. The clearest example of this was the opposition mounted to California's proposed 'Big Green' environmental protection bill. Companies spent some $35 million (16 million ECUs) on lobbying to prevent this bill becoming law by overcoming its initial popularity among Californians, and so by implication their own customers.

Criticism 3. The marketing concept is simply impossible

In relation to consumers the marketing concept assumes that they are well informed, rational, consistent and not interested in doing harm to themselves or others; and that they have clearly defined preferences. In many markets this is not the case. In green markets the problem of consumers being poorly informed (not to mention frequently misinformed and confused by much of the marketing communication regarding the environment) is particularly acute.

Criticism 4. Marketing in practice is poorly directed

Demand is only created where the desire to purchase a product is backed up by an ability to pay. Those that cannot afford to buy do not count in the demand figures and therefore cease to exist on the grey marketing agenda. Since all those exposed to the advertising for a product might be made to desire it, and at best, only those able to purchase the product will be satisfied by it, it is quite possible that the operation of marketing is creating more dissatisfaction than satisfaction.

Another focus for criticism of marketing's direction is that too much emphasis has been placed on creating intangible benefits within consumers' minds, rather than providing 'real' tangible benefits in terms of improved products. Medawar (1978) comments:

> 'In the US, there are some 200 brands of vodka, despite the fact that vodka is just plain alcohol treated so that it has no distinctive character, aroma or taste – and yet the best-selling US brand is also the most expensive. Howard Cohen, the chairman of an advertising agency, has commented: "Ninety-nine out of a hundred people could never tell the difference in vodka ... The difference is what you perceive and we in advertising are in the business of selling images that help people to add to their overall perception of themselves".'

CHALLENGING OUR ASSUMPTIONS ABOUT MARKETING

The marketing system provides all of us with the majority of the goods and services that we depend upon and enjoy. However, the benefits of marketing as a practice have also been challenged periodically. Drucker (1960) felt that the consumerism movement challenged four critical assumptions about marketing – assumptions which are also challenged by growing environmental concern:

1 Consumers really know their needs.

2 Businesses really care about those needs and understand how to meet them.

3 Businesses provide useful information to allow consumers to match products to needs.

4 Products and services really deliver what consumers expect and what businesses promise.

Assumption 1. Consumers really know their needs

In relation to environmental issues, consumers' lack of understanding of the problems and potential solutions makes it very difficult for adequate consumer-led initiatives. Consumers desire more biodegradable packaging without understanding what biodegradable means, and they are often against plastic packaging based on the misconception that plastic cannot be recycled. Even the most interested of consumers have relatively poor understanding of environmental issues. A survey of 1500 members of the US consumer group publication *Consumer Reports* found that out of 16 relatively straightforward questions the majority of respondents got at least ten wrong and no respondent got more than 12 answers right. The dangers posed by UV-B radiation as a result of the thinning ozone layer are considerable, but relatively few consumers understand that loose-weave clothing, light cloud and water provide little protection. Given the complexities of the issues it would seem appropriate for companies to attempt to lead rather than follow the customer.

Consumers are also typically ignorant about their most basic needs in relation to their status as 'human animals'. In a 'natural' situation, the availability of foods that are high in fats and sugars would be relatively low. They would therefore be indulged in when encountered as a valuable source of calories. Hunting and gathering are naturally energetic activities, and so the times during which food did not have to be gathered would be spent conserving rather than expending energy. The instinct to consume food which is high in fats and sugars and to rest after a 'hard day's work' remains, even though there is no shortage of available calories and our 'work' may involve little or no exercise. This does not mean that calorific foods must be demarketed. It does mean that companies should make information and healthy product alternatives available to consumers to allow them to make a choice – an informed choice. At present, food labelling often gives consumers a false impression of the fat and sugar content of foods.

Assumption 2. Businesses really care about those needs and understand how to meet them

Marketers have typically taken a relatively blinkered view of customer needs by seeking to address those which they can meet with their product offerings. Companies cannot necessarily be seen as passive and entirely subject to the demands of the customer in relation to eco-performance. Despite its emphasis on the environment, Volvo ran into environmentalist criticism over the relatively poor fuel economy of the powerful 850 model. Volvo's management defends this by stating that the powerful engine is what the Volvo customer wants (Rothenberg *et al* 1992). What Volvo does not say, according to Chris Agren (the Swedish NGO Secretariat on Acid Rain) 'is that they (Volvo) have a large influence on the consumers'. The defence that a course of action 'is what the customer wants' sounds a good deal more convincing when a company is doing something to improve its environmental performance rather than doing something to avoid improving its environmental performance.

Assumption 3. Businesses provide useful information to allow consumers to match products to needs

In the area of environmental issues, much of the information provided by companies has not been particularly useful. This has been the case particularly in the fields of green advertising, green labels and corporate environmental reporting. Many green claims have been shown to be misleading, inaccurate or downright false.

Assumption 4. Products and services really deliver what consumers expect and what businesses promise

In terms of delivering the products that businesses explicitly and factually promise, legislation (as opposed to the marketing concept) ensures that these promises are kept. Goods and services must reach the consumer as they were described and fit for their intended use. This legalistic approach is symptomatic of an economic and technical perspective, and of a product orientation. A marketing orientation on this issue should not take an interest in these elements, but in customer satisfaction. As Levitt points out:

'The consumer consumes not things, but expected benefits – not cosmetics, but the satisfactions of the allurement they promise; not quarter-inch drills, but quarter-inch holes; not stock in companies, but capital gains ...' (Levitt 1970)

In terms of these less measurable and often implicit promises about the benefits of products or services, businesses often do not deliver what consumers are encouraged by marketing communications to expect. In Advertisingland, buying a new car guarantees a blue sky and an open road, which perhaps leads to a holiday destination which is bound to be sunny and uncrowded. Levitt (1970) defends the fact that the images used in advertising are often unrealistic because of a need to see 'what life might be, to bring the possibilities we cannot see before our eyes and screen out the stark reality in which we must live' – a fairly convincing argument for advertising as the new 'opium of the people'. A green perspective would be that if people are made aware of the stark realities of life on earth, they may become motivated to do something to improve it.

THE MARKETING CONCEPT – SATISFACTION GUARANTEED?

Another key marketing assumption is that the consumption of marketed goods creates and increases satisfaction. Economic theory views human demands as insatiable, meaning that when one consumer need is satisfied, another takes its place. This poses the question as to whether marketing actually contributes to any overall increase in satisfaction within society.

The notion that the consumption of goods and services creates satisfaction is also challenged by Ivan Illich's philosophical doctrine of 'modernised poverty' (1981). This suggests that through the operation of the market economy individuals become dependent on the system to meet their needs. Without access to the money that employment or welfare provides us with, we become unable to feed or clothe ourselves, or to create adequate shelter. This dependence creates deep-rooted feelings of helplessness, frustration and vulnerability. The material satisfaction provided by modern consumption is counterbalanced, therefore, by emotional impoverishment and the dissatisfaction caused by a complete dependence on the availability of money to enable us to survive.

Evidence from psychologists also challenges the belief that our satisfaction is increased by consumption. During (1992) discusses the relationship:

'No more Americans report that they are "very happy" now than in 1957. The "very happy" share of the population has fluctuated around one third since the mid-fifties, despite near doublings in both gross national product and personal consumption expenditure per capita.'

Argyle (1987), in examining research on international comparisons in satisfaction, found that a wide range of countries' citizens ranked themselves near the middle of a 'happiness' scale, and that both low-income Cubans and their affluent American counterparts viewed themselves as happier than the norm. The level of satisfaction does not appear to be linked to the actual level of consumption, but there is a relationship to people's perceived position in the economic ladder. Therefore high income/consumption groups are generally more satisfied .with their lot (not surprisingly) than lower income/consumption groups (although it is worth noting that Scitsovsky (1976) among others relates this more to the difference in the skill levels and the psychological rewards of the type of work in which each group typically is involved). The argument that material consumption and actual satisfaction are not linked goes back to the philosophers of Ancient Rome and perhaps further. It has done nothing to prevent material consumption and progress, and could be viewed as being of little more than philosophical interest to marketing. However, it provides a potential future challenge to marketers if the thirst for happiness and satisfaction is chan-

nelled into alternatives to material consumption; and it also poses a current challenge to marketers in their role in contributing to the dissatisfaction of those on the lower rungs of any country's economic ladder.

One of the most obvious ways in which to create a satisfied customer is first to create a dissatisfied potential customer to whom a company's product can be presented as a source of satisfaction. As Goldman (1992) explains in great detail, advertising does a great deal more than signpost where a product can be found and what its features and benefits are. Advertising creates and disseminates an entire set of socio-economic values and images which links the consumption of products to social acceptance, achievement, self-worth, safety and happiness. For some consumers this will create or direct a form of dissatisfaction that will be converted into purchases; but for those unable to purchase it will create or enhance a sense of dissatisfaction which cannot be resolved.

There are certain markets where the emphasis on the creation of dissatisfaction has caused particular concern. Within the security products market there has been concern about the use of fear appeals to create and enlarge fears about crime among elderly consumers to stimulate demand. Feminist critics have also criticised marketers of beauty, fashion and diet products for a marketing approach aimed at making women dissatisfied with their bodies. The use of fashion models who are on average some 25 per cent underweight is creating a new female conception of beauty and attractiveness which does not fit the vast majority of the female population, and which may be at odds with the preferences of the people they would wish to attract. Charles Revlon is famous for saying, 'In the factory we make cosmetics. In the store we sell hope.' Cosmetic companies are open to the charge that in their advertising· they are spreading fear – fear of appearing old or plain and of becoming less attractive or less socially acceptable because of it.

Medawar (1978) takes a view of the market economy as driven more by the creation of dissatisfaction than the creation of genuine satisfaction, commenting that:

'It is true that dissatisfaction may be a driving force for progress – and also what passes for it – but the notion that we can make real progress by making dissatisfaction is very hard to swallow. To take the widest view, to be part of a system which does so much to continue dissatisfaction, in order to market palliative products to the few – in a world in which consumption for most means the salvage of human dignity, if not life and death – seems as fundamentally wrong as anything possibly could be.'

Economically based approaches to business tend to equate satisfaction with the ownership and use of a particular item. A consumer who wanted a car would therefore be satisfied by the acquisition of a car. In reality, people's satisfaction is largely determined by whether or not the benefits they enjoy from a given purchase meet their expectations. Marketing has always stressed the joys of product ownership because the aim of marketing is to present product offerings as the solution to particular problems. However, there are often responsibilities that come with the joys of purchase, and new problems that product ownership may pose. It may be issues of storage, maintenance, disposal, operation or insurance that turn the product of our dreams into something of a burden. This is not to say that it is better to be a 'have-not' than a 'have', but is a recognition that product ownership can have its drawbacks. Ottman (1992a) suggests that the members of the 'baby boomer' generation, in the quest for an increased quality of life, look to streamline and simplify their lives which may involve reducing and simplifying their consumption.

Rethinking the marketing concept

The transition from the selling era to the marketing era was marked by changes to the emphasis on customers and their needs, by changes to the role of the marketing function within the company, and by changes to the means by which profits were pursued. These three changes are being repeated with the greening of marketing which involves:

1 *A new customer orientation*. The marketing concept is often interpreted as making the cus-

tomers' needs the guiding force behind the companys' marketing efforts. This idea has its problems, however.

'It is quite certain that few, if any, of the really significant product innovations which have been placed on the market to date were developed because the inventor sensed that a latent pool of needs was yearning to be satisfied.' (Kerby 1972)

'The marketing concept is an inadequate prescription for marketing strategy, because it virtually ignores a vital input of marketing strategy – the creative abilities of the firm.'

'Twenty years of adherence to the marketing concept may have taken its toll on American enterprise. The marketing concept has diverted our attention from the product and its manufacture; instead we have focused our strategy on responses to market wants and have become preoccupied with advertising, selling and promotion.' (Bennett and Cooper 1981)

The green challenge does not call for an abandoning of the attention paid to customer needs and a return to the product, production or selling orientation. Instead it calls for a balance between the marketing, product and production orientations to ensure that the product and method of production are matched to the needs of consumers and other stakeholders.

2 *Even more integrated marketing*. The move from selling to marketing required the co-ordination of the efforts of the other business functions behind the effort to satisfy the customer. The green challenge expands the marketing effort to include internal parties and processes who were previously not thought to be of direct interest to customers. The integration challenge for the environmental marketer will cross many more levels of the hierarchy, SBUs and functional boundaries. Externally it may require close integration with suppliers to develop greener inputs into the production system.

3 *A new profit orientation*. Just as the marketing orientation moved the idea of how profit is generated away from sales volume to focus instead on customer satisfaction, environmental marketing shifts the focus on to the source of profit. Traditional marketing theory concen-

trates on the proposition that if you get the four Ps right (Product, Price, Place and Promotion), then success will follow in the form of a fifth P – profits. Environmental marketing involves generating success by ensuring the marketing mix meets the following 'S' criteria (Peattie 1990):

- *satisfaction* of customer needs;
- *safety* of products and production for consumers, workers, society and the environment;
- *social acceptability* of the products, their production and the other activities of the company;
- *sustainability* of the products, their production and the other activities of the company.

Consumer sovereignty

The most profound change in environmental marketing is the changed relationship between companies and consumers. The idea that the customer comes first is the very touchstone of the marketing concept. It also predates the marketing concept by some distance; Adam Smith back in 1776 stated that the purpose of production is to serve consumption, rather than the other way around. Unfortunately, consumer sovereignty can only be achieved by the market mechanisms of neo-classical economics under conditions of perfect competition. Since markets are imperfect in the real world, consumer sovereignty can only be achieved by the explicit inclusion of consumer needs in company's strategic thinking; in other words by companies adopting the marketing concept. For many years profitability was a key measure of business success, and was used as a proxy measure of customer satisfaction. Even before the marketing concept was fully developed, the idea that profits were not an assurance of satisfied customers began to emerge. Converse and Huegy in 1946 wrote:

> 'Business functions to satisfy the needs of consumers. The first measure of the success of any business is how well it serves the consumers. If an operation is not in the interests of the consumers, it is not justified, no matter how profitable it may be to its owners. He profits most who serves best.'

Both marketing and total quality management seemed to rediscover the importance of customer satisfaction during the 1980s. A popular adornment for British factory walls during this time was a poster featuring a rather sleepy looking lion, beneath which was emblazoned the slogan 'The customer is King'. This concept of the sovereignty of the customer as an element of marketing theory and practice has been accepted almost unquestioningly by those who preach the marketing philosophy.

In theory absolute consumer sovereignty may be the basis of both free market capitalism and marketing (Smith 1988), but in practice consumer sovereignty is relative and varies in extent among different types of market. Mulhern (1992) notes two important differences between the role of consumer sovereignty in economics and marketing. First, 'while neo-classical economic theory *assumes* consumer sovereignty, the marketing concept *proclaims* it by explicitly orienting a company toward the satisfaction of consumer wants.' Second, in economic theory consumer sovereignty is assumed to guarantee both liberty for the individual and the optimal level of societal welfare; while marketing is concerned with the satisfaction of consumer needs for the organisations' own ends. The classical marketing concept is therefore 'blind to the well-being of consumers'. The answer to this marketing 'blind-spot' is the societal marketing concept and the introduction of the concept of corporate social responsibility. This development relegates the customer from a position of sovereign, to that of a key constituency. This change of emphasis allows marketing to develop in ways that counter charges of passivity. Mulhern suggests that in considering customers' welfare as well as wants, marketing becomes more proactive in influencing fundamental customer perceptions and behaviour. While leverage marketing aims to influence consumers purely to make them consume more, environmental marketing would involve influencing consumer perceptions and behaviour in a way that improves both individual and social welfare.

The analogy of the customer as monarch is an interesting and perhaps a telling one. There are relatively few real-life monarchs around today, which suggests that monarchy is not a particularly easy system to maintain. Historically, monarchs have often ruled through fear and inspired little real loyalty among their subjects. The absolute power of the monarch can encourage them to wield it in pursuit of a whim, and can encourage subjects passively to follow to the detriment of both.

Blind allegiance to customers can result in companies taking actions which they know are not in the customers' interest because it is what the customers think, and say, that they want. McDonald's decision to switch to quilted plastic and paper burger wraps was justified by the fact that, despite being a retrograde step in environmental terms (compared to the polystyrene clamshell boxes once the offending CFCs had been removed), it was what the customer wanted.

The flaws in the analogy of consumer sovereignty are revealed by the fact that even when consumer sovereignty is discussed, the words that are used are those connected with democracy rather than those of a monarchy. When David Bellamy commented that 'Everytime you take your supermarket trolley out for a spin you are taking part in a referendum about the future of the planet', he was characterising the individual customer, not as a king or queen, but as one among many voters. For marketers the customer is not a monarch with a single wish to pursue, but a member of an electorate made up of many individuals with differing needs and opinions. In an election, the government that is elected has a mandate to represent not just the proportion of the population that endorsed them with a vote, but to represent all of society. The need for socio-environmental responsibility in marketing mirrors this mandate.

Conventional marketing places the responsibility for the companies' actions on the customer. Environmental marketing requires marketers to dethrone the customer as monarch, and instead to take responsibility for the customer. Mulhern (1992) terms this a welfare-based interpretation of the marketing concept. It involves defending consumers' welfare within the company as well as attempting to satisfy their wants. Just as marketing requires a balance between meeting

customer needs and generating profit, environmental marketing requires a four-way balance between customer wants, customer welfare, social responsibility and profitability. It may also mean an emphasis on consumers' welfare over the meeting of their explicit desires, or on trying to channel consumers towards products whose consumption and production will not compromise their welfare or the welfare of others. To some marketers this may smack of paternalism. To others it may seem a radical step involving the abandonment of a fundamental marketing principle. However, it is more akin to adopting the marketing approach of many of the professions. Patients do not usually approach doctors or dentists demanding a specific cure (even if they do, they are usually willing to be advised); they go with a problem which they hope can be solved. Consumers approach solicitors, accountants, architects, educators and a range of others from computer salespeople to hairdressers and ask 'What would you recommend?' The professional services marketing approach involves service suppliers taking responsibility for customers and solving their problems. The green challenge asks the same of all marketers. To be able to take this responsibility, marketers will first have to meet the credibility challenge so that consumers trust commercial marketers and the information they provide.

THE CREDIBILITY CHALLENGE

For the marketing philosophy to yield benefits, and for marketing activities to succeed, the marketing effort needs to be credible to the rest of the company and to its publics (and customers in particular). Many of the challenges to the marketing philosophy and the problems experienced by many companies attempting to implement it, relate to the tendency of marketing practice to revolve around the trappings of marketing as opposed to its substance (Ames 1970). Companies can employ marketers and set up departments handling market research and customer service, without ever embracing the substance of marketing as a philosophy. This tendency appears to be as much a feature of marketing in the 1990s as it was in the previous three decades in view of the comments of an anonymous but apparently eminent former marketing director:

'If it's going to work, marketing must run through the whole ethos of a company like letters through a stick of rock. Not having driven this point home is marketers' greatest collective failure – and the recession has proved it.' (McMurdo 1991)

Despite the fact that communicating the right image is a cornerstone of marketing practice, the marketing profession itself has always had something of an image problem. This is not a new phenomenon. When Plato attempted to create a universal hierarchy for all the 'occupations of man', he assigned the lowest status to 'those who sell, but do not produce the good'. Things may not have changed that much in the intervening 23 centuries in view of the findings of a 1983 Gallup poll on the ethical standards of various professions. This placed salespeople and advertising executives, two pillars of the church of marketing, bottom in terms of honesty and ethical standards. Farmer (1967), in an article with the thought-provoking title 'Would You Want Your Daughter to Marry a Marketing Man?', complains:

'For the past 6000 years the field of marketing has been thought of as made up of fast-buck artists, conmen, wheeler-dealers and shoddy goods distributors. Too many of us have been "taken" by the touts or conmen; and all of us at times have been prodded into buying all sorts of "things" we really did not need, and which we found later on we did not even want.'

In 1991 this theme was continued by BARB/Mintel's 1991 survey, *The Green and Ethical Shopper*, which revealed that 'irresponsible marketing' was the ethical issue in business of most concern to UK consumers.

Concerns about marketing relate partly to its methods and partly to its outcomes. In terms of methods, the use of persuasive advertising is a frequent focus of criticism. This has at times reached almost hysterical levels over issues like subliminal advertising. A marketing research experiment conducted in an American cinema exposed 45 000 customers to the messages 'Eat Popcorn' and 'Drink Coca-Cola'. These were shown at subliminal speeds (below the threshold of conscious perception) and lower light intensity than the surrounding film. Popcorn sales increased by almost 60 per cent and sales of the soft drink rose almost 20 per cent (Gist 1971).

For the purists, the defence of marketing is easy on the basis that the activities criticised by Farmer and others are really selling and not marketing. However intellectually satisfying this argument might be, it doesn't prevent marketing from developing a poor image among those outside the field. Societal marketing was an important step in trying to legitimise marketing and improve its image. Kotler talks about marketing's 'higher purpose' in the following terms:

'Ultimately, the enlightened marketer is really trying to contribute to the quality of life … Profits will still be a major test of business success in serving society. However, … profits are really a by-product of doing business well and not the moral aim of business. Business, like any other institutions of society, prospers only by maintaining legitimacy in the eyes of consumers, employees and the general public. Legitimacy is grounded in the institution's commitment to serve higher moral aims.'

In relation to the green challenge, marketing is faced with another credibility challenge. The idea that marketing managers can, and hopefully will, help to save the planet may seem curious to many of those outside the profession. Marketing and its role in stimulating consumption has made it something of a target within the green movement. In the UK Green Party's manifesto several important marketing tools including advertising, sales promotion and sponsorship are targets for increasing restrictions and tax penalties on excessive levels. Other areas of marketing practice like rapid model replacement, disposability as a product feature, and the addition of unnecessary features to create differentiation have all come under attack from environmentalists. However, these are very much features of perceived marketing practice as opposed to components of the marketing philosophy.

The marketing philosophy may champion the rights and needs of customers, but customers are not necessarily impressed with their self-appointed champions. In Gerstman and Meyer's *Third US Annual Survey of the Environment*, 91 per cent of Americans named marketers as the profession 'least concerned about the environment'; and only 12 per cent of Americans found environmental claims 'believable'. Much of the problem lies with companies viewing environmental concern as a selling opportunity rather than a marketing opportunity. Perhaps the most cynical example comes from Germany where the early stages of 'Green Dot' recycling ran into considerable problems, partly caused by a number of companies 'freeloading' by adding the symbol to their products without joining the scheme or paying the registration fee. When such stories become public, the result is a major 'credibility gap' between the concept of environmental marketing, and the perception of consumers about the sincerity of marketing strategies which use a green theme. This gap appears to be widening. In a 1990 Green Monitor survey of 1200 UK consumers, 56 per cent of them were 'suspicious' of environmental marketing claims, which by 1992 had risen to 63 per cent (Toor 1992).

It is not only consumers who are affected by this credibility gap. Business customers are not necessarily impressed by the depth of the greening efforts of their suppliers. In *Purchasing* magazine's (1993) survey of US purchasing managers, 50 per cent had been offered green products by suppliers but most felt that these were largely 'marketing hype'. Even marketers have their reservations. In a survey of leading UK marketers, the majority were critical about the level of 'bandwagon jumping' among other companies (Mitchell 1989).

The ethical challenge

Green issues can often pose ethical dilemmas for marketers when the short-term interests of the organisation and the interests of customers and society come into conflict. Imagine that the manufacturer of a certain food additive faces a domestic ban on its product because it has been named as a suspected carcinogen. Should it now try and market it in other markets where no such ban exists? Laczniak (1983) offers some guidance

for marketers on the horns of such dilemmas.

- *The Golden Rule.* Act in a way that you would expect others to act towards you.
- *The Professional Ethic.* Take only actions which would be viewed as proper by an objective panel of your professional colleagues.
- *Kant's Categorical Imperative.* Act in a way such that the action taken under the circumstances could be a universal law of behaviour for everyone facing those same circumstances.
- *The TV Test.* A manager should always ask, 'would I feel comfortable explaining this action on TV to the general public?'

THE PRACTICAL CHALLENGE

The greening of marketing

Creating a green concept of marketing, or putting environmental marketing into practice, is not a straightforward business. Part of the problem lies in the fact that green is a relative concept. Different people and different countries will have a different perception of what constitutes a green product according to their perception of different environmental problems, their urgency, causes and potential solutions. Air pollution, traffic congestion and rising levels of crime and drug usage may be key concerns among city dwellers. Those living on the coast may be more concerned with water pollution, littering by holidaymakers and the dangers of tanker spills.

What constitutes a green product also varies over time. It is perhaps a sobering thought that CFCs were originally marketed as being 'exceptionally environmentally inert'. As our understanding of the environmental challenge evolves, so do the issues of concern that may be translated into changed purchasing behaviour. Sudden interventions by the media or by newsworthy celebrities can also rearrange the priorities on the green agenda. Technology changes or competitor actions can also render a particular green product obsolete. Where HCFC-driven aerosols were once seen as a green alternative to CFC-driven

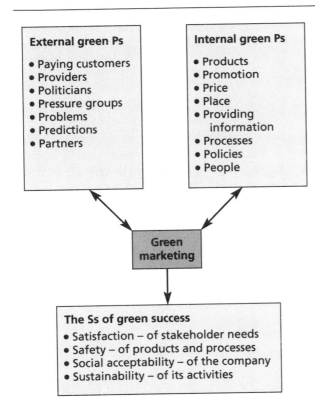

External green Ps	Internal green Ps

External green Ps
- Paying customers
- Providers
- Politicians
- Pressure groups
- Problems
- Predictions
- Partners

Internal green Ps
- Products
- Promotion
- Price
- Place
- Providing information
- Processes
- Policies
- People

Green marketing

The Ss of green success
- Satisfaction – of stakeholder needs
- Safety – of products and processes
- Social acceptability – of the company
- Sustainability – of its activities

Fig. 6.1 The green marketing process
(Source: Peattie (1992))

aerosols, the concern about HCFCs as greenhouse gases now make air-driven or pump-action aerosols the green alternative.

The environmental marketing process

The marketing process essentially involves matching the controllable internal variables of the marketing mix with the demands of the marketing environment. Environmental marketing is no different, in principle, although the internal variables and external demands which must be reconciled are a little different. Since marketers are used to dealing with groups of Ps, these can perhaps be most easily dealt with in terms of internal controllable green Ps and external uncontrollable green Ps. The model is summarised in Fig. 6.1.

The internal green Ps include McCarthy's (1960) classic '4 Ps' model of the marketing mix, together with other organisational factors.

- *Products*. How acceptable and competitive is their eco-performance in use and disposal, including their longevity and the environmental impact of components such as packaging and raw materials? (*See* Chapters 10 and 15.)

- *Promotion*. Will customers understand, believe and respond predictably to a green promotional message? A particular area for concern has been the accuracy of green claims (*See* Chapter 13).

- *Price*. Do prices need to be changed to reflect the differences in cost or demand for green products? How price sensitive are customers? What is an acceptable price for a green product? (*See* Chapter 16.)

- *Place*. Can our greening strategy be supported by using channels with suitably green credentials, and finding eco-efficient methods of distribution? (*See* Chapter 14.)

- *Providing information*. Do we have all the information available relating to the environment that internal and external stakeholders require? A green strategy requires a new level of openness and disclosure externally. Monitoring the internal and external issues which are relevant to environmental performance introduces an entirely new area for marketers. (*See* Chapter 12.)

- *Processes*. Can we improve our energy and material efficiency, and output of waste and pollution? (*See* Chapter 11.)

- *Policies*. Do they effectively motivate, monitor, evaluate and control environmental performance? (*See* Chapter 7.)

- *People*. Do they understand environmental issues, the company's performance, and their role in the greening process? (*See* Chapter 7.)

Externally the Ps that must be monitored and evaluated include:

- *Paying customers*. How green are they? How well informed about green issues are they? Do they want green products and, if so, what sort?

- *Providers*. How green are the companies who supply the business with everything including raw materials, energy, office supplies and services such as waste disposal?

• *Politicians*. The public can affect businesses directly through their purchasing behaviour. In a democracy they can also affect companies more indirectly through their influence on government. As the major political parties commit themselves to increasingly vigorous environmental protection policies, the green voter may become as powerful an influence on companies as the green consumer. Green pressure applied through political channels may take longer to affect business, but the effect of legislation may be more sudden and profound.

• *Pressure groups*. What issues are they currently highlighting? Who and what are they campaigning about? What new areas of concern are emerging?

• *Problems*. Has the company or any of its competitors been linked with environmental and social problems?

• *Predictions*. What environmental problems might affect the company in future? Issues take a while to pass from scientific discovery, through media and pressure-group interest, to reach the wider population and the political agenda. Companies observing the results of environmental research can gain a head start in the race to respond.

• *Partners*. Is the company linked to any other organisation whose environmental performance might affect the perception of the company's eco-performance?

The environmental marketing function

The green challenge obviously poses a practical challenge for marketers in terms of developing new marketing strategies, segmenting markets, developing new products, planning marketing communications campaigns, setting prices and all the other activities covered in the remaining chapters. Another practical dimension of the challenge relates to the way in which the marketing function is structured and managed. The philosophy of marketing is something holistic and all embracing, but this is at odds with the practicalities of marketing in many companies where marketing is perceived as a specific set of activities or as a particular business function. As Drucker states:

'Marketing is so basic that it cannot be considered a separate function on a par with others such as manufacturing and personnel ... It is the whole business seen from the point of view of its end result that is from the customer's point of view. Concern and responsibility for marketing must therefore permeate all areas of the enterprise.'

In practice relatively few companies have reached this total marketing orientation that Drucker envisages. For many others Carson's (1968) observation that marketing in practice is often merely 'the integration, just below senior management level, of those activities related primarily towards customers' still holds true. Responding to the green challenge will require marketing to become genuinely holistic in scope to ensure that all the activities of a company are acceptable to customers.

The role of the marketer

The marketer fulfils a variety of activities for a company, which will vary according to the breadth of the concept of marketing that the company adopts. Among the roles that the marketer is likely to have to fulfil are:

• *Advocate*. The terms of the marketing philosophy ensure that the marketer is the consumers' champion representing their interests when decisions ranging from the strategic to the mundane are made. In a company where the marketing concept has been fully embraced, there should be little or no need for marketers to fight internal battles on the customers' behalf. In practice, within even those companies that claim to be marketing-orientated, getting people to accept the principle that the customer is all important is one thing, while getting them to behave as though they believed this is quite another.

• *Missionary*. In promoting a customer and marketing orientation internally, the environmental marketer preaches a doctrine that is broadened out to include social responsibility and environmental sensitivity.

• *Sensor*. Through the activities of market research, environmental scanning and monitoring of marketing plans marketers act as an organisational sensory system. Marketers' close contact with the sales force and others in the distribution chain mean that they are often the first to learn about strategically important changes among customers and their needs, and among competitors. The marketer will often get the earliest warnings about the greening of the market.

● *Expert*, on the external environment. Marketers can contribute a good deal of important information regarding the market and the wider environment into a company's strategy formulation process.

● *Analyst*. Several of the tools and concepts that aid the formulation of company strategy such as segmentation and portfolio analysis originate from marketing.

● *Devil's advocate*. Wind (1981) views marketing as a motivator of change that prevents strategic management within the business from becoming too conservative. Adopting a greening strategy in response to the greening of consumers will require a good deal of corporate orthodoxy to be challenged.

● *Rapid response force*. Marketers have to deal with competitor initiatives, internal disasters or any mishaps involving customers. The crises that the marketer has to respond to will vary between grey marketers and environmental marketers, but both will undoubtedly spend a good proportion of their time fighting fires.

Marketing also has a very important leadership role to play within the organisation in relation to the environment. Coddington (1993) recommends that companies engaged in a greening process should set up an environmental task force in which marketers play a leading role. He identifies two sets of strengths that marketers can contribute to the greening process: the marketing perspective and the marketing skillset. The greening challenge requires creativity, the ability to work effectively across internal organisational boundaries and excellent communication skills. Coddington identifies marketing managers as being often 'superbly qualified' for the task in terms of skills for the following reasons.

● They can identify the marketing implications of corporate environmental exposures and initiatives. Marketers provide a much-needed 'voice from the marketing front', i.e. they can help management to understand the all-important marketing implications of a company's environmental strengths and weaknesses.

● Marketers can help to identify new business product and service opportunities that arise out of those same environmental exposures and initiatives. (More than one company has used its own hazardous waste clean-up obligations as a springboard for entry into the hazardous waste remediation business.)

● Marketers can work to ensure that when corporate environmental policies are developed, the marketing implications are given due consideration. It is much better to have input before the fact than to be left to gnash one's teeth after the damage has been done.

● As a matter of course, marketers must co-ordinate their activities across multiple departments (R&D, manufacturing, packaging, sales, public relations, etc.).

● In mapping their strategic directions, marketers take into consideration variables which come at them from a multitude of directions. What is the competition up to? What is coming out of research and development? What are the demographics and psychographics of the market-place, and how are they changing? What are the best advertising media? Both marketing and environmental management decisions are made in similar conceptual 'vortices'. In other words, marketers bring to environmental management the holistic approach to strategic planning that the consideration of environmental impact and initiatives demand.

● Finally, marketers are professional communicators. This skill is enormously useful in virtually every aspect of environmental management: on the task force itself, and in such areas as environmental management training, emergency response training, community relations and other domains which put a premium on communications. Bernstein (1992) suggests a variety of communication

Fig. 6.2 Key communication channels for internal green marketing

channels that marketers can use to meet the internal marketing challenge of environmental marketing (*See* Fig. 6.2).

The environmental leadership role of marketing is demonstrated in the environmental policy statement of home improvements company, B&Q, in the section relating to marketing:

'The marketing director is the main board director responsible for environmental issues and is therefore ultimately responsible for researching the issues, writing the policy and auditing progress. As marketing director he also has responsibility to ensure that the environmental policies and targets of marketing are implemented.

In market development B&Q shall monitor through market research customers' concerns and perceptions on environmental issues and customers' understanding and appreciation of B&Q's response to them. Market development will also incorporate environmental considerations into the strategic planning in the company and refer to strategic environmental issues in the five-year plan.

Marketing services is responsible for most of the purchasing decisions handled by marketing. They shall ensure that 'point-of-sale' material, carrier bags and all their other purchases consider environmental specifications. These include use of recycled post consumer waste, recyclability, and waste minimisation. Marketing services will ensure that no misleading environmental statements or claims are made on any POS material or other communications such as press enquiries. Marketing recognises that some of the products it sells have distinct environmental attributes, for energy efficiency equipment and home composting. We also recognise a need to inform our customers more about our environmental policies and the environmental performance of all products.' (From *How green is my hammer*, B&Q's Environmental Review, 1993)

The green brand steward

The traditional role of brand manager does not necessarily suit a greener approach to marketing. Brand management is typically a relatively tightly focused role. Environmental marketing calls for a more holistic and proactive approach to marketing. Ottman proposes a new role for marketing managers moving away from brand management and towards 'brand stewardship'. Brand stewardship involves taking responsibility for all aspects of a brand and balancing concern for its technical and economic success with concern for its social and environmental impacts. The concept of brand stewardship involves the manager becoming less focused on the brand itself, and instead taking a wider and longer-term view of its effects.

In practice the creation of new environmental marketing roles has been something of a stop–go affair. At the beginning of the 1990s, within large American companies there was a rash of new appointments to Environmental Marketing Manager posts (or similar). This was reflected in the formation of the Professional Environmental Marketing Association which evolved from a group of Californian companies. This trend declined sharply during 1992 and 1993, partly due to some of the backlash against environmental marketing hype. Many large companies eliminated the position of Environmental Marketing Manager, while still continuing the work of improving the eco-performance of products.

THE FUTURE OF THE GREEN CHALLENGE FOR MARKETING

Just as marketing was initially adopted by many companies as a 'bolt-on' extra, many companies attempted to superimpose environmental marketing on to grey marketing strategies and production processes. This explains why so much of the early green hype failed to convince the consumer. After a fairly inevitable backlash and something of a lull in environmental marketing during the early 1990s, there are signs that a more integrated and genuine approach to environmental marketing is emerging. Rehak (1993a) in tracking environmental marketing trends found that by 1993 green themes were not the subject of separate advertising campaigns but were integrated into more conventional campaigns which stressed the blend of performance benefits and environmental benefits.

Green consumerism and environmental marketing is likely to evolve in three phases during which it will sprout, grow and finally blossom (Peattie and Charter 1994).

1 *Substitution.* Characterised by green consumers differentiating between products on the basis of perceived eco-performance, much confusion over concepts and terminology, and with a great deal of sales and public relations activity dressed up as environmental marketing. There has also been a great deal of 'spotlighting', the singling out of particular industries, companies and products for praise or condemnation, sometimes with little relation to the actualities of eco-performance. Environmental improvements are often limited to end-of-pipe changes to production systems, the replacement of damaging ingredients such as CFCs and the elimination of excess packaging.

2 *Systemisation.* The establishment of BS7750 for Environmental Management Systems and the EU Ecolabel Scheme should move the entire 'game' on to a new plane of recognised (if flawed) performance criteria and evaluation. Businesses will move towards the redesign of products and production systems, and the implementation of environmental reporting and management systems. Better information for consumers will allow more informed and consistent green purchasing. Provision of environmental information and provision for the recycling of products will become standard practice, and governed by increasingly stringent legislation.

3 *Societal change.* The deepening environmental crisis will eventually lead to a more radical shift in consumer behaviour challenging the very basis of demand and consumption. This will be part of a wider social, political and economic upheaval to develop a more sustainable society. Consumers will increasingly become conservers and will seek opportunities to recycle or recondition products, and to achieve satisfaction through non-purchasing based activities.

When any given market will reach the first or the second phase of green consumption is anyone's guess. However, the longer the delay before reaching phase 3, the greater the upheaval involved will be.

CASE STUDY

Cultural Survival Enterprises

A pioneer in environmental marketing is Cultural Survival Enterprises, a human rights organisation in Cambridge, Massachusetts. It aims to defend people whose traditional cultures are threatened by modern economic life – like the Indians of the Amazon Basin, where every day 1400 acres of rainforest are cleared for timber, cattle raising or mining. Charles M. Peters of the New York Botanical Garden has shown that a Peruvian rainforest is worth more alive than dead: the fruit and rubber it produces are 14 times as valuable as its timber.

Cultural Survival Enterprises, headed by anthropologist Jason Clay, helps natives form co-operatives to harvest and sell rainforest products. In its first year, CSE sold fruits, nuts, and oils worth $447 000 (209 000 ECUs). It also opened a $100 000 (47 000 ECUs) nut-processing plant in Xapuri, where a rancher gunned down activist Chico Mendes in 1988. This year, with $2.6 million (1.2 million ECUs) of orders already in hand, CSE expects sales of $4.5 million (2.1 million ECUs).

CSE's biggest product is Rainforest Crunch, a peanut-brittle-like confection studded with cashews and Brazil nuts. It's sold as candy and used in Ben & Jerry's Rainforest Crunch Ice Cream. In addition, Clay has imported samples of 350 resins, oils, and pigments of proven usefulness in products from soap to furniture polish. Seventy-five corporations, including The Body Shop, Mars, Safeway, and Canada's Loblaw supermarkets, have been working with the samples; 17 are now steady customers.

More than nine million pounds of shelled Brazil nuts come to the US annually. What sets CSE apart from competitors is its effort to put the profit into the hands of forest residents, giving them less reason to sell out to miners and loggers. Says Clay:

'Poverty is as much a destroyer of the rainforest as greed. These people don't want to live in Stone Age zoos.'

CSE takes the same approach in Africa and Asia – selling killer-bee wax and honey from Zambia, for example. Clay is eyeing the mushrooms, berries, tars and resins found in North America's old-growth forests; some Native Americans have claims to a big share of revenue from products grown on their old lands. In this new environmentalism, entrepreneur and activist become one and the same.

Source: Adapted from 'Using Market Forces to Save Nature', *Fortune*, 14 January 1991, p. 42.

CHAPTER 7

The greening of the organisation

'As the environmental effects of the organisation may reach all parts of the world, the environment in this context extends from within the workplace to the global system.'
(British Standards Institute)

INTRODUCTION

Responding to the green challenge and meeting the needs of green consumers have implications which extend far beyond the boundaries of the marketing department. Marketing theory stresses the importance of the whole company in the marketing effort. In practice, however, grey marketing typically treats the rest of the organisation's production hardware and administrative software as something of a 'black box'. In political terms the rest of the organisation is high on the marketers' agenda because the marketing strategy will be constrained and guided by corporate strategy, marketing resources will have to be secured from the organisation, and political battles may have to be fought with other functions and philosophies in the pursuit of customer satisfaction. In practical terms, however, marketers' interest in the processes of other business functions is limited to the ability of their outputs to support the marketing strategy and mix. As long as a product which meets customer specifications is manufactured and delivered on time, and at a price which allows it to be sold at a profit, then all in the organisation is considered to be well.

Environmental marketing forces the marketer's internal perspective to change, because the customer's viewpoint has changed. In grey marketing the organisation helps to keep the customer satisfied, but usually according to the old proverb 'what the eye does not see, the heart does not bleed about'. To keep the customers satisfied they are presented with a carefully controlled vision of the business and its products through the marketing mix. In companies where there is pressure to 'go green' to keep pace with the market, marketers may be tempted to continue treating the organisation as a 'black box' for as long as possible. This is a rather short-sighted and dangerous view. Environmental pressure groups are becoming increasingly effective in putting a spotlight on companies whose environmental performance is poor or at least failing to live up to the image promoted by the company. Environmental marketing requires a more open and holistic approach in which the product, the production system and all the supporting administrative activities are openly managed and organised to keep the customer and other stakeholders satisfied.

THE CORPORATE RESPONSE

The green challenge is an issue which has some relevance to every business, whether or not the environment features in the marketing plan. Each business exists in the physical world and, however minimal its environmental impact, if the physical environment in which a business or its customers exist turns hostile, its future can be jeopardised. During 1993, floods, mudslides, earthquakes and drought-induced fires ensured that many environ-

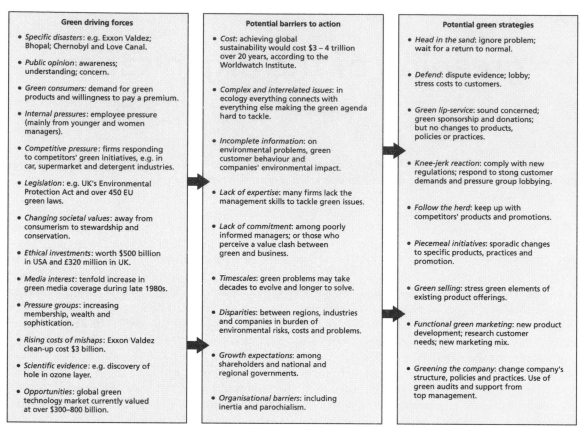

Green driving forces	Potential barriers to action	Potential green strategies
• *Specific disasters*: e.g. Exxon Valdez; Bhopal; Chernobyl and Love Canal.	• *Cost*: achieving global sustainability would cost $3 – 4 trillion over 20 years, according to the Worldwatch Institute.	• *Head in the sand*: ignore problem; wait for a return to normal.
• *Public opinion*: awareness; understanding; concern.		• *Defend*: dispute evidence; lobby; stress costs to customers.
• *Green consumers*: demand for green products and willingness to pay a premium.	• *Complex and interrelated issues*: in ecology everything connects with everything else making the green agenda hard to tackle.	• *Green lip-service*: sound concerned; green sponsorship and donations; but no changes to products, policies or practices.
• *Internal pressures*: employee pressure (mainly from younger and women managers).	• *Incomplete information*: on environmental problems, green customer behaviour and companies' environmental impact.	• *Knee-jerk reaction*: comply with new regulations; respond to stong customer demands and pressure group lobbying.
• *Competitive pressure*: firms responding to competitors' green initiatives, e.g. in car, supermarket and detergent industries.		
• *Legislation*: e.g. UK's Environmental Protection Act and over 450 EU green laws.	• *Lack of expertise*: many firms lack the management skills to tackle green issues.	• *Follow the herd*: keep up with competitors' products and promotions.
• *Changing societal values*: away from consumerism to stewardship and conservation.	• *Lack of commitment*: among poorly informed managers; or those who perceive a value clash between green and business.	• *Piecemeal initiatives*: sporadic changes to specific products, practices and promotion.
• *Ethical investments*: worth $500 billion in USA and £320 million in UK.	• *Timescales*: green problems may take decades to evolve and longer to solve.	• *Green selling*: stress green elements of existing product offerings.
• *Media interest*: tenfold increase in green media coverage during late 1980s.		
• *Pressure groups*: increasing membership, wealth and sophistication.	• *Disparities*: between regions, industries and companies in burden of environmental risks, costs and problems.	• *Functional green marketing*: new product development; research customer needs; new marketing mix.
• *Rising costs of mishaps*: Exxon Valdez clean-up cost $3 billion.	• *Growth expectations*: among shareholders and national and regional governments.	• *Greening the company*: change company's structure, policies and practices. Use of green audits and support from top management.
• *Scientific evidence*: e.g. discovery of hole in ozone layer.		
• *Opportunities*: global green technology market currently valued at over $300–800 billion.	• *Organisational barriers*: including inertia and parochialism.	

Fig. 7.1 Corporate responses to the green challenge
(Source: adapted from Peattie and Ratnayaka (1992))

mentally sensitive service businesses in California were temporarily put out of business by the environment. Every organisation has a physical presence which occupies land, uses resources and creates pollution and waste. Even with businesses which see themselves as 'pure', and therefore green, services will have some form of environmental impact. This might relate simply to the operation of an administrative office, since the average office worker generates an average of 180 kilograms of waste paper each year. As Bernstein (1992) comments:

'Every company burns fossil fuel; has a building which could be more efficient; needs to improve maintenance and planning; takes on supplies which could be greener; uses furniture which could derive from unmanaged tropical forests; employs people who drive cars; creates noise, smells, dirt and litter.'

Every business will also face some pressure to improve its eco-performance, if only from those employees interested in recycling office paper, or from an accountant seeking to reduce energy bills. This pressure will vary greatly in its intensity and its sources between different types of business. Each company also faces a variety of barriers to greening and a range of options as to the nature of the response that it makes (*See* Fig. 7.1). Companies' responses will vary in terms of the depth of greening and the degree to which they involve the trappings rather than the substance of improved eco-performance. Companies will also vary in the degree to which the greening process relates to the hardware (products and production systems) or the organisational software of the business.

For the majority of companies improving environmental performance has, until recently, been a question of legislative compliance and occasional reactions to external events and pressure. It has usually only been companies in 'front-line' sectors such as oil, chemicals, power and cars that have gone beyond a reactive and tactical approach to green issues. However, a 1992 survey of *Fortune 500* companies conducted by Abt Associates revealed a shift away from a technical, compliance-orientated approach towards a more proactive green strategy orientation (Hochman *et al* 1993). Companies were increasingly pursuing competitive advantage and product differentiation by increasing investment in environmental marketing, green design, and improving overall corporate eco-performance.

In addition to these externally motivated changes, Power and Cox (1994) point to a dawning realisation within industry that sustainability will not be reached simply by demand-pull from the market and compliance-push from regulations. The changes that are needed to safeguard the future of the environment and the economy must partly be driven from within the business community, which means they must proactively integrate eco-performance into the strategies, systems and cultures of their organisations.

The nature of the organisation's response to the green challenge will be important in setting the environmental marketing agenda for the marketing function. Marketers working in reactive 'laggard' companies will face a challenge if customers begin to discriminate on the basis of eco-performance. At the other end of the spectrum there are what Ford (1992b) describes as 'hyperactive' or 'Robin Hood' organisations which 'have their own system of environmental morality which transcends government and customer requirements'. This also provides a marketing challenge, since such ultra-green organisations may need to reassure customers about the functional as well as the environmental aspects of their products, and attempt to bring forward customers' expectations about eco-performance within their market.

THE ORGANISATIONAL DIMENSIONS OF GREENING

For the environmental marketer any aspect of the business can prove an asset or a liability in the quest to satisfy the customers' needs. The organisational dimensions of greening can be considered by using the McKinsey Seven S Framework (*see* Fig. 7.2). Each 'S' factor is an important influence on, and component in, the greening process.

Strategy

A dazzling array of different concepts and models to explain strategy exist, and this perhaps explains why there is often inconsistency and confusion in the way that strategy is discussed and developed. When a manager or academic speaks of strategy, they can mean one of several things, and this is reflected in five concepts of strategy adapted from Mintzberg's (1988) 'Five Ps' of strategy.

1 *As a plan of written or remembered intentions.* The environment is an increasingly important part of the formal strategic plans of companies.

2 *As a pattern of consistent actions which emerge.* Even companies which are not explicitly attempting to improve their eco-performance as part of a greening strategy may be becoming greener incrementally. Companies adopting TQM initiatives, lean production, value engineering, energy-saving campaigns, good citizen policies and enlightened employment practices may be improving their eco-performance more effectively than other companies making high-profile greening pronouncements.

3 *As a perspective on the world.* Greening requires a very different world view from companies. Marketers are used to viewing their companies as providers of benefits and solutions. It is perhaps difficult to reorientate themselves to view the company as also a cause of pollution, waste and other problems.

4 *As a pronouncement* – an intention announced to outwit competitors externally, to help to secure resources, or to influence key internal or external

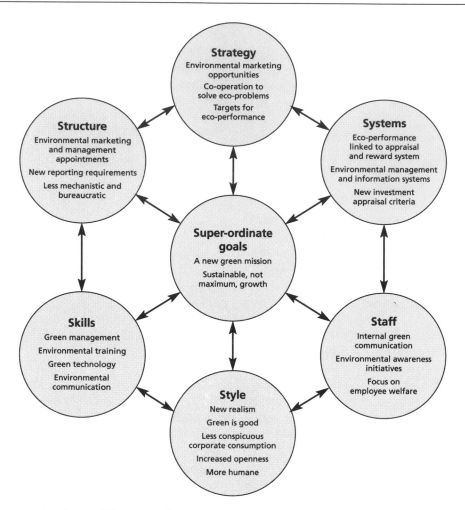

Fig. 7.2 Greening the Seven S Framework
(adapted from Waterman *et al* (1980))

stakeholders, which the company does not intend to implement. In addition to genuine strategic intent, formal plans often contain a certain degree of strategic rhetoric. There is little doubt that a number of organisations made environmentally orientated pronouncements in reaction to consumer concern during the late 1980s with little intention or ability to follow these through.

5 As a position that the firm occupies in relation to its environment. This is often described as the match or fit between the organisation's internal and external context. Whether it is internal pressure from concerned employees or external

customer concerns, companies are increasingly being forced to reposition themselves in relation to the environment. There are relatively few companies who will escape having to change or at least reassess some aspects of the match that their company achieves with its external environment as a result of the green challenge.

The environment has certainly emerged as a strategic issue among large companies. In a 1994 study of American top management by McKinsey & Co., they found that 92 per cent of CEOs and board members stated that the environment should be one of their top three priorities and 85 per cent claimed that integrating environmental considerations into corporate strategy should be one of their major goals. In practice though, only 37 per cent felt that they successfully integrated the environment into everyday operations, and only 35 per cent said that they had successfully adapted business strategy to anticipated environmental developments.

Superordinate goals

Superordinate goals are the fundamental ideas around which a business is built. They can be implicit, but are often made public through a corporate mission statement or philosophy. A commitment to the environment and society requires a company to take a fresh look at its mission statement, and to re-evaluate its objectives and the needs of the company's stakeholders. In some companies this has been expressed by amending the existing mission statement. A survey of top German and UK companies revealed that over two thirds had amended their mission statements to reflect increased environmental concern (Peattie and Ringler 1994). Environmental commitment can also be communicated through a specific environmental policy, strategy or statement. By 1991 over half of all European companies surveyed by Touche Ross had developed an environmental policy.

A key goal towards which the majority of corporate and marketing strategies strive, is the goal of growth. Growth is associated with many benefits for the company and its managers. Growth brings economies of scale, protection from predators, increased prestige and lobbying power. A growing business is also seen to be a normal one. During the 1970s' oil crises, the pre-eminence of growth was challenged by the addition of efficiency as a key corporate goal. The drive for efficiency was symbolised by the introduction of just-in-time management systems (JIT). The 1980s saw a reaction against the internal focus of JIT and the quantitative nature of growth. The new goal which gained prominence during the 1980s was quality, symbolised by the emergence of Total Quality Management (TQM).

The 1990s will see growth, efficiency and quality joined by a newly emerging corporate goal – sustainability. Although many in management might be sceptical about pursuing sustainability, it is worth remembering that JIT and TQM were also originally greeted with scepticism. Companies are beginning to confront the question of how and why they should pursue sustainable growth as opposed to maximum growth. In principle many companies have already signed up to sustainability through initiatives such as the ICC charter. In practice a move to sustainability will involve a major shift of perspectives and values among companies. Ruckelshaus (1991) captures the magnitude of the culture change that the shift towards sustainability will entail. He describes that whereas virtually all organisations in capitalist systems have a deep understanding of the concept of profit, in the former Soviet Union the concept was meaningless. This has hampered the progress of organisations in the wake of democratisation and the adoption of capitalist economic solutions. Sustainability repre- sents just such an alien concept to most managers in industrialised countries. Creating a culture which will support and reinforce the greening process can be a major challenge. Stead and Stead (1992) see the acceptance of sustainability as involving a change to the basic assumptions of organisations and their cultures. They point to the success of some TQM initiatives in achieving cultural change, however, and suggest that a quality-orientated route to sustainability is the most likely to succeed.

Organisational culture reflects the company's core values (what the company believes is important) and its beliefs (about the business, its environment and the relationship between them). In terms of values, during the 1980s the importance of achieving a fit between the values of the organisation and the people that it employs became increasingly clear. For environmental marketing the challenge is to create congruence between the values of the organisation, its people and society. Otherwise:

'Companies that do not materially adopt an environmentally responsible doctrine and norms will find their culture to be incongruent with the personal values of their employees.' (Hoffman 1993)

Otter (1992) highlights a survey within ICI Agrochemicals that revealed that only 30 per cent of employees thought that pesticides were essential for food production. A culture in which only 30 per cent of the employees believe in the product, and where society views its product as one of the least beneficial on the market, galvanised ICI to try and improve its eco-performance, culture and public image. Unless companies attempt to green their culture, they may find themselves engaged in an external struggle against societal influences and an internal struggle against staff who will increasingly wish to push the company towards better eco-performance, rebel against its culture or simply go elsewhere.

Style

Closely related to organisational culture is the issue of style, both of which are typically difficult to pin down, immensely influential and very difficult to change. Style is set by a number of things, not least by what senior managers say. Many top managers are beginning to talk about their companies in environmental terms. Frank Popoff, CEO of Dow Chemical, described himself as 'one of 62 000 environmentalists in the company'. Many managerial actions are also important in determining style because of their symbolic importance. Senior management's involvement in environmental training programmes and their willingness to commit resources to environmental initiatives are crucial proofs of commitment. One important corporate symbol, the annual report and accounts, witnessed a significant change in style during the late 1980s with the rise of the 'Golden Retriever Syndrome'. Reports became emblazoned with environmental policy statements, accompanied by pictures of CEOs stripped of the conventional icons of large mahogany desk and 'power' suit and instead shown half-way up a picturesque mountain with hiking boots and chunky sweater, accompanied by the ubiquitous golden retriever. Another important symbol is the company car. Many top managers in companies where every

person is meant to be deeply committed to the environment, are still driving around in large gas-guzzlers.

There are a variety of means by which a greener management style can be created. Davis (1991) talks about an 'orchestral style' which, as an orchestral conductor does, co-ordinates and inspires small teams of skilled and specialised professionals. Other authors view the difference in a green culture relating to how people are treated. Ledgerwood *et al* (1992) make the important point that successful greening in organisations is characterised by a co-operative spirit and the use of incentives rather than the allocation of blame and penalties. This is very much in line with the emerging concept of the 'humane organisation'.

Elkington *et al* (1991) stress the need for senior managers to break out of the 'corporate echo chamber' to confront and seek out the criticism and challenges that the green agenda will bring. They suggest that managers will need to:

- work on being approachable;
- avoid the trappings of power;
- provide occasions on which long-term or 'alternative' ideas and issues can be discussed;
- encourage people to speak up;
- encourage full and informed debate on major policy decisions.

Structure

Discussions of structure inevitably seem to degenerate into debates over the shape of the organisation and the division of tasks and responsibilities between different people and functional groups. This emphasis on compartmentalisation and the creation of boundaries runs against the principle of holism at the centre of environmental marketing. It is probably very natural, however, in the face of the sheer scale of modern enterprises. If we accept that people are tribal by nature, then a typical multinational company is far too large to be one tribe. Instead it splinters into its tribes of marketing, sales, production, R&D and finance – all with their own rituals, myths, language (jargon) and prejudices about the other tribes.

Structural change has been a favourite response of companies to a variety of different challenges, although this often involves superficial as opposed to real change. As Gaius Petronius Arbiter (Roman Governor of Britain around AD 55) observed:

'We trained hard, but it seemed that every time we were beginning to form up into teams, we would be reorganised. I was to learn later in life that we tend to meet any new situation by reorganising, and a wonderful method it can be for creating the illusion of progress, while producing confusion, inefficiency and demoralisation.'

For the green challenge the most usual approach has been the creation of new responsibilities for environmental issues and performance. At the top of the organisation, formalising green responsibilities typically involves adding them on to an existing board position such as Director of Quality or Director of Operations. At a line management level, new roles may need to be created to create integration across functions and departments, and cross-functional teams or task forces may be required to drive the necessary changes through. The creation of green posts is now mandatory for some countries and industries. For example, in Japan, all factories over a certain size must appoint an energy efficiency manager. Within the EU, 82 per cent of top companies have appointed an individual manager responsible for environmental issues in the last six years, according to Environmental Data Services (ENDS). Hopfenbeck (1993) suggests that the responsibilities for new green roles such as that of Environmental Affairs Manager should include:

● promoting environmental ideals throughout the company;

● advising on the development of eco-friendly products;

● planning and supervising the introduction of technical eco-measures;

● collaborating with development and investment projects;

● fixing regular minuted meetings;

● arranging appraisal procedures with the committee chairperson;

● assessing the costs of environmental protection;

● responding to regulations and overseeing payment of external duties;

● dealing with questions of product liability;

● setting up environmental information and control systems;

● carrying out environmental PR work;

● planning and carrying out environmental audits;

● acting as an agent for change;

● taking part in strategic planning;

● providing an ecological dimension to training programmes.

At a more 'grass-roots' level, organisations like British Airways and Exel Logistics have established 'green champions' within different parts of the business. These champions are responsible for maintaining the flow of ideas, information and enthusiasm regarding environmental issues.

Other key structural changes that can result from a greening strategy include the following:

● *The creation or redefinition of strategic business units to take advantage of green market opportunities.* Rockware amalgamated its various recycling activities into a separate subsidiary, Rockware Reclamation. Its mission was to create a profitable business by recycling a wide range of packaging materials.

● *Specifications of new internal and external information flows.* Over 80 per cent of major UK companies identified changed reporting responsibilities as a response to the green challenge (Peattie and Ringler 1994).

● *A reduction in the amount of structure that exists within organisations.* To escape from the reductionalist and compartmentalist nature of organisations (which are key factors underlying their environmental hostility) they will need to adopt a more fluid, organic and holistic structure.

Table 7.1 Human resource management's role in the greening process

Corporate identity – staff motivation and awareness	Training	Remuneration and incentive schemes	Work organisation and working time	Works council and trade union relations	Social services	Personnel administration
Company mission statements to all	Environmental education	Ecological incentives	Flexitime	Joint environment-related activities	Organise car sharing	Mode of business travel
Enterprise journal with environment section	Functional training programmes	Revise job evaluation and remuneration systems	Decentralise environmental responsibility		Promote use of public transport	Performance appraisal system
Involve families of staff members	Integration of environment into trainee programmes and professional training		Continuous work	Include environment in collective agreements	Healthy canteen food	Promotion credits
Community work				Assist works council to acquire environmental competence and profile	Environment-related books and journals in library	
					Participate in community activities	

Source: North (1992)

A key challenge for the green company is to ensure that environmental awareness spreads throughout the organisation's structure. Ledgerwood and Street (1993) point out that in determining environmental performance, all levels of the organisation are equally important since:

'the temporary employee can, by mistake, release toxic by-products into external water courses, and, if detected, the environmental programme of the company will be seen as ineffective, no matter how carefully drafted the Corporate Environmental Mission. Substantial fines and civil damages can result from poor training of site operatives.'

They suggest the use of self-directed teams emphasising the need to empower each employee and to make each team self-responsible. Although this might sound utopian, the use of self-directed work teams has proven effective in a number of organisations, and it certainly fits in with Schumacher's concept of 'good work' involving the creation of small autonomous teams within large corporations.

Staff

Staff are a vital stakeholder for the environmental marketer and an important component in the success of any greening strategy. They can be a vital source of pressure, ideas and enthusiasm for environmental improvement. One survey of 250 large companies across Europe found that almost half of them had experienced employee concern about corporate eco-performance. Nash (1989) found that over 28 per cent of directors of UK manufacturing companies named employees as a source of pressure to adopt an environmental policy. The key driving force behind Linpac Plastics' switch away from CFC-blown polystyrene (which cost over £100 000 (75 000 ECUs), required 300 000 square feet of factory space to be reorganised and involved retraining for 360 staff) was environmental concern among staff. Hoffman (1993) identified 'increased efficiency through improved employee self-esteem' as a key benefit of a greening strategy. Such an improvement is difficult to quantify and therefore receives less attention than other benefits, but Hoffman suggests that 'it may prove to be the most powerful and enduring'. The concern of a company for its staff and for the people involved in production back down the supply chain are an important test of the depth of a company's societal concern. Responsible working practices and purchasing policies should be supported by audits to ensure that exploitation is not occurring elsewhere in the supply chain.

For human resource managers, a greening strategy contains three distinct challenges. First, they are responsible for ensuring that the company has the personnel and the skills to implement a green strategy. In many cases environmental disasters have been linked back to the behaviour of relatively junior people in the organisation and to the training and recruitment practices of the organisations that employed them. Ledgerwood et al (1992) link the severity of the Exxon Valdez oil disaster back to mistakes in training, communication and expectations in areas such as maintenance, leadership and spillage prevention training. Second, they are responsible for ensuring that the working environment does not damage the health of workers. Finally, implementing a greening strategy is a massive internal communications challenge, and it is one in which the HRM specialists can play an important part. Table 7.2 shows the way in which the different elements of personnel management can be used to support a greening strategy.

Green concerns can affect the behaviour of potential employees in the same way that it can affect potential customers. With current demographic trends companies will find themselves competing in the labour market for new graduates and experienced managers. IBM has recorded an increasing number of questions being asked by potential recruits about the company's environmental policy. As the balance of power in the employment market swings away from companies, their social and environmental performance may become important in the recruitment battle (see Charter 1990 a and b). When it comes to recruiting suitably skilled people, good environmental performance can contribute to the attractiveness of a company as an employer. To respond to this, interviewers will need to be briefed on environmental performance. Companies in 'sensitive' areas, or with a poor track record on environmental and social areas may find it increasingly difficult to attract graduates in future. Alternative recruitment sources may need to be developed, or methods found to overcome negative perceptions among potential employees.

Skills

North (1992) suggests that for many manufacturers developing green products and responding to increasingly tough environmental legislation will be a considerable technical challenge. The need to develop new products and processes, the need to install and run complex pollution abatement technology and to run new and old processes to increasingly close tolerances all require a great deal of technical skill. In management terms, the complexity of the green challenge requires new skills and understanding among those devising and implementing new green strategies. One of the reasons that there is often a skills gap in terms of the ability of managers to understand the environmental aspects of their companies, products and strategies is that traditional business school education provides little or no teaching related to environmental issues (Post 1990). Managers are trained to focus on only one of the world's many subsystems when making decisions – the economic subsystem (Stead and Stead 1992), although this situation is now beginning to change, which brings the promise of a more environmentally aware generation of business decision makers emerging in the future.

By necessity, the green company will be a high skill company. Creating such high levels of skills requires a degree of investment, but this can pay handsome dividends, as the following example from North (1992) shows.

'The American company Geneva Steel is one of the few steel makers in the world with a good environmental reputation – and one of the world's most profitable. Its chairman began his career as a regulator in the United States Environmental Protection Agency. He therefore understands better than most industrialists how regulators work. At the age of 40 he is a good decade younger than most of his fellow steel bosses. Above all, his Utah plant employs a largely Mormon work-force with an average of one

college year of education. An intelligent work-force has allowed him to solve one of the most intractable problems of a steel mill and cut emissions from his coke ovens to less than a quarter of the permitted maximum. The secret is simply to take care of the oven doors. The fact that he is known to care about environmental problems encourages employees to come up with green ideas of their own. And because the company is profitable and he has a controlling stake in it, he has been able to take large investments in cleaner technology well before the state's regulations would have required it.'

Training needs which will have to be addressed include improving staff understanding of green issues and the company's environmental standards and performance, environmental regulations and standards, developing new skills such as environmental auditing and reporting. One of the benefits of pursuing British Standard BS7750 is the emphasis that it places on environmental education and training throughout the organisation.

Systems

In an organisational sense systems are the procedures through which the daily work of the organisation is accomplished (as opposed to production systems which are dealt with in Chapter 11). Improving the organisation's eco-performance will be impossible without changes to a number of its systems. Two key systems are central to many companies' greening efforts, an environmental management system and an environmental information system. The British Standard Institute has recently enshrined its own pioneering concept of an 'environmental management system' in the new standard BS7750. Grayson (1992) points out that this standard 'does not lay down specific environmental or operational targets' but rather it aims to protect the environment by assuming that the use of improved managerial means, will lead to an improvement in the environmental ends. In order to attain the voluntary certification under BS7750 the organisation must implement the following procedures:

1 commit itself to the establishment of an environmental management system;

2 conduct an initial review and assessment of the organisation's environmental position concerning its environmental policy and adherence to environmental standards;

3 formulate an environmental policy in the form of a corporate environmental programme (this will be the basis for a statement of targets and objectives towards which the environmental management system will strive);

4 complete an inventory of the organisation's activities, and an assessment of their environmental impact, in relation to the stated policy;

5 study the pertinent regulations and requirements to ensure compliance;

6 develop an environmental management plan and a supporting manual which details all the relevant aspects of the system;

7 apply the management plan in both the company's operations and record-keeping;

8 maintain a cycle of audits of the company's performance to test whether objectives and targets are being met.

A management system of any form is entirely dependent on the quality of the information that is fed into it. The green challenge provides a considerable informational challenge to businesses. It frequently requires information on a range of issues which companies may not have monitored before, such as the environmental concerns of consumers and the eco-performance of suppliers, marketing intermediaries and competitors. It also often requires new ways of handling information. In the US Johnson Wax had a profitable line of insect control products, but one which was subject to a growing number of environmental regulations. The legal checks necessary to monitor and register all products against changing state, national and international regulations were in danger of overwhelming the company's regulatory affairs department. This information challenge was solved by an expert system called REGI which automated the process of checking, registering and tracking the company's chemical products. REGI cut the workload for people in half and provided improved green product information for the whole company.

One important change that new information systems together with new technology may achieve is to free companies from the constraints of economies of scale. Japanese engineers have been developing production systems in which the application of information technology and robotics effectively eliminates the 'cost of variation', a principle which underpins the concept of economies of scale. As early as 1982 it was noted that the average set-up time for a heavy press was six hours in the USA, four hours in Germany, and 12 minutes at Toyota in Japan. A combination of automated production techniques, training which emphasised speed of set up, and a JIT ordering system allowed Toyota to provide customers in Tokyo with any one of 600 000 variations in the Corolla product line at only two days' notice. The implications of such techniques are that manufacturing production can be freed from the preoccupation with scale, allowing more variety, a closer (and therefore more efficient) match between products and consumer needs and opportunity for businesses to compete on a smaller and more local scale.

Other systems that may need to be revised include the following:

- Accounting and budgeting systems will need to be adjusted to reflect environmental costs and to use more environmentally sensitive timeframes and investment appraisal tools.

- Planning systems will need to be revised to encompass environmental and social objectives, audits and strategies.

- Reward and appraisal systems are already being used by companies to improve eco-performance. Companies like 3M offer cash bonuses, while Rover offers a free Mini to the most successful staff suggestions for environmental improvement. By contrast, air conditioning giant Carrier Corporation will dismiss engineers who break its strict environmental code and allow CFC discharges into the environment.

- New product development systems will have to be introduced. 3M has backed up its commitment to innovation with its '15 per cent' rule which allows the majority of company staff to spend 15 per cent of the time 'bootlegging' on any project they like, as long as it is product-related. A similar rule allowing even 5 per cent of people's time to be spent on environmental improvement would be likely to improve eco-performance and cost effectiveness significantly.

TOTAL QUALITY ENVIRONMENTAL MANAGEMENT

Tackling eco-performance through the mechanism of Total Quality Management is a popular strategy for greening, particularly with the emergence of the concept of Total Quality Environmental Management (TQEM) in America. TQM is an existing management doctrine which emphasises the elimination of waste by taking a holistic and customer-orientated focus. Using it to tackle environmental improvement makes it appear somewhat more manageable than the idea of doing something more revolutionary. James (1994) draws five parallels between TQM and environmental management.

1 TQM's emphasis on the importance of customers and its broadening of the terms beyond the purchasers of a product provide a useful framework for considering and responding to the demands of environmental stakeholders.

2 TQM's commitment to continuous improvement is very helpful to organisations wishing to move beyond mere compliance with environmental regulation.

3 TQM's focus on eliminating the root causes of problems rather than their symptoms fits with the growing awareness that pollution prevention is often a better approach to environmental problems than 'bolting on' pollution control equipment.

4 TQM's belief that quality is everyone's responsibility within a company fits well with the growing awareness that all employees have to make a contribution to environmental performance.

5 TQM's concern with calculating the cost of (non-) quality provides a useful framework for considering the total costs and benefits of environmental action or inaction.

The chief danger with taking the TQEM route to improved eco-performance is that in practice many TQM initiatives have become focused on internal conformance to standards rather than on the effect on external customer satisfaction (Kordupleski *et al* 1993). As James notes, the problem lies with companies adopting TQM as a set of management tools and techniques which are applied mechanistically, rather than as a 'radical management philosophy'. Companies may get more benefit out of TQM if it is adopted as part of a switch towards pursuing sustainability, rather than when the search for sustainability is subsumed within existing TQM initiatives. James notes that 'western' TQM has lacked some of the value-driven quasi-spiritual dimensions that have made it such a successful approach in Japan. The desire to protect society and the environment through environmental quality can perhaps give TQEM the human, moral and motivational dimensions that systems aimed at simply generating customer satisfaction and profit through better products and service may have lacked.

THE EVOLUTION OF THE GREEN ORGANISATION

Hunt and Auster (1991) describe the greening process of organisations as a progression through several stages of environmental commitment and management response. This progression is marked by changes to areas such as the mindset of managers, resource commitment, and support and involvement by top management, and has five distinct phases.

1 *Beginner*. Low financial commitment; no involvement of top management; no environmental programmes; management sees no need for environmental programmes.

2 *Fire fighter*. Ad hoc project funding; minor top management involvement; no formal environmental programmes but attempts made to resolve issues as they arise.

If these statements decribe your company's general approach to environmental, health and safety (EHS) management, then they are likely areas needing attention and change.

1 EHS is an outsider

- Environmental affairs are disconnected from key business processes such as R&D, marketing and finance.

- Management tactics to improve environmental performance are incremental, with no consideration of the environmental dimension of other critical business processes.

- EHS professionals have little contact with top management and few opportunities to transfer in or out of corporate or divisional line positions – a few stars emerge when companies bolster their legal and engineering resources to tackle high-stakes problems.

- While EHS staff are convinced they know how to make the right decisions, they still expect line management to make sure the right decisions are made and the work gets done – although line managers pass money back to EHS to tackle the problem.

2 The focus is on a fire-fighting mentality

- The EHS function is relegated to manage problems rather than opportunities – a preoccupation with accidents, liabilities and fines has isolated environmental affairs from making contributions to other parts of the business.

- Environmental management is considered a necessary cost of doing business rather than a resource to improve overall performance of the business.

3 Staff is isolated from decision makers

- The environmental managers report too far down the corporate ladder – several levels down from the CEO.

- The EHS function is housed in a staff area, isolated from direct access to key decision makers.

4 The tail wags the dog

- Although line management has ultimate responsibility for EHS performance, management systems are not in place to hold them accountable.

- The understaffed and overworked environmental staff are expected to lead corporate environmental performance and keep the company on its toes.

5 EHS professionals are specialists

- EHS issues are left to specialists: engineers to solve technical plant problems, and regulatory experts to decipher complex laws and manage legal vulnerabilities.

- Little effort is made to educate line and staff managers in other functions about the importance of environmental factors to their disciplines and overall company performance.

- EHS professionals are rarely given the support to develop business skills.

- Information on environmental concerns is dispersed inefficiently, making it difficult to make the best decisions.

6 Financial and human resources are limited

- EHS almost always loses out in the bidding to get its share of shrinking corporate operating budgets.

- Downsizing at most companies means that the EHS function has to make do with less, at the same time that pressures grow for better environmental management.

7 Decisions are based on hindsight, not foresight

- EHS decision makers look to past problems to assure they will not be repeated. This hindsight approach focuses on reducing the problems with existing processes, rather than considering how to redesign or change the process

8 Cultural hurdles are a barrier to excellence

- It is difficult to motivate managers because EHS culture tends to stem from negative perceptions – isolated and understaffed department, a backwater in the promotion chain, and undervalued because no one understands the advantages of state-of-the-art environmental management.

- Without clear goals communicated from top management and resources to back them up, neither line nor staff managers with EHS responsibilities are sure about what they are trying to achieve.

9 A soft approach is used to measure environmental performance

- The CEO often bases his judgement of environmental successes on number of programs in place rather than actual measurable performance.

- Corporate EHS staff are incorrectly identified as best people to provide a perspective on the quality and achievements of waste minimization on the shop floor, or similar measurements of progress thoughtout the company.

- Compared with measures of profitability, EHS data is considered soft and evaluated less regularly – accounting tools are not in place to quantify the benefits of cost avoidance.

- Measurements dwell on negatives rather than evaluating return on investment in environmental improvements.

10 Too few motivators are in place to implement environmental excellence

- Without clear goals, neither line or staff managers are sure about what they are trying to achieve in environmental performance terms.

- On the shop floor, those assigned a specific task – such as reducing stack emissions – may not know how to start without someone there to advise them.

- There is inadequate attention and resources given to employee training.

- Very few personal motivators (e.g. through individual performance reviews) are in place.

Fig. 7.3 Where traditional environmental management falls short: ten critical areas for examination

(Source: Greeno and Robinson (1992))

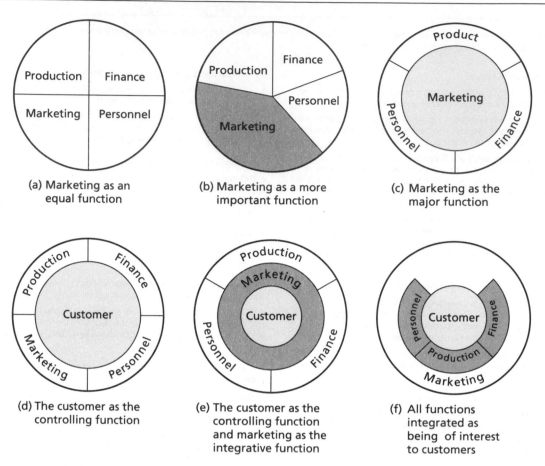

Fig. 7.4 The evolution of marketing within companies
(adapted from Kotler (1988))

3 *Concerned citizen.* Small consistent budget; top management theoretically involved; management believes environmental policy worthwhile; policies show corporate responsibility.

4 *Pragmatist.* Sufficient funding; top management theoretically involved; management believes environmental management is important; policies attempt to minimise firm's environmental impact.

5 *Proactivist.* Open-ended funding; active involvement of top management in environmental policy setting; policies attempt to include active management of environmental issues.

Polonsky *et al* (1992) challenged Hunt and Auster's life cycle approach and the notion that 'an organisation is in one stage of environmental management at one time'. Their Australian-based research suggests that organisations can be in more than one stage of environmental management at one time, often because there is not necessarily a consonance between the commitment to environmental policies and the commitment to implement those policies. Green actions, in other words, may tend to lag behind the green corporate intentions and pronouncements.

Concern for the environment is at a relatively early stage in most business organisations. A lot of companies have reacted with a response which is mainly structural in creating some form of environmental management department, function or post. Greeno and Robinson (1992) observe that:

'As long as environmental, health and safety issues continue to be managed as a separate function, com-

Fig. 7.5 The green strategy iceberg
(Source: Peattie and Ring (1993))

panies will run into resource and organisational problems. Any function that is treated as distinct from the key business and profit centres in the company is prone to critical scrutiny about whether or not the environmental affairs function is under-resourced or over-resourced. Is the corporate staff too large? Should it be centralized or decentralized? Is there enough or too much or too little money being spent?'

If this sounds vaguely familiar, it is not surprising. It is very much a reprise of the struggle that marketing often has in trying to exert an influence within companies. Many companies created marketing departments during the 1970s and 1980s, often large and well resourced departments that were 'bolted on' to the existing organisation and regarded with jealousy and suspicion by those they were meant to influence. A concern for the environment and a concern for the customer (which are inextricably linked) will only really influence a company when it stops being contained in a part of the organisational structure and instead forms part of its culture. A checklist of ten critical areas for the management of 'environmental health and safety' (EHS) is suggested in Fig. 7.3. Any company that recognises its treatment of the green challenge in the ten statements is not practising any form of green marketing and management. It is simply another grey company with a green box on its organisational family tree.

MARKETING WITHIN THE GREEN ORGANISATION

The evolution of the organisational role of marketing is charted by Kotler (1994), who suggests that it represents something of a struggle against the other more established and entrenched functions who will resist what they perceive as the increasing domination of marketing. Progress is made by emphasising that it is not marketing but the customer that becomes dominant with the increasing marketing orientation. Eventually the customer becomes central to the perspective of the business, with marketing as the integrative function. Figure 7.4 charts this evolution. The conventional end point of the evolutionary process is the 'marketing-orientated company', but this represents a grey rather than an environmental marketing perspective since the marketing function appears to distance the other internal functions from the customer. The need for all elements of a green business to satisfy, and be visible to, the green consumer means that a model in which marketing is still an integrative function, but in which all other functions are still directly connected to the customer, is more appropriate. Figure 7.4 (f) therefore takes Kotler's sequential model of the evolving role for marketing one step further into environmental marketing.

A NEW VISION OF THE ORGANISATION

During the early phase of environmental marketing, the greening effort has often been marketing-led, rather than market-led. The market wants greener products from greener companies. The evidence from research suggests that many companies are changing their products, the marketing mix which supports them, and even their production processes (Peattie and Ring 1993, Vandermerwe and Oliff 1992). The companies who are making these changes are not, as yet, making changes to themselves in terms of the seven S factors (Peattie and Ring 1993). This situation is reflected in the Green Strategy Iceberg model (*see* Fig. 7.5). The extended marketing mix is visible above green C-level (the point where change occurs); the larger part of the organisation still remains submerged, largely unseen, and a danger to shipping.

The move towards the environmentalist paradigm in society may need to be mirrored in the creation of a new organisational paradigm. Stead and Stead (1992) attempt to define this paradigm and identify the following dimensions.

● *Organic structures*. Instead of the classic mechanistic, rigid, controlled and hierarchical form of organisation, structures will become flatter, more flexible, fluid, informal, participative and knowledge-based. Such structures will allow companies to respond quickly to turbulent environments, and will accommodate trends such as teamworking and the increasing concentration of key knowledge at the bottom of organisations.

● *Smart growth*. Halal (1986) argues in favour of an economic transition 'from more, to better, to less' or from 'hard growth' to 'smart growth'. Competitive advantage in the 21st century will be achieved through factors such as 'speed, flexibility, quality, design, and skill upgrading' (Stead and Stead 1992) rather than through expansion and cost reduction.

● *Holistic thinking*. In this case organisational problems are not attacked from a linear 'cause-and-effect' perspective, but understood in terms of organisational cycles, interrelationships and patterns.

● *A multiple-stakeholder orientation*. A more complex agenda of potentially conflicting goals for managers to pursue instead of the classical management aims of growth and profit.

● *A new work ethic* based on Schumacher's concepts of 'good work' and 'smallness' with an emphasis on teamwork, relationship building and autonomy.

CASE STUDY

Volvo's drive to be green

Volvo has been one of the leading contenders for the green car mantle, and it has also taken a lead within the car industry in terms of organisational change in pursuit of improved eco-performance. The company has emphasised its social responsiveness since 1927 when it made a formal commitment to pursue outstanding product safety. Volvo's social principles were gradually expanded to deal explicitly with the issue of process safety and also with the environment. This has resulted in a range of technical changes aimed at improving eco-performance. In terms of products the combination of catalytic converters with Volvo's Lambdasond oxygen sensor technology removes 95 per cent of harmful elements from car exhaust emissions. In the trucks division Volvo's FH series of trucks are powered by one of the cleanest diesel engines in the world. In the management of chemicals, Volvo's MOTIV database provides detailed information on around 90 per cent of the chemicals used at Volvo plants. The database monitors chemical use to help minimise the risks to employees and the environment, and it will even suggest replacements for any potentially dangerous chemicals. In the management of emissions and waste Volvo has also implemented aggressive emission reduction and recycling programmes, particularly at its Torslanda plant.

Product and process technology have not been the only focus for Volvo's greening efforts. In 1988 an ambitious new green strategy was launched and an Environmental Task Force set up with the aim of improving eco-performance. The company aimed to make environmental concern a 'cornerstone' of the company, and to develop a unique corporate image that would allow its products to be marketed on the basis of personal safety and environmental excellence. Volvo's goal was 'to lead the transportation industry in implementing efficient environmental care programmes, in the firm belief that progressive programmes of this nature also contribute to healthy long-term growth and profitability.' The key elements of the greening strategy were:

- the setting up in 1990 of a programme of systematic environmental audits of all its plants;

- a commitment to proactively improving eco-performance ahead of legislation;

- an emphasis on active and open communication with stakeholders on environmental issues;

- a commitment to develop eco-efficient technologies to create vehicles with a superior eco-performance (albeit with the proviso that this would not be at the expense of technical performance);

- a pledge to adopt manufacturing processes with the minimum impact on the environment;

- contributions to the Environmental Car Recycling in Scandinavia research facility aimed at developing new car recycling technologies.

Volvo has a culture which reflects its Swedish origins by emphasising consensus, caring and training rather than formal control. This was very much the hallmark of the environmental strategy which relied heavily on an environmental training programme, which in the first three years involved more than 10 000 people. Envi-ronmentalist groups were often involved in the training initiatives which had the effect of strengthening ties between the company and these groups, and also of helping to legitimise the company's greening programme to any sceptical employees.

One problem that can act as a barrier to any company's greening strategy is the short-term nature of conventional investment appraisal techniques. Volvo tackled this by making a commitment to use environmentally superior technology, wherever possible, and by insisting that investments in environmental inferior technologies could only be made with specific senior management authority. This policy counteracts the tendency for grey investments to be considered 'normal' and for green investments to be considered to be extraordinary.

Another element of the greening strategy was an attempt to take a holistic view of the environmental impacts of new products, such as the 850 model, during the design process. This was assisted by the development and use of Environmental Priority Strategies (EPS), a system for life cycle assessment that evaluates and compares the environmental impact for different materials at each stage of the physical product life cycle. For each material an 'environmental load unit' is calculated enabling the car designers to compare the eco-performances of materials when specifying each component. The new emphasis on the physical life cycle of the products also led to an increased level of environmental auditing activity. For many companies, the adoption of so many environmentally related changes might have proved disruptive, but for Volvo, it seemed to have been a very natural progression. As Olle Boethius, Volvo's Environmental Affairs Manager, explained:

'To understand the change at Volvo, you need to consider that as a Swedish company we have a certain tradition ... there is a certain caring attitude in the organisation – it's a backbone of the company ... and when it comes to environmental issues, people react – it is easy to connect the two.'

Adapted from Rothenberg S *et al* (1992) 'Issues in the Implementation of Proactive Environmental Strategies', *Business Strategy and the Environment* vol. 1 (4) pp. 1–12, and other sources.

CHAPTER 8

Developing an environmental marketing strategy

'In the past, it has been argued that successful marketing strategies should be based on a solid foundation of knowledge about the customer and competition ... firms allocate considerable resources to carefully monitor consumer behaviour and competitor actions. Today, successful marketing strategies must be built on a foundation that includes the customer, the competition and environmental knowledge.'
(McDougall 1994)

INTRODUCTION

Successful marketing rarely happens by chance. It usually reflects the successful implementation of an effective strategy, driven by entrepreneurial flair, careful strategy planning or a mixture of both. A variety of benefits are ascribed to developing strategies using formal corporate and marketing planning processes. Four of the key benefits are also important in improving the eco-performance of a company.

● Planning ensures that the potential moves of competitors will be considered and planned for, helping to keep the company market- and marketing-orientated.

● Planning allows resources to be allocated more efficiently.

● Planning encourages the systematic gathering and analysis of information and the consideration of different alternatives which provide opportunities to make more effective strategic decisions.

● Planning encourages marketers to take a broader, more systematic and longer-term view of the marketing environment.

There is a long running debate over the degree to which formalised approaches to the development of corporate and marketing strategies help or hinder companies. Although most companies like to consider themselves as being 'strategically managed', formal strategic management and planning approaches have received something of a bad press in the early 1990s. Books like Mintzberg's (1994) *The Rise and Fall of Strategic Planning*, or conferences and training seminars promoting 'euthanasia' for corporate planning systems are symptomatic of a rebellion against the type of strategic planning which was popular during the 1970s and 1980s. Successfully eschewing formalised planning approaches is relatively rare among larger companies (although the early success of the likes of Anita Roddick and Debbie Moore suggests that it may be more common among successful companies run by women). Possession of a good plan for a business is analogous to having a good script on which to base a comedy show. It is quite possible to be very funny without a script, but it usually relies on the exceptional talent of a small number of performers. For those with more modest talents, or as the size of the cast increases, it is important to have a script.

This ensures that entrances, exits and cues are not missed and that there are neither embarrassing silences nor a babel of conflicting voices.

A formal marketing planning process usually exists as a component of a larger corporate planning process. On paper the marketing strategy may appear to be just one of several functional strategies. In practice it should be a great deal more than 'just another' functional strategy. All functions are important, but marketing has a justifiable claim to pre-eminence because of its customer orientation. A company can hire an inappropriate person or buy an unsuitable piece of machinery, and these would be expensive and inconvenient mistakes.

These are internal affairs, however, which often remain invisible to the market. They may be embarrassing or worse for the managers involved, but will usually be put down to experience by the company. Marketing mistakes, by contrast, are potentially fatal for the company concerned, because they can alienate customers. Marketing is also important within corporate planning because of the need to market the business as a whole, and the significance of marketing research and intelligence in supplying crucial information into corporate level planning about customers, competitors and market developments.

Developing an environmental marketing strategy does not involve different planning process steps, but it does create new challenges within the marketing planning process. There are four key elements of a greening strategy that need to be resolved within the marketing planning process:

● developing holistic environmental marketing strategies which encompass the whole business;

● creating an appropriate match between the company and a marketing environment increasingly influenced by the green challenge;

● creating and maintaining competitive advantage in relation to grey products and companies;

● making decisions which are both strategically effective and eco-efficient.

STRATEGY AND HOLISM

The marketing concept is holistic in the sense that it involves organising the entire company's activities behind the drive to satisfy the customer at a profit. In practice, planning processes tend to divide the totality of marketing strategy among the different management functions and hierarchical levels. Many strategic marketing decisions, such as which markets to enter or what products to develop, may be taken in a corporate-level strategic planning process in which the marketing function may not even be represented (Peattie and Notley 1989). The corporate strategy will also usually contain the marketing plans associated with promoting the company as a whole. The functional aspects of gathering marketing information and implementing the marketing strategy through the management of the marketing mix is likely to be contained within the marketing strategy of each SBU plan. This subdivision of the total marketing process to fit in with the structure of the organisation and its planning processes creates considerable dangers of gaps, conflicts and duplications emerging among the different parts of the marketing strategy (Peattie and Notley 1989).

A failure to co-ordinate an environmental marketing strategy across different sections of the organisation can be fatal. If one SBU is attempting to compete in its market on the basis of eco-performance, its strategy may be tarnished by any environmentally hostile actions taken by other SBUs or the company as a whole. Some companies with high profile greening strategies such as Monsanto and Ciba-Geigy have gained Friends of the Earth Green Con of the Year awards on the basis of a poor eco-performance by one subsidiary or product. Similarly, if an SBU's competitive strategy is based on its environmental performance, this will need to be reflected in all the functional strategies and not only the marketing plan. Strategic market planning is a concept that attempts to integrate strategic- and operational-level marketing decisions. Figure 8.1 illustrates the sort of integrated strategic marketing planning in which green strategists need to be involved.

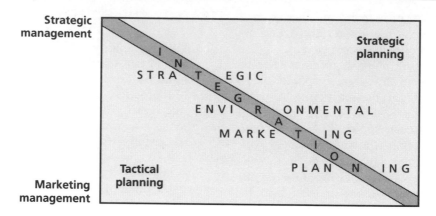

Fig. 8.1 Strategic environmental marketing planning

APPROPRIATENESS

Although managers tend to view strategy in pragmatic, often pseudo-militaristic terms (see page 142), theoretical approaches to strategy often view the formulation of strategy as a matching process between the organisation and its environment (Ansoff 1984). This approach to strategy has more in common with biology and other life sciences that see organisms and species as shaped by their environment. Following this logic, the strategies and plans that companies develop will tend to reflect the demands of the competitive and the wider environment as the company searches to adapt and evolve to ensure an appropriate match. Appropriateness is a key theme within the green agenda in areas such as appropriate technology or appropriate business conduct and even, in industries such as tourism, encouraging appropriate consumer behaviour.

A green approach emphasises the need for the economic and technological dimensions of a company, product or project to match appropriately with its social and physical aspects. This is in contrast with the grey techno-economic paradigm in which economic and technical changes, rather like a war, are often imposed on social and physical systems in ways which disrupt them. This is demonstrated by Robinson's (1990) description of the Aswan Dam project:

'Egypt's Aswan Dam was supposed to provide much needed hydroelectric power, which it did. What it was not supposed to do was silt up. In turn this silt held back in Lake Nasser used to fertilise fields and fisheries downstream as well as provide brickmakers with their raw materials. Environmental factors were not fully considered during planning. Fertiliser imports were forced up and fisheries and brick manufacturers' interests were affected. On top of that irrigation problems affected agricultural production still further and people living alongside the new lake and irrigation canals suffered in an epidemic of schistosomiasis, a water-based parasitic disease.'

Creating an appropriate match between the internal and external marketing environments is very dependent on the level of understanding that strategic decision makers have about the business and its environment. In addition to their physical sustainability, the appropriateness of products and companies will also relate to the degree to which they are accepted and tolerated by society. Products including tobacco, handguns and drugs are restricted by their social acceptability.

Stakeholder analysis

One way to develop 'appropriate' strategies is through stakeholder analysis. This involves relating the companies' activities to needs other than those of customers and shareholders. The stakeholders with an interest in any large organisation will include suppliers, creditors, local communities, special interest groups, employees, trade unions and society. In addition to balancing these different and sometimes conflicting stakeholder requirements, the green challenge is creating changes in the needs of different stakeholders that need to be considered. Two of the most important stakeholders from a green perspective, which are ignored in grey marketing, are the earth itself (Stead and Stead 1992), and the consumers, shareholders and workers who have yet to be born. While the conventional concept of stakeholder analysis aimed to give marketing strategy societal breadth, green stakeholder analysis also attempts to give it futurity.

SWOT analysis

One simple but potentially helpful technique developed to help managers keep a business appropriately matched to its environment is SWOT analysis – an analysis of its Strengths, Weaknesses, Opportunities and Threats. SWOT involves scanning the external environment in search of any changes which pose a significant opportunity or threat, and scanning the internal environment in search of significant strengths or weaknesses. SWOT has been criticised as too simplistic, and is often misused by managers who focus on the opportunities and strengths, while neglecting the threats and weaknesses. To use the technique effectively it is important to include only those factors which are likely to affect the company's competitiveness and to recognise that any factor can be a mixed blessing. The technique should be used to help in visualising which strengths and opportunities can best be capitalised upon and which weaknesses provide the greatest vulnerability.

The green challenge calls for a reanalysis of the SWOT factors which form the basis of many corporate and marketing strategies. A whole range of new opportunities and threats can be presented by the green challenge, and the nature of existing opportunities and threats may appear subtly different from a green perspective. Internally the green challenge means that factors which were previously 'housekeeping' concerns can now influence purchase decisions and therefore need to be considered when discussing strategic strengths and weaknesses.

Auditing key internal strengths and weaknesses

Each element of the business needs to be considered in terms of whether it represents a benefit or a burden to the eco-performance of the company. Waste disposal arrangements, sources of supply and product packaging can all become a source of potential competitive advantage or disadvantage. This is a very different form of auditing challenge for marketers, and one which has helped to fuel the growth in the environmental auditing business. The first formally recorded environmental audit took place in the USA in 1977 when the Security Exchange Commission required Allied Chemicals regularly to review its policies and procedures to ensure a clean environmental bill of health following its failure to notify shareholders of potential environmental liabilities. Since then, environmental auditing has become a big business in its own right. An outline of the steps involved in conducting an environmental audit is contained in Fig. 8.2. Between 1988 and 1990 there was an 88 per cent increase in the number of organisations offering environmental consultancy registered in the Environmental Data Services (ENDS) directory, while turnover for the sector rose by 75 per cent. Eco-information can be gained for input into the marketing audit from a range of green audit approaches including:

- corporate audits
- issues audits
- activity audits
- process/safety audits
- occupational health and safety audits
- energy audits
- site audits
- compliance audits
- waste audits
- supplier/customer/contractor audits.

Another important form of audit, particularly for the marketing of new products or new ventures is an environmental impacts assessment (EIA).

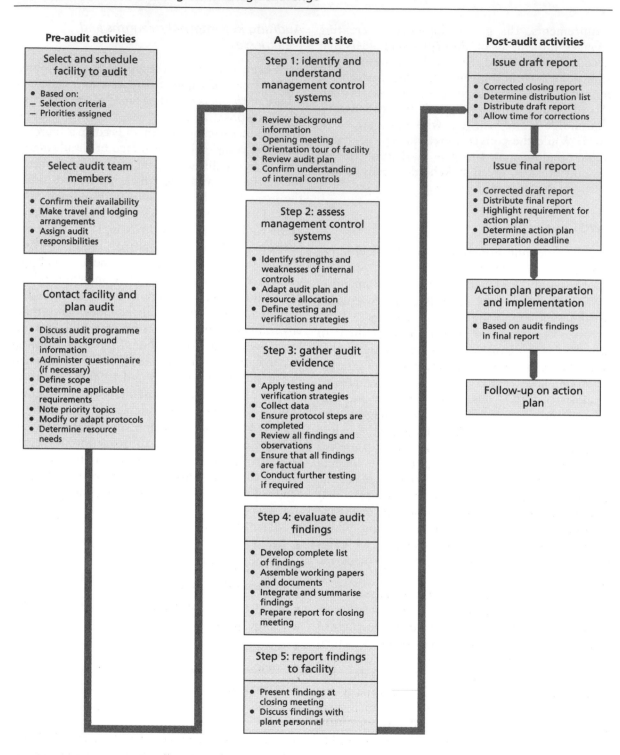

Fig. 8.2 Outline of an environmental audit
(Source: International Chamber of Commerce)

During the 1960s awareness increased that quantitative cost–benefit management decision-making techniques tended to ignore, undervalue or oversimplify the impact on the environment. EIAs were first formally developed as a management tool in the US National Policy Act of 1969. They aim to promote a better appreciation of the full environmental implications of individual development projects. An unfavourable EIA can screen out environmentally poor marketing strategies, while a favourable EIA is a valuable proof of a strategy's green credentials. EIAs have become mandatory in many countries for the development of new projects in areas such as agriculture, civil engineering, tourism and transport. Other useful techniques for auditing eco-performance include life cycle analysis and eco-balance research (see page 275).

Key external opportunities

The green challenge is often spoken of as a threat to businesses, but the growth in demand for many types of product from waste-disposal services to energy-efficient light-bulbs is a clear opportunity. Environmental concern can increase the demand for a particular company's products, either through consumer 'pull' or legislative 'push'. Demand pull in the market for natural plastics is forecast to create growth of over 12 per cent between 1992 and 2002. In the automotive market European legislation enforcing the use of catalytic converters has pushed a £7 billion (5.25 billion ECUs) opportunity in the direction of the three companies that dominate the market. There are many examples including food products, investment products and even pesticides, where the green segment of a particular market provides the fastest growing segment of the market.

The new emphasis on the eco-performance of products and the companies that produce them can create a whole new range of opportunities including:

- forming a new basis on which products can compete and gain competitive advantage;
- providing access to new markets geographically or in terms of new uses for existing products;
- creating tactical opportunities by creating difficulties for direct or indirect competitors;
- creating opportunities for diversification.

Key external threats

The green challenge presents two types of potential threat to companies. The first is that the deterioration of the environment will change the nature of the industry in ways which will affect the company's ability to do business. Ironically this can place market growth (traditionally an unqualified opportunity) in the threat category where this growth is not sustainable. The decline in demand for holidays to certain destinations has shown that too much success in attracting customers in the short term can pose a long-term threat in terms of lost competitiveness. A range of industries are now threatened by the consequences of environmental degradation. The fishing industry faces the threat of dwindling fish stocks; agriculture faces the threat of soil erosion, climate change and overdependence on a small number of crop species; the holiday industry may suffer from the overexploitation of resorts and rising concern about ultraviolet radiation; all industries may be affected by the rising costs of protecting the environment, particularly if measures such as carbon taxes are introduced to tackle global warming. The second type of threat is presented to companies who fail to respond to the green challenge to keep their eco-performance competitive. Hutchinson (1992) outlines a range of such threats.

- Corporate image deteriorates.
- Customers prefer products and services which do less damage to the environment.
- Investors become more difficult to attract if the company cannot meet the criteria for environmental and ethical screening.
- Material costs rise faster than for competitors who use materials more sparingly and recycle resources.
- Penalties for pollution become greater – in money terms as well as in damage to reputation and possible health.

- Insurance premiums increase because environmental damage is likely to be greater than it is for competitors who reduce their pollution risks.
- Recruitment becomes increasingly difficult and it becomes harder to keep good people as more seek companies which provide scope for personal growth and development as well as companies that care for the environment.
- Failure to give early attention to re-focused R&D and management development creates a time lag so it becomes increasingly difficult to catch up with competitors.
- Alienation from the local community with the consequences of a hostile neighbourhood.
- Failure to act may provoke stricter legislation or closer attention from regulatory authorities.
- The long-term future of the company may be jeopardised.

Legislation can ban a product or service completely, restrict its use or promotion, or enforce changes to its nature or production processes which increase its costs. Legislation to ban or restrict the use of products has previously been applied to products with a societal impact, such as alcohol, drugs or weapons. Increasing environmental concern has led to a rapid increase in the level of green legislation and the impact it has on companies. In the USA the 1990 Clean Air Act has been called 'the most expensive piece of legislation of all time' with annual costs to industry put as high as $25 billion (11.7 billion ECUs) (Williams 1991). Legislation typically applies to an entire industry rather than to specific companies, and if it affects all companies equally, it will not affect the balance of competition. In some cases legislation which focuses on a particular product type or ingredient may threaten some companies without affecting others. In other cases legislative change which aims to enforce a certain minimum standard will only pose a threat to those companies currently below that standard.

Industry structure and maturity

The structure and nature of the industry in which a company competes will influence the marketing strategies that it can and will adopt. Although environmental marketing is affected by industry structure, there can be a reciprocal pressure on industry structures to change in response to the greening of the market. Davis (1991) suggests that in industries such as food production where over many decades a once fragmented system has given way to an industry dominated by huge capital-intensive processing plants backed by massive international distribution systems, the process may need to be reversed. Porter's (1979) model of industry structure examines the relationship and balance of power between the different players in a particular market (*see* Fig. 8.3).

1 *The bargaining power of buyers.* Despite the widespread acceptance of the marketing philosophy, in consumer markets the influence of individual consumers over companies can be infinitesimally small. Buyers only have power over the suppliers when they act in concert. Combined consumer action can be implicit as when consumers follow a particular fashion, or explicit as in the case of consumer group campaigns. In Japan the pioneering Seikatsu Club Consumers' Co-operative was founded to combat the increasing incidence of 'greenwashing' within Japanese markets for products such as fresh fruit and vegetables. The club aims to promote green and ethical purchasing, and views unity as the most effective weapon that the consumer can use. Alternatively buyers for intermediaries may be sufficiently powerful to dictate terms to the manufacturers that supply customers through them. Migros, as one of two giant supermarket chains controlling 70 per cent of the Swiss grocery market, has used its influence to insist upon higher environmental standards among the companies that supply it. (Issues relating to environmental marketing through intermediaries are covered in greater depth in Chapter 14.) In industrial or business-to-business markets the customer can be many times the size of the supplier, and may account for such a major share of the company's turnover that the power of the buyer is almost absolute. British Telecom, a company with between 20 000 and 30 000 suppliers, now requires them to provide assurances about various elements of eco-performance and has threatened to de-list any

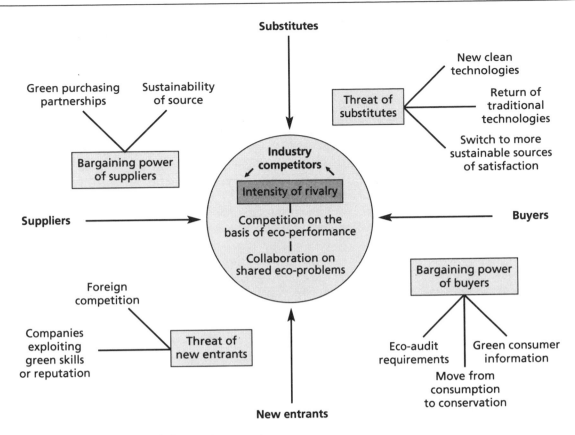

Fig. 8.3 Industry structure and the environment
(adapted from Porter (1979))

companies revealed to be 'dirty'. In this way large green companies can make a considerable impact in a range of industries other than their own by setting up a 'supply-chain reaction'.

2 *The bargaining power of suppliers.* This can be considerable, particularly if the number of suppliers is limited and they refuse to be drawn into price-based competition. In some cases suppliers have the power to resist pressure for greening, or insist upon considerable price increases. In the contract aerosol packaging market, companies seeking to improve their eco-performance have been squeezed between powerful chemical companies who have raised the price of the propellants they supply, and customers who have refused to accept increased prices by threatening to handle their own packaging. The marketing concept and the principle of consumer sovereignty creates the

expectation that the power in the supplier–buyer relationship will reside with the buyer. The green challenge can cause some reappraisals of customer–supplier relationships, however. Nash (1989) in a survey of UK directors found that just over 9 per cent of directors in manufacturing industries named suppliers as a source of pressure on their companies to develop a formal environmental policy. In extreme cases, a supplier may refuse to do business with customers because of their poor eco-performance. Cross-channel ferry operators have refused to carry truck-loads of live animals bound for European slaughterhouses because of the public outcry over the treatment of the animals in transit.

3 *The threat of substitutes.* All companies have indirect competitors who can pose a threat if they can persuade companies to switch products as

opposed to switching brands. Typically the emergence of a new technology creates a substitute for an existing product. In green markets the reverse can happen, with consumers switching to low technology, traditional products in search of improved environmental as opposed to technical performance. In the USA the diaper (or nappy) market provides a good illustration of the opportunities for environmentally based substitutions. The $6 billion disposable diaper industry found itself under attack from the product that disposables replaced – the terry cloth diaper. The perceived environmental disadvantages of disposables have led to their market share being eroded by cloth diaper services which also enjoy a cost advantage ranging from 100 to almost 300 per cent (Scerbinski 1991). Following this development, Procter and Gamble hit back by conducting and publishing research which showed that in terms of total environmental impact (including factors like energy use and water pollution) disposable diapers were not at a disadvantage to cloth diaper services which were marketed on the specific issue of reducing landfill waste. P&G's response helped to establish the concept of measuring the total impact of products through life cycle analysis. The whole controversy illustrates the difficulties that can be involved in creating products with demonstrably superior eco-performance.

4 *The threat of new entrants.* In some countries greener products and technologies are being imported from other countries such as Germany, in which green markets are at a more mature stage of development. The threat of new entrants is partly determined by the existence of entry barriers such as economies of scale, access to distribution channels, high levels of differentiation or government policy. To continue the US diaper market example, a new entrant into the market, Family Club Inc, attacked both disposable diapers and cloth-based services with a new reusable diaper called a Dovetail which is used in conjunction with a disposable pad or a washable terry pad.

5 *Degree of rivalry.* The final element of Porter's model is the intensity of the competition that exists within a market. Conventional wisdom

which viewed investing in the environment as an optional extra indulged in by large dominant companies in relatively uncompetitive markets no longer applies. Environmental performance is now a focus for some very intense and sometimes bitter rivalries. In the battle to market the green, non-chlorine bleached, disposable nappy, Procter and Gamble ended up being taken to a Swedish court by Molnlycke, the parent company of Peaudouce. The court found against P&G, stating that its claims about the non-chlorine bleached nature of the nappies was misleading to consumers and discrediting to companies whose products were genuinely chlorine-free. In other markets, the increasing tendency towards co-operation is helping to reduce the degree of rivalry. A significant trend within many markets is an unprecedented level of collaboration between rivals in the development of new technologies to solve common environmentally related problems. Many environmental problems are of a scale that threaten an entire industry, prompting companies to work together to find a solution. In the electronics industry, concern about the use of CFCs as a solvent has encouraged many companies to develop alternative solvents, and also to redesign production processes to reduce the number of cleaning steps involved. The Industrial Coalition for Ozone Layer Protection, a consortium of American and Japanese companies, has been formed to facilitate the free sharing of research concerning these green innovations and to allow electronics companies all over the world to reduce their usage of CFC solvents.

Sustainability

The ultimate measure of whether companies and their products are appropriately matched with their environment is whether or not they are sustainable. The less sustainable a company or product is, the shorter the time that the company's environment will be able to tolerate its existence. There is a great deal of similarity between what might be called a 'strategic' approach to marketing and management, and environmental marketing and management. Strategic management attempts to treat the organ-

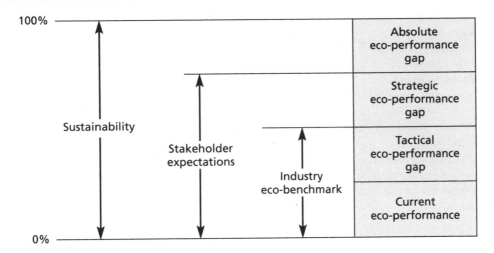

Fig. 8.4 The eco-performance gap

isation in a holistic way in order to gain economic and technical performance improvements. Greening encourages an holistic view in search of improved social and ecological performance. A strategic approach to management echoes the green theme of sustainability in attempting to ensure that a business succeeds not only today, but also survives and thrives in future. The difference being that while strategic management involves a change of focus from the short term to the long term, sustainability involves taking an open-ended approach. Both approaches also encourage businesses to think of themselves as open, rather than closed systems.

Gap analysis and the eco-gap

Gap analysis is a common technique to evaluate the appropriateness of a company's chosen strategy. It involves projecting the likely future results of a strategy, usually in terms of growth in sales or profit, and comparing them against the planned objectives. If a gap exists, the strategy may need to be reconsidered or the objectives possibly amended. The same approach can be taken in terms of eco-performance (*see* Fig. 8.4). Two forms of eco-performance gap will tend to exist. The *tactical* eco-performance gap will be the difference between the current eco-performance and the most sustainable eco-performance possible under pre-

vailing market conditions. The tactical eco-performance gap needs to be closed if the company is not to be put at a competitive disadvantage. The *strategic* eco-performance gap is the gap between the best possible current eco-performance and true sustainability. This will only be closed gradually as the industry is pushed and pulled towards sustainability. Companies will only be able to close the strategic eco-performance gap through changes to their industry's 'rules of the game'. This could involve introducing new technologies or working practices, legislative changes or improvements to 'downstream' industries. Market leaders such as The Body Shop, Shanks & McEwen and Dow Corning have been actively involved in trying to move their entire industry towards sustainability.

COMPETITIVENESS

Another reason behind the widespread adoption of a strategic approach to marketing and management is the intensely competitive nature of contemporary markets. In markets that were once characterised by relatively gentle rivalry in pursuit of the largest share, there is now a fiercely competitive struggle to survive and thrive. One of the most commonly cited barriers to improving eco-performance at the level of a company, an industry or a nation is fears that it will damage economic competitiveness. For some industries which are major users of natural resources and major polluters, concern about the financial costs of environmental improvement is understandable. It is not particularly defensible, however. Industries do not face rising environmental compliance costs because they are being in some way victimised, but because of the environmental damage they have caused and the eco-subsidy that they have enjoyed for many years. For most industries, the effect of environmental improvement on competitiveness should not cause concern. As Stevens (1993) explains:

'The relative stringency or laxity of environmental standards has little or no impact on the general competitiveness of countries or their trade balances. This conclusion has emerged from countless empirical studies of the relationship between the costs of compliance with environmental regulations and international trade patterns. Environmental compliance costs are not a large share of overall costs to industry: in most sectors they constitute approximately 1–2 per cent of total costs ... they have not been large enough, relative to other costs, to influence competitiveness ... This picture is not expected to change much even if environmental standards are tightened further in the pursuit of sustainable development.'

As the competitiveness of a market increases, so the need to develop a distinctive competitive advantage grows in importance. Ohmae (1982) identifies four ways to achieve and sustain a competitive advantage.

1 Identify the key success factors within an industry, and focus efforts on opportunities to gain significant advantages over competition.

2 Exploit the company's existing areas of superiority.

3 Attempt to change the key success factors of the industry in the company's favour, by challenging the basic assumptions and practices within the industry.

4 Innovate through new products and the opening up of new markets.

Eco-performance is becoming a key success factor in many industries, but demonstrating competitive advantage can be difficult where environmental concern is a consensus issue, or where performance differences between companies are relatively slight. The concept of 'benchmarking' became popular during the late 1980s and early 1990s to allow the performance of different companies to be compared. Unfortunately, in a green context, as Hocking and Power (1993) found:

'One of the major problems with benchmarking is that there is no standard format or benchmark available. Environmental performance measurement is still in its relative infancy. Different parties calculate their performance on different bases and sets of assumptions. It is very difficult, if not impossible, at present, to compare directly one company's performance with that of another.'

Marketing as warfare

The competitive dimensions of marketing strategy are usually discussed using concepts that originate from military warfare. The very word 'strategy' derives from the Greek word 'strategos' which roughly translates as 'the art of the general'. This analogy is rather frightening when one considers that, with the application of modern technology, there is no activity more destructive to the environment and the societies which it touches. It is usually those on whose behalf a war is fought, and their environment, that suffer most from its conduct. The environment was certainly one of the key victims of the Vietnam War, during which it absorbed some 72 million litres of herbicides (in addition to 25 million tonnes of conventional bombs), the effects of which on human health are still apparent today.

The parallels between business and warfare are often discussed within industrialised countries in the relatively positive context of liberating a country from an oppressor. The use of the military analogy to illustrate strategy therefore became somewhat more popular after Operation Desert Storm than it had for some years (even though the environmental destruction of the Gulf ecosystem was another consequence of the conflict following the torching of the Kuwait oilfields). Examining the wars that have taken place in countries like Rwanda, Liberia, the former Yugoslavia and Ethiopia reveals that wars are often fought around complex, confused and deep-seated differences between peoples with little in the way of positive outcomes for any of the parties involved.

The proposition that the development and implementation of corporate and marketing strategy is the commercial equivalent of warfare has been put forward in the books *Business Wargames* (James 1985) and *Marketing Warfare* (Reis and Trout 1992). As Ries and Trout comment, 'We think the best book on marketing was written by a retired Prussian general, Karl von Clausewitz. Entitled *On War*, the 1832 book outlines the strategic principles behind all successful wars.' They go on to suggest that because all major companies have become customer-orientated, there is no strategic advantage in being customer-orientated. Instead, by being competitor-orientated, companies can seek out and attack their competitors' weaknesses. Concepts of aggression, eradicating 'the enemy' and disregarding the environmental consequences, are seen as acceptable in business, just as they are in battle. However, the business/warfare analogy is flawed. In warfare, there is usually one or possibly two enemies, a relatively simple objective of gaining enough territory and inflicting enough damage on the opposing forces to make them surrender on your terms, and a relatively limited time span of a few days, months or years. Business is very different. In the European shoe industry there are around 20 000 small companies. For each of these, deciding who the enemy is and where the battlefield lies is virtually impossible. Similarly a monopolist would find it difficult to reconcile its strategy with military concepts other than viewing itself as an army of occupation (which is not a very attractive image). The complexity of the relationships involved in business is also very different from warfare, although it is perhaps more akin to the related field of diplomacy. For an industrial firm, a particular company may be its key competitor in one market, its sole supplier in another and its partner in a third. Such interrelationships make the all-out aggression of warfare inappropriate for business.

A further problem with viewing companies as armies is that modern war machines are very unnatural creations. Conflict is undoubtedly a natural part of human nature, but the application of economics and technology allows for the creation of war machines capable of destroying the world many times over. An alternative to viewing strategy as analogous to the unnatural acts of modern warfare, is to view it as analogous to the survival and expansion strategies of natural populations. Plant and animal populations compete, co-exist and co-operate in ways which enable each to survive and expand as far as possible within the limits imposed by the environment. As marketing theory becomes greener we may witness a more ecological approach to strategy, where other companies are regarded as 'natural competitors' rather than as enemies to be destroyed. Perhaps instead of seeing the strategists as military generals, we shall come to see them more like tribal chieftains. Such chieftains often had to engage in armed struggle against competing tribes, but they would also engage in a great deal of more positive activities. Tribal societies are generally very good at caring for the environment that supports them, caring for their members, and managing their growth to suit their available resources. Faced with competition for resources or territory, warfare would be only one of a chieftain's options along with co-operation and trade.

Market position

A firm may occupy one of several positions within the total market and the objectives and strategies it adopts will reflect its market position. Each type of company may adopt a greener strategy to satisfy different objectives.

For *market leaders*, such as McDonald's, IBM and Dow Corning, a green strategy is part of their effort to maintain their market dominance, and possibly aims to expand the market by attracting new green consumers. Greening can also reflect the feeling of responsibility that large dominant companies often have for the communities within which they exist. For the next group of companies, *market challengers*, who are actively fighting to become the market leaders, a greener strategy can represent a new way of attacking the market leader. For Varta, its greening strategy was a key factor in its successful attack on the leaders of the UK battery market. *Market followers* are smaller companies typically more concerned with protecting their current share than challenging for market leadership. Their response to the green challenge is typically reactive and will follow the greening of the market leaders and challengers by introducing 'Me Too' products or promotions. During the early stages of greening, almost all green companies were small *market nichers,* serving market segments which the larger firms had failed to satisfy. A green strategy can help to serve or protect a niche, but there is a danger that the niche may attract larger companies as the interest in greener products grows. Ecover had occupied a niche worth under or around £1 million (750 000 ECUs) in the UK detergents market for several years. Between 1988 and 1989 this niche expanded to over £10 million (7.5 million ECUs) which was enough to draw the attention of the soap giants.

EFFECTIVE DECISION MAKING

A key benefit claimed for the strategic approach to management is that it leads to better decisions and more effective strategies. This has an intuitive logic, since the information that will be provided by a systematic internal and external strategic audit, and its formal and explicit discussion and analysis *should* lead to a better strategy than one which is intuitive and based on partial information and discussion. However, this is not always the case since formal strategic audits can be far from comprehensive and objective, and the information they provide can overwhelm just as easily as it can empower a strategic decision maker.

The emphasis on strategic decision making during the 1980s was on pursuing effectiveness (concerning technical and economic outcomes) over efficiency (concerning methods and the use of resources). For the environmental marketer the difference between strategic effectiveness and efficiency has less meaning since achieving the desired outcomes (customer satisfaction) relies on the eco-efficient use of resources as well as the

effective manipulation of the marketing mix. There are some important strategic decisions into which environmental considerations will increasingly need to be incorporated.

Establishing strategic direction

An overall strategic direction is important for any company to possess. Ansoff's Growth Vector Model proposes four basic corporate growth strategies, each of which involves potential consequences for eco-performance (*see* Fig. 8.5)

● *Product development.* Maintaining market share in a greening market is likely to require new product development. Within the car market, initiatives have included recyclable cars, lean burn engines, electric cars, diesel-electric hybrids, and gas-powered cars.

● *Market development*, through finding new markets for existing products. This can be viewed as a relatively green strategy in terms of extending the use of existing products and avoiding the resource consumption involved in new product development.

● *Market penetration*, through increasing sales of current products in existing markets. The eco-performance implications of market penetration depends on whether it involves stimulating new demand, or on switching competitors away from less green competing brands or products. Some green products have achieved substantial market penetration, for example phosphate-free detergents which over a three-year period expanded from a minority niche to dominate the German market.

● *Diversification.* Particularly grey companies and industries may be forced to diversify away from the traditional product market base. Tobacco companies have expanded into many other sectors such as food and drink. Some companies noted for good eco-performance can become owned by other companies with a poor image. For example, Jacobs Suchard (see page 277) is owned by American tobacco conglomerate Philip Morris. This can pose problems for both marketers and consumers when assessing the credibility of a greening strategy in such compa-

Product

		Present	New
Mission/ Market	**Present**	**Market penetration** Capitalise on expanding green markets for current products Promote eco-performance to enhance existing customer loyalty	**Product development** Investment in 'clean' and alternative green products Support of products through new green services (e.g. reconditioning)
	New	**Market development** Reposition a 'classic' product for green consumers Extend product life cycle through export	**Diversification** Develop green skills (e.g. waste disposal) into new businesses Acquire into new green markets (e.g. the investment by Group 4 in Ecover)

Fig. 8.5 A green growth vector model
(adapted from Ansoff (1984))

nies. Should the children be held responsible for the sins of the parent? For other companies diversifying into green markets may simply reflect the normal practice of spreading risks and seeking out growth opportunities.

Once overall strategic direction has been set, the next key task is to identify the markets and market segments in which the company will compete. For many companies green market segments will represent a potential new target for their marketing strategy (*see* Chapter 9 for details on segmentation).

Selecting investment opportunities

Portfolio analysis is a popular strategy formulation approach which attempts to guide strategic investment decisions by analysing the competitive position and the investment 'portfolio' of the company. Portfolio models include the famous Growth Share Matrix (aka the Boston Box), the General Electric Business Screen and the Shell Matrix. The Boston Box aims to aid corporate investment decisions by contrasting the market growth and/or investment needs of SBUs or products against their market share and/or cash generation capacity. Although it is a widely used

and accepted model, it has been criticised for a variety of omissions and questionable assumptions. The model can also be criticised from an environmental standpoint. It assumes that high growth markets are the most attractive, rather than markets with sustainable growth, stable growth or even long-term growth potential. The underlying logic of the model also says that new products should be financed by the surplus cash provided by the 'cash cows'. This milking of the 'cows' and the starving of the 'dogs' can result in mature products being abandoned too early as a result of underinvestment, while a succession of resource-intensive new products are launched. An alternative to a portfolio based on competitive position, is a portfolio that accounts for eco-performance. Schaltegger and Sturm (1992) developed a green portfolio as part of their 'eco-rational path method' for developing environmental strategies. An adapted version of their matrix is presented in Fig. 8.6.

A decision to enter a particular new market, or develop a particular new product, will usually involve new investment. For such an initiative to succeed, the strategic logic of a new investment must be matched by a positive investment appraisal. A major barrier to greener strategy is the use of discounted cash flow (DCF) techniques

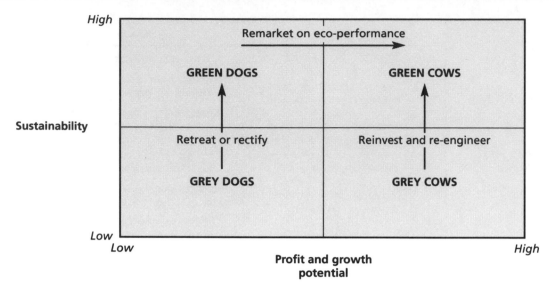

Fig. 8.6 A green marketing portfolio
(adapted from Schaltegger and Sturm (1992))

to evaluate investment projects. The whole idea of DCF techniques is to place a greater weight on costs incurred today, as opposed to those that will be incurred in the future. It therefore works entirely against the long-term approach that sustainable development requires.

Choosing the basis of competition

Within any market, a company must select a basis on which to compete. Porter's (1985) generic competitive strategy model suggests three alternatives reflecting the basis of competition and the extent of the market coverage a company pursues (*see* Fig. 8.7).

● *Cost leadership*. Greening is not associated with a cost-leadership strategy because of the general, but often mistaken, assumption that improved environmental performance involves a cost burden. Increasing opportunities to reduce costs by reducing resource inputs, and the increasing costs of poor environmental performance will push the issue of greening up the agenda for low-cost strategists in future.

● *Differentiation*. Mass market products which are differentiated from the competition on the basis of superior eco-performance are becoming increasingly widespread. Switching to compete on the basis of eco-performance can have a miraculous effect on company strategy. In Eastern Germany in 1992 refrigerator manufacturer DKK Schjarfenstein faced liquidation until it showed its prototype propane/butane-cooled fridge to Greenpeace. After a hastily assembled advertising campaign funded by Greenpeace the company had 50 000 firm orders for the new product and was talking to potential buyers instead of the receiver.

● *Focus*. A focus strategy involves targeting a product which is differentiated or low in cost at a particular segment of the market. In the early days of environmental marketing the lack of mass consumer interest in green issues limited most green companies to a focus strategy. Many green products, such as Body Shop cosmetics or unleaded petrol, have moved on to gain mass market acceptance. Others, such as green investment products, are still targetted at specific segments of the market.

Competitive advantage

	Low cost	Differentation
Broad	**Green cost leadership** E.g. P&G eco-bag Detergent refill	**Eco-excellence** E.g. Body shop cosmetics
Narrow	**Green cost focus** E.g. Kyocera Ecosys Computer Printers	**Green nichemanship** E.g. Ben & Jerry's ice cream

Market scope (label at left, between Broad and Narrow rows)

Fig. 8.7 Generic strategies for green competitive advantage
(adapted from Porter (1980))

The logic of Porter's model originally dictated that companies should consistently pursue only one of these strategies. The 1990s have seen an increasing trend in companies attempting to be both low-cost and highly differentiated. This comes partly from the ability of new technology to create production flexibility and allow for 'mass customisation'. It is driven partly by necessity. The creation of the Single European Market has acted to create price convergence and a reduction in margins while also creating an increased need for service and differentiation. Environmental marketing based on improving eco-efficiencies provides an opportunity to reduce costs (by reducing resource inputs and waste disposal costs) and using the environmental benefits as a basis for differentiation.

The early part of the 1990s has seen a relatively consistent trend arising in terms of the basis of a green response. Niche players with a focus strategy are developing relatively 'deep green' products, while the mainstream companies are concentrating on minor changes to existing products (such as the use of more efficient packaging) or the introduction of new green variants.

The timing of market entries and exits

The timing and method of market entry and market exit are important elements in the execution of marketing strategy. In some cases timing decisions will be based on consumer readiness or on competitor moves. The delay by major soap powder manufacturers in launching green detergent brands related partly to the evolution of the green agenda, with the launch of Procter and Gamble's Ariel Ultra coinciding with an upswing in consumer concern about phosphates and bleaches.

Market entry can be achieved through acquisition, collaboration or internal development. Entry through acquisition or partnership brings with it the risk of problems associated with the target or partner's eco-performance. Screening acquisition targets for eco-performance is almost universal among large American companies. It has not been as widely practised in the UK, where several companies have acquired their way into major environmental liabilities. Beazer Homes acquired American aggregates company Koppers, only to find themselves faced with an unexpected $200 million bill for environmental liabilities.

Market exit for products or the company as a whole may become an increasingly important challenge for marketers of products which are environmentally or socially harmful, and therefore need to be demarketed despite being profitable and popular with customers. Ciba-Geigy withdrew 40 dyes from the market because they were unable to change the production process to make them both economically and environmentally efficient.

IMPLEMENTATION

Good strategies and plans ultimately count for nothing in terms of successful marketing. What counts is what the company actually does to meet the needs of its stakeholders, to generate profits and to respond to the demands of its competitive and wider environment. This is not to say that the two activities of planning and implementation are distinct; they are not, or at least they should not be. Many of the strategic problems that companies encounter relate back to the consideration of implementation after, rather than before, strategy formulation. Effective implementation can be difficult to diagnose. If a company succeeds in the market-place, it can be symptomatic of a good strategy, a lot of hard work going in to make the best of a poor strategy, a failure among competitors, or simple good fortune. Kotler (1994) suggests that instead of trying to judge the effectiveness of implementation from the final result, it is better to evaluate the company's implementation efforts. Kotler's checklist of questions can be adapted for an environmental marketing strategy.

● Is there a clear environmental marketing theme, backed by strong leadership and a culture that promotes and provokes excellence?

● Is there subfunctional soundness in the company's environmental marketing activities? Are sales, distribution, pricing and advertising effectively and efficiently managed?

● Do the company's marketing programmes integrate and deliver environmental marketing activities to each stakeholder group?

● How good is marketing management at interacting with (a) other marketing-related staff, (b) other functions, and (c) customers and the trade?

● What monitoring efforts are being used to measure eco-performance and changes in the marketing environment?

● How good is marketing management at providing time, people and money to tackle green issues?

● How is management organised, both to do marketing tasks and to deal with customer interactions? Are there open 'organisational doors' for customers and the trade?

Figure 8.8 presents a simple matrix to diagnose the effectiveness of companies' planning and implementation. This framework can be used to plot companies' overall competitive economic performance, or socio-environmental performance. As the green challenge deepens and eco-performance influences competitive success, so the positions on the matrices relating to competitive performance and eco-performance will converge. The matrix identifies four general categories of planner.

1 *Entrepreneurs*: typically smaller companies which are capable of creating and implementing very successful strategies with little or no formal planning to back them up. Interestingly The Body Shop, one of the most successful of green companies, based its early success on a sometimes fierce avoidance of conventional strategic and marketing planning approaches. Entrepreneurs often reject formal planning systems as part of a mechanistic way of doing business.

2 *Rabbits*: neither develop formal strategies nor implement an effective informal strategy. The life expectancy of any company who remains in this sector is likely to be low. Grey Rabbits will typically be frozen when the green spotlight is turned upon them. To address the green challenge Rabbits need to be provided with both the motivation and the skills.

3 *Bureaucrats*: companies who pay a great deal of attention to planning, and yet produce plans

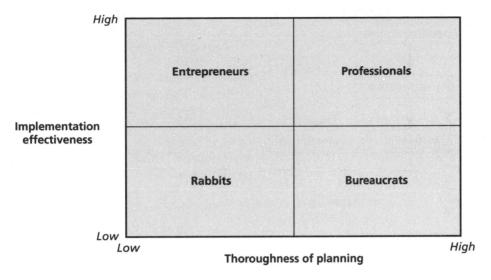

Fig. 8.8 Planning *versus* implementation effectiveness

which are not effectively implemented. In environmental marketing terms they become victim of TEAPOTS Syndrome – The Environmental Action Plan On The Shelf. Green Bureaucrats include many companies who are adopting a procedural approach to eco-performance. This may involve the introduction of an environmental management system (possibly in pursuit of a recognised standard such as BS7750), and the development of detailed but unrealistic environmental strategies and policies.

4 *Professionals*: companies whose success is based on effective planning and implementation. A company may move towards planning professionalism from any of the other three boxes. A Rabbit might adopt an effective approach to planning which creates realistic plans; an Entrepreneur might lose its founder or might experience problems and a decline in performance which encourage it to embrace more formalised planning; and a Bureaucrat might abandon an overly formalised planning system which created 'paralysis by analysis' in favour of something more streamlined and effective.

As competitive performance and eco-performance converge, it becomes important for companies to move towards Green Professionalism or Green Entrepreneuring quickly, and not use their professional or entrepreneurial competitive position as an excuse for leaving environmental performance languishing to the left of the matrix.

Managerial dimensions of implementation

Greenley (1986) provides a model of the managerial dimensions of implementation which includes five interrelated components (*see* Fig. 8.9). *Delegation* gives those responsible for implementation the power to make decisions and take actions. Charter's (1990) research showed that environmental concern is strongest among younger managers and women managers. Given that hierarchical position often equates roughly with age, and that the operation of the 'glass ceiling' keeps the concentration of women at the lower levels of the hierarchy artificially high, increased delegation can allow for more effective green strategy implementation. Such delegation should not compromise the important *leadership* role of top management in the execution of a greening strategy. Strong leadership is particularly important because greening involves a change to established corporate culture. It needs to be value-driven and in many cases it requires vision, patience and some bravery.

Fig. 8.9 Management components of implementation
(Source: Greenley (1986))

Participation is important during both the planning and implementation of a strategy, and it is closely linked with another important component – motivation. Participation is a key feature of the type of humanist, open and democratic approach to society, its government and institutions, including corporations, that is central to the green agenda. *Motivation* is closely associated with participation, since people are likely to be more motivated to support the implementation of a strategy whose formulation they have participated in and towards which they will feel some degree of 'ownership'. Green strategies are likely to have an edge over grey strategies in implementation simply because they can create enthusiasm among the staff responsible who feel they are doing something relatively positive.

Monitoring and control

Strategies need to be more than formulated and implemented; they also need to be monitored and controlled. The greening process can require a number of changes to the methods of monitoring and control of strategies. Green audits are as important for monitoring a strategy as they are for informing it (through data inputs into the strategy formulation process) in the first place. In terms of how things are measured, environmental marketing implies an increased emphasis on qualitative control because of its emphasis on the quality and sustainability of growth as opposed to its level. This is not to say that quantitative approaches to monitoring eco-performance are not important. All of Sandoz Corporation's 350 facilities world-wide now report on ten safety and environmental (S&E) performance measures on a regular basis:

1 Lost-time accident rate
2 Lost-work day rate
3 Total energy consumption
4 Total water consumption
5 Total liquid and solid waste
6 Total S&E investments
7 Total S&E expenses
8 Total S&E personnel
9 Total production
10 Total personnel

To aid in its greening process, Novo Nordisk, the Danish health care and industrial enzymes group, has developed an 'eco-productivity index'. The index is created by dividing the volume of output sold by the volume inputs, including water, energy, raw materials and packaging. The company knows that in the four years since 1994 it has improved its eco-productivity on energy by 33 per cent, water by 31 per cent and packaging by 19 per cent. Annual improvement targets of 4 or 5 per cent have now been set for the eco-productivity of each input.

Ledgerwood and Street (1993) stress the importance of linking environmental programmes to rewards and incentives, when creating effective control for green strategies. This means that environmental auditing avoids a focus on fault finding and blame, but instead concentrates on translating problems into 'training opportunities'.

SUCCESS FACTORS FOR ENVIRONMENTAL MARKETING PLANNING

Successful environmental marketing planning is only likely to succeed where the planning process incorporates the Five I Factors:

- *Informed*. Planning a strategic response to the green challenge requires a great deal of information, much of which will be new to the company.
- *Innovative*. The green challenge calls for innovative solutions to new or established problems. Whether it is creating the recyclable car, the refillable fabric conditioner bottle or the reusable printer cartridge, the emphasis is very much on innovation.
- *Involving*. The planning process needs to involve (in the sense of both participation and enthusiasm) a wide range of internal stakeholders together with key external stakeholders such as key suppliers or distributors.
- *Integrative*. The holistic nature of eco-performance means that the strategic and marketing planning processes need to become virtually seamless in their integration.
- *Iterative*. Planning needs to be iterative. The environment that companies exist within is dynamic, and the strategies which they develop to cope will constantly evolve. Formal planning processes tend to produce periodic snapshots of this evolution, and to make a contribution to strategy, green issues cannot be considered in a once only environmental review.

Getting the planning process right provides no guarantee of creating the right strategy, but it does improve the likelihood. To succeed, the environmental marketing strategies which are the product of the planning process need to follow the 'Seven Green Cs':

- *Customer orientated*.
- *Commercially viable*.
- *Credible* to customers, senior managers and other stakeholders.
- *Consistent* with corporate objectives, strategies and capabilities.
- *Clear* by avoiding environmental or technical jargon.
- *Co-ordinated* with the operational strategies and plans of the other business functions.
- *Communicated* effectively internally and externally.

CASE STUDY

Varta batteries – green power in action

In absolute terms, a battery is not a very green product. During manufacture the average battery consumes seven times the energy it can store, and conventional batteries include harmful components such as mercury and cadmium. However, the modern lifestyle requires power on the move for personal stereos, cameras and torches, and a variety of products including toys, clocks and radios require batteries even when stationary. Batteries are big business. In 1988 the UK market was dominated by Ever Ready and Duracell who held just over 60 per cent of the market. The leading company in Europe as a whole was Varta with sales of over £600 million (450 million ECUs), but it had experienced difficulties in expanding its share from among the many 'minnows' in the UK market who combined to form 30 per cent of the market.

In the summer of 1988 Varta relaunched its range in the UK with improved easy-to-open packaging (which market research had revealed as an important issue with female consumers), accompanied by a major campaign of sales promotion. The hoped-for penetration of the UK ▶

market failed to materialise. At the same time the company was launching a mercury-free zinc-chloride battery in its home market of Germany. In the autumn of 1988 environmental interest in the UK was on an upswing following the publicity over Mrs Thatcher's speech to the Royal Society, and the publication of *The Green Consumer Guide* (Elkington and Hailes 1988) which advised UK consumers', 'If "green" (mercury-free) batteries come on to the market, give them a try.' Spotting an opportunity, Varta had the UK's first mercury-free battery on retailers' shelves within four weeks, six months ahead of the competition. When Ever Ready launched its own mercury-free battery in the spring of 1989, Varta replied by also removing cadmium from its zinc-chloride batteries. The effect on Varta's UK market position was spectacular. Over the first 18 months of the greening strategy its market share grew from below 4 to around 15 per cent.

The success of Varta's green products owed much to the rest of the marketing mix. The early sales growth was achieved largely on the strength of some very positive media coverage of the product launch. This was reinforced during 1989 with an advertising campaign targetted at women in publications such as *Homes and Gardens*, *Good Housekeeping* and *Family Circle*. Sponsorship of the Green Awards run by *The Grocer* in 1989 was followed up by a packaging switch to use recycled card and biodegradable plastic. Finally the company launched an innovative return-and-recycling scheme for its 're-charge-ables' range in which consumers were offered a cash incentive for recycling. In distribution terms Varta tripled its distribution base in the first year of its 'green' strategy. What began as a relatively opportunistic transfer of a product from one market to another, evolved into a comprehensive and effective environmental strategy.

CHAPTER 9

Segmentation and positioning within green markets

'The only issue more complicated than the environment, is the human psychology that affects consumer perceptions of the environmental issue and how it motivates their purchasing habits.'
(*Financial Times*, 28 May 1992, p2)

INTRODUCTION

Through its reliance on the techniques of segmentation and targetting, grey marketing emphasises the needs and characteristics that divide people. It concentrates on attempting to categorise people in the market into a subgroup whose members are in some meaningful way different from those in other subgroups and from the mass of consumers. Such market segments become targets within the marketing strategy, and are offered specifically tailored versions of the marketing mix. A green philosophy, by contrast, concentrates more on the things that unite people. These include the common generic needs for fresh air, food, clean water, health care, rewarding work, freedom, choice, fulfilment and the pleasure of seeing future generations growing up in a viable world. At present, what differentiates 'green consumers' from the mass of consumers and from those who are generally concerned about the environment, is that green consumers consciously connect the ability of product purchase and use to satisfy their specific needs, with the ability of the environment to meet their own generic needs and those of others.

The green movement is often associated with conformity because of the implied reduction in consumer choice that the search for eco-efficiency involves. Issues of diversity and unity are central to green thinking in terms of creating social and political unity, while maintaining biological and cultural diversity. Johnson (1991) comments:

'(Unity) should not be confused with uniformity which is characterised by indistinguishability between the parts or individual constituents ... It is the combination of unity and diversity which is of interest to greens ... the ability of essential expressions of individuality, of diversity, to form coherent wholes, unity, without the need to sacrifice that diversity in the process. Many trees make the diversity of the unified forest. The frequent demand for conformity in grey culture and human affairs is an expression of weakness, of insecurity in the whole, rather than an expression of the strength it is intended to illustrate. It is uniformity rather than unity.'

Segmentation, it could be argued, attempts to divide people by reinforcing economic and socio-political boundaries, while also attempting to enforce uniformity within particular groups. Fashion can be viewed as an attempt to enforce cultural norms within segments by marketers, while marketers would probably argue that through fashion consumers are offered the ability to express the individuality that the green philosophy champions. Fashion marketing during the 1980s and 1990s has certainly changed from the fashion marketing of the 1960s and 1970s in its emphasis on individuality over conformity. However, in many areas, international marketing is creating social, cultural and technical uniformity where previously there was diversity.

It is not only green thinkers who have expressed reservations about the use of marketing segmentation. Marketing practitioners have run into a range of difficulties when trying to apply its principles (Piercy and Morgan 1993). These include understanding the difference between a market and a segment, creating internal 'ownership of segments', reconciling segments with existing marketing plans and budgets and the difficulties of getting the information with which to define meaningful segments. Despite these difficulties, companies continue to talk in terms of 'the green segment of the market' and to attempt to identify, define and understand the green consumer.

THE HUNT FOR THE GREEN CONSUMER

The concept of the green consumer is at the heart of environmental marketing. A great deal of effort has gone into attempting to define who green consumers are, what characteristics define them, what motivates them, and what they will or will not do and buy. For over 20 years, researchers have been trying to identify consumers who can be labelled as environmentally concerned/conscious, socially responsible, green or ethical. For our purposes the label 'green consumer' covers all of the others since the distinction between them tends to be misleading. Most consumers' concern about global warming or ozone depletion relates to the potential impact on society. In terms of attempts to isolate 'environmentally conscious' consumer behaviour, Flodhammar (1994) produces a useful summary of 40 studies from 1973 to 1993 which cover a range of definitions and observed behaviour. The definitions used vary in terms of their scope. While some emphasise purchase choices, others emphasise the full range of behaviour within the consumption process. Some definitions emphasise products purchased, while others emphasise non-purchase decisions. Some definitions emphasise the nature of the environmental effects of the products involved, while others emphasise the consumers' motivation for purchasing a green product. Examples include:

'a person who knows that the production, distribution, use and disposal of … products lead to external costs, and who evaluates such external costs negatively, trying to minimise them through (his or her) own choices.' (Balderjahn 1986)

'a person who, in his or her consumption behaviour, consciously attempts to have a neutral or positive effect on the earth, its environment, and its inhabitants.' (Rolston and di Benedetto 1994)

If we pause for a moment to consider what constitutes consumer behaviour, we find it defined by Loudon and Della Bitta (1993) as 'the decision process and physical activity individuals engage in when evaluating, acquiring, using or disposing of goods and services' (which parallels the purchase process outlined in Chapter 5). The hunt for the green consumer has mostly focused on the acquisition part of consumer behaviour. Troy (1994) argues that 'consumer purchases don't seem to reflect their intentions as measured by environmental surveys'. Such observed differences are usually blamed on an overreporting of environmental concern, but perhaps can be understood by taking a wider view of the consumption process. In terms of purchase evaluation, given the confusion and lack of understanding of green issues exhibited by many consumers, and the wealth of information, claims and counter-claims to which they are exposed, it is not surprising that green consumers' purchase intentions and actual purchase impacts do not always match up. The 'green purchase gap' may also reflect environmental concern finding expression, not in purchase, but in the consideration of alternatives (including non-purchase decisions), product use and product disposal. In countries such as Germany and the USA a sufficiently large proportion of the population is involved in recycling to view green consumption as the norm, simply on the basis of product disposal. An individual can operate as a green consumer by incorporating environmental concern into any phase of the consumption process.

Unfortunately, as discussed in Chapter 5, the green consumer is likely to remain to some extent a mythical creature. Although environmental concern and consumption are not so irreconcilable that the label 'green consumer' must be consid-

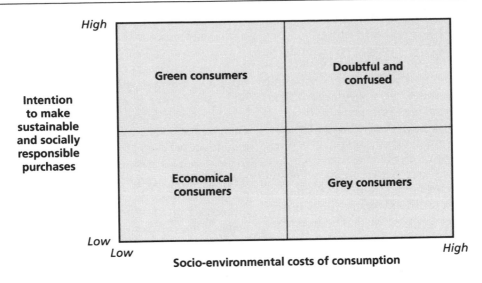

Fig. 9.1 Consumers in relation to the environment

ered an oxymoron, the two are more like opposing magnets which can be held together, but only with a good deal of conscious effort. Consumers who consider themselves deeply green will, by accident or design, purchase many products which are less sustainable and less socially responsible than competing products. Conversely, the most environmentally sceptical and economically minded consumers may still use lead-free fuel or grow their own largely organic produce because they find it economical or enjoyable. Green consumption has two key dimensions: the intent to buy as sustainably and socially responsibly as possible and the socio-environmental impact of the actual purchases. If we plot these two dimensions on a simple two-by-two matrix (*see* Fig. 9.1), four possible consumption positions are created:

1 grey consumers;

2 economical consumers;

3 the doubtful and confused;

4 green consumers.

The vast majority of people, if offered credible green products with similar prices and technical performance to conventional products, would discriminate in favour of the green product. This means that the basic difference between people whose consumer behaviour tends towards the green consumer box, and others is that they have a belief in both the problems caused and the solutions offered by the market system. For marketers of green products, the challenge is how to identify those that have this belief in order to market products to them. For those without the belief, the question is whether and how they can be converted. The early phase of green consumption has seen relatively few people consistently adopting or consistently and deliberately avoiding green purchasing behaviour, which defines the majority of consumers as predominantly economical or doubtful and confused.

DEFINING GREEN MARKET SEGMENTS

Markets are no longer the cohesive entities they once were. According to Loudon and Della Bitta (1993) 'the mass market became fragmented in the 1980s and is now dissolving into particles'. In any market a key challenge is deciding how to segment the market and successfully target particular segments. Marketers need to identify customer groups who share similar characteristics which make a variation of the marketing mix particularly suited to meet their needs. In trying to identify and target green market segments, marketers could also be excused for feeling 'confused and doubtful'. Miller (1993), in examining the problem of reconciling conflicting market research data, points to environmental marketing as an area where this is a particular problem. Commercial advertising and market research agencies have typically developed green consumer profiles based around demographic variables. However, the majority of academic research suggests that the relationship between environmental concern and socio-demographic variables is unclear, and that they fail to work as predictors of environmentally related behaviour. The benefit of segmentation in green markets perhaps lies in Wind's (1978) observation that segmentation approaches are more important in helping marketers to better understand their market, than they are in turning that market into a set of identified targets.

There are an almost infinite number of ways in which a market can be segmented. There are also different levels at which segmentation can be used. *Strategic* segmentation can be used to aid the development of a company's mission and general strategic direction. *Managerial* segmentation is used in developing marketing strategies and allocating marketing resources. *Operational* segmentation attempts to pinpoint the needs of segments for the customisation of the marketing mix. At the operational level, for a segmentation approach to be successful, it must be able to identify segments which are:

1 measurable;

2 accessible;

3 substantial;

4 unique, in that the purchasers within it are in some meaningful way alike, and unlike the members of other segments;

5 stable;

6 likely to provide additional revenue to justify customising the marketing mix for a particular segment, rather than attacking the market as a whole;

7 well matched to the competitive strengths of the business;

8 compatible with the other segments targetted by the business.

Most segmentations come under one of four main headings. *Demographic* segmentations focus on who people are in terms of their gender, age, ethnic origin or socio-economic classification. *Geographic* segmentations concentrate on where people are, and adjust the marketing mix to cater for differences between continents, nations and regions. *Psychographic* segmentations tackle what people are like in terms of their characteristics, interests and lifestyle; while *behaviouristic* segmentations differentiate between people on the basis of what they do.

In practice, the segmentation that companies use can be highly detailed, identifying ten or more carefully quantified segments, created by cross-referencing a number of segmentation bases; or it can simply classify customers intuitively into two types. British Rail segments its customers into three groups: realists, fatalists and analysts (Elgie 1990). Since rail journeys have often been used as a metaphor for the journey through life, this simple classification is perhaps an appropriate starting point for a discussion of consumer types in relation to the environment.

Demographic segmentation

Much of the discussion of environmental concern and green consumption has been based around socio-economic and other demographic divisions. This is despite the fact that several studies have found no significant link (Kinnear *et al* 1974, Gerstman and Meyers 1981, Neuman 1986). Samdahl (1989) characterises the relationship between socio-demographic characteristics and environmental concern as 'still poorly understood'.

Socio-economic grouping

In much of the industrialised world there has been a continuing belief that concern for the environment is primarily a 'middle-class' attitude. This is partially a hangover from 1970s' environmentalism which was demonstrably strongest among the middle classes. In the UK, figures produced for the National Trust in 1973 and the RSPB in 1979 showed that 96 per cent and 66 per cent of their respective memberships were accounted for by people in the ABC_1 socio-economic grouping (Lowe and Goyder 1983). Another 1982 study of environmentalist group membership revealed it to be strongly skewed towards students, the self-employed and those in service, welfare or creative professions (Cotgrove 1982). Such studies have been used to justify the labelling of green consumers as 'middle class'. However, there are dangers inherent in using environmental group membership as a proxy measure for environmental concern. There is a marked tendency among the middle classes to form and support voluntary organisations in general (Stacey 1960, Goldthorpe et al 1969), which in the case of pressure groups may reflect more widespread concern.

Demographic factors

One of the reasons why attempts to segment consumers on demographic bases have not been more successful probably relates to the fact that different types of people relate to different parts of the environmental agenda. The 1986 UK Department of the Environment (DoE) Survey on attitudes towards the environment examined concern about sixteen different issues, and broke the results down by age, sex, social class and area of residence. The survey produced the most surprising results in relation to social class. It was unskilled workers who were the most deeply concerned on half of all the environmental threats mentioned in the survey. This contradicts the accepted wisdom that the middle classes are the bastion of environmental concern. In terms of social class, the grouping expressing the strongest concern on each issue varied as shown in Table 9.1.

Gender

In the DoE study the differences between men and women were relatively slight, with women being one or two percentage points more concerned on most issues, but markedly more concerned about nuclear waste, litter and fouling dogs. In terms of

Table 9.1 Concern for the environment, according to occupational group (1986)

Group	Nature	Greatest concern
1	Professional occupations	Chemicals in rivers; urban decay; factory fumes (jointly)
2	Intermediate occupations	Car exhaust
3	Skilled non-manual work	Agrochemicals; factory fumes (jointly)
4	Skilled manual work	Nuclear waste; dirty beaches; acid rain
5	Unskilled	Loss of wildlife; litter; oil slicks; fouling dogs; hedge loss; traffic noise; ugly new buildings; countryside access

environmentally responsible behaviour, Hines et al (1987), commenting on four surveys, found no relationship with gender. This is in marked contrast to other studies. Schann and Holzer's (1990) study of German consumers found that although women knew less about environmental problems, in terms of concern and behavioural response they were significantly ahead of men.

Age

The 1986 DoE survey showed the 18 to 24 age group to be less concerned about most green issues than adults aged 25 to 64, except on the issue of loss of wildlife. By the late 1980s, concern among young adults in particular had broadened. Research 2000 found that young adults (aged 16 to 24) were more concerned about environmental issues which were global and of concern to the future of the planet, such as ozone depletion, global warming, deforestation, nuclear power and chemical waste. Older consumers aged 65 and over were more concerned with local and current environmental problems such as litter, air pollution, traffic congestion and noise. The 18 to 24 age group was generally more concerned than the over-65s on most of the issues.

A 1987 McCann–Erikson survey contrasted the attitudes of the 15 to 19 age group (New Wavers) with the 20 to 35 age group (the Baby Boomers). Concern for the environment was expressed by 54 per cent of New Wavers compared to 61 per cent of Baby Boomers, and the New Wavers showed greater enthusiasm for market forces and less enthusiasm about state control. This suggests that the 1980s have produced a generation with an interest in the environment, who will seek to tackle it more through their purchasing power than through a belief in state control.

Lifestage segmentation

Although age is a popular basis on which to segment markets, it is not necessarily a reliable choice for the environmental marketer. Hines *et al* (1987), analysing ten different studies, found only a tenuous relationship between age and environmentally related behaviour. There is an argument that age is not an influence on people's consumption behaviour as much as an indication of the 'lifestage' that people have reached. It does not matter, therefore, if people are 25, 35 or 45, if they are parents of young children they are likely to be buying a whole range of products for the first time (and putting a range of other products away in a safe place to be consumed again some years later when life returns to something like normal); and they may begin to worry about the consequences of their purchase decisions on the environment of the future.

Geographic segmentation

Although environmental problems do not respect human geo-political boundaries, experience of the environment and the green challenge does vary geographically. Water supply is the key concern in many African countries; water quality worries many European consumers; while water levels in relation to the greenhouse effect occupies the thoughts of low lying areas such as the Maldives. Such differences translate into different concerns among consumers. Fiori (1989) compared consumers from Spain, France, the UK and Germany.

She contrasted the four countries on lifestyle habits, such as smoking or pressure group membership, product use and product availability to compare greenness. She found some wide variations. While the UK was the lowest for recycling, it was the best for availability of organic produce. Spain scored poorly on many of the criteria, and was the only country where lead-free petrol was more expensive than leaded, but it was second only to Germany in the use of returnable bottles. Germany had by far the largest membership for Greenpeace, but only in Spain had a lower percentage voted for the Green Party in the 1989 European Election. Green products were well established in most German markets, with the exception of organic produce which had the lowest availability. In France many green products were at a relatively embryonic stage, but 53 per cent of consumers claimed to choose 'environmentally friendly' products, and the growth in markets such as CFC-free aerosols had been very rapid. Often the differences between nations in terms of overall environmental concern are relatively slight, while there are considerable differences over specific issues. While Britons are highly concerned about water pollution, Swedes worry about acid rain and Germans worry about the links between the environment and personal health.

At a national level there can be differences between metropolitan, urban and rural dwellers. In the 1986 UK attitude survey (DoE 1986) these were relatively slight, with some predictable exceptions. Whereas litter was a much lower priority for rural dwellers, hedgerow loss was relatively important, and metropolitan dwellers were markedly more concerned about urban decay and car exhaust.

Psychographic segmentation

Lifestyle

A person's lifestyle will partly reflect his or her demographic characteristics and culture, but it will also reflect a person's activities, interests and opinions. Products aimed at particular 'lifestyles' became a popular segmentation approach during the 1980s, particularly among manufacturers of food products and consumer durables. Volkswagen, for example, developed a car for the 'good citizen' which emphasised economy, safety and eco-performance. Since the environmental impact of consumption relates as much to people's lifestyles and product use as to their purchases, categorising people according to their lifestyle may prove useful.

Level of education

There is a belief that environmental concern is directly related to a consumer's level of education. Balderjahn (1988) found that household energy-saving behaviour was strongly influenced by level of education. Samdahl and Robertson (1989) found the reverse to be true and in a study of over 2000 residents of Illinois found a negative correlation between educational level and perceptions of environmental problems and support for environmental regulations. Perhaps this reflects that, until recently, outside of the environmental sciences, relatively little education was given over to an appreciation or understanding of the environment. Typically environmental issues are most prevalent in the schooling of young children, which all consumers share, but this declines drastically with progress through the educational system. The farm worker who left school at 16 is therefore quite likely to have a much deeper understanding of the environment than a marketing director with an MBA in an agrochemicals company. New initiatives to integrate the environment into education, such as the Toyne Report in the UK (Toyne 1993), may bring a stronger correlation between education and environmental concern in future. A higher level of education also typically brings the economic power to insulate the individual from many of the effects of environmental degradation, in the short term at least. While well educated managers might live in the suburbs, therefore, less educated people within city centres or rural districts may have a greater experience of environmental degradation in their daily lives.

Personality

Another interesting and popular challenge is to try and define a 'personality profile' for the green consumer (Henion 1976). Anderson and Cunningham (1972) studied socially conscious consumers and looked for demographic and socio-psychological predictors of socially responsible consumption. This approach was followed up by Kinnear *et al* in 1974. They found that ecological concern related less to socio-economic variables, and more to personality traits. Such early green consumers were often characterised by an openness to new ideas and a strong desire to understand how things work. Hines *et al* (1987) found that a sense of personal responsibility was an important influence on environmentally related behaviour. Personality traits are often grouped together to form three basic types.

1 *Tradition-directed* – behaviour which follows well established patterns making it easy to predict. Dunlap and Van Liere (1984) found that those least concerned about the environment were traditionalists in terms of supporting key elements of the 'dominant social paradigm' such as support for laissez-faire government and private property rights along with a belief in economic growth and material abundance.

2 *Outer-directed* – often thought of as behaviour which seeks to conform to society, one's peer group or some other third party. Balderjahn (1988) sees the 'socialisation conditions' within which consumers operate as important, and affected by factors such as number of friends, friends' social status and place of residence. At a broader level, since society is itself grey at present, green behaviour is not exactly about conformism. Balderjahn views green consumers as relatively 'alienated from the core culture'. So perhaps outer-directed green consumers are concerned about the future of society, without wanting to conform to its current values. Webster (1975) linked socially responsible consumption to high levels of 'social involvement' among consumers.

3 *Inner-directed* – behaviour which aims to please oneself first and foremost without

reference to others. Green consumption was initially considered as something of a 'self-indulgent' form of consumer behaviour involving self-actualisation or conscience salving. More recently the link between environment and health put much greater emphasis on green consumption to protect personal health and welfare, and in this sense is becoming more inner-directed.

The basic idea behind psychographic segmentation is that it is who we are that will determine what we will or will not buy. A reversal of this concept comes from the sociology of consumption literature in which it is proposed that consumers create and maintain a sense of personal identity through their purchases (Baudrillard 1988, Bocock 1993). So purchases determine identity, not vice versa. This has profound implications for the attempts to limit consumption in the face of environmental concern.

> 'This suggests that *there are no limits to consumption*. If it was that which it was naïvely taken to be, an absorption, a devouring, then we should achieve satisfaction. But we know that this is not the case: we want to consume more and more. This compulsion to consume is not the consequence of some psychological determinant etc., nor is it simply the power of emulation. If consumption appears to be irrepressible, this is because it is a total idealistic practice which has no longer anything to do (beyond a certain point) with the satisfaction of needs.' (Baudrillard 1988)

Baudrillard sees consumption not in terms of pre-existing needs, but as a symbolic process in itself in which the idea and anticipation of consumption are as important as the actual act of consumption and where 'the more they consume, the more they will desire to consume' (Bocock 1993).

Ogilvy & Mather developed a typology which combines demographics and psychographics to create four general segments.

1 *Activists* (16 per cent of the population). Typical profile:

● aware of green issues; likely to buy green products and services;

● concerned for their children;

● believe in people;

● optimistic about future technological development;

● place environmental protection above economic growth;

● home owners with older children;

● Conservative voters;

● relatively up-market consumers.

2 *Realists* (34 per cent). Typical profile:

● young parents;

● worried about the environment;

● perceive a conflict between profit and environmental protection;

● not confident that problems will be resolved;

● sceptical of the 'green bandwagon';

● Labour/Liberal voters.

3 *Complacents* (28 per cent). Typical profile:

● up-market consumers with older children;

● optimistic about mankind, business and government;

● see the solution as somebody else's problem;

● not very aware of green issues;

● to the right politically.

4 *Alienated* (22 per cent). Typical profile:

● less well educated, down-market consumers;

● young families and senior citizens;

● unaware of green issues;

● view green concern as a transient issue;

● pessimistic about possible solutions;

● to the left politically.

Behaviouristic segmentation

While geographic, demographic and psychographic segmentation describes customers in terms of their characteristics, behaviouristic segmentations classify customers according to what they do. Even a company that has not even heard of segmentation will categorise the available market into two behaviour-based segments – people who buy from us and everybody else. One method that is popularly used is to segment people according to the degree to which environmental concerns influence their purchasing behaviour. Although potentially interesting, this approach does not help to predict people's purchasing behaviour since it already describes it. One behaviour which Hines *et al* (1987) found to be a reasonably good predictor of environmentally responsible behaviour was the verbal expression of good intentions.

The way in which knowledge of environmental problems is reflected in people's behaviour varies considerably. Environmental concerns may be dismissed to allow behaviour to be continued as before, behaviour may be modified to accommodate the environmental concern, or behaviour may be changed to respond to the concern. This is demonstrated by responses to the thinning of the ozone layer and the increasing threat of skin cancers caused by overexposure to ultraviolet radiation. A visit to a beach in midsummer will demonstrate that many people are denying the problem to enable them to 'lie and fry' as before. Others will be adapting by plastering themselves and their children with sunscreen.

Marketing Diagnostics define green consumers in terms of four different behaviour-related shades of green:

- *Green activists*: members or supporters of environmental organisations (5 to 15 per cent of the population).

- *Green thinkers*: will look for new ways to help the environment and seek out green products and services (up to 30 per cent of the population including activists).

- *Green consumer base*: includes anyone who has changed his or her consuming behaviour in response to green concerns (45 to 60 per cent of the population).

- *Generally concerned*: people claiming to be concerned about green issues (includes almost 90 per cent of the population).

Neilssen and Scheepers' (1992) research in The Netherlands found distinctive clusters of consumers who varied in both their environmental consciousness and their environmentally related behaviour in relation to energy consumption, consumption of green products, use of transportation and disposal of rubbish. This allowed the identification of four distinct segments (which map relatively well on to the segments suggested by Fig. 9.1):

1 *Consistent non-ecologists* (24 per cent).

2 *Inconsistent-consciousness ecologists* (34 per cent): who profess concern about the environment but have not translated this into any changes in behaviour.

3 *Inconsistent-behaviour ecologists* (20 per cent): who are strongly concerned about the environment and have begun to change their behaviour in response.

4 *Consistent ecologists* (22 per cent): who back up strong ecological consciousness with a willingness to translate it into action.

These segments were demonstrably linked into socio-economic and political factors. The consistent non-ecologists and inconsistent-consciousness ecologists were more likely to be those with the lowest incomes, while the inconsistent-behaviour ecologists were more likely to include the higher skilled and higher paid workers and socialist voters. Consistent ecologists were more likely to be older consumers and those with green political leanings.

THE ROLE OF ENVIRONMENTAL KNOWLEDGE

Another popular attempt to explain differences in purchasing behaviour in relation to green issues is in terms of knowledge. The theory is that consumers who are knowledgeable about environmental problems will be motivated towards green consumer behaviour. This is a difficult relationship to prove, however. Martin and Simintiras (1994) comment on a number of attempts to examine the link between environmental knowledge and behaviour in the early 1970s and conclude that they fail to identify any clear link. Krause (1993) discovered that the ability of people to answer questions on environmental issues correctly did not correlate with professed environmental concern (although a broader range of questions may have changed this result).

The problems stem partly from the difficulties of measuring environmental knowledge, and partly from the fact that general knowledge about environmental problems does not necessarily translate consistently into specific consumer behaviour. Hines *et al* (1987) found that it was not simply knowledge of the environmental issues which influenced consumer behaviour, but also awareness of the action strategies needed to respond to the issue. Similarly Schann and Holzer (1990) in a study of German consumers found that while abstract knowledge about environmental problems did not affect the relationship between attitudes and behaviour, what they term 'concrete' knowledge concerning action strategies and potential solutions did. For the environmental marketer to benefit from environmental knowledge among consumers, the link between a specific environmental problem and the attributes of the product or company as part of the solution may need to be made very clearly and explicitly.

Amyx *et al* (1994) found that subjective knowledge about the environment was a better predictor of green purchasing intentions than objective knowledge. In other words the people who thought they knew about environmental problems were more likely to buy green than the people who really knew about the problems. Those with higher levels of subjective knowledge were generally those with higher incomes (which helps when it comes to targeting) but there was no clear link between higher levels of subjective knowledge and individuals' age, education, gender or home ownership (which doesn't help when targeting). They also identified an ultra-green segment who have a lifestyle highly orientated towards the environment, and suggest that this segment may be worth companies trying to exploit, although success here would very much depend on reaching that segment with a credible green offering.

THE ROLE OF ATTITUDES TOWARDS THE ENVIRONMENT

Attitude towards the environment is another popular choice as a suggested predictor of green consumption. Research again throws doubt on this seemingly logical proposition, however. Hines *et al* (1987) analysed 51 studies dating from 1971, and found only a moderate correlation between attitudes towards the environment and environmentally sensitive behaviour. However, Martin and Simintiras (1994) point out that many of these studies measure general environmental concern while purchase decisions will relate to specific environmental issues. A consumer, therefore, who is generally concerned about the environment but not particularly concerned about animal welfare, might be happy to consume veal and might not buy free-range eggs. An animal lover with no general interest in the environment might be careful to seek out free-range eggs and avoid veal. This makes it important when segmenting consumers on the basis of attitudes to do it on the basis of attitudes to issues which relate directly to the product and its attributes (including the producer and production processes involved) rather than on environmental awareness and attitudes in general.

Environmental attitudes are themselves shaped by a number of influences beyond knowledge. Feldman (1988) found that core beliefs shaped attitudes, and Eckberg and Blocker (1989) found religious beliefs to have a significant influence. Krause (1993) implies that where once environmental attitudes were shaped by information that people received from external sources, increasingly the realities of their environment and people's personal experience are shaping their attitudes. Therefore even 'those who did not get angry about the slaughter of baby seals in Alaska, or who were not worried about the disappearing rain forests in Brazil, began to pay attention when their own community's air became dangerous to breathe, when local beaches began to close in summer because of polluted water, or when they began to face restrictions on home water use because of shortages.' The 'nearness to home' of

Table 9.2 A green segmentation of the UK Market (1989)

Group	Level of knowledge and concern	Comparison with 1988	Main environmental concerns	Comments
Girls 15	Low – main focus is on self	Same	Animals – cosmetic testing; whale and seal hunting	Could grow into green consumers later on
Men 16–22	Moderate concern, but limited personal involvement	Increased knowledge	Whatever the current media focus is on	Cynical about government and manufacturers' motives
Women 18–30	Moderate	Increasing knowledge, trial of green products	General	Will try green products, but can revert if functional performance is poor
Women under 30, 1 child	High	Growing activity – definitely becoming greener	Those affecting children's health: food production, pesticides, leaded petrol	The most obvious green consumers
Women 35–45 Children 13–18	High	Growing knowledge and activity	All major issues that will affect their children's future	Children acting as educators
Retired men and women	High	Increased knowledge and activity	Deterioration in quality of life	'Have to regard the fight for the environment like the Blitz – all do your bit'
Men and women 25–45 embarrassed capitalists	High	Growing sense of individual responsibility. Greater knowledge	General – depends on media focus	Environmental concern becoming normalised
Men and women (no children at home)	High	Growing concern	Environmental issues have become the greatest threat of the 20th century (replacing communism)	Every little bit helps

Source: Brand New and Diagnostics Market Research

the perceived threats was found to influence attitudes by Grieshop and Stiles (1989) and Gunter and Finlay (1988).

SEGMENTING GREEN INDUSTRIAL MARKETS

It is not only consumers that can be grouped into segments. Companies can be segmented on a variety of bases including location, size, age and level of technology. Drumwright (1994) examined environmental concern as a buying criterion in companies, noting that, like consumers, the majority of organisations see themselves as environmentally concerned. She found green purchasing to be stimulated by a corporate context in which social and environmental concern was viewed as an extension of the founder's ideals or where it was viewed as a symbolically important component of corporate strategy. In terms of targeting corporate buyers, Drumwright's results suggest that purchasing managers are likely to respond to socially responsible buying opportunities that relate to socio-environmental issues that are perceived as relevant to the company's core businesses.

SEGMENTING GREEN MARKETS – MISSION IMPOSSIBLE?

In trying to segment markets into consumer groups who vary in their environmental concerns and the way in which these influence their consumption behaviour, market researchers have tended to combine a range of segmentation bases. Table 9.2 shows a segmentation of the UK market developed in 1989 by Brand New and Diagnostics Market Research which uses a combination of demographic, lifestyle and lifestage approaches. Relating such segmentations to the purchase of individual products poses a challenge. A key problem is that the same purchase can be made for many different motives. For example, the major reason behind the purchase of a BMW could be:

- *prestige* – for the insecure;
- *reliability* – for the mechanically inept;
- *comfort* – for the high mileage user;
- *safety* – for those prone to worry;
- *eco-performance* – for the green consumer who cannot do without a car.

It could also be a combination of several of these factors, each of which will be influenced by the consumer's demographic profile, personality traits, lifestyle and lifestage, knowledge, attitudes, values, past experiences and social contacts. No wonder trying to explain green consumer behaviour is so difficult.

Analysing all the research that has been conducted into the driving forces of environmental concern and green consumer behaviour, it becomes clear that there are no easy answers. Many of the studies exhibit conflicting results; others fail to find consistent relationships and the interactions that are revealed are usually complex and require further research to untangle. Perhaps the answer is that consumer behaviour in relationship to the environment can only be understood holistically, and will not reveal itself in any neat and demonstrable interplay of cause and effect that can be isolated by adherence to the scientific method. This would be altogether appropriate.

ECO-POSITIONING

We exist within the world of our perceptions, and everything that we know and think is held in our minds in a vast array of perceptual maps. What a given word means, how far one place is from another, the nature of people of different races and regions are all mapped out within our minds. As each of us matures and learns, we will learn to position words closer to their true meanings, to visualise relative distances accurately and to understand the differences between peoples in terms of cultural diversity rather than simple prejudice.

The products and services that we consume are similarly positioned on a mental map which also includes the known direct and indirect competitors of that product. Our mental maps are multidimensional, and a product will be positioned relative to its rivals on dimensions such as price, value, durability, convenience, reliability and after-sales service. Consumers position products within their perceptual maps on the basis of their experience of the product or the information that they receive about it. This provides marketers with an opportunity to influence the position which their product occupies within the consumer's mind by using the management of the marketing mix proactively to position or reposition the product.

There are a number of positioning strategies that can be adopted.

1 *Find a new position.* By mapping out the various products within a market it may be possible to identify an undefended gap in the market-place and then fill it. Since environmental performance is a relatively new performance dimension in many markets, there are frequently opportunities to find a new position as a green product, or beyond that a green high-performance product, or a green low-cost product.

2 *Reposition the product.* A great deal of advertising expenditure is taken up with attempts to challenge people's preconceptions about a brand and to reposition it. This is notoriously difficult to do by advertising, and is perhaps more successful through sales promotions aimed at stimulating trial and altering people's perceptions of a product by giving them a new experience of it.

3 *Reposition the competition.* It may be possible to reposition a product's competitors to their detriment by challenging their credibility. Shanks and McEwen's lobbying campaign to introduce tougher controls on eco-performance in the waste disposal industry has involved repositioning many of its competitors as environmentally irresponsible.

4 *Position close to the market leader.* Where it is unlikely that a product can credibly reposition itself ahead of the market-leading brands, it may be possible to position the product as close as possible to the market leader on one dimension and build an advantage on another. The Boots Natural Collection was sufficiently similar in its packaging and promotion to be seen as an attempt to position itself very closely to The Body Shop.

The golden rule when attempting to position or reposition a product through marketing communications is to keep the message simple. Consumers in the information age are bombarded and frequently overloaded with information.

The green challenge, and the growing importance of eco-performance has not only provided a new and important dimension to our perceptual maps, it has challenged many of the existing positioning dimensions. In extreme cases greening can invert a particular dimension, or, using the ladder analogy that is popular in envisaging positioning, it can turn the ladder upside down. A product which previously used disposability as a positive means of positioning, may find that a shift to greener values leaves it lagging behind companies who instead emphasise reusability. The challenge for the marketer is to isolate the key dimensions which influence the buying decisions of consumers and attempt to position their product offering ahead of the competition. Being positioned poorly on environmental performance can be an expensive business to correct. When McDonald's became widely, but mistakenly, associated with rainforest destruction, it had to mount one of the largest customer education programmes of all time.

The concept of an eco-position for a product is a relatively new idea, which relates to relatively few products as yet. On the technical/economic axis of the STEP Framework (*see* Chapter 1), the positioning of a product depends on the degree to which the product is perceived as potentially relevant as a solution to a particular problem or need. Eco-positioning of a product along the social/physical environment axis depends on the consumer's perception of the product and producer in relation to environmental and social problems and their potential solutions (*see* Fig. 9.2). The eco-position and market position of products will tend to be separate entities in the minds of consumers living in a culture where economics and the environment are kept artificially separate. As the importance of the relationship between the environment, society and the economy becomes increasingly clear, so the market positions and eco-positions of products and companies will begin to merge in consumers' minds. An excellent market position may not be compromised by a poor eco-position today, but this may not hold true tomorrow. The more a company can distance itself and its products away from environmental problems and towards their solution, the stronger their eco-position will be.

BRANDING

A brand is a name, symbol, design or image which identifies the product of a particular business and helps to communicate its competitive advantage. Loyalty to a particular brand helps to simplify the buying process for the consumer. Instead of having to analyse a product against a range of performance attributes in order to evaluate it each time a purchase is made, loyalty to a particular brand allows the consumer to forget the detailed reasons why they buy a particular brand. The only question they need to answer when purchasing is 'Which brand do I prefer?'

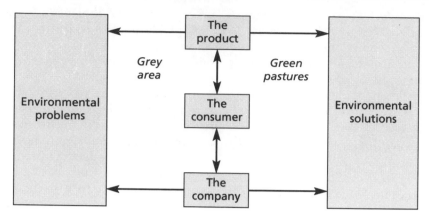

Fig. 9.2 The eco-positioning challenge

The aim of positioning is to put the company's brand at the top of the customer's actual or mental list of alternatives, or, better still, to have it named as the preferred purchase on the shopping list. A particular brand might be purchased by a consumer because it has become fashionable, regardless of its performance in comparison to the competition.

Creating successful green brands

One problem for the environmental marketer of a new product is that the process of branding tends to entrench patterns of demand for established brands backed by heavy promotional investment. New products launched by relatively unknown companies often find it difficult to wrest market share away from the household names. It can be easier for a trusted brand to realign itself as green, than for a green brand to gain consumer trust. When under attack from new green detergent products, Fairy Liquid both addressed the green challenge and reasserted its trusted nature by stressing on its package that it was biodegradable, and always had been.

Technological innovation is perhaps the best way to create a green brand and to compete with established household brands. Emerging green brands are often then faced with green product variants being launched by household brand names, however. While DKK Schjar-fenstein's future seemed assured by the launch of the 'green fridge', within a matter of months major European appliance manufacturers were launching their own equivalents and business growth for the German fridge manufacturer suffered a reversal. The increasing rate of technological change means that products and their capabilities are changing at such a rate that manufacturers may be unable to rely on individual products having more than a few months' demonstrable competitive advantage. This has led to manufacturers attempting to build brands around the relatively enduring aspects of their companies as opposed to the more transient products and technologies. This shift towards the company being the brand is clearly very much in line with the move towards environmental marketing in which the whole company has become the product.

These new company brands of the 1990s and beyond will attempt to communicate the identity of the business, its values and its philosophy in a way that will position itself, and all its current and future product offerings, in the mind of consumers. The interest that the green consumer takes in how the product is made has already been reflected in a demand for products from businesses with a good environmental track record.

CASE STUDY

McDonald's

McDonald's is one of the most successful marketing organisations that the world has yet seen and it is also one of the companies that has been most profoundly affected by green consumer pressure. The McDonald's story demonstrates how association with environmental problems can position a company poorly, and the challenge that repositioning a company on the basis of environmental excellence represents. McDonald's also shows how environmental initiatives need to be reflected in different elements of the marketing mix, and as such it provides a suitable introduction to Part Three of the book dealing with the environmental marketing mix.

In the 1970s, when dwindling resources were a key environmental issue, McDonald's switched from paper-based containers to polystyrene containers made from petroleum waste in an effort to 'save trees'. During the 1980s concern about the volume of plastics in landfills, and the ozone damage caused by the use of CFCs as agents for blowing plastic foam to make polystyrene, left the McDonald's hamburger box as a focus for environmental pressure. Despite switching to non-CFC blown foam containers in 1988, and establishing a pilot polystyrene recycling programme in its New England outlets, McDonald's came under continuing environmentalist pressure. In the USA, McDonald's heartland, a nationwide campaign was launched in which children mailed their old polystyrene clamshells back to the corporate headquarters in Illinois. The company responded with the creation of a 'Solid Waste Task Force' in conjunction with leading green group, the Environmental Defense Fund (EDF). This produced a 42-point action plan which included the replacement of polystyrene containers with paper and plastic-quilted wraps. These were lighter and more compact and created a 70 per cent saving in landfill space. The environmental downside of the wraps was that being made of a composite material they could not easily be recycled.

When the shift away from polystyrene came, McDonald's was quick to underline the customer orientation which was behind its decision. Company President, Edward H. Rensi, explained that the switch was made 'because our customers asked us to'. The decision came under attack from many who debated the environmental merit of the change. The decision also proved a major setback for the emerging US plastics recycling industry whose future plans had been highly dependent on McDonald's contribution to the plastic recycling process. The partnership with the EDF proved to be particularly valuable for McDonald's when faced with this sort of criticism. In the face of controversy over the switch away from polystyrene the unsolicited support for McDonald's provided by EDF executive director, Fred Krupps, ensured that a potential public relations disaster left McDonald's looking responsive to customers and responsible towards the environment.

Burger packaging was not the only element of McDonald's eco-performance to come under attack. The McDonald's hamburger itself became the focus of environmentalist criticism with claims that beef for McDonald's hamburgers came from ranches established on cleared rainforest land within Amazonia. This prompted McDonald's to launch a massive consumer education counter-attack. Newspaper advertisements, in-store posters, tray liners and 'McFact Cards' were produced to highlight McDonald's efforts on abandoning the use of CFC-blown foam, on recycling and to dispel fears about the source of McDonald's beef. At the peak of its customer education programme the campaign was reaching 18 million customers each day, making McDonald's the biggest environmental educator in history. With the McFact Card Number One, McDonald's met the claims about rainforest destruction head-on by saying:

▶

'Let's put the record straight. Nowhere in the world does McDonald's use of beef threaten or remotely involve the tropical rainforests ... McDonald's restaurants in Central and South America ... only use suppliers who document that their beef has come from long established cattle ranches – not rainforest land.'

The card concludes with a pledge:

'The Company will continue to monitor and adapt policies and practices as necessary to protect the global environment on which we all depend.'

This commitment has prompted McDonald's greening efforts to go far beyond its original concerns related to the packaging which delivers its products into the hands of the customer. Some 80 per cent of the waste generated by McDonald's is relatively invisible to customers since it occurs on the other side of the counter. In the early 1990s pilot projects looking at composting were established, together with schemes to experiment with the use of refillable cups and biodegradable cutlery. In 1993 the company was even testing out vegetarian burgers in The Netherlands. What had begun with concerns about the impact of post-consumer packaging waste ended with initiatives to improve eco-performance in terms of waste-processing, customer service and even changes to the product offerings. It is therefore not surprising to find that McDonald's went from being a key target for environmentalist pressure during the 1980s to being voted the greenest fast food firm in the *Advertising Age* and Gallup consumer surveys in the 1990s.

PART 3

Environmental marketing: the operational challenge

CHAPTER 10

Less is more – green products

'The family which takes its mauve and cerise, air-conditioned, power-steered, and power-braked automobile out for a tour passes through cities that are badly paved, made hideous by litter, blighted buildings, and posts for wires that should long since have been put underground. They pass on into a countryside that has been rendered largely invisible by commercial art. They picnic on exquisitely packaged food from a portable icebox, by a polluted stream and go on to spend the night at a park which is a menace to public health and morals. Just before dozing off on an air mattress, beneath a nylon tent, amid the stench of decaying refuse, they may vaguely reflect on the curious unevenness of their blessings.'
(John Kenneth Galbraith, 1968)

INTRODUCTION

The product is the cornerstone of the marketing mix. It does not matter how attractive the price is, how persuasive the marketing communications effort is, or how accessible the product is; if the customer does not want the product, all else is in vain. Changes to conventional grey products and the emergence of new green products have been two of the main areas of activity in response to the green challenge. Vandermerwe and Oliff's (1991) survey of multinational companies revealed that 92 per cent had changed their products in response to the green challenge. Table 10.1 shows the growth in new green product introductions in the USA. In some markets the importance of green products is greater than such averages would suggest. For example, while in the USA in 1991 13.4 per cent of packaged goods made some green claims, for household products the proportion reached a startling 44 per cent.

A wide variety of products are now being marketed on the basis of their eco-performance. Where once it was the province of 'alternative' brands, retailers' shelves are now increasingly populated with green products from mainline brands. I can now word-process this book on a 'Green PC' from IBM, wearing my 'Rugged Wear Earth Wash Jeans' from Wrangler and sipping Coca-Cola from a bottle made from 25 per cent recycled PET (polyethylene terephalate); or, if I need a break, I can go skiing in a pair of Benetton's Nordic ski boots made from recycled materials, or watch a totally recyclable television set from Grundig.

Table 10.1 The growth in green product introductions

	Number of US green product introductions	Green share of all product introductions (%)
1985	24	0.5
1986	60	1.1
1987	122	2.0
1988	160	2.8
1989	262	4.5
1990	728	11.4
1991	810	13.4

Source: Marketing Intelligence Services

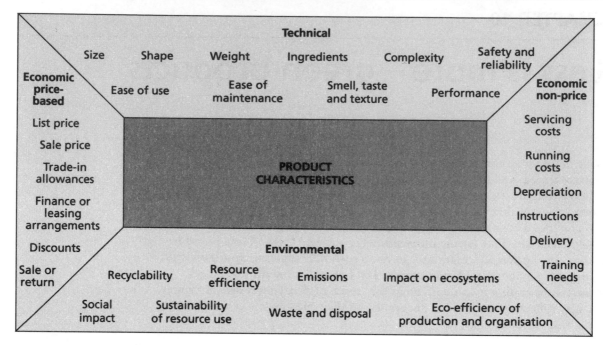

Fig. 10.1 Product characteristics
(adapted from Rothwell *et al* (1983) and Evans and Berman (1982))

PERSPECTIVES ON PRODUCTS

Kotler (1994) defines a product as 'anything that can be offered to a market for attention, acquisition, use, or consumption that might satisfy a want or need'. Such a wide definition covers everything which can be marketed including physical products, services, people, places, organisations and ideas. The emphasis on markets, consumption, wants, needs and satisfactions makes this an essentially economic view of goods and services, as outputs of a production or service delivery process, and as inputs into a consumption process. The technical/economic view of products has dominated marketing thought and is reflected in the definition of product characteristics provided by Rothwell *et al* (1983). In keeping with the spirit of the STEP Framework (*see* Chapter 1), it is possible to take some alternative views of what a product represents. A useful first step is to expand Rothwell's framework by adding in the environmental characteristics which define the sustainability of the product (*see* Fig. 10.1).

A physical view of products: products as a combination of resources

Every product is created by bringing resources together. In classical economics, production involves the combination of land (natural resources), labour (human resources) and capital (financial resources). In marketing terms it is more usual to consider products in terms of the relative contribution made by intangible service components and tangible physical components. Although 'goods and services' are typically spoken of as alternatives, most products can be located on a continuum of tangible/ intangible inputs. Products vary in the degree to which they are physical product or service orientated. A product may be:

- *a pure physical product* (for example, a box of soap powder);
- *a physical product supported by services* (car marketing is supported by after-sales service);
- *a service supported by physical products* (during an evening's entertainment in a restaurant, the food will be a key component);

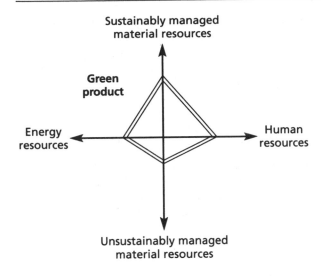

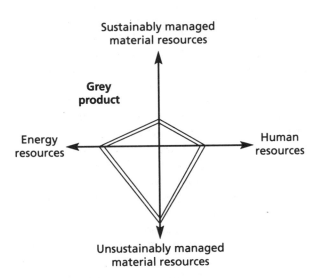

Fig. 10.2 A resource consumption profile

- *a pure service* (such as a haircut).

The green challenge may relocate consumers' purchasing tendencies on this spectrum, away from relatively resource-hungry goods towards seeking satisfaction through more labour-intensive services. However, this approach is slightly simplistic, because it ignores the actual environmental implications of manufacturing compared

to service delivery. A product that is manufactured in a sustainable manner from renewable and recyclable resources can be relatively green. A service delivered in an over-heated, brightly lit retail environment which uses and discards a great deal of non-renewable materials in creating in-store displays can be relatively environmentally hostile. Attempting to create a more balanced picture of the resource implications of different forms of business, we can divide the resources consumed into four groups: human resources, energy, renewable materials and non-renewable materials. This can be plotted on a matrix (Fig. 10.2) to provide profiles of the resource consumption impact of different types of product.

Another effect of the green challenge will be to change the nature of the physical resources that are brought together to form products. Environmentally harmful ingredients will gradually be replaced by less harmful ingredients, and eventually by environmentally benign alternatives. For example, CFCs in air-conditioning systems are being replaced by HCFCs (which generally break down before reaching the stratosphere, thereby reducing ozone layer damage) in the short term, while companies work on systems which use water as a refrigerant. While it is conventional to market a product on the basis of inherent or added features and benefits, environmental marketing is unusual in its emphasis on the removal or absence of disbenefits. Products marketed on the basis of what they do not contain include lead-free petrol, additive-free foods and cruelty-free cosmetics.

A combination of environmental concern and market mechanisms will also lead to scarce and non-renewable resources being designed out of products, and reclaimed or waste materials replacing virgin raw materials. Product designers are already exhibiting considerable ingenuity in the reuse of materials. Déjà Shoes, based in Oregon USA, has developed a shoe with a sole made from old tyres, an upper made from the plastic leftovers from the manufacture of disposable nappies, eyelets made from recycled metal, and a range of other green ingredients including recycled brown paper and used coffee filters.

A societal view of products: products as symbols

Levy (1957) observed that 'people buy things not only for what they can do, but also for what they mean'. Levitt (1970) viewed products as 'promises of satisfaction', his famous example being that consumers do not buy quarter-inch drills – they buy the ability to make quarter-inch holes (although from personal experience of home improvement, possession of a tool does not necessarily equate with an ability to do the job). A societal view of products puts the satisfaction that products provide in the social quadrant, rather than the conventional economic and technical quadrants, of the STEP Framework (*see* Chapter 1). In other words a consumer might buy a particular drill in order to make an impression rather than a hole.

Many forms of product have a social/psychological meaning which can symbolise a consumer's age, gender, social position, ethnic origin and aspirations. Symbolic consumption reached new heights during the 1980s with the cult of conspicuous consumption, but it remains a difficult area for marketers to deal with. The economic and technical performance of a product will be familiar and measurable, and even the environmental impact of a product can be objectively ascertained with some certainty; but the social significance of a product is highly subjective and, like its beauty, very much in the eye of the beholder.

A good example of the collision between symbolic consumption and environmental performance comes in the form of company cars. The company car allocated to a person has long been a popular surrogate measure of status. Any newcomer or visitor can be placed on a mental map of importance before they have even entered the corporate reception area, according to the make and model of car deposited in the car park. The concept that greening should be led from the top is generally endorsed by green companies, and yet this rarely goes beyond using lead-free petrol when it comes to applying a greener perspective to the company car as a corporate symbol. In a survey conducted by *Marketing* magazine, a majority of marketing managers expressed a willingness to accept a smaller company car to help to protect the environment. In practice, it is unlikely that such sentiments would be matched by actions unless the symbolic role of the company car changes.

Products as a focus: the product orientation

The marketing orientation is meant to focus a company on customer needs. This does not prevent many companies who are very enthusiastic about 'marketing' from exhibiting a product orientation. This is often demonstrated in the way that companies define themselves. It is more usual to hear managers speaking about car companies, computer companies or biscuit companies than personal mobility, information processing or taste and nutrition companies. Partly linking a company to its product makes for simpler semantics, but it also indicates deeper problems in defining a company according to the marketing orientation and the customers' needs. A key difficulty is that different customers may purchase one product to fulfil different needs. Furthermore, one product (such as a car) may be used for a variety of tasks and may meet a different set of needs at different times. The product will be the common denominator in such purchases, so it is not surprising that companies anchor themselves to it.

A product orientation can exacerbate environmental problems and also hamper their resolution. For example, in terms of energy use, the emphasis among energy producers has been to concentrate on investment to expand output, rather than in delivering the same benefits to customers through energy conservation. This is despite the fact that consumers have no need for energy itself, only for the benefits that it provides in terms of heating, lighting and the ability to operate equipment. Now energy companies are becoming aware that investment in energy saving can allow customers to satisfy their needs more cost-effectively. Power utilities such as Wisconsin Power and Light in the US have shown that the marketing of 'negawatts' (energy savings) can be more profitable than the marketing of megawatts. MacKenzie (1990), writing in *New Scientist*, showed how rising concern about CFCs prompted chemical companies to focus on the need for new (and therefore costly) replacement chemical products. However, approaching the problem from the point of view of the customer needs to be addressed, revealed that alternative and often cheaper technologies to using CFCs already existed.

Some companies have attempted to redefine themselves in terms of customer needs as a specific response to the green challenge. Where a company's products are fundamentally grey, there may be some advantages in tying the company less closely to the product. Audi Volkswagen has recently redefined its mission so that it is no longer a car company, but is now a transportation company. Such redefinitions can lead to changes to a business and the products it offers. Electrolux in Belgium has instigated a programme of installing centralised 'textile care centres' of leased washing machines in apartment buildings on the basis that people have no innate desire to own a washing machine; they simply require clean clothes. Other companies have found themselves in the strange situation of turning fairly publicly against their cherished products on account of their socio-environmental consequences – for example, Du Pont's offer of a 'reward' for the company developing the most effective CFC-substitute, or the policy of some Japanese car manufacturers of encouraging workers to use public transport to commute to reduce the traffic congestion caused by their product.

PRODUCTS, FIRMS AND THE ENVIRONMENT

The relationship between the environment, the businesses that operate within it and their products is many-faceted. It is worth noting that although we very often talk about 'the natural world', there is very little left in the world that could be labelled as 'natural'. In most cases the landscape that we see is not natural, but the result of the products that we demand and consume. The mighty grain belt of the USA and Canada is a reflection of the world's enormous demand for a variety of foods from cattle feed to bread and breakfast cereal. The land which once held over half of the world's total area of tropical rainforest stands as a monument to our demand for tropical hardwoods, cheap beef and exotic plants. Even national parks, which symbolise nature to many people, only exist in the form that they do, in order to meet people's needs for open space and beautiful landscape for recreation and leisure. The extent to which the planet on which we all depend is being rapidly reshaped by the forces of economics, marketing and technology is so profound as to be disconcerting.

The physical environment plays a range of roles in relation to the products of different types of business. The physical environment can represent the following:

● *The product.* A part of the environment is often sold or used as all or part of a product or service. Real estate transactions, visits to national parks and the trade in wild animals all involve consumption of a part of the environment. In an industry such as tourism, the environment itself forms the heart of the product offering. This helps to explain why the tourism industry is one of the few that has made a serious effort to come to terms with what sustainability will mean in practice (Peattie *et al* 1992).

● *The raison d'être of the product and/or company.* Umbrellas, suntan lotions and earthquake-proof buildings only exist because of the nature of the physical environment and the needs and wants of people in response to it. Any substantial change in the nature of the physical environment can alter the extent, nature and timing of the demand for a particular product.

● *A design influence.* Nature has continually provided inspiration for products and the technologies that go into them. The term bionics may be popularly associated with the 'Six Million Dollar Man', but it applies to the study of nature for engineering and design application. This has helped to provide us with aeroplanes, medicines, valves and building materials.

● *The supplier of raw materials and energy.* The environment supplies all the raw materials and energy that businesses rely upon. This seems a very obvious statement to make, but the 1970s' oil crises underlined the fact that the marketing plans of many businesses are based on an implicit assumption that resource supplies will not be interrupted by economic, political or environmental upheaval.

● *The production process.* For many primary producers environmental processes form part or all of the production process. In many cases natural production systems are being impaired. For agriculture, climatic instability caused by global warming, plant damage caused by pollution or ozone layer depletion, or loss of soil and soil nutrients due to erosion and salinisation, all pose a threat to the continuation of production.

● *The research and development facility.* Nature has always been an important source of new substances and innovations for companies. An obvious example is the pharmaceuticals industry, where around 25 per cent of all drugs on the market originate from rainforest plants. The disappearance of the rainforest has been likened to someone burning down one of these companies' research and development laboratories.

● *A source of product support.* Many products will simply not work without some form of support from the environment. Surfboards need waves, kites need wind, skis need snow and solar panels need direct sunlight. Environmental stability is often vital for product support. The future of the skiing industry at lower altitudes looks bleak if forecasts about global warming prove accurate.

● *A waste disposal unit.* Since matter is redistributed rather than destroyed, and since relatively little man-made material makes it into space, the environment becomes the final resting place of all products or their constituent components once they become waste.

● *A competitor for resources.* In a few industries, the environment can provide a form of competition. The European fishing industry, in the wake of over-fishing, dwindling fishstocks and increasing legal regulation of the amount of fishing they can do, tends to regard other species such as seals as key competitors.

LEVELS OF PRODUCT

When we speak about a product, we usually have a relatively narrow concept in our mind. If consumers say that yesterday they 'had a McDonald's', the chances are that they are consciously thinking about the hamburger, when in reality what they had was the 'McDonald's experience'. When a customer makes a purchase, he or she consumes more than the physical object that is carried away, or the service that is experienced. Kotler (1988) explains this in terms of different levels of product.

The *core product* provides the central benefits which satisfy the customer's primary wants or needs. Some companies are responding to the green challenge by repositioning their products to address new customer needs and wants in a way which redefines the core product. A suntan lotion in the 1990s is less the glamour-enhancing browning agent that it was in the early 1980s and is much more a skin protector. The *tangible product* includes all the elements that the customer experiences directly in consuming the core product. The early phase of environmental marketing has been relatively product-orientated and focused on their tangible dimensions. This reflects environmental concern about product packaging, quality, features and ingredients. Packaging has been an important focus for environmentalist and consumer concern, and for company response (*see* Chapter 15). The *augmented product* includes the supporting products and services which the customer consumes indirectly. A conventional core product can become greener through environmental improvements to the tangible product components which support it. Some companies are developing new green services as a means of adding a green dimension to products. Agfa in the USA launched a programme called EARTH (Environmental Awareness and a Response That Helps) which provides assistance for corporate customers with waste-disposal problems. Agfa experts will analyse effluents, assessing waste-treatment processes and suggesting any necessary improvements. Even companies with no obvious link to key environmental issues are creating green augmented products. A scheme by American Express in Italy, in which card use created an automatic charitable donation linked to a coastline conservation appeal, boosted card usage by over 20 per cent.

To these conventional three levels, environmental marketing requires the addition of a final fourth concept – the *total product*. The total product includes all the activities of the producer organisation which contribute to the creation of the augmented product. The total product includes all the organisation's hardware and software. It concerns marketers because the green consumer may reject a satisfactory augmented product due to dissatisfaction with the company that makes it. In the wake of the Exxon Valdez disaster, when former Exxon consumers boycotted Esso filling stations and returned their Exxon credit cards, they were not reacting to the augmented product which was satisfactory, but to a total product they could no longer accept.

To meet the green challenge and the new customer needs it brings, companies have now begun to change their production systems and organisations as well as their tangible products. The implication of this is that the eco-performance of a product can be improved without any form of change to the end product. Rod-and-line caught tuna is a green product because the means of production is environmentally safer than the use of drift nets. Some products can improve their eco-performance by virtue of the organisational changes that happen around them. In the USA Kodak's disposable camera was suffering because of concerns about solid waste and the resource inefficiency of disposable products. It was reborn as the 'recyclable camera' once a recycling programme was announced. The greening of production systems is the focus of Chapter 11, while the greening of the supporting organisation is discussed in Chapter 8.

CATEGORISING PRODUCTS

The world contains a seemingly infinite variety of different goods and services to be marketed. To make it possible to study marketing, it is essential to group products into categories for discussion, and 'green products' is a recent addition to the range of categories. Although it is a new classification, it also overlays the established categories of products. Therefore, one can have green industrial goods as well as green consumer goods; green consumables and green consumer durables. The process of compartmentalisation has the somewhat unfortunate effect of creating false dichotomies that products are either goods or services, either green or grey, either differentiated or undifferentiated. Such categorisations usually obscure a continuum of change with no clear boundaries. Some of the classifications of products are important to consider in the context of environmental marketing, because the green challenge and the opportunities for greening can vary significantly according to which end of a particular continuum a company's products tend towards.

Public *versus* private goods

Economic theory distinguishes between public goods (which can be enjoyed by all) and private goods (which are owned and consumed by a limited number of people). Many of the earth's resources such as land, minerals and oil reserves are treated as private goods and have well developed markets. This means that owners have property rights which can be enforced to protect the resources from external damage, or at least gain compensation for damage caused. Ownership imposes a duty on those who do not own a resource to respect it; the problem is that it imposes no duty on the owner to care for the resources, only a responsibility which can be shirked. Other public goods such as clean air and water, natural fisheries and natural landscapes have no market, or have an incomplete market which creates a danger of disruption or exhaustion from misuse (Dasgupta 1982). In general terms it is the negative externalities (or external diseconomies) involved in the marketing of private goods, which is acting to damage the public goods which we all depend upon and should have the right to consume and enjoy.

Goods *versus* services

Service industries are often referred to as being 'smokeless', and they indeed typically have a lower environmental impact per ECU of wealth created than manufacturing. This does not make the green challenge irrelevant for services. Tourism is the largest industry in the world, and it has a very direct and obvious impact on the environment. The financial services industry is another service industry that has been picked out by the environmental spotlight, particularly for its role in creating the burden of debt among less industrialised countries and the financing of environmentally damaging developments such as the power sector loans for Brazil. On the positive side, many service industries are benefiting from the green challenge. Although tourism is often associated with the destruction of beautiful areas through the process of 'Benidormisation' (overcrowding combined with uncontrolled development) the eco-tourism market is a major growth sector for the industry. By 1992 nature-orientated travel was accounting for between 4 and 6 million international trips annually among American tourists alone (Dunne 1992). Environmentally related services such as waste disposal and eco-consultancy are also major growth areas. The OECD puts the market for green services (not directly related to the installation and servicing of equipment) at $48 billion (22.4 billion ECUs) in 1990 with a forecast growth rate of 7.4 per cent (Stevens 1992). There are also opportunities for entirely new green services. In America the company Naturalawn was formed in 1987 to offer organic lawncare services to local customers in Maryland. By 1991 turnover exceeded $2 million (930 000 ECUs) and the service had been franchised into a further ten states and Canada.

Durables *versus* consumables

Tangible products can be differentiated between non-durable consumables (such as foodstuffs) which are generally consumed in one or a few uses and durable goods (such as domestic appliances) that are used many times over a long period. The environmental concerns relating to products vary with their durability. For consum-

ables the accumulation of packaging material as solid waste is a key issue, while for durable goods it is their durability as waste that causes concern. Energy efficiency is an important issue for many durables, while ingredients, such as additives in food, cause concern in consumables.

The degree to which consumer durables actually endure has become an important issue within environmental marketing (Cooper 1994). In *New Scientist* a survey examining the lifecycles of domestic appliances found that a high percentage of appliances discarded on rubbish dumps had little wrong with them and required only simple and cheap repairs (Hunkin 1988). Products can become obsolete in terms of the following factors:

● *Function.* Technological change can render products obsolete because some other product fulfils the same needs. In the production of food crops, some pesticides are being replaced by integrated pest management systems or made obsolete by genetic engineering.

● *Quality.* Products can simply cease to function, and during the 1970s there was considerable concern over the concept of 'built-in-obsolescence' in which products were designed to have a limited functioning lifespan in order to ensure regular repeat purchases. Environmental marketing emphasises the need to allow products to continue functioning through design for longevity and repairability. Agfa Gevaert switched from a policy of selling photocopiers to leasing them on a full-service basis. This led to a design brief based around durability, and the upgrading of the copy drums from a lifespan of under 3 million copies to over 100 million (Roome and Hinnells 1992).

● *Desirability.* Fashion, economic conditions and technological advance can render a product no longer desirable. The rising cost of fuel and insurance, environmental concern and problems associated with urban parking all conspire to reduce the desirability of large, high-performance, low-fuel economy cars.

Industrial *versus* consumer goods

In industrial markets, the concept of customers taking an interest in how a product is manufactured is well established. Customers might audit a potential supplier to reassure themselves about the likely quality and security of supply. They might also need to audit suppliers as part of their own quality or environmental management systems. Greening brings consumer marketing closer to industrial marketing in the concern about how the product is made, and the need for an open dialogue between producer and customer. While in the past companies might have been used to opening the factory doors to the purchasing and quality managers of their industrial customers, in the future it may be representatives from consumer watchdogs, the media or environmental groups that will be receiving the guided tours.

Homogeneous *versus* heterogeneous goods

Products vary in terms of their heterogeneity, ranging from commodities such as oil or wheat to unique works of art or talented footballers. The concept of heterogeneity is generally applied to the physical product itself. The only way to create differentiation within a commodity market is by creating a distinctive brand image, which can be very expensive and risky within markets which are notoriously price competitive. Greening offers an opportunity to differentiate commodities on the basis of the method of production. Organic cotton, sustainably sourced hardwoods and nonchlorine bleached paper are all differentiated from the grey competition by the method of production.

PRODUCT CHARACTERISTICS

Products which are placed into a category such as convenience goods, consumer durables, white goods or unsought goods will usually share particular characteristics. Miracle (1969) devised a set of nine product characteristics which can be used to group products into particular categories. For any category of products, each of the nine characteristics may need to be reconsidered in the light of the green challenge.

1 *Unit value.* Resources can often be conserved by purchasing in larger quantities by reducing the amount of packaging per unit of product. The Body Shop encourages consumers to buy products in larger unit sizes on the basis of reduced packaging and refilling requirements.

2 *Significance of each purchase to the customer.* Products vary in terms of the level of involvement with the product that the consumer engages in during the purchase process. A loaf of bread and a house are clearly very different purchases in terms of the significance to consumers. However, the green agenda is placing a new importance on even everyday purchases. Consumer guides and environmental groups are reinforcing the message to the consumer that every purchase is a vote which can be used for or against the environment. The perceived consequences of buying the 'wrong' loaf of bread might once have been seen as no worse than mild personal inconvenience. For the truly green consumer, buying anything other than conservation-grade bread might be perceived as contributing to the destruction of the environment.

3 *Time and effort spent purchasing by the customer.* Related to the significance of the purchase is the effort that a customer is willing to put into the purchase process. Purchasing equipment such as washing machines or office printers requires time and information. Providing detailed environmentally related information in brochures for such products can help to attract the green customer. For more habitual purchases, a visible green label may be all that is needed to attract the green consumer.

4 *Rate of technology-driven or fashion-driven change.* The greening of markets is likely to slow the rate of technology- and fashion-driven change, both of which contribute to the consumption of resources, often for superficial improvement. The 'New Traditionalism' of the environmental marketing era may see a return to relatively simple and traditional technologies as replacements for new and technologically complex products, and an emphasis on enduring 'classic' styles.

5 *Technological complexity.* In many markets the technological complexities of the products and the features that they offer is outstripping the ability of consumers to benefit from them. Con-

sider the following comment on the personal computer market (Brake 1993):

'Why don't manufacturers work harder on making inexpensive 386s for the masses? Intel has a lot to answer for: it has spent hundreds of millions of pounds to convince consumers that they need a 486. Application writers are also to blame. In the race for market dominance, they have squeezed more and more features into their software and the size of applications has grown out of all proportion to their usefulness.'

The technological paradigm seems to call for products which are bigger, better, more complex and costlier. Schumacher's (1973) vision of 'intermediate technology' was for technologies that were smaller, simpler, cheaper, more human in scale and more benign in their effect on the environment.

6 *The customer's need for service before, during and after the sale.* As green consumerism becomes reflected in a desire for products that are built to last, so the demand for after-sales service to maintain, recondition and repair products will rise. This will provide further business opportunities for companies in the face of slowing purchase rates for brand new products.

7 *Frequency of purchase.* Convenience goods such as groceries, newspapers and petrol are frequent, often habitual and low-involvement purchases. Other products, such as shoes, washing machines and cars, are bought infrequently leading to more considered and involved purchasing. It was often the high-value, low-frequency purchases where consumer guides played a part in influencing consumer choice through information on product performance including eco-performance. With the publication of *The Green Consumer's Supermarket Shopping Guide* (Elkington and Hailes 1988), consumers had the opportunity to make a more environmentally informed choice on even the most everyday purchases.

8 *Rapidity of consumption.* The green challenge is creating a swing back away from the wide range of single-use disposable items that proliferated during the 1970s and 1980s.

9 *Versatility of the product in terms of satisfying different needs.* A typical family car is called upon to do a number of very different tasks. It will make numerous short journeys carrying one person to work or to shopping centres and then may be asked to take an entire family and luggage all the way across Europe once a year. The compromises involved in creating a car that can fulfil both tasks results in considerable environmental inefficiencies. Nieuwenhuis and Wells (1994) suggest that in the search for environmentally optimised vehicles there may be a move towards using more efficient, use-specific vehicles. This would allow a family to own an efficient small commuter car, and then to hire a larger car for its holiday.

GREEN PRODUCTS

Green is one of the newest product classifications to arise, but is also one of the most difficult to apply. The question of what constitutes a green product is almost as intractable as the question of what constitutes a green consumer. The implications of our definition of environmental marketing is that a green product is one that meets consumers' needs, is socially acceptable, and is produced in a sustainable manner. Using sustainability as a criterion for labelling products as 'green' appeals to the deep ecologists, but it creates problems in developing and marketing products. Because markets are imperfect in relation to the environment, the costs of a grey product are substantially lower than for a sustainable product which will cover the true costs of pollution and resource use. It is unrealistic to expect consumers to cover the entire price difference that would exist between a grey product and a green product, particularly in view of the conflicting information they receive from different producers, environmental groups and government agencies.

If only sustainable products qualified for the green tag, there would be no incentive for companies to develop products with an improved, but not sustainable environmental performance. Treating sustainability as a fixed hurdle to clear also removes any incentive to introduce products which actually enhance the environment rather than simply sustaining it. Until our economic and legislative systems begin to reflect the true costs of poor environmental performance, it is unrealistic to restrict our definition of green products to those which are sustainable.

We can define a product or service as 'green' when its environmental and societal performance, in production, use and disposal, is significantly improved and improving in comparison to conventional or competitive product offerings. This definition has the following important characteristics.

● *A dual focus on environmental and societal performance*. Performing well on only one dimension is unlikely to create a credible green strategy.

● *A continuous improvement orientation*. Since what constitutes 'green' is constantly changing, it requires improvement to be a continuous process rather than a single event.

● *A use of both competitor offerings and past products as a yardstick for comparison*. A company could still become green while lagging behind competitors in terms of eco-performance, therefore, providing it could demonstrate significant and continuous eco-performance improvement.

● *An emphasis on significant change*. This means significant in the eyes of consumers and other stakeholders. In this way it becomes a question of marketing realities instead of marketing images.

Such a broad definition can be criticised as being vulnerable to abuse by unscrupulous marketers. In an earlier book (Peattie 1992), I defended taking a broad approach to defining a green product on the grounds that:

'Improved green performance can be viewed as a ticket which allows a company to compete in the green marketing game. Once in the game, it is the level of performance which will determine a company's success. It will be better for the environment and society to have a game which is closely refereed, but open to the majority of companies, rather than one in which only the most talented élite can compete.'

The early phases of the game will inevitably be made more difficult by the presence of companies who are 'riding the green bandwagon'. It will become more orderly as legislation regarding green products and product claims tightens, and is increasingly closely monitored by the media, pressure groups and consumers.

Within this definition of green products will be a variety of shades of green and types of product, as shown in Fig. 10.3. *Absolute* green products are those which can contribute to the improvement of society or the environment. Examples include health care, pollution abatement equipment, the services provided by charities, or a bucket of earthworms bought to improve the soil quality of a garden. The other group of green products are '*relative* green products', whose claim to greenness lies in the reduction of the actual or potential harm they cause to society or the environment. The standards by which to judge such green products have led to some controversy. There are several elements that can influence the perception of a product's greenness.

1 *What goes into it* – including the quantity, sustainability, efficiency and safety of the raw materials and energy that go into a product, together with the social acceptability of the conditions under which human resources contribute to production.

2 *The purpose of a product*. However sustainably a missile is produced, it would seem difficult to perceive it as a green product.

3 *The consequences of product use and misuse*. Products whose use is harmful are tolerated where the benefits are also high (as with cars) or where the consequences of use are controversial or take many years to manifest themselves, as was the case with CFC damage to the ozone layer (*see* page 75). Cigarettes are unusual in that they are the only product which will kill the consumer if used as directed. In this case the power of the corporate lobby and the size and voting potential of the product-addicted market have allowed the product to survive. Misuse of a product can also colour the perceptions of eco-performance. In agrochemicals markets there has often been difficulties with correct product use in countries with low literacy rates among farmers. For some companies the concept of brand stewardship involves

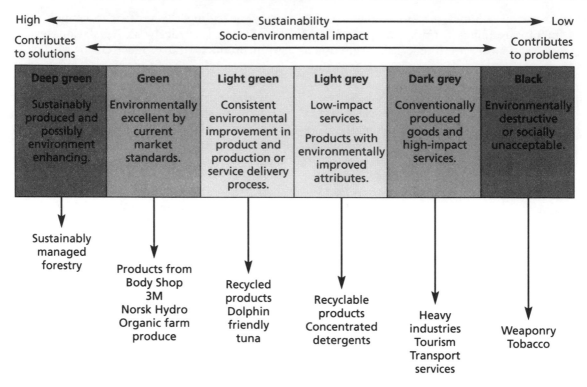

Fig. 10.3 The eco-performance continuum

taking responsibility to ensure that products are used correctly. Dow Corning places the following responsibilities on its sales staff (Elkington *et al* 1991):

● Inform customers about known hazards relating to the products.

● Advise customers to use products in accordance with label recommendations.

● Insist that distributors pass on handling, use and disposal information to their customers.

● Report and respond vigorously against cases of misuse.

● Co-ordinate visits by company staff to customer sites, to ensure safe use and disposal of products.

4 *The risks involved in product use.* Beck (1992) sees a key development of industrialisation as the replacement of harmful elements of society with risks. While water supplies in pre-industrial times were frequently harmful due to contamination, 'clean' water supplies in the industrialised era carry the risks involved in the cumulative consumption of additives such as aluminium. Many products carry a heavy burden of environmental or societal risk. Nuclear power is a target for public and environmentalist concern because of the risk of product failure combined with the magnitude of the potential consequences.

5 *Product durability.* How long a product lasts may become an important consideration for consumers, both environmentally and economically. An example of a lifespan-based product is the development of alumina and zirconia ceramic razor blades which would offer the same level of performance as high quality steel blades, but would last 15 times longer and 40 times longer than cheap disposables. (*See* also page 178.)

6 *Product disposal.* Product stewardship approaches can require companies to take a very proactive and responsible approach to the safe disposal of their product. Shell pooled resources

with the Niger government and the aid agencies, USAID and GTZ, to retrieve and safely destroy residual stocks of the insecticide dieldrin.

7 *Where it is made.* Countries can gain a reputation for the technical quality of a certain product, and this may be repeated for environmental quality. So while Swedish and German cars have an established reputation for technical quality, they also have an emerging reputation for environmental quality. Davis (1991) predicts that 'locally made' will gain strength as a mark of excellence, possibly as a reaction against the delocalised economy.

A final complicating factor in considering the greenness of a product is that perception of environmental and social performance is influenced by situational factors related to the product's use. One consumer might have a very different opinion of the social and environmental impact of a syringe if asked to visualise it either in a children's hospital or lying discarded by a drug addict in a children's playground.

PRODUCT PERFORMANCE

The conventional view of product performance relates to the satisfaction of consumer needs at the moment, or during the period, of consumption. The green challenge has added a whole new scope and timescale to the concept of product performance. The performance of green products relates to their impact on society and the physical environment before, during, and after consumption. While performance in the kitchen may have been the key to success in the 1980s, performance in the landfill may become a key success factor in the 1990s. Product quality in the 1990s often means removing those features or additives which were used to improve quality in previous decades. As Davis (1991) notes:

'It is not only that purity has been added to the list of desirable quality characteristics. The whole process of production is reinstated as an element of quality. For example, free-range eggs are considered superior to factory-farm eggs.'

Table 10.2 The eco-performance matrix

Product attribute	Comparative green performance				
	Best possible	Among the best	Above average	Better than some	Poor
Raw materials					
Energy efficiency					
Waste					
Pollution					
Packaging					
Lifespan					
Reusability					
Recyclability					
Effect on customer behaviour					
Green associations and linkages					
Socio-economic impact					

Source: Peattie (1992)

Evaluating product performance

For marketers of products faced by the actual or potential greening of their market, it is important to evaluate the green performance of existing and new products. Green audits will provide useful information on products and the company. Choosing the criteria on which to judge green performance and making valid comparisons with competitors and their products can be difficult and dangerous, however. A company may focus on one set of performance measures and market a product as green. Pressure groups, the media and consumers may then focus on a less favourable group of performance measures resulting in a backlash of negative publicity and consumer rejection. To be able to demonstrate that a product's performance is better than conventional or competitive alternatives, a marketer must ensure that the product's green strengths are not outweighed by any significant weaknesses. A quick way to evaluate a product's green performance and to seek out the areas which could be improved is to score it on the matrix shown in Table 10.2.

Perception and performance dissonance

The success of a green product will depend on the consumer's perception of both its green performance and its primary performance. Sometimes performance differences can be actual (such as the reduced tensile strength of recycled paper); sometimes they are perceptual or they can be a mixture of both. The majority of consumers assume that improved eco-performance will involve a reduced technical performance. In many cases this may be acceptable, as long as technical performance differences are slight. The successful zero-added mercury Green Power battery from Ever Ready is a comparable price to its standard product, but has only 90 to 92 per cent of the service life.

In other cases the assumed environmental/technical performance trade-off may simply not exist. In some cases companies, in the course of developing greener products and technologies, have actually enhanced their primary performance. ICI's Aquabase range of waterborne car paints were developed to cut solvent emissions by 60 per cent, but were also found to have a better primary performance than conventional paints. Other attempts to develop green products have floundered because their technical performance was simply not competitive. 3M is one of the leaders in terms of developing technically and environmentally excellent products. Its attempts to develop an audio tape using a water-based rather than a solvent-based process failed to meet quality targets, however, despite substantial research and investment (Bringer and Benforado 1989).

Expectations about performance can heavily influence consumers' experience of a product. In one famous market research experiment, consumers were asked to compare Coca-Cola (which they all said they liked) with a new 'Diet Coke'. The new product was universally condemned as 'awful, with a bitter aftertaste' – even though it was exactly the same Coca-Cola which they had praised moments earlier (Stander 1973). Green products are subject to similar effects. Green detergents do not generally contain the foaming agents found in conventional competitors. These create bubbles, which give the customer the impression of high cleaning performance. The absence of foaming agents and extra bubbles makes the customer perceive green detergents as less effective at cleaning, beyond actual performance differences. The assumptions about a trade-off between environmental and technical performance can work both ways. A naturally produced foodstuff may be perceived as tastier than a more commercially produced one, regardless of the results of blind taste tests. Although actual performance is important, therefore, it will be market-place perceptions that determine a product's success or failure. Figure 10.4 contrasts perceived technical performance and perceived eco-performance to create four categories of product.

1 *Underperformers.* Products whose perceived environmental and technical performance is relatively poor are unlikely to survive for long in the market unless they are extremely price competitive.

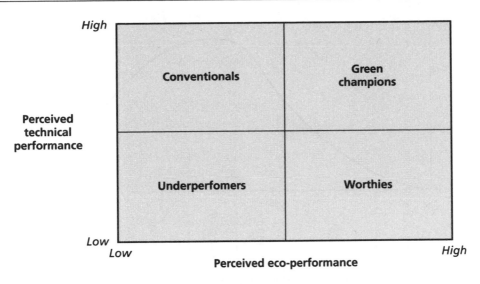

High

Perceived
technical
performance

Conventionals

Green
champions

Underperfomers

Worthies

Low

Low

High

Perceived eco-performance

Fig. 10.4 Environmental *versus* technical positioning

2 *Conventionals*. A product may suffer from a poor green image despite a good primary and green performance. A long-standing brand can have its green performance overlooked compared to new green market entrants, or be seen to be 'jumping on the green bandwagon' when it begins to emphasise eco-performance.

3 *Worthies*. Strong eco-performers can succeed in spite of poor perceived technical performance in comparison to conventional brands. In the household cleaners market the cleaning power of green alternatives does not match that of synthetic chemical-based cleaners. Future success relies on continuing interest in the relevant green issues, and an ability to maintain an eco-performance lead over conventional rivals.

4 *Green champions*. Products from companies such as The Body Shop, 3M and Ben & Jerry's have proved that a product can be perceived as sound in terms of primary performance and eco-performance. There will be some companies who occupy this section more on the basis of skilful selling than on the basis of truly excellent eco-performance. As information about relative eco- performance among companies becomes more widely available, it will become harder for

companies to maintain this position without making substantial improvements to their eco-performance.

Internal perceptions of green products and technologies will also be important in determining whether or not they reach the market. Often green technologies are lying dormant because at the time they were first developed and tested their performance was not technically superior, or they failed to meet the requirements of corporate investment geared to short-term payback for investment projects. Solar energy is generally perceived to be a 'failed' technology, and despite steady improvements in costs and energy yields, it has never fulfilled the optimism of the early 1970s. However, in the case of a business called Real Goods which specialises in solar and alternative energy products in the USA, solar energy provided the company with 1993 sales exceeding $10 million (4.7 million ECUs). As Elkington *et al* (1991) ponders:

'How many green technologies of the future are currently sitting unnoticed on the shelves of R&D laboratories around the world, ignored today because they failed to meet yesterday's criteria for success?'

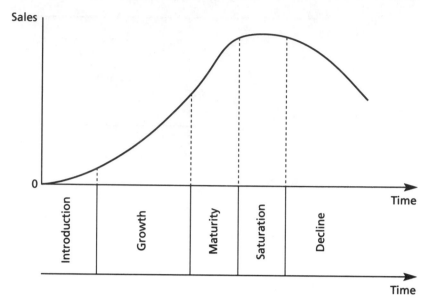

Fig. 10.5 The product life cycle

THE PRODUCT LIFE CYCLE

The product life cycle (PLC) model is one of the most widely used and enduring marketing concepts (Wood 1990). It proposes that products follow a fixed birth–growth–maturity–death life cycle, analogous to living organisms, in which levels of sales and profits rise and fall as a product moves along a typical S-curve (Fig. 10.5). The use of the model as a guide for marketing management decisions has been criticised on the basis that the PLC concept is:

● *Too standardised.* Although the S-curve is almost universally accepted as the likely pattern for a product to follow, Tellis and Crawford (1981), in a review of the PLC literature, found fourteen documented alternative patterns to the classic S-curve.

● *Potentially misleading.* The approach of deciding upon marketing strategies on the basis of a perceived PLC stage ignores the fact that sales patterns are partly determined by marketing strategies and actions. Cox (1967) in a study of drug brands found that it was common practice to revive mature brands with a promotional 'thrust'.

● *A self-fulfilling prophecy.* If young, 'growing' products are allocated more marketing resources, and ageing ones are given less, those starved of marketing resources will quickly decline and be phased out.

In environmental terms, the danger of the PLC model is that mature products will be 'killed off' and replaced once sales growth begins to decline. Seeking to sustain sales growth through constant new product/model introduction is a very resource-intensive approach to product management. A green approach to product management would emphasise measures aimed at lengthening the PLC and boosting sales of existing products.

The Lazarus Effect

Environmental concern has thrown the conventional PLC view of many products into some confusion. In particular, the 'Lazarus Effect' is witnessing products coming back from the dead. Otter (1992) explains:

'The event of chemicals leaving the market due to either bans or companies deciding not to incur the massive costs of tests requested for re-registration can allow old products to return from the marketing death zone. With detailed knowledge of the regulatory criteria and the performance of certain products in the environment, this so-called "Lazarus effect" can be predicted and should be included in marketing plans.'

In the USA consumers are turning away from 'modern' cleaning agents to return to 'new traditional' cleaners which are perceived as less environmentally toxic. Heinz reported an unexpected 5 per cent increase in gallon and half-gallon sizes of white vinegar; Dial Corp's borax sales jumped by 16 per cent between 1988 and 1990; and Church and Dwight reported 10 per cent growth in baking powder sales during 1990 (Scerbinski 1991).

Environmental life cycle models

The conventional PLC model charts the life of a product type in economic terms by measuring sales over time. An alternative view of the life cycle of a product is its physical life cycle from 'cradle-to-grave'. Like the conventional PLC model, the cradle to grave life cycle has its problems. The key difficulties involve knowing how far back down the supply chain to proceed, how many branches of the supply chain to pursue (should you worry about the companies that supply capital equipment to your suppliers, or just their suppliers of energy and raw materials?) and where to get information on the eco-performance of each link in the supply chain. The challenge of working out the components of any product and their eco-performance is illustrated by the musings of Lovins (1973).

'The typewriter I am now using probably contains Jamaican or Surinam aluminium, Swedish iron, Czech magnesium, Gabonese manganese, Rhodesian chromium, Soviet vanadium, Peruvian zinc, New Caledonian nickel, Chilean copper, Malaysian tin, Nigerian columbium, Zairean cobalt, Yugoslav lead, Canadian molybdenum, French arsenic, Brazilian tantalum, South African antimony, Mexican silver, and traces of other well-travelled metals. The enamel may contain Norwegian titanium; the plastic is made of Middle Eastern oil (cracked with American rare-earth catalysts) and of chlorine (extracted with Spanish mercury); the foundry sand came from an Australian beach; the machine tools used Chinese tungsten; the coal came from the Ruhr; and the end product consumes, some might say, too many Scandinavian spruces.'

The difficulties involved have not prevented some companies from forging ahead with life cycle analysis (LCA). Novotex, the Danish textile manufacturer, has implemented full LCA of all aspects of T-shirt production. This includes analysing the cultivation of the cotton including the use of agro-chemicals, soil management, irrigation, working conditions of labourers and transportation; the manufacture of the finished product including thread spinning, fabric knitting, dying, cutting, stitching and packaging; and even analysing the opportunities for future recycling and likely eventual disposal.

The product stewardship element of environmental marketing involves taking responsibility for a product all the way through its physical life cycle. For example, Black and Decker in Canada has established a programme to take back old products from customers to allow its components to be recycled. Given the lifespan of the products, customers taking advantage of this service will have made their purchase long before green concern became widespread, and it is not a service which will be of importance to new customers since it should be many years before they need it. What the service does, is to provide an unexpected benefit to former customers, and an ideal marketing opportunity to sell them a new product when they bring the old one in for disposal.

CREATING GREEN PRODUCTS

Faced with the emergence of green consumer demand, marketers can adopt a variety of product strategies. A grey, business-as-usual, marketing strategy will ignore the emergence of green consumerism. Emerging green consumer demand can be met using existing products. As long as the existing product is sufficiently eco-efficient to be a credible green contender, this strategy can have advantages over an attempt to create a new green brand which may have to overcome years of trust building between conventional products and consumers. Bernstein (1992) points out, however, that existing products represent limited opportunities for environmental marketing because renaming or redescribing an existing product in a green light has a relatively low market impact. The most obvious response to green consumers is the launch of brands specifically geared to meet their needs, but where they are also competitive in terms of their cost or technical performance, they may also be marketed to non-green consumers. Even the greyest of consumers may well enjoy a tub of Ben & Jerry's 'Chunky Monkey' ice cream because they listen to their taste buds rather than to any pronouncements about Ben & Jerry's socio-environmental excellence.

In addition to product changes inspired directly by a response to consumer demand, the green challenge has prompted manufacturers to develop new green products where:

● Existing conventional products have reached the decline phase of their product life cycle.

● Competitor products have developed a technical lead in the market-place which existing products cannot challenge by conventional strategies.

● New laws or technical standards have outlawed existing products. The inter-governmental agreement to phase out CFCs by 2000 has led to a race to develop a green alternative.

● An existing product has become uneconomic to produce because of rising costs which cannot be passed on to consumers. In the UK the rising green costs of environmental protection and waste disposal acted to make the nuclear power station building programme uneconomic in the newly privatised electricity industry.

● A shortfall in the supply of existing products requires the creation of substitutes. A shortage of supplies of whale oil is one of the reasons behind the development of vegetable-based alternatives such as jojoba oil.

The new product development (NPD) process itself has been a focus for environmentalist criticism. Companies have been accused of using leverage marketing techniques backed up with rapid product replacement to create the demand for a succession of minor model changes within

consumer durables markets. Such changes are designed to encourage regular additional purchases among consumers and is relatively wasteful of resources. New products are still an important part of environmental marketing to meet the new and changing needs of green consumers. The focus of green NPD is on improving the primary and eco-performance of a product rather than cosmetic changes aimed simply at improving economic performance. It also involves designing out what is not needed. Value analysis or value engineering approaches to product design can improve eco-performance by simplifying designs to their essential parts so that materials and money can be saved.

Designing green products

The environment has become an increasingly important aspect of product design, as revealed by Lent and Wells' (1992) survey of top US companies. The concept of 'design for environment' has entered the product designer's vocabulary. There are various ways in which a product can be 'designed for environment'. It can be changed in terms of:

● *Contents*, by switching to more sustainable components or ingredients, or eliminating environmentally harmful substances. In the USA organic fertilisers account for over 10 per cent of a $1 billion market (467 million ECUs). Carrier Corporation redesigned some of the components for its air-conditioning systems to remove toxic solvents, which also reduced annual manufacturing costs by $1.5 million (700 000 ECUs).

● *Manufacture*. While products are normally designed to meet the requirements for performance in use, green products may be changed to improve their eco-performance during manufacture.

● *Performance*. A car can be redesigned to improve the fuel performance of its engine, or the impact resistance of its body.

● *Use*. The invention of the soap powder dosing ball means that millions of consumers bypass the dispensing drawer built into the machine. This allows them to use less powder and eliminate the pre-wash cycle, saving time, energy and water.

These factors are not particularly new territory for product designers. More unusual is the need to consider product performance after use. This can require a radical new perspective among product designers, involving a need to 'think about your product's death at the moment of its conception' (Wheeler 1992). Product designers who may have spent years perfecting a product which hangs together even in the most hostile circumstances, are suddenly faced with making it easy to disassemble for recycling. Improving post-use eco-performance is usually achieved by building one or more of five R-factors into a design.

1 *Repair*. A modular design approach and good after-sales service provision can make repairing products cost effective and extend their useful life.

2 *Reconditioning*. In the automotive market a wide range of reconditioned parts, from tyres to engines, can be purchased. Davis (1991) quotes a survey conducted by the Batalle Research Centre in Geneva which showed that by the use of a reconditioning strategy for the car industry, France could halve its consumption of materials and energy in car manufacturing. In addition, the increased garage servicing needed would produce a substantial increase in overall employment, while motorists would benefit from a reduction in the cost of motoring.

3 *Reuse*. Some products are designed to be reused for the same purpose: for example milk bottles in the UK are reused on average twelve times. Other products are designed with a 'cascade' approach to use. Some product packages are designed to be reused as kitchen storage containers or even drinking glasses.

4 *Recycling*. Products ranging from beer cans to BMWs are now designed to be recyclable. Getting involved in recycling can move a manufacturer into a very different business mission. Anheuser-Busch are the world's largest brewer with sales of over $12.6 billion (5.9 billion ECUs) in 1991. They are also now the world's largest recycler of aluminium cans, recycling one can for every one of the 17 billion it sold during 1991. The strategy also paid off in terms of cost savings, since manufacturing from scrap saves 95 per cent of the cost of manufacturing aluminium from ore (Simon 1992).

5 *Remanufacture*. To create new from old, such as the remanufacture of used laser-printer cartridges performed by Onyx Associates.

Building recycling or reusability into a product design can present quite a challenge. A key problem is that the information and measurement techniques needed to work out the environmental impacts of different design choices may simply not exist (Ashley 1993). This is now beginning to change with the development of techniques such as Volvo's Environmental Priority Strategies system. Heeg (1984) produced a checklist for incorporating recyclability into new products.

1 *Design products to be as reusable as possible*:
- Build longevity into non-expendable parts.
- Locate expendable parts for ease of dismantling.
- Attach components for ease of dismantling.

2 *Anticipate the need for updating*:
- Provide room for expansion, use modular rather than integral construction.
- Build the possibility for expansion into the technology (reserve performance capacity, ability to plug in enhancements).

3 *Provide for the possibility of different uses after irretrievable obsolescence*:
- Adapt exterior design for the possibility of new uses.
- Make allowances for conversion.

4 *If products are not suitable for reuse, ensure that components are reusable*:
- Combine components into functional units that can be dismantled.
- Standardise components.
- Arrange for easy dismantling.
- Code reusable components.

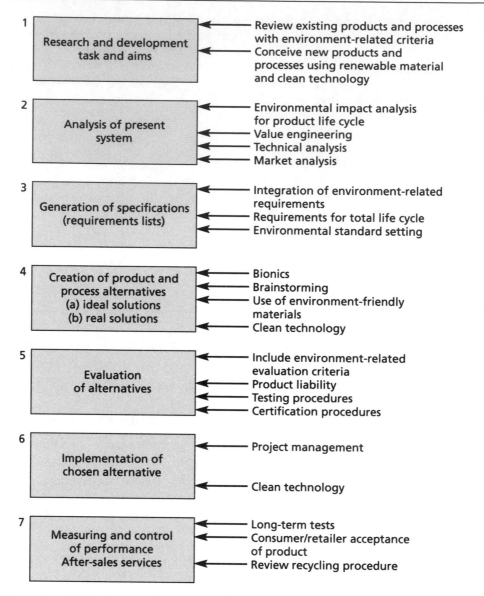

Fig. 10.6 Research and development methodology for green products
(Source: North (1992))

5 *Do not forget possible additional uses.*

6 *Do not forget about exploitation of raw materials.*

7 *Use only one material in production, or as few as possible.*

8 *Plan for easy re-exploitation of materials:*

● Only use compatible materials.

● Reduce the proportion of incompatible materials to below the permitted level.

● Design high proportions of incompatible material for easy removal.

● Reliable coding of all materials used.

9 *Plan carefully the use of restricted or non-exploitable materials*:

- Substitution with exploitable materials.
- Use only in long-life products if possible.
- Improve the quality of materials with restricted exploitability, to increase the number of usage cycles.

Due to the complex interrelationship of different aspects of a product's eco-performance, designing an improvement in one aspect of eco-performance can cause problems with another. For example, in washing machine design, increased spin speeds of 3000 rpm, rather than the conventional 500–1000 rpm, reduces the moisture content of clothes sufficiently to save 50 to 60 per cent of the energy required for tumble drying. However, this saving is partly negated by the wear and tear caused by increased vibration and the need for additional materials to provide stabilisation. AEG solved the problem of this trade-off by developing an electronic system to control the distribution of clothes and spin phasing to reduce vibration and allow a 20 per cent reduction in the weight of raw materials required.

Research and development

'The challenge for research and development will be to find materials with inherent recyclabilities, to use materials or modules that are easy to separate from others, to develop long-life characteristics for products, to develop new uses for by-products, and to find ways to use fewer materials.' (Wheeler 1992)

This challenge will need to focus on both products and production processes. Such a dual focus may act to dilute the green R&D effort going into innovation of the core product, so that the market is presented with a better product less often, yet with a better produced product more often. This would help to decelerate the rate of product introduction and lengthen product life cycles. A summary of the steps involved in the green product research and development process is shown in Fig. 10.6.

Key success factors for the development of green products

A green product strategy involves more than simply creating new green products. They also need to be launched, managed and integrated into the company's overall product portfolio. To succeed in the market, the following conditions must hold true for a new green product.

- It must be aimed at a genuine green need or want among consumers.
- It must perform acceptably in terms of both primary function and environmental quality, and also be perceived to perform acceptably by consumers.
- Its environmental quality must be communicated successfully to consumers through the naming, branding, design, packaging and promotion of the product.
- Consumers must be willing and able to pay any price premium which is associated with improved environmental quality.
- It should aim to equal, or better, competitors' products in terms of green and primary performance, price and availability.
- It must be supported by the genuine pursuit of environmental quality from the producer to create a credible green total product.

CASE STUDY

The Fiat Cinquecento – small is beautiful

The idea of a green car is considered to be a contradiction in terms by many environmentalists. No product more clearly symbolises the grey culture of the industrial era than the motor car. Although a deeply green car is probably a number of years, and a number of technological breakthroughs, in the future, an innovative car in terms of its impressive eco-performance by current standards, is the Fiat Cinquecento. Small cars with smaller engines are environmentally preferable to larger cars because they use less fuel, produce fewer emissions and are easier to park. Small cars have often suffered in terms of technical comparisons when it comes to long distance driving at the legal speed limit, however, in terms of comfort and refinement and in terms of driver safety in the event of an accident. The Cinquecento, by contrast, attracted positive reviews when it came to handling and performance on the motorway and was considered to be lively, stylish, fun and surprisingly refined. It proved that a small car need not lack flair, or restrict consumer choice. Fiat persuaded some of Italy's leading design houses to work on the project, leading to a four-wheel drive pick-up version from Pininfarina that can also convert into a coupe, sports car or van; and a one-seater version from Zagota, with an on-board bike for the growing trend in cycle-drive commuting.

In terms of eco-performance, the Cinquecento was designed from scratch with the aim of minimising pollution of all types, and creating as close to total recyclability as current technology allows. Fiat developed a 'materials ecology' approach to designing the car to minimise the direct and indirect environmental damage related to the manufacture, use and disposal of the car. The material innovations in the Cinquecento include CFC-free plastics in interior padding, organic pigments used in colouring components and lubrication instead of the conventional cadmium- and chromium-based pigments, a special zinc-aluminium plating called Dacromet instead of chromium for nuts and bolts, asbestos-free brake pads, clutch linings and sealing rings, and the elimination of aromatic solvents. The 'design for recycling' approach to the Cinquecento has involved the marking of every plastic component weighing over 50 g with a recycling code. The plastic and rubber components that cannot be reused will be burnt and the energy will be used in the construction of new cars. The aim is to ensure that the Cinquecento, and other future Fiat models, are 100 per cent recyclable.

Adapted from Derrick, M. 'Fiat proves that Beautiful doesn't have to be Big', *The Independent*, 30 June 1993 and other sources.

CHAPTER 11

Inside the black box – processes and policies

'A business that makes nothing but money is a poor kind of business.'
(Henry Ford)

INTRODUCTION

The conventional marketing concept focuses the operation of a company on the satisfaction of customer needs and on why purchases are made. It superseded the earlier product concept (emphasising what is purchased) and the selling concept (concerning how purchases can be made to happen). The production concept, emphasising how a product is made, is possibly the least fashionable of all the managerial orientations, but environmental marketing is set to bring production issues back to centre-stage. The original production philosophy emphasised the need to drive production volumes up, unit costs down, and to make the product as widely available as possible. Environmental marketing emphasises production, but in terms of its quality rather than its quantity; and it will aim to blend a production orientation with a marketing orientation. Already the issue of how a product is made is causing a shift in demand patterns towards products such as organic fruit and vegetables, sustainably harvested wood or traditionally baked breads. This renewed emphasis on the product and its manufacture may help to correct what some marketing commentators have seen as a counter-productive overemphasis on customer needs (see page 104). As the potential for the technologies and policies of a company to influence the competitiveness of products increases, so the opportunity for marketers to treat other aspects of the organisation as a 'black box' will diminish.

The environmental impact of a tangible product will be divided into product use, product disposal, production itself, and the inputs of materials and energy into the production process. Although in general it is the post-production use of products which has the greatest environmental impact (Hindle *et al* 1993), environmental impacts during and before production (or service delivery) are an important component of eco-performance. For some makes of car, for example, the production process consumes up to 50 per cent more energy than the car will consume in its lifetime. The concept of taking responsibility for the product during, and prior to, production represents something of a new frontier for marketing and marketing managers. This is not to say that marketers do not already work closely with production and R&D managers on issues of product and process development, or with purchasing managers in the specification of raw materials and components. However, issues of production and purchasing are ultimately 'somebody else's problem' unless they affect the pricing, profitability, quality or technical performance of the product. As the greening of consumers and legislation deepens, so the need for marketers to influence and integrate the management of eco-performance at all stages of the physical product life cycle will intensify. In the early phases of environmental marketing it has often been the eco-performance of the production system which leads to a hostile reception for an otherwise worthy green product or organisational effort.

When ICI unveiled its liquid soda crystals as a green industrial cleaner they were accused of hypocrisy because the production process was polluting the River Weaver. IBM, a company usually associated with good environmental performance, had plants ranked number one and three in a 1989 list of America's top ten CFC emitters compiled from Environmental Protection Agency figures.

Many of the trends within production management are improving the eco-performance of business, even though they are motivated by concerns about costs rather than the environment. Philosophies such as lean production aim to reduce inventories and reduce the number of steps in the production process. This leads to a reduction in energy consumption, waste and materials handling costs. Total Quality Management (TQM), with its emphasis on 'getting it right first time' and zero defects, is also contributing greatly to the reduction in waste among manufacturers. Environmentally motivated changes to production systems are also now becoming the norm among manufacturers with 85 per cent of multinational companies claiming to have changed their production processes in response to the green challenge (Vandermerwe and Oliff 1990).

THE COMPANY AS AN HOLISTIC SYSTEM

Green marketing views a company as an holistic entity, and not just as a collection of functions, divisions, hierarchical levels or SBUs. This holistic system is a blend of both 'software' and 'hardware' dimensions. The emphasis of many companies in improving their eco-performance has been a technological one, with products and processes being redeveloped to become more environmentally sound. Other companies are putting more emphasis on the organisational software of the business and are seeking to improve their policies and practices, often in pursuit of some environmental quality standard such as BS7750. The priority given to hardware and software initiatives varies among companies, industries and nations. Peattie and Ringler (1994) in a comparison of leading German and UK companies concluded that although German industry is acknowledged to be leading the European field in terms of environmental technology, UK companies showed greater enthusiasm for many of the organisational dimensions of greening.

THE COMPANY AS A PHYSICAL SYSTEM

A company's green philosophy can be demonstrated in the nature and management of the buildings and sites which it occupies. The concept of designing offices and factories to be environmentally sensitive is reflected in the rise of eco-architecture, which involves the following principles (Krusche 1982):

- consideration of environmental and energy use issues in the choice of site, conception and form of the building, positioning, choice of materials, use of space and landscaping;

- minimum use of energy and natural resources for construction and operation;

- use of natural resources such as natural light, solar radiation and green space;

- minimisation of pollution, waste and use of land for building;

- enrichment of surrounding plant and animal life;

- integration of buildings into the landscape in terms of environmental sensitivity and aesthetics.

The aim of eco-architecture is to produce buildings with an emphasis on the environmental and human consequences as well as the economic and technical performance.

Workplace design

The design of company facilities impacts on people as well as their environment. The human effect of the workplace has received attention recently, and switched in focus from the factory floor to the office with the emergence of 'sick building syndrome' (SBS). In industrialised countries office workers make up more than 50 per cent of the work-force, but are increasingly affected by poor ventilation, inadequate natural lighting, noise and pollutants such as ozone released from office equipment. These result from a grey economic and technical approach to workplace design, which ignores environmental and human impacts. Field and Phillips (1992) view the failure to properly 'manage' the workplace environment as an inefficient and costly failure to get the best out of the company's human resources. Research by Building Use Studies in the UK indicates that among 4300 office workers from 47 buildings, 80 per cent suffered from at least one ailment caused by their working conditions while over a quarter blamed their working conditions for significantly reducing their productivity. In The Netherlands annual losses due to SBS-related absence are estimated at between 27 and 36 million Belgian francs (Develter 1992). Field and Phillips (1992) suggest a five-point framework (PLANS) to create a healthy workplace:

● *Privacy.* People should be allowed access to visual privacy and speech privacy and the company should ensure that their level of accessibility and 'interruptability' is appropriate.

● *Lighting.* Good levels of (preferably natural) lighting measurably increase productivity, accuracy, motivation and job satisfaction. Low-pressure sodium lighting may appear economical for companies, but is a false economy in offices since workers consider them to be harsh, unnatural and unsatisfying to work in.

● *Air quality.* One of the by-products of the 1970s' oil crises and the economically and environmentally motivated desire to conserve energy that followed was that natural ventilation was much reduced in buildings. Office buildings used increasingly 'sealed' designs and relied on air-conditioning and ventilation systems to circulate air. Air circulation was further reduced by variable-air-volume systems which reduce the air flow while office temperatures remain relatively stable, and shut off outside business hours. The result of these energy-saving economies is that, according to architect and environmental consultant, Elia Sterling, 'People in modern offices aren't breathing air but a photo-chemical smog.'

● *Noise.* The spread of office technology has increased noise levels to a point where it impairs productivity.

● *Space.* The ergonomics and allocation of space and office furniture can impact on productivity and motivation (as well as providing a lot of fun in the political machinations of the typical office). The US National Institute of Occupational Safety and Health found that workers using properly designed workstations were 24 per cent more productive than those using poorly designed workstations.

Constructing an office environment which maximises worker health and welfare following this PLANS framework might appear to be costly, but the annualised cost of office construction and maintenance is a fraction of the salary costs of those working in it. If workplace attendance and productivity are improved, it can produce net savings; an approach that Ecover took in the economic justification for the investment in its 'ecological factory' and accompanying offices (Develter 1992).

Location decisions

Location decisions are one of the most difficult decisions that a company must face, economically, environmentally and socially. Faced with the need to locate almost any form of industrial or commercial development, powerful forces can be unleashed. The location of unpopular facilities provides a severe marketing challenge to the green company, since the reaction of most people faced with the prospect of living near an incinerator, a chemicals plant or a landfill dump is 'Not in my back yard' (or NIMBY). The conventional approach to siting such operations is the 'decide-announce-defend' sequence which relies upon presenting a *fait accompli* which is pushed through the local planning system against local opposition. Alternatively, potentially unpopular facilities are proposed for economically disadvantaged areas. In such areas the demand for inward investment and the creation of employment is usually so great that almost any form of development will be welcomed, regardless of its effect on the local environment and population. A fresh approach to such difficult siting decisions is environmental dispute resolution, a technique pioneered in the USA by Professor Patrick Susskind. It involves extensive public consultation throughout the decision-making process, allowing the community to influence the final choice and providing some form of benefit for the community as compensation (Cottam 1993).

THE COMPANY AS A TRANSFORMATION SYSTEM

Another physical perspective on businesses is as systems which bring together human labour, ingenuity and technology in order to transform material and energy inputs into marketable products. This is eloquently expressed in a simple but striking observation about our industrial economy from Laughlin and Varangu (1991).

'Observing our earth in the late 20th century would surely make a visitor from another planet scratch his head in confusion. A simplified description of our industrial-based manufacturing economy consists of the following four steps:

1 digging stuff out from a hole in the ground, creating greater or lesser environmental damage;

2 refining and using the stuff to make products;

3 using these products for a time ranging from a few minutes for some packaging products to a few decades for some domestic appliances and durable goods;

4 putting discarded stuff back into another hole in the ground with greater or lesser environmental damage.'

Despite its over-simplification, this description remains apt for a wide range of industrial activities. It could, however, be made a little more precise if step two were amended to mention that while 'stuff' is refined and used to make products, unwanted 'stuff' is ejected into the atmosphere and water system as well as being discarded into holes in the ground, again with more or less environmental damage.

Such an earth-to-earth, input–processing–output approach to production systems has always underpinned management thinking and the majority of academic business disciplines, in particular accounting, managerial economics and operations management. This approach is also being used to evaluate companies eco-performance through resource-flow/input–output analysis, which can be used to trace, record and assess all resource flows through the company. Figure 11.1 shows how Glaxo charts the environmental inputs and outputs related to its production of medicines.

Since the production systems outlined by Laughlin and Varangu involve several opportunities for lesser or greater environmental damage to occur, there are several different ways in which environmental improvement of the overall transformation system can be achieved.

● *End-of-pipe pollution control*: installation of equipment to remove pollutants from the waste streams of a production process.

● *Waste minimisation*: technologies and techniques to minimise waste streams per unit of input, including the replacement of polluting raw materials with ones which give rise to less downstream pollution or facilitate a less polluting production process.

● *Clean technology*: installation of alternative production techniques which inherently produce less polluting waste streams.

● *Waste management*: technologies and techniques to handle, treat and dispose of waste by the most environmentally acceptable means.

● *Recycling/resource recovery*: minimising disposable wastes by reusing waste streams.

● *Clean products*: minimising environmental impact through their design, production, use and disposal.

● *Environmentally optimised sourcing*: purchasing from the supplier who is creating 'the neatest holes in the ground'.

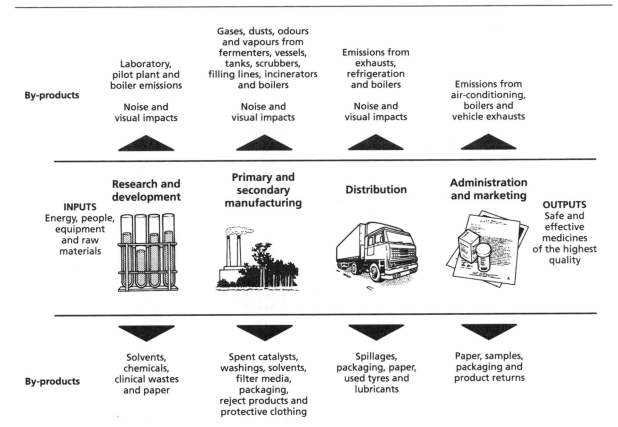

Fig. 11.1 Environmental inputs and outputs for the production of medicines
(Source: Glaxo)

GREENING THE PRODUCTION SYSTEM

The production function

The idea of being held responsible by the consumer for the way in which a product is made might seem like a rather novel and unsettling idea for production managers within a green company. However, many of the essentials of green production management such as using planned maintenance to ensure that production systems work efficiently and safely, or planning production schedules to keep factories working as efficiently as possible, are familiar territory for production managers. A summary of the key activities for the green production manager is shown in Table 11.1.

The environment and innovation

Technological innovation is the focus for many people's optimism about the future of the planet. This is despite the environmentalist criticism that it is a rather blinkered approach to the application of technology to our environment that has led to the current crisis. Historically, environmental applications have not been a focus for intensive research and development activity or innovation. Many of today's end-of-pipe filtration and scrubbing techniques are little different to when they were first developed in the nineteenth century. For many years a lack of environmental legislation provided little incentive for investment in research and development for environmental innovation. As legislation has become more

Table 11.1 Production management's role in the greening process

Definition of production philosophy	Investment planning	Implementation of new equipment, technology and work organisation	Continuous improvement of systems performance
New philosophies in line with environmental protection	Clean technology, and resource saving as investment cause	Workers and management training commitment to environmental protection	
		Environmental impact assessment	Good housekeeping
Simplification	Environment friendliness as decision criterion	Testing of new equipment according to environmental criteria	Resource saving programmes
Inventory reduction			Suggestion systems
JIT	Cost-benefit of environment-related investments	Decentralisation of environmental responsibilities to supervisors and work groups	Performance review of production systems
Product vs. process orientation	Environment-related production costs		

Source: North (1992)

stringent, so companies have begun to invest and innovate. Often the countries with the strictest regulations have gone on to produce companies with world-beating new technologies as is the case with Germany and flue gas desulphurisation or Japan and nitrogen oxide control technologies. These two countries have taken a lead in the development of environmental innovations, with Germany originating some 43 per cent of eco-patents for products reaching international markets (Hopfenbeck 1993).

One of the difficulties of making the technological systems side of a business responsive to the needs of the customer, society and the environment, is that those working in technological fields are often not used to thinking in those terms. It is understandable for technologists to adopt a product or production orientation. Most people who have worked in marketing have at some time found themselves locked in a battle of wills with someone wearing a white coat, who is convinced that a certain technology is so good, all it requires is a little bit of selling to the customer. The techno-myopia of scientists was noted by C. H. Waddington (1941) in his book, *The Scientific Attitude*.

'Responsible scientists, looking at their colleagues, saw the obvious fact that most specialists were quite unfitted to play an important part in the evolution of general culture; but, far from acknowledging that this was a sign of science's failure, they accepted it almost with glee as an excuse which let them out of the necessity of thinking about wider issues.'

To create greener technologies, the people working on them will need to become sensitive to and knowledgeable about many of these 'wider issues'. Saemann (1992) attempts to broaden the scientific perspective to create 'sustainable engineering' within companies. He proposes a ten-point code of ethics for engineers and technical scientists developed for the Swiss Academy of Engineering Sciences (*see* Fig. 11.2). The aim is to balance the economic, social and environmental responsibilities involved in technological development and to contribute to the coming 'ecological social market economy'.

1 **Principle of responsibility**
Engineers/technical scientists are responsible for their own actions and for their input in decision making by other authorities or groups. This personal responsibility cannot be delegated.

2 **Subjects of responsibility**
The ethical responsibility of the engineers/ technical scientists applies to three principal areas.
• Caring for humanity and society. Aim: Contributing to humankind's well-being.
• Protecting the environment/nature. Aim: Maintaining the basis for life.
• Ensuring economic success. Aim: Satisfying legitimate requirements of corporate partners and society.
These three responsibilities must be borne simultaneously and optimally, as well as globally and in the long term.

3 **Freedom in technical research**
The changing needs of individuals and society call for a constant expansion of technical knowledge, which in turn necessitates the basic freedom for technical research. This entails taking personal responsibility for respecting limits in the search for knowledge; in the choice of research objectives; because of harmful effects of the research activity on humanity and the environment; owing to the limitations of available resources.

4 **Maintaining the basis for life**
The unrestricted consumption of limited resources has an adverse effect on the basis of life and well-being of subsequent generations. The same applies to the increasing environmental pollution through wastes and emissions. Engineers/ technical scientists promote products and technologies which reduce environmental pollution and the consumption of limited raw materials to an acceptable level.

5 **Benefits versus risks and damages**
The provision of products and services and the construction and operation of plants always affect humanity and the environment. Engineers/technical scientists must on the one hand increase desirable positive effects while on the other hand reducing undesirable negative effects (as far as possible: a safe, environment-friendly and economical technology and meaningful products).

6 **Innovation**
Inevitably linked with the task of the engineers/technical scientists is innovation, i.e. the implementation of new technical knowledge.
• for optimising the ratio of benefits to risks and damages relating to the technical activity.
• as a driving force for raising living standards or for fighting poverty.
• for creating and maintaining a healthy economic basis in a geographical region.

7 **Technical competance and advanced training**
Engineers/technical scientists have the personal task and responsibility, for themselves and their colleagues, to continue training and to keep pace with the state of the art by learning and teaching, especially in their area of expertise, but also in related technical disciplines.

8 **Comprehensive view**
In order to take responsibility from the social, ecological and economic points of view and hence be able to realise optimal overall solutions in complex projects and tasks, it is not only technical competence that is necessary but also a knowledge of economic, cultural, social and ecological relationships and the willingness to co-operate in interdisciplinary working groups.

9 **Communication**
In the interests of communication with the public (citizens, authorities, media) bases on mutual understanding, the social responsibility of the engineers/technical scientists also includes their personal involvement in an open dialogue. This allows the public to assess technical matters from a well informed standpoint and permits industry to take greater account of social aspects in its work.

10 **Truthfulness**
Truthfulness towards society and towards oneself is an essential part of the personal ethics of engineers/technical scientists. It must form the unshakeable basis of all technical activity; it may also entail the refusal to carry out irresponsible technical work.

Fig. 11.2 Ethical code for engineers and technical scientists
(Source: Saemann (1992))

GREEN PURCHASING

The need for environmental improvement requires careful analysis of the inputs of material resources which are purchased for the organisation. From where and from whom production inputs have come and how they were produced have important implications for the eco-performance of the finished product. In some cases, this may require marketing managers to work directly with suppliers. Redesigning products and their packaging to eliminate harmful components or to aid recovery and recycling will often require the expertise of those responsible for manufacturing and developing the materials. In other areas, such as the purchase of pollution control equipment, or the selection of CFC-free solvents, or the choice of fuel which powers the production process, the purchase decision will not directly involve the marketing function. The environmental marketer should stay informed about such purchasing decisions for two reasons. First, such issues may conceivably form the basis of questions from customers interested in the environmental performance of the company. Second, addressing the environmental effects arising from a company's purchases of goods and services is a requirement for companies wishing to pursue BS7750 or similar eco-standards.

Raw material choice

The choice of the material inputs into the production process has traditionally been specified by product designers and process engineers on the basis of cost and technical performance. Welford and Gouldson (1993) suggest a new checklist for raw material assessment.

- Is the raw material renewable?
- Is the raw material recycled?
- Is the raw material ultimately reusable?
- Is the raw material ultimately recyclable?
- Is it possible to replace high quality raw materials with lower grade inputs which meet the desired performance standards?

- Is the input supplied in a form which is instantly usable?
- Has the quality of inputs been assessed in relation to output defects and therefore waste generation?
- Are toxic or hazardous inputs used only where there are no alternatives?
- If the quality of raw materials degrades with time, can the ordering schedule be altered to minimise waste?
- Does the company practise stock rotation in order to minimise wastage?
- If the nature of the output varies with time, can the ordering schedule be altered to minimise waste?
- Are local suppliers used, wherever possible?
- Can the packaging of the raw materials be reduced and returned to the suppliers?

From a technical point of view, product designers and production managers tend to prefer virgin materials since their quality tends to be more uniform and predictable. Therefore recycled raw material inputs need to have economic advantages and/or advantages in terms of their customer appeal and green promotional opportunities.

Energy savings

The potential that existed for businesses to save energy, and to save money in doing so, was highlighted by the 1970s' oil crises. This focused the attention of process engineers on the energy efficiency of production systems, albeit for economic rather than environmental reasons. Since that time there has been a relatively steady decline in the energy inputs needed to create a unit of output. A range of initiatives can allow energy to be saved, including careful selection of energy sources, proper battery management and maintenance, improving the energy efficiency of production processes, switching to low energy/high output lighting, recovering waste heat and combined heat and power schemes for large facilities. Cost constraints are often raised as a barrier to increased investment in energy efficiency, but energy savings can often be achieved through very simple changes. For example, American companies, anticipating future growth, have tended to buy larger industrial motors than they currently need. Large motors are inefficient if run at less than their optimal speed, however. According to World Resources Institute figures, equipping all such motors with a simple speed control device would reduce total US energy consumption by 7 per cent.

Supplier choice

Although some leading green companies such as IBM, The Body Shop and 3M have thoroughly integrated environmental issues into purchasing management, for the majority of companies it is unexplored territory. In a 1992 survey conducted by BRMB International on behalf of Business in the Environment among purchasing managers in companies with an environmental policy and the companies that supply them, it was shown that:

● the integration of environmental management into purchasing is not well developed;

● data collection on supplier eco-performance tends to involve very general letters or questionnaires with little useful feedback for suppliers;

● little work had been done in validating information provided by suppliers (reasons cited included trust in suppliers and a lack of time and resources);

● 65 per cent of customers and 71 per cent of suppliers said that addressing environmental issues had improved relationships;

● there was universal agreement that environmental issues would become more important in future.

There can be some difficult issues involved in working back down a supply chain. Identifying the actual producers of products bought and sold as commodities can be virtually impossible. Furthermore, when purchasing ready-made machinery, the variety of components and the diversity of sources can make them very difficult to track down.

Auditing within the supply chain is a complex and time-consuming process which relies a great deal on co-operation and information being provided by suppliers. One of the companies to rearrange its supply chain management on the basis of a systematic analysis of supplier eco-performance was Scott Paper. Scott own life cycle analysis revealed that many of the factors hampering its own eco-performance, which had been the subject of some environmentalist pressure, were imported into the company. So Scott sent suppliers (initially focusing on pulp suppliers) a questionnaire asking for details of energy consumption, energy sources, pollution releases and waste disposal. Using a weighting and scoring system devised in conjunction with environmental experts, Scott's was able to identify and de-list the 10 per cent of its suppliers with the worst environmental performance. The company also notified all suppliers that top eco-performers will be actively preferred in future purchasing decisions (Elkington 1994).

In terms of specifying environmental standards for suppliers there is considerable variation across Europe. Although 30 per cent of UK companies surveyed by Touche Ross in 1990 considered the environmental performance of suppliers important, no companies imposed specific environmental standards on suppliers. This compared poorly to other European countries in which the percentage of companies imposing environmental standards on suppliers ranged from 38 per cent in Germany, to 60 per cent in Belgium and reached 80 per cent in Denmark.

Partnership approaches

The competitive ethos which was so strong in the early 1980s stressed individual efforts and did little to promote the benefits of co-operation and partnership. A green approach to business tends to stress co-operation rather than competition, and looks for opportunities for companies to work with their competitors, customers and suppliers in pursuit of mutually beneficial improvements. *Buying into the Environment: Guidelines for Integrating the Environment Into Purchasing and Supply*, published by Business in

Table 11.2 Environmental risk evaluation for suppliers

Ranking	Action
Low	Communicate your company's policy.
Low/Medium	Request specific information on non-hazardous processes, materials and wastes/emissions.
Medium	Carry out an initial supplier evaluation covering the points above, and basic environmental management systems, involving correspondence and management meetings.
Medium/High	Carry out periodic vendor rating against key specifications and management systems requirements involving correspondence and management meetings.
High	Carry out a full supplier evaluation involving site visit and collecting evidence on environmental performance and management systems.
High	Carry out periodic vendor rating against all environmental requirements involving site visits and collection of evidence.
High	Provide information on hazardous materials, processes and wastes/emissions as a result of company specification.
High	Provide training on hazardous materials, processes and treatment/disposal of wastes/emissions as a result of comany specification.
High	Provide direct financial or other resources to support the organisation to improve environmental performance.

Source: *Buying into the Environment*

The Environment, strongly stressed the adoption of a 'partnership style'. This does not involve the development of formal partnerships, but instead involves moving away from a traditional 'win–lose' style of negotiated purchasing towards a 'win–win' approach of mutual problem solving. A key advantage that such an approach offers is the more open exchange of information and the opportunities for pooled ideas to help new and improved solutions to be developed. Although The Body Shop has become known for its stringent screening of the eco-performance of its 200 or so suppliers, its approach is based around partnership and the exchange of information rather than the direct application of pressure (Barry 1990).

Managing supplier and purchasing risk

Evaluating the eco-performance of suppliers can be a daunting task for companies who may have no very accurate picture of their own environmental performance, and whose supplier list may run into tens of thousands. The two key criteria in setting priorities for eco-auditing suppliers is whether their product or service is known to be linked to any specific environmental issues, and whether the supplier or supplies pose any form of known environmental risk. Risk management is an important issue in purchasing, and eco-performance of suppliers is becoming an increasingly important component of supplier risk. Purchasers seek to protect companies against the risks posed by an interruption to supply, sudden price increases and any failures of suppliers to meet quality standards. Environmental risk was once viewed as an additional and secondary category of risk, and one which may have to be traded off against other risks regarding price, quality and security of supply. The green challenge has brought these different elements of risk together with the integration of eco-performance with quality management and the high financial and supply security risks posed by an environmental disaster befalling a company's suppliers.

Many companies are developing risk criteria with which to screen suppliers and risk categories into which they can be placed. IBM operates a sophisticated five-tier risk categorisation of suppliers which reflects the depth of IBM's involvement with suppliers and the extent to which they are supplying to IBM's specifications. AT&T have added environmental criteria to its 'Quality Program Evaluation' of suppliers. The logic behind this being that in the long term, poor eco-performance is likely to increase vendor cost, and may lead to complications in terms of liability. Pedigree pet foods operates a simpler categorisation of suppliers as posing a high, medium or low risk. Suppliers may be classified as high risk and require particular scrutiny when:

● they supply materials of strategic importance;

● they supply a particularly high volume of a material;

● they have a history of quality management problems;

● the materials or processes they used are known to cause environmental problems or risk.

A suggested scheme for basing environmental actions and decisions regarding suppliers on their perceived environmental risk categorisation is provided in Table 11.2.

In the long term increasing mandatory environmental disclosure is likely to provide a great deal more information, but in the short term, green companies may face something of an information shortage on supplier eco-performance. In some cases, such as with the purchase of tuna fish from Ecuador, it can be assured through the presence of an independent accreditation body which actively inspects and approves suppliers according to agreed standards. Where no such independent accreditation exists, companies are typically reliant on the suppliers themselves to provide the information on which to judge their performance. The use of questionnaires has been pioneered by companies such as The Body Shop. It operates a five-star supplier accreditation scheme which depends on suppliers' responses to a series of progressively more searching questionnaires which explore issues of manufacturing, processing and packaging. All suppliers that supply over £100 000 (75 000 ECUs) of material must be accredited. A supplier's willingness to make modifications to its products and processes, and to provide information are also taken into account in the accreditation process.

The ability of companies to get information from suppliers or to effect change in the eco-performance of suppliers will obviously reflect the relative balance in size and power between supplier and customer. The operation of stringent supplier screening policies by a company the size of IBM will obviously have a profound effect on the supply chain. Site visits, inspections and full supplier audits can be powerful tools for gathering information about supplier eco-performance, and also for building a positive, problem-solving relationship with suppliers. They are resource intensive to operate, however, and can lead to conflict between suppliers and customers if badly handled. For small companies it can be more difficult to implement green purchasing initiatives.

GREEN PROCESSING

For many manufacturers, significantly improving their eco-performance will involve the application of 'clean technology' which aims to produce the same end result as conventional technology, but with reduced environmental consequences. Clean technology is about process change and the elimination of problems. It can be contrasted with 'end-of-pipe' treatments which simply seek to transfer pollution from one medium to another through *post-hoc* modifications. There are several ways in which a particular technology can be made cleaner.

1 *Increased efficiency.* Many clean technologies aim to create the same result with less environmental damage. An award-winning example is ICI's Electrodyne Sprayer. This electrically charges pesticide molecules so that they stick to the plants to which they are applied. In some circumstances this can allow an area of crops to be treated with one hundredth of the conventional amount of pesticide.

2 *The replacement of harmful process components.* Sericol, a subsidiary of Burmah Castrol, for example, has developed a range of water-based screen printing inks which have the potential to eliminate the release of organic solvents into the environment by screen printers, which amounts to 5000 tonnes per annum in the UK alone.

3 *Turning waste material into profit-earning by-products.* Packaging giant TetraPak has developed a pilot plant in Germany which shreds and presses discarded drinks cartons into a colourful chipboard which can be turned into anything from briefcases to wall clocks.

In some cases clean technology development is an evolutionary approach to change which means redesigning existing products to reduce their environmental impact. In other cases it involves a switch to an entirely different form of technology which is still capable of producing the same results, but working more 'symbiotically' with the environment. Table 11.3 demonstrates the difference between developing a new chemical pesticide and developing an 'agrobiological' solution which solves the same pest problem through more natural means. In 1992 sales of such biorational pesticides accounted for £350 million (263 million ECUs), which equates to almost 5 per cent of the global market for insecticides valued at $7.8 billion (3.6 billion ECUs). While the value of the total market is forecast to decline to $7.3 billion (3.4 billion ECUs) by 2005, the share for green pesticides is forecast to rise to over 12 per cent.

In addition to improving environmental quality, the benefits accruing from the adoption of clean technology are said by the OECD to include:

● an overall improvement in production processes;

● savings in raw materials and energy leading to increased profitability;

● a reduction in the costs of pollution abatement;

● the diffusion of new processes creating market opportunities and further stimulating innovation.

These predicted benefits were borne out in Irwin's (1992) study of seven companies implementing new clean technologies, five of whom reported accompanying technical quality improvements. Savings on raw materials and/or energy costs were also experienced by all the companies involved, ranging from 'modest' savings to annual savings of up to £1 million (750 000 ECUs) per annum. Four of the companies also reported reduced costs for waste treatment and disposal, resulting from waste reduction. A French study also found that among companies who redesigned their production process to eliminate pollution, 70 per cent also achieved cost-saving benefits over plants operating the conventional production systems (North 1992).

Barriers to clean technology

Despite the exciting prospects that clean technology appears to offer, there are a number of factors which would seem to favour investment in end-of-pipe approaches.

● End-of-pipe approaches are generally cheaper in the short run and therefore more attractive using conventional investment appraisal techniques. This, combined with the narrow definition of costs and benefits used, can make clean technology appear a poor investment.

● 'Add-on' technologies are typically highly visible and can be useful symbols of environmental commitment.

● End-of-pipe changes are typically less disruptive to current production processes and working practices.

● The market for end-of-pipe technologies is well developed, and can use relatively standardised products. The redesign involved in clean technology requires specifically tailored products and services.

● Clean technology initiatives can be overtaken by regulatory pressures aimed at the faster improvements offered by end-of-pipe solutions. So while car companies attempted to develop lean-

Table 11.3 The alternative technology potential: two ways to target a pest

	Agrochemicals	Agrobiologicals
PRODUCT DEVELOPMENT		
R & D costs	£12 million	£400 000
New products discovery	Screen 15 000 compounds, discover afterwards what targets they control	Target selected on market need; microbial control agents often easy to find
Market size required for profit	£30 million per year to recoup investment: limited to major crops	Markets under £600 000 can be profitable due to low development cost
PRODUCT USE		
Kill	Often 100%	Usually 90–95%
Speed	Usually rapid	Can be slow
Spectrum	Generally broad	Generally narrow
Resistance	Often develops	None yet shown, but microbes also adaptable
PRODUCT SAFETY		
Toxicological testing	Lengthy and costly – £3 million	£40 000
Environmental hazard	Many well known examples	None yet shown
Residues	Interval to harvest usually required	Crop may be harvested immediately

Adapted from Robinson (1990)

burn engines from scratch, like Ford with its Zeta engine, they were overtaken by legislative change enforcing the use of catalytic converters, even for small cars.

● The majority of corporate and regulatory strategies emphasise emissions and engineering standards. This has the effect of diverting attention away from more structural changes in the underlying technology.

● There is a lack of appropriate knowledge and technical expertise to support clean technology development. By its very nature, clean technology requires companies to 'step outside' their conventional way of dealing with environmental problems.

So while the concept of clean technology has strong support among environmental groups, governments and many industrialists, many technical, economic and organisational factors would seem to favour the gradual 'adding-on' of new technology, rather than the more radical innovation needed for clean technology. At present some 80 per cent of European investment in environmental technology is 'end-of-pipe', compared to 20 per cent in clean technology.

Ensuring efficient use of resources

The green challenge has mainly focused on unwanted outputs in terms of pollution and waste. Another important measure in terms of environmental performance is the resource efficiency of the production systems in terms of the ratio of economically valuable outputs to material and energy inputs. The environmental impact of a particular production process relates to the nature of the technology being used, and the safety and efficiency with which it is used. There are a number of ways in which a company can ensure that the production system runs as efficiently as possible including:

- ensuring that those who operate and supervise the system are suitably trained and experienced;
- planning production schedules to minimise set-up delays or the need for process interruptions and restarts;
- controlling production to ensure that good working practices are followed to allow optimal consumption and recovery of resources and to ensure that the production of pollution and waste is controlled;
- using planned maintenance to keep equipment running efficiently, to avoid breakdowns and pollution leaks and to extend the lifespan of capital equipment;
- encouraging and rewarding suggestions for improvements from those who operate and supervise production processes.

WASTE MANAGEMENT

Emission control

A great deal of concern has been expressed by environmentalists and communities about the level and nature of the pollution that companies release into the environment. In the past companies have tended to be relatively complacent about their emissions as long as they were within legal limits. It was not until forced to do so by a Congressional subcommittee in 1984 that Dow Corning attempted to calculate its total pollution emissions. When it performed the calculations, the company was shocked to discover that it was releasing ten million pounds of dangerous chemicals into the environment. The initial reactive response to this was the introduction of expensive end-of-pipe measures such as filters. After this, a more proactive pollution prevention programme was established, which saved money, halved pollution levels and led to improved relations between Dow and the communities within which it operates.

New control technologies are being developed which reduce emissions and improve both environmental performance and conventional product quality. Leading American manufacturers are increasingly using real-time expert systems to monitor and adjust manufacturing processes to minimise leaks, waste, emissions and energy consumption while simultaneously maximising quality and yield.

Waste minimisation

Some 60 per cent of the solid waste generated by societies in western Europe is generated by industry and commerce, with the remaining 40 per cent coming from consumers and households. Waste has always been a low priority for marketers and production engineers. While a pollution incident could be very damaging to the business in terms of cost and image, the legal disposal of waste has attracted relatively little interest. A combination of rising waste-disposal costs, tougher legislation, increasing liability for the long-term effects of waste and the requirement to improve eco-performance, have made the waste outputs of the production system the subject of the sort of attention that was previously reserved for products.

Hazardous waste is a key concern for environmental groups and for the communities within which it is produced, transported or stored. For companies the disposal of hazardous waste has become an expensive business. Corbett and Wassenhove (1993) show that in the USA in the space of 11 years the cost of disposing of hazardous waste rose 8000 per cent for landfilling and between 400 per cent and 4000 per cent (depending on type) for incineration. For some products, the cost of disposal is greater than its value. The cost of disposing of a gallon of methanol is over 40 per cent more than its market value (Buckholz et al 1992). Waste reduction can therefore provide financial as well as environmental benefits. Dow Chemicals' total waste reduction between 1988 and 1990 cost $12.5 million (5.8 million ECUs), but the resulting 30 per cent reduction in waste produced an average payback period of only ten months on waste reduction projects.

Maintaining compliance and proactive strategies for increased legal and environmental pressures

Improved efficiency and proactive strategies to address increased input prices

Environmental, health and safty benefits

Benefits of a waste management strategy

Reduced risks and liabilities

Identification of new internal and external reuse and recycling opportunities

Cost savings in inputs, management and disposal

Development of clean technologies and techniques

Marketing and stakeholder benefits

Fig. 11.3 The benefits of a waste management strategy
(Source: Welford and Gouldson (1992))

Chevron's SMART (Save Money and Reduce Toxins) campaign by the end of 1991 had achieved a 60 per cent reduction in waste.

Pollution prevention is effectively a question of companies perfecting their manufacturing process so that there is no waste and no inefficiency. This mirrors the zero waste ethos of TQM. It is worth bearing in mind that zero waste is rather like total quality or 100 per cent customer satisfaction in being better as a goal to strive towards, rather than as a target that must be achieved. In search of this goal, companies are developing integrated waste minimisation strategies. The benefits of such strategies are outlined in Fig. 11.3. Crittenden and Kolaczkowski (1992) outline a five-step hierarchy of waste management strategies:

1 Total elimination of waste by radical process changes (clean technology).

2 Reduction of waste by changes in materials or process procedures. Process changes which can help to reduce waste include the scheduling of production to reduce the amount of equipment cleaning needed, or the separation of wastes during production for easy recovery.

3 Recycling of wastes for reuse or materials recovery or energy production.

4 Treatment by chemical, physical or biological

means to render the waste less harmful (for a summary of the available techniques see Allen 1994).

5 Disposal to air, water or land in compliance with the law.

Recycling

The amount of suitable space in which waste can be buried in the majority of developed countries is relatively limited, but the volume of waste produced is growing rapidly. In Holland there is virtually no suitable landfill space left, and in some American states such as California and New York, the costs of landfill dumping have reached as high as $100 (47 ECUs) per ton. The result is increasing financial, consumer and legislative pressure to recycle waste.

An important element in recycling is closing the loop between the consumer and the producer so that the elements of the tangible product which survive can be fed back into the production process. In a curious twist, the consumer can then become the company's supplier. At one end of the spectrum this can be as minor as supermarkets paying customers a penny to reuse their plastic shopping bags. At the other it can be a significant transaction such as the trading in of an existing car when buying a new one, with the customer only paying the difference between the value of the two cars.

SAFE TECHNOLOGY

Production systems have an impact on the people that operate them as well as the environment within which they operate. Exposure to radiation, noise, heat, vibration and potentially toxic chemicals all pose threats to the health and safety of workers. It is not always in the context of manufacturing that such hazards exist. In 1981 Oxfam put the number of accidental pesticide poisonings at 75 000 each year and in Europe there has been recent concern over the effect of sheep dip on farm workers.

To develop a working environment that is as safe as possible for workers, the following steps can be taken to go beyond mere compliance with health and safety regulations:

● Prevent health and safety hazards through safety conscious and ergonomic design.

● Where health and safety hazards cannot be eliminated through design, they should be isolated from the work-force as effectively as possible. This could be achieved through the physical layout of the facility, by controlling access to particular areas, by adding in systems to minimise the problem (e.g. ventilation systems) or by providing protective clothing for workers.

● Develop regular cleaning and maintenance procedures to reduce the possibility of the release or build-up of hazardous substances.

● Monitor the level and concentration of any potential hazards that do occur in the working environment.

● Regularly check workers who are exposed to any form of working environment hazard for any ill effects.

● Organise work schedules to shorten exposure periods, and ensure that worker training, production manuals and workplace signs all reinforce the safety-at-work message.

● Make appropriate contingency plans to deal with any foreseeable workplace accidents and ensure that these are linked into the monitoring and management process allowing them to be put into effect without delay.

Production systems need to be safe, not only for those who work with them, but also for those who live near them. The release of methyl isocyanate at Bhopal in 1984 and the release of dioxin at Seveso in Italy in 1976 are only two examples of incidents in which accidents at production facilities have led to deaths, injuries and the destruction or evacuation of local communities. Hazards to the community from production facilities usually stem from the use or storage of toxic, flammable, explosive or radioactive substances. Many of the steps needed to reduce the risks posed to local communities are the same as those needed to protect the work-force. Safety-conscious design, regular maintenance, inspection and monitoring, effective staff training and planning for emergencies all contribute to the reduction of risk. The UNEP promotes its Awareness and Preparedness for Emergencies at the Local Level (APELL) programme with the aims of ensuring that companies and communities work together to be aware of potential hazards and are prepared to respond in a planned and effective manner to any emergencies that occur (UNEP/IEO 1988).

CASE STUDY

Ecover

Ecover, the manufacturer of green cleaners and detergents based in Belgium, grew out of the green washing products marketing and distribution business set up by entrepreneur Frans Bogaerts in 1979. In 1982 the business became Ecover, and in 1988 it began manufacturing its own liquid cleaners. Ecover has an explicit aim of striving towards 'minimum environmental impact' during each stage of product manufacture and use. When it comes to raw materials the company, whenever possible, sources natural raw materials and avoids the synthetic petrochemical products which have become the mainstay of the cleaning products industry. For example, surfactants based on sugar and soap are used which use renewable sources and quickly biodegrade unlike their more modern petrochemical counterparts. To keep pollution and waste during usage down to a minimum, the company uses minimum packaging, modular packaging of washing powder bleach (to allow it to be used in white washes but not in coloured washes) and even warns its customers against using too much of its product.

The Ecover vision went far beyond the usual concept of green products. The company saw its product range as:

'far more than a series of ecological products. It is a symbol, a statement, a point of view: we can no longer continue like this. We want to be able to swim again in our rivers, drink water from the tap without being afraid, and look forward to our children's future with confidence.'

The only difficulty with developing a strategy of minimal environmental harm which went beyond the product itself was that conventional production processes and facilities could not provide the sort of green production performance that the Ecover vision entailed.

The company therefore set about creating the world's first 'ecological factory' based on a number of green principles. It aims for 'closed-loop processes' and has neither a chimney nor a polluting discharge pipe. The 1.5 million litres of water used each year is purified and recycled using a reed bed. Energy consumption is kept to a minimum through the use of solar power and heat recovery. Solid waste is sorted to maximise recycling opportunities. The building itself is a product of 'organic architecture'. It is made from entirely biodegradable materials including an insulating and aesthetically pleasing lawn roof garden supported by wooden rafters (sustainably sourced), and exterior walls made from recycled coal slag. In the choice of building materials, criteria for environmental quality pioneered by the Technical University of Eindhoven were used in addition to the conventional technical parameters. The building was also designed to cater for the health and welfare of its inhabitants through good thermal and acoustic insulation, and good natural ventilation and lighting.

Company policies include car-pooling, the provision of company bicycles and allowances for using public transport or switching to a fuel efficient car. (Although it might seem inappropriate that any workers at a factory like Ecover's should contribute to global warming by commuting to work, the company has calculated that the volume of carbon released into the atmosphere by the journeys of their staff will equate to the annual atmospheric carbon absorbed by the grass roof.) Office staff are networked on computers to reduce consumption of recycled stationery, and can take advantage of flexible hours and working from home via their portable computers.

Building the ecological factory involved a premium of 30 per cent additional cost compared to a conventional plant. However, due to its choice of materials for reuse, recycling or easy disposal, decommissioning the plant will cost only one tenth of that for a conventional plant.

(Adapted from Develter, D. (1992), *Ecover – The Ecological Factory Manual*, Ecover Publications.)

CHAPTER 12

Opening the doors – sustainable communications

'While compliance is now given attention by most organizations, fewer organizations seem to have a handle on communication, and it is the latter that spells success or failure in your effective transition to a new Green World.'
(Harrison 1992)

INTRODUCTION

Marketing communications is often perceived as synonymous with promotion, one of the four Ps of the classic marketing mix. In some companies it is even more narrowly associated with advertising. However, there is a great deal more to marketing communications than promotion, and a great deal more to promotion than advertising. This becomes particularly apparent in relation to the greening of marketing. The role within society of marketing communications, and advertising in particular, has been a contentious one. Marketers and advertisers have usually responded to criticism of the effects of their communication campaigns by claiming that they are a mirror which simply reflects society without altering or influencing it. Critics claim that this mirror is distorted, and that the inaccuracies in the reflection can change society and its values in undesirable ways. A green perspective reveals the communication process in grey consumer marketing operating like a one-way mirror between the consumer and the company. It reflects back images of the consumers with their real or imaginary problems solved by the company's product. The production system and much of the company is presented as a 'black box' into which the customer may not look (the situation is different for business-to-business marketing. The growth of green concern has produced powerful forces which are attempting to prise this box open. In many countries, legislation is forcing companies into unprecedented levels of environmental disclosure. Customers, together with the consumer and environmental groups who may influence them, are demanding to know more about what goes into products, their manufacture and disposal. What customers do or do not learn about the production processes, ingredients or the manufacturer of a product is increasingly likely to influence their consumption decision. When the green spotlight falls on to a company, the one-way mirror will suddenly become transparent, and the company behind is revealed. As Bernstein (1992) puts it:

'We are entering the age of corporate *glasnost*. Consumers want to know about the company. Companies won't be able to hide behind their brands. Who makes it will be as important as what goes into it since the former may reassure the customer about the latter. How can they trust a so-called "green product" unless they know something about the company's environmental performance?'

There are two dimensions to the environmental marketing communications challenge. The first involves providing information about the company, its products and production processes, and their socio-environmental implications. This is the focus of this chapter. The second challenge is to integrate eco-performance into promotional strategies, which is dealt with in Chapter 13.

THE MARKETING COMMUNICATIONS PROCESS

The development of marketing communications theory has been dominated by models developed in the 1940s, 1950s and 1960s which take a physical/technical approach to understanding communication. These present communication as a process involving a 'sender' who encodes a message and sends it in the form of a signal to be decoded and interpreted by a 'receiver'. As Buttle (1989) puts it:

'The adherence of marketing communication authors to the ancestral writings of Lasswell, Shannon and Weaver, Schramm and Berlo and Klapper has produced a contemporary literature which has failed to take account of recent advances in communication theory generally. What we have is outdated, ill-informed and in need of radical revision.'

In most consumer markets the dominant form of communication has been advertising, which conforms very much to Schramm's (1954) early concept of communication as a 'magic bullet' that transfers information from one party to another. Advertising communication is typically a relatively uni-directional process involving two parties, and its dominance has reinforced the conventional mechanistic view of the communication process. This means that any other messages that the target audience are receiving are dismissed as 'noise' that may interfere with the message. In practice this 'noise' may be messages about environmental issues from green groups being broadcast to a company's target audience more effectively than the company's own green message.

Contemporary approaches to communication emphasise more human and social aspects of communications such as sharing and understanding. It is these aspects of communication which are particularly important to environmental marketing. Communicating successfully is not simply a question of putting out positive messages

regarding eco-performance. It involves becoming involved in the multi-party dialogue about business and the environment.

THE COMMUNICATIONS MIX

The promotional mix comprises a company's marketing communications efforts over the four major controllable channels (advertising, sales promotion, personal selling and public relations). The importance of each type of channel varies between industries, companies and products. While advertising and sales promotion are the dominant channels in consumer marketing, personal selling remains more important in industrial markets. Public relations and selling are the two elements of the mix which are most commonly used for the provision of information to customers and other stakeholders; advertising and sales promotion are more commonly used for promotion.

These four channels are the main ones through which a marketer's carefully designed messages are sent. Communication, in the broader sense of sharing with consumers and influencing their understanding of the company and its product, also takes place through a number of other media. Everything about a company and its marketing mix communicates including the following.

● *The product.* This can proclaim its own eco-performance through energy-saving features, compact size as in nappies, or the use of 'bionic' design (*see* page 175).

● *Prices.* These are often interpreted as a measure of quality by consumers but can also be used by companies to put across an image of a company that cares more about its customers than about profits.

● *Availability.* A product that is available through a channel which is known for its environmental excellence will communicate by association.

● *Packaging.* The package and its labelling can say a great deal about the product and the company. The use of packages to provide information about the company, the product and the packaging materials can all contribute to a good eco-performance.

● *Names.* Almost any value can be communicated by the name of a product, brand or company. An increasing number of products are being marketed with names that involve 'natural', 'earth', 'whole' or 'green'. The use of 'eco' is interesting, in that the words 'ecology' and 'economics' have a common root in the Greek word for 'house'. This makes it very suitable to communicate a resource-reduction/cost-saving green strategy. For example, Kyocera's 'Ecosys' printer has been marketed both on the environmental benefits and the cost benefits of its reduced consumption of paper and toner cartridges. One of the problems for communicating eco-performance through naming is that in today's international market-place, different words can mean very different things in relation to the environment.

● *Actions.* These are meant to speak louder than words, and as Bernstein observes:

'Everything communicates. But does everything communicate coherently? A buyer takes a supplier to task for operating environmentally unsatisfactory manufacturing processes and then gives him a lift in the company 3-litre car. The chief executive sends out an environmental statement on non-recycled paper … The local environmental group is called in for a community meeting around the boardroom table of tropical hardwood veneer. Conversely a favourable message will be conveyed by converting part of the reserved car park to a bike rack.'

● *Procedures and policies.* When customers interact with companies they will typically come into contact with a company's policies and procedures, and these can communicate a great deal. Safeway's 'Refund and Replace' policy to replace unsatisfactory own brand goods while also refunding their price communicates confidence in its own brands, a commitment to customer satisfaction, and unusually but perhaps most importantly, great confidence in the integrity of its customers.

● *Facilities.* The buildings and land that a business occupies can be an important communicator.

As Bernstein's quote above illustrates, even the layout of the company car park can communicate something. The reception area of the corporate headquarters is typically decorated with the company mission statement and any awards for technical achievement or export performance. Environmental awards, copies of a corporate environmental policy (CEP), summaries of environmental audits, even real plants instead of plastic ones can all help to communicate a company's environmental commitment.

This list of communication methods is by no means exhaustive. Developing strategies has been likened to many things, including conducting an orchestra or playing in a jazz band. Managing the environmental marketing communications process is perhaps somewhere between these two analogies in being like conducting a 'big band'. The four major channels of communication are the soloists, and at times they may have to do a little improvisation. All the other elements of the organisation represent the other instruments who need to stick to the tempo and the melody in the score to prevent the message becoming ragged or discordant.

TOWARDS A SUSTAINABLE COMMUNICATION PROCESS

For green companies the challenge is to move from unsustainable to sustainable communication. McDonagh (1994) defines sustainable communication as:

'an interactive social process of unravelling and eradicating alienation that may occur between an organization and its publics or stakeholders. Based on the notion of totality or holism it embraces conflict and critique through information disclosure, access to and participation in organizational policies and processes and structures allowing open ended dialogue. Thus by use of "green eco- or environmental marketing communications" the organization builds trust in the mind of those in society and permits the approach of a utopian situation of high levels of … consensus as to how mankind should exist.'

Table 12.1 Comparison of sustainable and unsustainable communication

Sustainable communication	Unsustainable communication
• manages expectations	• manipulates emotions
• acknowledges poor past performance as a serious matter	• ignores or denies mistakes, or treats them lightly
• looks for options that make sense to all stakeholders only	• looks out for number one
• presents evidence to support positions and ideas	• does not disclose relevant raw data and back-up work
• asks and tries to answer questions	• disseminates news and decisions
• focuses on core publics to create relationships	• does PR to the public
• treats stakeholders as customers who need to be understood	• believes stakeholders and audiences need education
• interacts with stakeholders at their respective levels of awareness, with a consistent commitment	• delivers a variable message to various publics
• is always open	• is open when convenient

Source: Harrison (1992)

The characteristics of sustainable and unsustainable communication are contrasted in Table 12.1 (Harrison 1992). McDonagh integrates the different elements of the sustainable communication process into a comprehensive model presented in Fig. 12.1. It demonstrates how as companies move towards increasingly green and sustainable marketing strategies, so their marketing communications process will need to evolve into something much more holistic and complex than the conventional grey models of marketing communications. Some of the key principles of this model include the following considerations.

● *Trust.* The loss of trust and confidence in businesses and business leaders is well documented (*see* page 44). Sustainable communications aim to rebuild that trust.

● *Access.* The issue of openness of information has become an increasingly important issue on the green agenda, partly driven by the secretive tendencies of businesses and governments over issues of environmental degradation. Johnson (1991) proposes:

'Openness is essential in all public/social functions. A lack of openness is usually a mark of hypocrisy, of protection of position, of exclusivity; the closed group and closed mentality are hallmarks of grey culture.'

Investors who screen companies for socio-environmental performance are increasingly using the openness of a company to external enquiries and its level of disclosure as one of their criteria. Openness is not simply a matter of keeping consumers, investors and environmentalists happy. In the case of major environmental hazards posed by companies, it can become a matter of life and death. During the two years before the 1984 Bhopal gas leak, Union Carbide denied reports of faults in the plant. Even the local toxicologist was not given data about the lethality of the escaping gas. An open information policy might have created enough community concern to stimulate the company to take steps which would have prevented the leak. It almost certainly would have stimulated the local community to make contingency plans which might have saved some lives. It also would have made the company less vulnerable to accusations of criminal negligence (Kleiner 1991).

● *Disclosure.* Secrecy breeds distrust and a lack of confidence. As Fig. 12.2 shows, there appears to be a correlation between the familiarity of an industry and the perception that the general public holds about it. Generally speaking, the more people know about an industry, the more favourably it is viewed. This provides a strong incentive for companies to come out from behind their traditional veils of secrecy. Over time companies appear to be becoming reconciled to the principle of disclosure. In the USA, when the

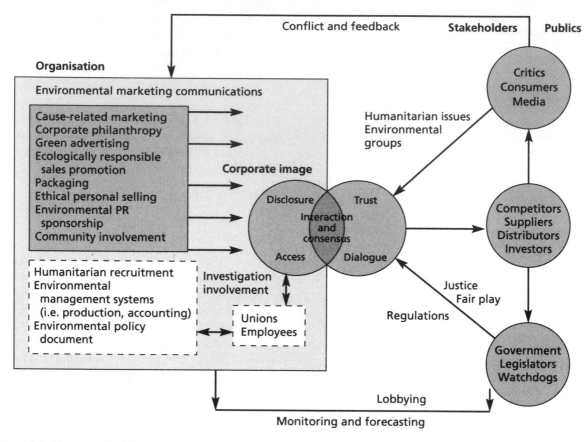

Fig. 12.1 The sustainable communications process
(Source: McDonagh (1994))

Council on Economic Priorities began sending out questionnaires on social and environmental issues in the early 1970s, the response rate was only 2 per cent. By the end of the 1980s this figure had risen to 85 per cent.

● *Promotion.* The name of the communication game is still promotion. Whatever the company discloses should still be with the ultimate aim of promoting the company or its product to their publics.

Buttle (1989) sees one consequence of the emphasis on the traditional physical/technical models of marketing communications as an overemphasis on the short-term effects on the target audience. This leads to a failure to appreciate longer-term cumulative effects of marketing communications

on people, families, institutions and cultures. This influence, although largely ignored, is immense. Its effect is also so widespread that it is impossible to isolate the degree to which the world view that we each possess is created by it. The business community has put a great deal of energy and communications resources over the years into portraying environmentalists as scaremongers, pessimists, Luddites and as being anti-business, anti-growth, anti-profit and anti-libertarian. The influence of marketing communication beyond our attitudes to products and producers is emphasised by Nohrstead's (1993) assertion:

'The common aspect of these processes (PR, information management strategies, and lifestyle advertising) ... is that they not only intend to influence attitudes towards certain organizations and policies, but basic

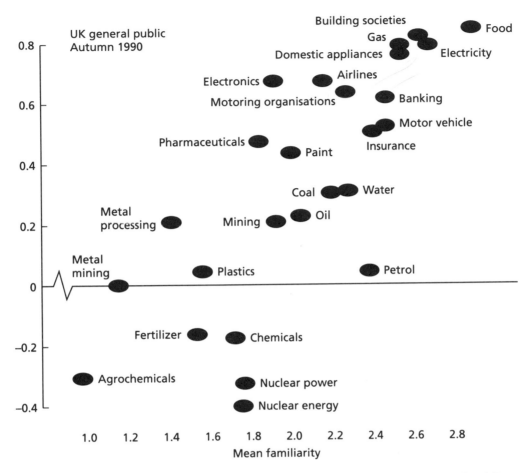

Fig. 12.2 FT perceptual map showing industry favourability and familiarity – UK general public, Autumn 1990
(Source: MORI)

value structures of society, concerning, for example, whether material growth or ecological care is the most important value or whether efficiency or democracy should have the highest priority.'

Sustainable communications requires companies to address the longer-term and the socio-environmental effects of their communication efforts. Taking a longer-term view may allow companies to become more open about the poorer aspects of their environmental performance. In a competitive world in which the vociferous media are hungry

for sensational stories of environmental failure among companies, the managerial instinct is to hide weaknesses from competitors, customers, investors and other stakeholders. Hiding a problem produces an illusion that it has been dealt with, whereas it actually creates a new problem, an informational time-bomb buried in the organisation which could go off at any time. A longer-term focus can allow a company to announce any environmental weaknesses in the context of launching a credible initiative to improve them.

THE GREEN COMMUNICATIONS CHALLENGE

The implications of the green challenge for a company's marketing communications strategy will reflect the actual and perceived eco-performance of the company, its products and the industry to which it belongs. For companies with a strong eco-performance, there is clearly an opportunity to gain competitive advantage by communicating this to the market-place. For those whose environmental performance is poor, or poorly perceived, the communications challenge will centre around damage limitation and clarification together with accurate and rapid communication of any improvements. For companies somewhere in between, their communications strategy is likely to involve promoting themselves on other dimensions of competitive performance, while also ensuring that they are perceived as open, honest and environmentally acceptable.

Developing a green communications campaign is fraught with danger for the company that simply attempts to climb aboard the departing green bandwagon. Campaigns such as Friends of the Earth's 'Green Con of the Year Awards' ensure that there is a great deal of negative publicity awaiting the unwary company. There are Seven Green Cs which companies need to negotiate successfully.

1 *Complexity.* Environmental problems are mostly complex in nature and rarely involve simple answers. Consumers are frequently poorly informed about environmental issues even though they are interested in environmentally and socially responsible consumption. Schlossberg (1993a) suggests that the lack of factual environmental information represents the 'greatest environmental hazard'.

2 *Cacophony.* Another problem for marketers is that consumers are currently bombarded by information and images about the environment, which can make it difficult for a company's environmental message to stand out and communicate. A survey of newspapers and magazines monitored by *Marketing* magazine revealed that during June 1989 the word green was used 30 777 times. This compares with 3617 occurrences for the same publications

for the same period five years earlier (Mitchell and Levy 1989). Research International, when surveying 28 countries, concluded that an excess of messages about the environment was leading to information overload among customers.

3 *Credibility.* The content of many green messages lacks credibility in consumers' eyes. Mintel's 1991 survey revealed that 90 per cent of UK consumers were highly sceptical about green promotional campaigns. Research by Gerstman and Meyers suggests that only 15 per cent of US consumers feel that current environmental claims by manufacturers are believable. The aim of all forms of environmental marketing communication is to develop credibility for the company and its product. However much money is set aside for communications, and however well the green messages are designed and executed, credibility may not be developed unless the message is consonant with the target audience's perception of the company and the environmental issues being addressed. Some companies will find it easier than others to develop a credible, consonant message connected to some parts of the green agenda.

4 *Confusion.* Kinnear *et al* (1974) found that consumers mistakenly viewed enzymes in washing powders as pollutants along with phosphates, leading to a subsequent avoidance of enzyme claims by manufacturers. One might have expected the increasing level of environmental media coverage to have produced a new generation of more environmentally informed and confident consumers. However, BRMB/Mintel's research showed that 63 per cent of UK consumers said that they found what companies said about the eco-performance of their products 'confusing'. This is not surprising given the information overload and conflicting messages from different parties that consumers are faced with.

5 *Cynicism.* The motives of marketers seeking to communicate a green message are also often open to doubt. Mintel's 1991 survey revealed that 40 per cent of green shoppers felt that retailers selling 'environmentally friendly' products were seeking to exploit the market rather than to protect the environment. According to Sian Morrissey, a researcher with the Consumers' Association:

'In all our discussion groups on Green issues consumers have shown a high degree of scepticism. They are very, very suspicious about manufacturers jumping on to the environmental bandwagon.'

6 *Co-ordination.* It is unwise for a marketer to make green claims for a product unless they are certain that the environmental credentials of the product, its ingredients, its packaging, its manufacturing process and the entire company are behind it. This perhaps explains why many companies' environmental marketing efforts are centred around packaging reductions which, in addition to leaving the core product untouched, are fully under the control of marketing management.

7 *Commercial confidence.* In countries such as the UK there is a tradition of secrecy and of using 'commercial confidence' as a reason for keeping hidden much of what goes on within a company, including environmental impacts (Irvine 1990). This is set to change with the introduction of the EC Directive on the Freedom of Access to Information on the Environment (90/313/EC), which guarantees individuals access to information concerning any company's environmental performance without them having to prove an interest.

MARKETING COMMUNICATIONS STRATEGIES

The degree to which different companies in a market integrate environmental information into their marketing communications strategies varies widely, and is not always a fair reflection of eco-performance. It was interesting to note that it was not until rivals gained competitive advantage from putting a CFC-free sticker on their aerosols that Johnson & Johnson were prompted to market their aerosols as CFC-free, even though they had been since 1976.

There are three key V variables in environmental marketing communications: the *virtue* of the product offering in its eco-performance; the *visibility* of the environmental performance and the information relating to it; and the *volume* of noise which the company makes about its environmental performance. A backlash from environmental groups and the media followed some of the early green campaigns which were high in terms of the volume of communication, but not backed up by either particularly virtuous eco-performance or visible evidence to back up the green claims. Since then, many companies have turned down the volume, but continued to improve in terms of virtue and visibility. One example of this is the removal of the word 'recycled' from products such as refuse sacks on the shelves of some supermarkets. The product is still made from recycled materials, but is not being proclaimed as such for fear of being viewed as cashing in on green concern. A further V factor which will become more important as environmental marketing moves towards its second phase is *verification*. The use of independent third parties to substantiate environmental claims can be a vital weapon in overcoming problems of credibility and cynicism.

ENVIRONMENTAL DISCLOSURE

Information about corporate environmental and social performance can reach the public domain in a number of ways. Mandatory responsibilities require companies in countries such as France and the UK to register some of their environmental impacts by the completion of pollution registers. America took the lead in legislation with the 1986 Emergency Planning and Community Right-to-Know Act, which obliges all but the smallest companies to compile and publish a Toxic Release Inventory (TRI). This information is used by organisations such as the Council on Economic Responsibilities and the Investor Responsibility Research Centre to keep consumers and investors informed. There has been relatively little legislation forcing environmental disclosure within Europe until recently. Norway's 1989 amendments to its Enterprise Act and Accounting Act made it mandatory for companies' annual reports to include pollution levels together with details on remedial and preventative measures undertaken or planned. In practice, however, the majority of Norwegian companies affected have limited their response to a short statement confirming that they comply with all the relevant regulations.

Table 12.2 Methods of environmental disclosure

Style	Characteristics	Examples
INVOLUNTARY		
The Green Spotlight'	Involuntary disclosure as campaigners turn spotlight on 'polluters', 'despoilers'	Targets have included Albright & Wilson, Bayer, British Gas, Du Pont, Exxon, Hoechst, ICI, McDonald's, Mitsubishi Corporation, Norsk Hydro, Shell, etc.
MANDATORY		
'The Doomsday Book'	Compilation of registers of emissions, effluents or wastes – often open to public scrutiny	HMIP and NRA registers in UK, TRI in USA. FoE has made extensive use of such data, as has Greenpeace's 'Dirty 50' campaign
'The Bottom Line'	Provisions and continent liabilities in annual reporting	Potentially, in every corporate annual report. Accountancy profession still must decide which liabilities are probable, quantifiable and 'material' (i.e. likely to be *financially* significant)
VOLUNTARY		
'The Corporate Nod'	A paragraph or two in the annual report	Legion – and growing
'The Green Gloss'	A separate evironmental publication, often featuring frogs or butterflies, generally put together with PR in mind	Legion, with growing numbers in Japan – but under fire in Europe
'The United Front'	Initiatives by industry federations	Mainly defensive (e.g. nuclear energy, PVC, packaging), but some proactive (e.g. Responsible Care, GEMI)
'The Tax Return'	Ranging from the bare facts, as required in Norway and Sweden, through to Toxic Release Inventory-style reports	e.g. Monsanto's TRI-style reporting transferred to Europe
'The Confessional'	A warts-and-all exposé of a company's problems	Very few, although elements crept into ICI's 1992 report (e.g. mention of prosecutions, fines). Not popular in Japan
'The Pledge'	Specific, auditable targets set, as with companies participating in the US EPA's '33/50' Program	Lead taken by US chemical corporations (e.g. Monsanto, Dow, Du Pont) and some oil companies (e.g. Shell Canada's Sustainable Development Report), followed by EU chemical majors (e.g. ICI) and then by others (e.g. British Telecom)
'The Environmental Balance Sheet'	Full environmental cost accounting	e.g. BSO Origin
'The Whole Picture'	Integrated financial, environmental and sustainability accounting and reporting	Who will be first?

Source: International Institute for Sustainable Development

Other forms of environmental disclosure can be involuntary. 'Whistleblowing' by internal employees, the penetration of the organisation by investigative journalists or environmental activists, or revelations resulting from legal investigations can all bring the most carefully guarded company secrets out into the open. Finally there is a wide range of voluntary forms of disclosure that companies may engage in as part of a corporate communications and promotion strategy. Annual reports, information on product labels, press releases and information hot-lines can all be provided. Figure 12.2 details some of the most common forms of disclosure.

Although many companies are viewed by environmentalists and the media as secretive in relation to eco-performance, there is an alternative explanation for the lack of information coming from many companies. *Coming Clean: Corporate Environmental Reporting* (produced by Deloitte Touche Tohmatsu International, in conjunction with SustainAbility and the International Institute for Sustainable Development) found that many companies are simply poorly prepared to answer the growing number of questions about eco-performance coming from customers, regulators, lenders, insurers, accountants and environmentalists. Within such companies, the lack of disclosure reflects an inability rather than an unwillingness to answer the questions. Being unable to answer such fundamental questions from key stakeholders is itself an act of communication, and the message it presents is not one of professionalism. Elkington (1994) sees the expectations about acceptable levels of disclosure among key stakeholders as rising and comments that:

'Business leaders must now get actively involved in defining and managing the process of environmental communications. Failure to do so will increasingly pose the risk of their company's real present (and potential future) value being challenged; their position as a responsible corporate citizen being undermined; and competitive advantage draining away as customers and consumers turn to others who are – or are seen to be – more environmentally responsible.'

The benefits of environmental disclosure

There is a difference between openness, which is reactive, and active disclosure which is more proactive. Each carries a particular form of risk. Where companies disclose information but do not actively disseminate it, there is a danger that understanding will not be widespread leading to misunderstandings. Elkington (1994) cites the example of Danish health care and enzymes company, Novo Nordisk. It opened up by inviting groups of environmentalists, regulators and others into the company to discuss how to make progress towards sustainability. Although this provided a range of benefits, information released to environmentalists by the company during a visit later resurfaced in a distorted fashion as part of an environmentalist campaign against enzymes in Switzerland.

Active disclosure can also be something of a gamble. When British Telecom published its award-winning environmental report, it 'shattered the public delusion that BT was a "clean" company' according to Deputy Chairman Mike Bett (Tennant 1993). The report identified that BT was a major user of CFCs, that it consumed more than 1 per cent of the nation's electricity and consumed 125 million litres of fuel each year. According to Mr Bett:

'Some time ago, we in BT projected that all companies, in all industrial sectors, would soon be expected to address the environment as a serious business issue and, more especially, would need to demonstrate to their shareholders that they were doing something positive about it.'

Ben & Jerry's reporting strategy shows that such a gamble can pay off. It publishes two audits within its annual report: one financial, the other social. The social audit covers employee benefits, community involvement, ecological impact, plant safety and customer service. These external audits have been quite critical of aspects of the business. The 1992 audit highlighted concerns over plant safety after an 87 per cent increase in accidents and injuries, and criticised the lack of 'follow through' on its employee ownership pledge. Despite this, the openness has acted to enhance the company's credibility as a socially responsible company.

Norsk Hydro are another company at the forefront of environmental reporting initiatives (see case study at end of chapter) which cites five main benefits of public disclosure:

1 as a spur to continuous improvement;

2 to secure competitive advantage;

3 corporate communications benefits which accrue from presenting an honest and open picture of eco-performance to employees and local residents among others;

4 enabling the company to contribute to, and influence the environmental debate;

5 contributing to the education of the general public, and children in particular.

Corporate environmental reporting

The *Coming Clean* report surveyed corporate environmental reporting (CER) practices in the triad of major world markets: Europe, Japan and the USA. The survey included a sample of 70 companies that had produced 'free-standing' environmental reports, and also a sample of the 'users' of these reports. A wealth of information and recommendations were contained in the report, and it described an evolutionary life cycle for CER within companies:

Stage 1   Green glossies, newsletters, videos. Short statement in the annual report.

Stage 2   One-off environmental report, often linked to an initial formal policy statement.

Stage 3   Annual reporting, linked to an environmental management system, but consisting mostly of descriptive text without quantification.

Stage 4   Provision of full performance data on an annual basis, and made available on diskette or on-line. Environment report cross-referenced with annual report.

Stage 5   Sustainable development reporting linking environmental, economic and social aspects of corporate performance, and supported by indicators of sustainability.

The companies surveyed in *Coming Clean* represented the pioneering early adopters of CER, rather than the majority of companies. In some companies the development of CER has reached a point where it resembles the financial reporting process. The Body Shop's *Green Book*, for example, was designed to complement its annual report and accounts by providing an equally detailed and accurate picture of the environmental performance of the company. This contrasts with the environmental reporting of the majority of companies who use CER which, according to a study by the Institute of Chartered Accountants, is 'highly selective ... public relations driven ... with a distinct tendency to err on the side of self-congratulation'. A study of CER across France, Germany, The Netherlands, Sweden and Switzerland by Roberts (1991) found a similar situation, concluding:

> 'Whilst the majority of companies disclose at least some environmental information, the level of disclosure is generally low'.

Environmental Data Services (ENDS) also found that where information is provided, it is rarely quantified or adequately explained.

The motivation for CER

The motivation behind voluntary forms of environmental disclosure varies widely between companies and between countries (Wong 1988). It is often adopted as a response to reduce the pressure for increasing mandatory disclosure. Jones (1993) points out that the corporate environmental reporting which represents the most comprehensive reports from American companies are nearly all in 'high-profile, potentially very environmentally unfriendly industries'. The reasons provided by companies engaged in CER in the *Coming Clean* report are presented in Fig. 12.3. A cynical reader might interpret these findings as companies putting a positive and proactive face on an initiative which in many industries appears to be relatively defensive and reactive, at least in its early stages. The effect of pressure groups is barely acknowledged outside of Japan, but it would be interesting to know how many companies would be engaged in CER if environmental pressure groups did not exist.

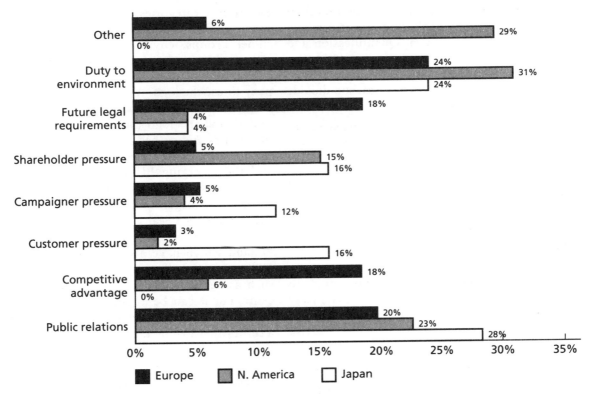

Fig. 12.3 Motivations for corporate environmental reporting
(Source: International Institute for Sustainable Development)

Mastrandonas and Strife (1992) conducted focus group research among church and governmental institutional investors along with individual investors who 'screen' their investments on the basis of socio-environmental performance. They found that investors were interested in companies' eco-performance including their compliance record, liabilities, policies and programmes and the results of audits. They also note that:

'historically, corporations have been reluctant to expand communications with 'outsiders' beyond legally mandated reports, incident-generated press communications, advertisements, new product announcement and 'good news' stories. Requests for information regarding the operations within the four walls of the company were considered intrusive and, as a rule, were not acceded to.'

A corporate evironmental report needs to be marketed as carefully as any other element of the communications mix. This means that it should be targetted at key stakeholders, developed to meet their needs and made user-friendly and accessible. Companies can also use it as a process of creating dialogue on green issues with key stakeholders, by introducing feedback mechanisms such as a green telephone hot-line with a freephone number. Mastrandonas and Strife (1992) make the following general recommendations for Corporate Environmental Reports, based on the marketing-orientated concept of meeting the needs of shareholders and other stakeholders.

● A report should be a corporate-level report, covering employee health and safety as well as environmental, legal requirements, trends and concerns.

● A report should demonstrate the corporate values, philosophy and commitment to improved eco-performance.

● A report should describe clearly environmental and health and safety goals, and report candidly progress made against them. Quantification and benchmarking is important; Cottam (1992) suggests the use of indicators such as waste generated per employee or unit of output, or carbon dioxide output per unit of sales.

● A report should describe relevant management systems, structural changes, compliance programmes and audits.

● A report should detail the compliance record, and in the case of non-compliance explain the remedial and preventative actions taken.

● A report should highlight the main green challenges relevant to the industry sectors that the company is involved in.

● The company should take the opportunity to discuss in the report any criticism of the company from special interest groups, communities or the media.

● The company should include financial data to demonstrate the implications of eco-performance.

● The company should include third-party reviews where possible to validate the contents of the report.

As the *Coming Clean* report put it:

'(A) successful free-standing report can be seen as the "jewel in the crown" of a corporation's environmental communications strategy.'

Product disclosure – green labelling

At the product level, the issue of disclosure has also become important, particularly in relation to green labelling. There are more than 30 different green product identification schemes in action across the world. Germany's Blue Angel scheme, founded in 1978, is the forerunner to a range of government-sponsored, voluntary membership schemes that have been implemented in countries including Japan, Canada, Australia, New Zealand, France, Finland, Portugal and the USA. Around 4000 products carry the Blue Angel label (Fig. 12.4a), showing that they meet the specific environmental criteria laid down for one of the

64 product categories. These criteria are agreed by a panel including representatives from consumer groups, environmental groups and the industry. The scheme is a voluntary one, with costs covered by an annual fee paid by the company to use the logo. A 1989 survey revealed that 80 per cent of German households recognised and understood the logo (Salzman 1991), although this understanding has since become confused by the creation of the 'Green Dot' recycling scheme and the emerging EU Ecolabel (Fig. 12.4(b)). Another group of schemes involving private sponsorship have begun to emerge, such as the Green Cross and Green Seal schemes in the USA and the environmental labelling schemes in Norway and Finland which have also been introduced since 1991. Green labelling is associated with products such as aerosols, washing machines and detergents, but it can be applied to a wide range of products. In Denmark, new homes must be given a certificate showing their energy efficiency before they are sold.

Consumers demonstrate a mixture of support for, and ignorance about, green label schemes. In 1989 the Consumers' Association interviewed 1930 UK consumers about green labelling. It found that around 60 per cent of shoppers had seen green labels in shops, and nearly 60 per cent of those had bought a green-labelled product on their last shopping trip. When shown a supermarket's own green label, 55 per cent wrongly assumed that it had been officially approved, usually by the government. Among those who knew that green labels were not subject to official scrutiny, 83 per cent believed that they should be (Consumers' Association 1990). The situation had not improved by 1993, when a further survey of UK consumers found that 67 per cent felt they were 'confused' about green labelling (Vallely 1993).

Labelling schemes can either work on a simple pass/fail basis, or can involve some form of gradation of performance. Consumer groups favour the grading schemes which are more informative to consumers, and because the simple pass/fail approach provides no incentive for qualifying companies to continue to improve their eco-performance. Two key problems with implementing such schemes is deciding how full a product

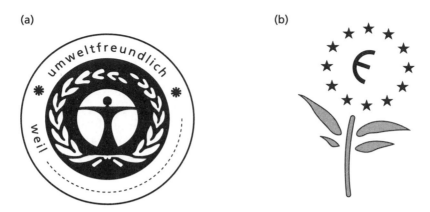

Fig. 12.4 Key green labels: (a) The German 'Blue Angel', (b) The EU Ecolabel

life cycle to examine, and how often to regrade products. A scheme which reassessed products on a three-yearly basis, as has been suggested for the UK, might not keep pace with the rapid evolution of technology in some markets.

It is not only environmentally based labelling schemes that are being introduced. The 'Fair Trade' label covers a range of products such as coffee, tea and a range of craft items which are produced in local co-operatives in less industrialised countries and sold under trade terms which aim to benefit them. There are also product specific schemes such as the 'Rug Mark' for Indian carpets, which ensures that the rugs are produced without the exploitation of child labour.

Do green labelling schemes work?

One product in which pressure group action and consumer concern led to changes in industry practice and a new green label being introduced is canned tuna fish (Sykes 1993). 'Dolphin-friendly' tuna can be found on most supermarket shelves, but customers will have to look more closely at labelling information to find out where the fish came from and how it was caught. The Whale and Dolphin Conservation Society (WDCS) reached an agreement with the tuna industry for a 'dolphin-friendly' quality standard which would be awarded to products meeting the WDCS criteria. In 1991 the industry agreed to set up an independent body to monitor the tuna fleets and

canneries to ensure that they were not producing tuna using 'wall-of-death' drift netting. Two years later no independent monitoring body had been established. The six biggest tuna producers in the UK who signed an agreement with the WDCS and adopted the 'dolphin-friendly' logo were also found not to be operating on-boat inspection of tuna fleets, which formed one of the conditions of the agreement. According to Alison Smith, Conservation Projects Manager at WDCS:

'It is fundamental that we get inspectors on board the boats to check the fish at source. Anyone can write things on a piece of paper but this is leaving a company open to mistakes and forgery. At sea anything can happen – trans-shipment, offloading on to factory ships. Companies can get away with murder just because they have a piece of paper saying it's all OK.'

Until the industry begins to live up to the agreements that it has signed in order to make use of the 'dolphin-friendly' logos, customers will have to look more closely at labelling information to find out where the fish came from and where it was caught. Rod and line caught tuna provides the best protection for dolphins, and tuna from Ecuador (such as that marketed by Heinz) is also a safe choice given the Ecuadorian government's 'no dolphin deaths' policy and the presence of independent inspectors from the Inter-American Tropical Tuna Commission on every boat (Sykes 1993).

Another question is whether labelling schemes work in terms of creating the intended response from consumers. Holloway and Wallich (1994) suggest that consumers can only process about five different pieces of information attached to a product. Adding environmental information on to a food product label which will already contain ingredients information, nutritional analysis and perhaps a free recipe could lead to information overload instead of to more informed or thoughtful purchase decisions. A key problem is that many environmental issues are complex, controversial and constantly changing, which does not make for easy encapsulation on the label of a product which may be very small. A short environmental claim may leave the company open to accusations of 'sins of omission' but too long an explanation may overwhelm both the package and the consumer with details. One alternative, pioneered by Scientific Certification Systems (SCS) in America, is the 'environmental report card' (Schlossberg 1993b). This provides a label similar to nutritional labelling, detailing the environmental impacts of a product established by a life cycle analysis. It grades companies on five 'environmental burdens': resource depletion, energy use, air pollution, water pollution and solid waste. This information is presented in a numerical and pictorial form which can be absorbed by consumers in the one or two seconds during which they will pick up a product to inspect it. As SCS President, Stanley Rhodes, points out, the strength of the report card is that it 'does not set a standard, it only reports what is. Standards are set on pre-set criteria. Those types of position are controversial. We'd rather communicate and educate.'

Another solution to the problem that many marketers face of trying to communicate complex environmental information using a small (and preferably shrinking) package, is to simply include upon it an address to which the consumer could write for full product information. This misses out on the opportunity to use a green claim as a trigger for the green consumer, but it avoids the potentially damaging criticism that can result from the use of simplistic or misleading messages. Procter and Gamble provides customers who write in with a double-sided information sheet on each of its products including details on

ingredients and environmental information, together with a copy of its environmental policy and environmental newsletter.

A final criticism levelled at green labelling schemes is that they often represent an informal environmentally-based trade barrier in an era when trade barriers within Europe and elsewhere are being dismantled. For the German Blue Angel scheme, about 12 per cent of all label holders are non-German companies, a figure which is inconclusive in relation to the trade barrier debate.

European eco-labelling scheme

The most significant development in green labelling within Europe is the EU Eco-labelling Regulation agreed at the end of 1991. The initiative aims to provide purchasers with clear independent and authoritative guidance on those products in any category which have the lowest cradle-to-grave environmental impact. The product categories first chosen for use in the scheme were washing machines, kitchen towels, detergents and xerographic paper.

Once a category becomes open for an eco-label, companies can apply to have their products assessed. The companies pay the administrative costs associated with processing and assessing their application, and must pay a fee to use the label if one is awarded. Progress has been predictably slow with a good deal of wrangling over how the life cycle assessments involved should be conducted and what criteria products should be assessed against. The proposal for eco-labels on cosmetics and toiletries ran into considerable difficulties over the issue of animal testing. There has also been much discussion on whether the criteria should be strictly ecological, or whether they should cover ethical, health and social issues. A range of products are now being studied to develop eco-label criteria including insulation materials, toilet rolls, batteries, paints and varnishes, shampoos, cleaning agents, building materials, packaging materials, refrigerators, soil improvers and shoes.

Information and auditing

Both CER and product labelling schemes rely on environmental auditing for the information that makes them meaningful. In some cases audits are used as an input into the corporate environmental report, in other cases entire audits are being published. As Bernstein (1992) notes, audits themselves are an important communications tool. They signal management's commitment to tackling eco-performance to internal and external stakeholders, and they are an important means of sparking and structuring a debate about eco-performance internally. A question which is bound to grow is whether audits should be made compulsory and public. While organisations like the Trades Union Congress (TUC) have lobbied to make environmental audits open and compulsory, the International Chamber of Commerce has argued to keep them voluntary and confidential. There appears to be a common perception among managers that in forcing green audit to be disclosed, it would turn into an exercise in green promotion which would lead to problems being buried rather than uncovered (Peattie and Ringler 1994).

It is interesting to apply the same thinking to financial audits. They are compulsory and must be published in order to protect the interests of economic stakeholders such as shareholders and creditors. To try and ensure that they are accurate and revealing, they must be conducted by external third parties. This is considered to be a normal part, and cost, of doing business. Why should environmental and social audits not be considered in the same light, with the aim of protecting the interests of other forms of stakeholder? In some pioneering companies, such as Danish Steel, the two concepts of financial and environmental disclosure are converging with the move towards full-cost accounting which includes environmental costs.

BUILDING A GREEN CORPORATE IDENTITY AND REPUTATION

Since environmental marketing involves communicating with the customer about the whole company rather than just its products, public relations (PR) and corporate identity campaigns have assumed a new importance. In many ways the emphasis on 'corporate identity' is a development from the traditional concern about a company's 'reputation'. In the USA Opinion Research Corporation did some research into the components of a company's reputation, and the importance that the public attach to each element. Among those interviewed, 44 per cent of respondents named environmental responsiveness, effective environmental self-regulation and effective waste minimisation programmes as 'of the highest importance' in determining a company's reputation. This was the same proportion that nominated good-value products and services as crucial. A further 46 per cent named environmental policies which demonstrate a definite concern for the environment as 'of the highest importance'; the same proportion that nominated dependable product and service quality. The only factors that a higher proportion of respondents viewed as crucially important were social responsibility and strong corporate ethics.

Bernstein (1992) views greening as a public relations 'catalyst, forcing the most reticent of companies to communicate, raise its profile and state what it stands for'. Robin Sadler of the consultancy New Perspective suggests:

> 'No doubt there is a huge opportunity for major corporations to be seen as environmental saviours, because individuals feel powerless, and they feel the government is not doing enough.' (quoted in Bond 1989)

The companies that seem to have been the most active in green PR, however, are not necessarily those providing potential environmental solutions. In many cases they represent those industries most fiercely criticised by green groups. In a 1990 special green issue of *Public Relations,* the industries that were represented in articles were waste management (Cleanaway), nuclear power (British Nuclear Fuels Limited), chemicals (ICI), and refrigeration (the Heating and Ventilating Contractors' Association).

For industries under pressure, PR can certainly succeed in altering public perceptions. Research on visits to BNFL's £5.5 million (4.1 million

ECUs) visitor centre at Sellafield found that while 57 per cent of people described themselves as favourably disposed towards nuclear power before the visited, this figure had risen to 79 per cent after the visit. The 16 per cent of people who expressed unfavourable attitudes before the visit had dropped to 9 per cent following the visit. Impressive results, although it must be doubtful whether many of those genuinely opposed to nuclear power would venture inside Sellafield to be convinced. As Peter Melchett (1990) of Greenpeace put it:

> 'good PR is only as good as the product. Any PR company asked to give the nuclear industry or oil or chemical industry a green image will have an uphill task. At any moment all their work can be swept aside in a rush of spilt oil from an Exxon carrier in Alaska, or a tide of lethal chemicals flowing down the Rhine from a Sandoz factory in Switzerland.'

PR strategies

PR is a very flexible form of communication and in the area of corporate communication it is becoming increasingly important as a strategic tool and weapon. There are a variety of different forms of green PR strategy adopted by companies depending on the nature of the challenge that confronts them. *Offensive strategies* are often adopted by the greenest companies to generate competitive advantage, or by their grey rivals seeking to set a different competitive agenda. Following the publication of its second green audit, waste management company Shanks & McEwen mounted a campaign to highlight the poor performance of its competitors commenting:

> 'We are convinced that others are getting away with lower standards. It is important that our example is followed. The regulatory authorities must implement controls over those who operate to the lowest possible standards. In this respect we welcome any legislation.' (*Euromonitor* 1990)

Defensive strategies are typically adopted in response to external pressure or any form of disaster. Perrier's clean and natural image was badly tainted by the exposure of potentially harmful levels of benzene contamination caused during bottling. Perrier mounted a comprehensive and expensive global product recall campaign. They later used the 'social responsiveness' of the recall campaign in PR messages aimed at repairing the damage. *Pre-emptive strategies* are adopted by companies who can foresee potential criticism of their eco-performance. Abbey National pre-empted environmentalist criticism by announcing that it would plant enough trees to replace those consumed to make 450 tonnes of flotation prospectuses. *Opportunist strategies* are adopted by companies who see an environmental issue or competitor action that they can turn to their advantage. In 1987 after the British 'hurricane', Esso put a major advertisement in national newspapers publicising its involvement in a major tree-planting initiative.

Corporate communications

Public relations also includes a range of opportunities for the company to communicate a green message internally and externally, through actions or specialist media.

- *Speeches.* Managers can increasingly be found addressing conferences and other audiences on green issues.

- *Literature.* Companies like Kellogg's and Coca-Cola have developed environmental teaching materials for schools.

- *Audiovisual material.* The visual appeal of a green message based on natural images has led to a boom in green corporate videos. These can be very effective communications tools. Shell has been one of the most consistent users of video to carry a green message. ARC developed an award-winning video showing the re-landscaping of a derelict quarry into a wildlife-friendly environment. ICI launched a £20 000 (15 000 ECUs) video promoting its CFC substitute (KLEA 134a) aimed at capitalising on concern about ozone depletion.

- *Information services.* Some companies and industries are providing green information lines to answer queries and advise customers. ICI is one of many companies in agrochemicals markets that has set up information services aimed at improving the safety and eco-performance of its products in use.

● *Joining or forming green groups.* For example, Business in the Environment, Industry and Nature Conservation or any one of a growing list of green business networks.

● *Charitable donations.* Donations are a long established method of enhancing a company's social responsiveness. In the USA business annually donates over $5 billion (2.3 billion ECUs) to charities. Environmental charities have benefited from the green challenge with significant increases in corporate donations to charities such as The Woodland Trust or the Worldwide Fund for Nature.

● *Adopting codes of conduct.* These can be general codes, such as the Valdez Principles drafted in the wake of the Exxon Valdez disaster by the Social Investment Forum, who control over $150 billion (70 billion ECUs) in institutional investment; industry-specific codes, such as the chemical industry's Responsible Care programme; or company-specific codes, with companies adopting codes relating to ethics, the environment, customer care or good citizenship.

● *Lobbying.* This generally has negative connotations and is associated with large and powerful companies using their influence on legislators to keep restrictive legislation at bay. Some green companies have been lobbying to try and enforce stricter legislation and higher standards within their own industry. Excel Logistics, for example, have lobbied to remove the 10 per cent tax penalty on low-sulphur Scandinavian-grade diesel whose use in distribution would significantly reduce emissions (Penman 1994).

Whatever the media and the content of the message, it must be backed up by meaningful changes within the company; otherwise green public relations and corporate communications will simply present what Boorstin (1962) refers to as 'a change of face rather than a change of heart'.

CASE STUDY

Norsk Hydro

Norsk Hydro is the largest employer in its home country of Norway, and one of Europe's 50 largest companies. It therefore has a very public profile among Norwegian companies. As a pioneer in the production of inorganic fertilisers and now the world's largest fertiliser producer, a major producer of PVC and a major producer and user of energy, it has also attracted the interest of environmentalist groups.

The late 1980s saw its image become increasingly tarnished by a series of environmental incidents including the discovery of extensive groundwater pollution around its Rafnes plant, contamination of two fjords and oil contamination at another plant. In 1987 the Porsgrunn works in Norway were broken into by an environmental pressure group. This group publicised its findings that soil samples taken were contaminated with mercury. The following year witnessed a major fire at the Rafnes plant. These incidents attracted media attention and made newspaper headlines. As a result, Norsk Hydro decided to undertake a complete environmental review of all its sites in Norway and to publish the results and inform people of a programme to improve eco-performance. The philosophy behind the new corporate environmental communications initiative was summed up by company President Torvild Aakvaag:

'I believe that openness is the best policy. The public has a right to information. If we have a problem, it is in our best interest that it should be presented, and explained, in a totally honest manner. We must not leave the impression that we are trying to keep something hidden; at the same time, we don't want the public view of us to be determined by one individual matter.'

The resulting 36-page 'Miljorapport' (environmental report) was published in 1989. Copies were circulated to key stakeholders including employees and their families, local and national government, and summary copies were sent to residents, schools and colleges in areas surrounding every Hydro site. The report was an instant success. Public confidence in the company was restored, and the company's image evolved from a 'dirty' company to a leader in proactive environmental management and particularly a leader in environmental reporting excellence. In subsequent years the company was voted as 'the best company to work for' in Norwegian opinion polls.

The Norwegian report was followed by a world-wide report and a UK environmental report in 1990. In the UK six of the company's main factories were independently assessed by Lloyd's Register who concluded that the environmental performance of the company was 'above average'. The UK environmental report was important for Norsk Hydro UK, not just because it provided comprehensive and credible communication about eco-performance, but because it helped to raise the profile of the entire company. Prior to the release of the report, despite being one of the UK's 150 largest companies and despite the majority of its business units being in the top two of their particular markets, the company remained largely unknown or ignored, even within the business community. When the UK report was released it was promoted in a *Financial Times* advert, and gained widespread media coverage including prime-time television programmes such as 'Tomorrow's World' and 'Business Matters'. To ensure that the report helped to raise the company profile within the business community it was mailed to the leaders of *The Times* top 1000 companies. The advertising and publicity resulted in over 700 requests for copies, and over 10 000 copies were mailed out in total. For its efforts the company was awarded two prizes: one from the Campaign for the Freedom of Information and the first Environmental Reporting Award (jointly with British Telecom) presented by the Chartered

Association of Certified Accountants. Charles Duff, the Corporate Development Manager of Norsk Hydro, commenting on the reporting initiative in *Long Range Planning* said:

'We are in the world league of producers of each of our products, and we believe that we therefore have a responsibility to provide a wide audience with full and factual information about them ... We are committed to communicating to everyone why we are in business – how, in particular, our products contribute to daily life, and, in general, to explain the vital part that industry plays in society.'

The success of Norsk Hydro demonstrates that an open and socially responsible commitment to corporate communication can be by far the safest option for industries in environmentally sensitive sections. The grey tradition of secrecy and 'commercial confidence' will only create new generations of ever more distrustful stakeholders.

Adapted from Duff (1992) and other sources.

CHAPTER 13

Putting the message across – green promotions

'The major part of *informative* advertising is, and always has been, a campaign of exaggeration, half-truths, intended ambiguities, direct lies and general deception ... Advertisements of the *non-informative* kind present a psychological museum of rare interest, but with some depressing exhibits.'
(ASJ Baster, from *Advertising Reconsidered*, 1935)

INTRODUCTION

Although it is tempting to believe that if a company builds a greener mousetrap, the world will beat a path to its door, it is not true. Any product needs to be promoted to ensure that consumers are aware of it, understand it, and view it as a potential solution to an actual or potential need or want. The process of promoting products and companies is itself a big business. Buttle (1989) estimates that some 15 per cent of the USA's Gross National Product is spent on the combined activities of advertising, personal selling, sales promotion and publicity. Not only is it important economically, it is something which is so deeply woven into every aspect of our society that it is virtually inescapable, and its impacts are very difficult to isolate. Advertising agency, Ogilvy and Mather, has estimated that each of us is exposed daily to some 3000 different messages designed by marketing managers to communicate something to us.

Promoting green products presents a particularly difficult challenge. It means trying to communicate complex issues in an age where the consumer is used to messages delivered in snappy 'soundbites'. It involves communicating issues which threaten all of mankind in an age when marketing communication is expected to be upbeat and entertaining. It also brings the risk that by highlighting eco-performance, the company will attract the critical attention of green interest groups. Advertising is the most obvious means by which to spread the company's green message, yet advertising has been a focus for environmentalist criticism. Curiously though, green products also pose a promotional problem for grey rivals. How does a company attack a green competitor without appearing anti-environment? Will an attack on its technical performance appear like a cross between sour grapes and a desire to destroy the earth?

A great deal of marketing activity in the early phase of environmental marketing has been driven by communication, or more specifically promotion (Vandermerwe and Oliff 1990, Peattie and Ring 1993). Before a company ventures into the realms of green promotion, the eco-performance of the product and the organisational hardware and software behind it should have been scrutinised and moved as far as possible towards sustainability within current constraints. The eco-performance of the company should be audited and made public before any attempt is made to use it as a basis for promotion. As Bernstein (1992) puts it, 'There has to be an iceberg beneath the tip'. In some ways this reverses the traditional link between brand and corporate image. Strong corporate images were often forged from the collective strength of a raft of brands.

For green brands, they need to draw their strength from the secure base that a green corporate identity provides.

GREEN PROMOTION OBJECTIVES

Simintiras (1993) poses the question: 'What are the advertising objectives and strategies of companies practising environmental marketing?' Clifton and Buss (1992) answer this by saying that:

'There is, of course, no magic green method or style of promotion. Quite the opposite; it cannot be emphasised too strongly that greener communication should be approached in just the same way as any other communication: the basic disciplines are the same.'

The broad objectives of the green advertiser will be similar to those of a grey advertiser. One aim may be to *inform* the target audience about the company and product, so that they become aware of a new green product, how it works and what its environmental and other advantages are. A second aim may be to *persuade* consumers to switch to a green brand, to change their preconceptions about a product, or even to find out more about it, perhaps by sending for a brochure. Finally, promotions can aim to *remind* customers that they will need a product soon, and to emphasise where and how it can be purchased.

FUNDING GREEN COMMUNICATIONS CAMPAIGNS

One of the socio-environmental criticisms that is levelled at promotion, and advertising in particular, is that it consumes resources which could be invested in more directly benefiting consumers. Saatchi & Saatchi estimates that during 1989 organisations in North America and Europe spent $138 billion (64 billion ECUs) on advertising. In terms of the proportion of the economy that this represents, Jain (1987) calculates advertising as accounting for 2.4 per cent of the USA's Gross National Product, 1.09 per cent of British GNP and 0.7 per cent of German GNP. Major advertising campaigns are vulnerable to accusations of waste

when they are matched successfully by competitors, negating any competitive advantage. This simply consumes resources and raises prices without benefiting either customers or producers. The detergent market and cola markets are used as examples where major companies fight an expensive but inconclusive advertising war, which achieves little beyond driving out small competitors and so reducing consumer choice. The £20 million (15 million ECUs) advertising campaign for the privatisation of the UK electricity industry was also criticised because it equalled the industry's entire annual budget for promoting energy efficiency.

The idea that advertising represents an added cost burden to the consumer has an intuitive logic. However, this logic is challenged by the work of Reekie (1979) who found that among 65 heavily advertised food brands, the effect of advertising was to intensify competition, thereby holding prices down. Given that there is concern about the level of advertising expenditure, environmental marketers may find that a frugal approach to promotional expenditure pays dividends. There are several green brands which have achieved considerable success with communications expenditure of a fraction of their grey competitors. The most striking example is The Body Shop which has built up a business on an international scale without the use of advertising. When Fort Sterling launched Nouvelle, the recycled toilet tissue, it used a comparatively small advertising budget of only £500 000 (375 000 ECUs) within an industry characterised by heavy advertising expenditure. Despite this modest outlay, the Nouvelle brand captured a 3 per cent share of a market worth over £500 million (375 million ECUs) in its first year.

TARGETTING GREEN PROMOTIONS

Targetting green promotional campaigns involves identifying distinctive target audiences who will relate and respond to a green promotion. This process shares many of the difficulties of segmenting green markets over issues such as environmental awareness and understanding, separating general concern from issue specific concern, and the lack of consistency among green consumers. It also involves hitting a moving target since the audience's green understanding, awareness and concerns will be constantly evolving. Iyer and Bannerjee (1993) identify three types of target: they are people interested in:

- planet preservation;
- animal life preservation;
- personal health preservation.

Fiori (1989) recommends the use of two prime targets: first, women (preferably mothers) who are attracted to green products which appeal to their nurturing instincts: second, children, because their exposure to environmental education at school has turned them into important green purchase initiators. Ironically, it may often be the children in a household who are best able to comprehend the environmental issues highlighted within marketing campaigns. Certainly schools have become a favourite target for environmental marketing communications among a large number of companies. Schools are generally more than willing to take advantage of free educational materials, and companies can be seen to be making a real contribution to both social and environmental improvement. However, targetting children would be a dangerous strategy for a company with an eco-performance that was only superficially good. A misleading promotional strategy will always draw criticism from the media and green groups. The chorus of disapproval would be at least twice as loud if the target audience was children.

Targetting promotional messages accurately can help to tackle some of the key environmental and social criticisms of marketing. Advertising is often criticised for the effects that it has on audiences for whom the message was not intended. The effects of advertising for alcoholic drinks and cigarettes on children have created concern, particularly when it has been consistently shown that the most highly promoted brands of cigarettes are those that are most popular with child smokers. An environmentally related social question is the effects of advertising on those unable to afford the products advertised.

The problem of poorly targetted campaigns has led to the direct mail industry becoming something of a target for the environmentalist lobby. This has resulted in media coverage declaring that 'every year two trees are posted through your letterbox' (Cobb 1989). The challenge for marketers who rely on direct mail, is how to promote without polluting. Research by the Recycling Council of Ontario suggests that 98 per cent of all Canadian third-class mail (mostly direct mail) and all privately delivered inserts are simply thrown away (Mason 1991). In the USA seventh Generation have tackled this problem by charging $2 for each catalogue issued and running an ongoing programme which aims to keep its mailing list 'clean'. At present most database marketing companies promote themselves on the basis of the size of their databases and the breadth of coverage. In future this will need to change to an emphasis on the precision that they can offer. The increasing volume of customer information held on databases by manufacturers, credit card companies, retailers and database marketing specialists has the potential to combine with emerging geodemographic targetting methods to create direct mail so precisely targetted that 'junk mail' ceases to be a relevant term.

STRUCTURING THE MESSAGE

Any promotional message will contain a theme designed to appeal to the target audience. Themes fall into one of three general types. *Rational appeals* aim at the customer's self-interest by stressing the value or performance of the product. *Emotional appeals* aim to create an emotional response in customers which will motivate them to purchase. Green adverts relating care of the environment with children's welfare or stressing the dangers of environmental degradation are aimed at people's emotions. *Moral appeals* aim at people's sense of right and wrong. The launch of Nouvelle toilet tissue included the wonderful piece of moralistic copywriting that 'it feels a little uncomfortable using toilet tissue that wipes out forests'. Although the environmental accuracy of the claims caused some debate, the campaign undoubtedly hit the right moral note with consumers.

Fiori (1989) suggests that environmental marketers should use rational appeals which promote self-interest, rather than social conscience, as the key product benefit. The logic is that most people will respond to issues that directly relate to themselves or their families rather than those which appear to tackle a problem for society in general. Therefore unbleached nappies will appeal to people on the basis that they are good for their babies' skin rather than for the national sewerage system. In practice though, advertisers use a variety of appeals based around environmental issues, many of which are not strongly related to self-interest. Iyer and Bannerjee (1993), in researching green print advertising, identified six appeal themes used:

1 *Zeitgeist appeals* – which attempt simply to join in with the prevailing green climate, either through 'bland statements' such as 'brand x is environmentally friendly', or by a bandwagon-jumping attempt to link the product to the green movement;

2 *emotional appeals* – evoking fear, guilt or a sense of empowerment;

3 *financial appeals* – involving price reduction (possibly passed on from resource conservation) or donations to causes;

4 *euphoria appeals* – invoking a sense of well-being by emphasising the healthiness or naturalness of the product;

5 *management appeals* – in which companies imply that the company itself is involved in the green movement;

6 *others* – including comparative advertising or celebrity endorsement.

In addition to the rational appeals, emotional appeals have been very prominent, particularly fear-based appeals. Strong fear appeals can be counter-productive, however. Kinnear *et al* (1974) found that consumers who were most concerned about personal harm were the least concerned about the environment. Kinnear *et al* postulated that those potentially most worried about the potential dangers of pollution may react to the threat by ignoring or denying the environmental problem. They recommend a formula when targetting the green consumer of:

1 arousing and meeting a consumer's need to understand, perhaps by providing some factual evidence on the benefits of a green product;

2 stressing how using the product will enable the consumer to contribute to reducing environmental damage, and demonstrate his or her own social responsibility;

3 gently play to people's desire for harm avoidance by mentioning the environmental consequences of consumers not using a green product.

Some of the messages that a green advertiser will have to communicate will be difficult because they do not suit the typical advertising approach of hyperbole and 'glitz'. For many new green products their superior eco-performance may be achieved by a reduction in technical performance. Although the majority of consumers profess a willingness to accept 'slight' technical performance disadvantages in green products, promoting their virtue is difficult in a world where advertising has always relied on 'whiter than white' absolutes and exaggerations. Where any technical performance gaps emerge there will be a considerable marketing communications challenge.

Message content

It is the content of a promotion that will most differentiate the green from the grey. The question of what constitutes green content is yet another of the seemingly endless intractable questions in environmental marketing. One simplistic answer is to define green adverts as those that promote environmental solutions, while grey adverts are those promoting the causes of the problems. Such straightforward dichotomies rarely work in practice where eco-performance is not black or white, but instead involves shades of grey and green. Another problem is that although it is simple enough to identify explicit green claims, it is very difficult to delineate implicit green claims. Many adverts use rural backdrops to advertise their product; this could be an implicit message that their product is at one with nature, or it could be the most attractive background the advertising agency could think of.

McDonagh (1994) seeks to define messages in relation to advertising on a scale of conventional (grey) to sustainable (green) on the basis of environmental disclosure. The nature of that disclosure can also focus on different elements of the cradle-to-grave life cycle. Iyer and Bannerjee (1993) subdivide green promotional messages as dealing with issues of production (divided between raw materials use and processes), consumption or disposal. Carlson et al (1993) in an analysis of magazine advertisements making green claims identified five categories:

- product-orientated claims relating to green attributes;

- process-orientated claims relating to technologies and methods of production or disposal;

- image-orientated claims linking the organisation to a green cause;

- environmental fact-based claims which inform consumers about relevant environmental issues;

- claims which combine more than one of the above themes.

By analysing the content of these claims further they also found that only 40 per cent of advertisements were 'acceptable' in terms of avoiding misleading claims. The other 60 per cent featured claims which ranged from the ambiguous to the downright false.

Bernstein (1992) recommends making marketing communications honest and participative, wherever possible, since involvement encourages message retention, and the presence of any 'bad news' will make the 'good news' all the more credible. In some cases partial disclosure is more misleading than no disclosure. Strid and Cater (1993) highlight Chevron and General Motors as running high-profile advertising campaigns highlighting their environmental achievements. What the advertisements failed to mention was that the achievements were all enforced by legislation and the intervention of government agencies.

Davis (1993) classifies advertisements according to the degree to which environmental claims are specific, present concrete tangible product benefits to consumers, and are supported by factual objective information. Kangun et al (1991) and Davis (1993) revealed that consumers are able to differentiate between the woolly and the concrete when it comes to green claims. Consumers responded negatively to claims perceived as vague, and positively towards claims perceived as specific which identified real and meaningful benefits. An advertising campaign in Japan which won plaudits for its unusually frank approach came from Volvo. As Strid and Cater (1993) explain:

'A full-page Volvo ad in a major daily read quite simply "Our products create pollution, waste and noise." An explanation followed, recognizing that although the automobile was an asset to society, it is also bad for the environment. The copy listed what Volvo is doing to make its cars cleaner and quieter. The ad was a sensation and got extensive media attention. Good business for everyone.'

Creating the right tone

Messages communicate through the tone that they use, as well as through the appeal and content they involve. Kinnear et al's (1974) theme of gentleness was picked up by Fiori (1989). She put forward a prescription for green advertising which, in addition to dealing with practicalities such as ensuring that green claims are backed up by product and company eco-performance, made several style-orientated suggestions.

- Be gentle on consumers who may be confused or relatively ill-informed.

- Be positive and reassuring by stressing products' abilities to contribute to solving perceived environmental problems, rather than intensifying consumers' fears.

- Address consumers' existing environmental concerns rather than creating new worries.

- Be in keeping with the spirit of the green conscience by making sure that it is credible and has style.

- Make consumers feel part of the green movement, and that through their purchase they will be making a contribution.
- Treat the consumer as an intelligent human being.

A clever example of setting the right tone through the style of the advertisement came from the first 'mainstream' advertising campaign for Ecover products. The campaign involved posters commissioned by 52 artists who were told to take old advertising posters and literally recycle them.

Bernstein (1992) notes that although humour has proved a popular and effective element of advertising, it must be used with more care in promoting a green image where many of the underlying issues are very serious. International Paper was on the point of launching a totally biodegradable refuse sack 'The Great Green Bag' when the company's chairman intervened because 'he didn't want to create a flippant marketing statement that would undermine the seriousness of the product' (Penzer 1990). This is not to say that all green communications are deadly serious, but outright humour tends to have been replaced by wit and wordplay.

New values and language

One of the principal challenges in environmental marketing is getting the terminology right. Bernstein (1992) points out two key linguistic problems with environmental marketing. The first is that the language of marketing is warfare (campaign, targets, strategy), while the language of green is that of peace. The second is that marketers cannot assume that the vocabulary and interpretations of the customer will be the same as their own. He warns against using abstract or extravagant language, and against undermining a green message with spurious or absolute claims.

Choosing the right terms to describe a green product can be difficult. 'Sustainable development' and 'green growth' are both frequently used terms, but green organisations such as the Environment Council view them disapprovingly as contradictions in terms. 'Environmentally friendly' has slipped into everyday language despite the fact that it is both vague and meaningless. In Sweden the term 'environmentally friendly' can only be used to describe products which actually enhance the environment. Terms like 'environmentally friendly' and 'environmentally sensitive' also tend to anthropomorphise products and endow the product itself with some form of environmental attitude. One example of this was the advertising of an energy-efficient CD-player advertised on the Eurosport channel during the Barcelona Olympics on the basis that it 'loves the Earth'. The term 'recycled' invites a debate about how much of the new product's content needs to be recycled and whether or not the waste that has been recycled is post-consumer or not. A key problem in developing factual green claims for a product, which are safe from any charge of being misleading, is that there is no clearly agreed set of environmental marketing terms to assist the evaluation of claims. Terms like 'biodegradable' and 'recyclable' have been the subject of varying interpretations and much academic debate.

During the 1970s and 1980s terms such as 'disposable' or 'pre-packaged' were highlighted in advertising as key benefits, while in the 1990s the associations of such terms would make them a potential liability. Instead terms such as 'organic', 'additive-free', 'sustainably sourced', 'recycled', 'natural', 'unbleached' and 'energy efficient' are the new purchasing keywords. Ottman (1992a) even suggests that the marketer's favourite word 'new' is perceived differently by 1990s' consumers who see new as risky and who are potentially more interested in the reassurance of classic and traditional products.

Green marketing has begun to subtly change the values as well as the language emphasised in advertising. Values such as caring, sharing and nurturing are more prevalent; while values such as affluence and convenience have become less prominent. Procter and Gamble, in marketing its new green non-chlorine bleached paper-based products such as nappies, now stress their 'natural creamy whiteness'. This replaces the emphasis on 'brilliant snowy whiteness' which was endemic in the advertising of paper products and detergents during the 1970s and 1980s. The Co-op when advertising its new nappies used copy explaining that 'They may not look quite as white as the old disposables, but they'll be just as good for babies – and even better for the environment.' A startling example of the shift in values of 1990s' marketing communications came from Mercedes-Benz in a campaign which downplayed their luxury car image under the headline 'Our idea of a luxury car. Nothing on it is a luxury.' The advertisment went on to highlight virtues of safety, reliability, durability, functionality and simplicity. Anybody within an advertising agency during the 1980s proposing that a Mercedes-Benz should be marketed on its functionality would probably have had a relatively prompt career change.

MEDIA CHOICE

Marketers can choose from among a number of media to promote a product, and the choice will tend to reflect the nature of the product, the communications objectives being pursued and the size of the available budget. Every campaign needs the right choice of media, but for green communication, the media need to be appropriate for both the product and for the relevant green issues. A paper company wishing to communicate its efforts to replenish tree stocks would be ill-advised to do so using a glossy direct mailshot.

Advertising

Mass media advertising is the most powerful channel in most consumer markets with an ability to reach a large or dispersed market repeatedly, and persuasively. Adverts can be dramatic and glamorous as well as entertaining in the search for a message which creates favourable customer perceptions of a given brand.

The 1980s witnessed a gradual shift of marketing communications away from advertising and into other media such as sales promotion. This reflects growing doubts about the cost effectiveness of advertising in the face of rising prices and increased advertising 'clutter'. Between 1983 and 1987 the revenue produced by a given level of advertising dropped by almost 20 per cent (Peattie and Peattie 1994). A lack of conclusive evidence directly linking advertising to consumer preference and buying behaviour, and increasing consumer hostility towards advertising have fuelled these doubts. The advent of videos and remote controls which allow adverts to be 'zapped' has also eroded television advertisers' confidence in their ability to reach their target audience. Green mass media advertising has been an important element of environmental marketing strategy for many companies, but it is worth noting that the use of advertising poses some particular difficulties for the environmental marketer (not least the medium's grey associations) and the success of many leading green companies such as The Body Shop has been built on an avoidance or minimal use of advertising.

The socio-environmental impact of advertising

In its role as the highest profile marketing communications channel, advertising has attracted the most attention from practitioners, academics and critics of marketing. Criticisms of advertising tend to fall into two types. *Practical criticism* concerning 'sins against the consumer' focus on the techno-economic dimensions of advertising and whether the images of the products, their use and their benefits are accurately portrayed and delivered in practice. These can include misleading by overemphasising product virtues, presenting incomplete information, emphasising the experience of atypical users or generating unrealistic fears. *Socio-environmental criticism* relating to 'sins against society' concentrates on the role and effect of advertising beyond influencing market exchange processes and the satisfactions they create. These include compounding the harm done by already harmful products or promoting an inappropriate product to a non-target group, debasing tastes and values through an appeal to the lowest common denominator, contributing to the homogenisation of global culture through the expanding mass media, and providing overidealised or stereotyped images of people, which may be alienating or offensive to those who do not belong to, or identify with, the target group.

Advertising undoubtedly influences more than just consumer attitudes towards products, brands and companies. Advertising is a powerful force which influences our attitudes towards ourselves, our lifestyles and the society and world in which we live. As the availability of commercial mass media and levels of literacy have grown throughout the century, so have the power and reach of advertising. In 1985 the International Advertising Association pronounced:

'The magical marketing tool of television has been bound with the chains of laws and regulations, in much of the world, and it has not been free to exercise more than a tiny fraction of its potential as a conduit of the consumer information and economic stimulation provided by advertising. These chains are at last being chiselled off.'

Although television advertising may be increasing in markets where commerical television is expanding rapidly (such as in India), in its established industrialised markets, some of the momentum has been lost. One problem for advertising is that its sheer success and growth have created a backlash that threatens to reduce its effectiveness. As Goldman (1992) puts it, 'By the end of the 1980s a chief sociocultural consequence of advertising and the commodification of culture was the ripening of cynicism and distrust.' There is also growing and widespread concern about the impact of advertising on society. A 1993 survey of 1000 UK adults by *Marketing Week* and *The Human Factor* indicated that nearly half of the population claim to be 'advertising-immune' and over one third felt that advertising was 'a bad influence on society'. Increasing legislative controls and the establishment of advertising watchdogs such as the Advertising Standards Authority reflect this growing concern about the role and effect of advertising within society.

It is curious that while advertising is accused of having a negative influence on society, the advertising industry and the marketers who use it are quick to underplay its influence. This is particularly the case with tobacco advertising in which tobacco companies and their advertisers have steadfastly argued that advertising does not increase overall consumption, and that it merely affects the choice between competing brands. On the other hand, when advertising is not under any form of attack, the industry and the marketers that use it are typically enthusiastic about its ability to influence. As a former Chairman of McCann Erickson commented:

'I am always amused by the suggestion that advertising, a function that has been shown to increase consumption of virtually every other product, somehow miraculously fails to work for tobacco products.' (Foote 1981)

The claims of consumers to be advertising-immune are probably an indication of wishful thinking given that major advertising campaigns are frequently linked to otherwise inexplicable increases in sales of a brand. One example is the UK and European relaunch of Levi 501 jeans into a relatively saturated market, which featured a 1950s theme and two TV/cinema commercials (including the famous scene featuring Nick Kamen in a launderette). Following an all-time low in non-American sales of 501s, Levi saw sales of 501s jump from 60 000 in 1985 to over 650 000 in 1986 following the campaign. Perhaps consumers are becoming more immune and resistant to 'conventional' forms of advertising and the stereotypes and direct selling messages they involved. A new generation of advertisements (often described as post-modernist) has emerged which uses pastiche, ambiguity, disconcerting images, puzzles and self-mocking humour. The advertisement is no longer an intrusive 'salesman' that enters into our living rooms, it has become part of the video entertainment culture which communicates through stylish and symbolic messages instead of overt selling.

Green advertising

Advertising as a medium is a considerable consumer of resources; 17 000 hectares of primeval Canadian forests are cut each year to provide the newsprint on which American daily papers publish their advertisements (Durning 1992). However, green criticism of advertising is more usually related to its effects rather than to the resources that go into it. Much of the criticism that has been levelled at advertising from a social perspective has been reprised in relation to the environment. The accuracy of the claims involved in green advertising has been one focus of concern. The other has been the use of and misuse of persuasive advertising, which is criticised for providing few benefits for customers, for attempting to persuade customers to replace serviceable consumer durables with 'this year's model', for using 'leverage' techniques to create, rather than satisfy, consumer needs, and for emphasising the human motivations for buying to create dissatisfaction, rather than the qualities and benefits of the product.

Advertising's role in stimulating over-consumption has also drawn heavy criticism from environmentalists. The UK Green Party Manifesto complains:

'The message of advertising is always more consumption. It disfigures towns and landscapes. It encourages waste, from unnecessary model changes to gimmicks which supposedly differentiate identical products. Its bottom line can only be environmental destruction.'

It goes on to propose:

- the ending of large-scale advertising as a legitimate business expense;
- the progressive taxation of all expenditure on sales promotion above a minimum level;
- the tagging of environmentally hostile products with 'environmental health warnings';
- complete bans on advertising for the most damaging products, such as cars.

In the short term at least, it is difficult to imagine a situation where the Green Party Manifesto gets the opportunity to be translated into UK government policy, just as it is difficult to imagine commercial television without car advertising.

The use of mass media advertising may also dilute the credibility of the green message because, although consumers get most of their environmental information from the mass media, they do not find it very believable. In a survey by Abt Associates (Abt 1990) the least credible source of environmental information was an advertisement placed by a major company (the most credible source being environmentalist groups).

Advertising may also be an unsuitable medium to carry the communications burden for the green company given that, according to Bernstein (1992), the green communication challenge is broader in terms of content (since the brand and the company must be promoted) deeper in coverage (providing more information) and delivered to a wider audience (which embraces audiences beyond customers). As Rawsthorn and Zagor (1990) observe:

'the conspicuous consumption that characterised consumer attitudes in the 1980s was ideally suited to advertising. The archetypal 1980s ad – men in bright Gordon Gekko braces barking down portable phones and femmes fatales in boxy Chanel suits – sought to persuade people to buy things with images of unapologetic affluence.'

Advertising is very effective at demonstrating a product, its direct benefits and the enjoyment which consumption brings. Demonstrating an absence of environmental harm or the additional pleasures involved in consuming a green rather than a conventional brand is much less easy. For the green marketer, mass media advertising therefore poses a dilemma. It may be impossible to compete effectively without it, but difficult to communicate the product's competitive advantage credibly when using it. A company such as Ecover originally managed to grow using advertisements which used specialist media such as Friends of the Earth's *Earth Matters* magazine. When growth put them in more direct competition with the likes of Lever and Procter and Gamble, the company somewhat reluctantly embarked on a mainstream advertising campaign.

The problems of implicit messages make it difficult to draw exact definitions of green adverts, and therefore to measure the extent of their use. Certainly advertising using explicit green claims grew dramatically at the end of the 1980s. According to J. Walter Thompson's *Greenwatch*, green advertising claims quadrupled between 1989 and 1990. The problem with such growth is that environmental claims and images will become much less effective if overused. As Rawsthorn and Zagor (1990) note:

'Scenes of rural serenity and cloud-encircled globes have joined the "new man" with his stubbly chin and chuckling baby as the advertising clichés of early 1990s advertising.'

Although advertising may not appear to be an ideal medium for promoting a green image, it clearly has worked for many companies. In 1989 AEG launched a green UK advertising campaign for its dishwashers and washing machines. The campaign stressed the energy and water efficiency of its products and the fact that by contributing less to acid rain and water pollution they were good for endangered aquatic species such as newts. Although the 'Save the Newts' campaign was met with scepticism from some advertising industry commentators, it produced a 30 per cent sales uplift in an otherwise stagnant white goods market.

Procter and Gamble are the world's largest advertiser spending some $138 billion (64 billion ECUs) annually (Dahringer and Muhlbacher 1991). P&G was also the company most often named as 'environmentally conscious' in a sample of American consumers conducted by *Advertising Age* and Gallup (Chase 1991). This raises the question of whether this is achieved by the volume of its advertising, rather than strictly by the virtue of its environmental performance. In a 1989 survey conducted among senior marketers within the UK, Procter and Gambler was one of the firms identified as responding relatively poorly to the green challenge (Mitchell 1989).

Green advertising claims

The claims used in green advertising have been one of the most controversial issues in the emergence of environmental marketing. According to the UK's Advertising Standards Authority:

'Some advertisers seem to be paying more attention to making sure their wares are perceived as sitting on the right side of the green fence than to checking the factual accuracy of their claims.'

Much of the early research work examining green advertising or labelling has concentrated on the issue of unsubstantiated and misleading advertising claims (Kangun *et al* 1991 and Strid and

Cater 1993). It should be noted that there is a difference between the use of falsehood in advertising, and misleading advertising. Aaker and Myers (1987) suggest four types of advertising that can be misleading.

1 Adverts can contain factually correct information, but still convey a misleading impression.

2 Adverts can be ambiguous in their meaning, and subject to multiple interpretations.

3 Adverts can omit information which would be important to consumers and whose absence creates a false impression.

4 Adverts can make subjective and extravagant statements about product quality, which, although impossible to disprove, can mislead the consumer who takes them literally.

The advertising claims that have led to companies being criticised by environmentalists and advertising watchdogs vary from the inept (such as BP's initial claim that its *Supergreen* unleaded petrol was emission free) to the cynical. One of the most cynical must be the claim by Higgs Furs that its fur products are 'environmentally friendly' because, unlike fake furs, their processing did not involve ozone-depleting chemicals. Such incidents have led to an increasing number of codes governing the use of environmental claims in advertising, and one example from France is shown in Fig. 13.1. The *New Scientist* blamed the 'splendidly incompetent copy-writing by advertisers' as a major cause of growing cynicism about green claims. Consumers are already concerned about the validity of advertising claims in general (Varadarajan & Thirunarayana 1990). Add the growing scepticism about environmental claims into these doubts about advertising and the challenge to convince the green consumer through advertising becomes a considerable one.

On-pack promotion

Another important area for green promotion and for concerns over the accuracy of the claims used is the use of labelling and other on-pack information. In the face of complex issues and

The objectives
All references to the environment must correspond with one or more of the following objectives:
• Present with accuracy the significant action(s) undertaken in environmental matters.
• Present with accuracy the positive environmental characteristics of a product.
• Inform about the positive environmental balance of a product.
• Inform in order to modify or correct the preconceptions and unfounded or incorrect rumours concerning the products, their components and contents.

The rules
1 Publicity has to avoid all information that misleads the consumer directly or indirectly on the actual advantages or the ecological properties of products as well as on the actual actions that the enterprise takes in favour of the environment.
2 The enterprise must be in a position to produce all evidence to justify its claims, indications or publicity presentations.
3 Publicity cannot include demonstrations or scientific conclusions relating to the environment which are not based on renowned scientific works.
4 Publicity cannot use improperly the results of research or citations taken from technical or scientific works.
5 Publicity must not reproduce or make statements which are not true or linked to the experience of the person who gives them.
6 Publicity must not give or appear to give a total or complete guarantee of harmlessness in the field of the environment, when the ecological qualities of the product only concern one stage of the product's life cycle or only one of its properties.
7 Advertisements must indicate how the product presents the qualities that it is attributed to have and in what context.
8 It must not be alleged that the product presents particular characteristics with regard to regulation and its uses, since all similar products present the same characteristics relative to the protection of the environment.
9 A claim must not infer a false superiority and/or allow a product to distinguish itself unfairly from other similar products or products which possess similar characteristics in their contribution to the protection to the environment.
10 The advertising enterprise must not take advantage, in an action in favour of the environment, of superiority or anteriority which rests on the facts which cannot be objectively verified.
11 A sign or a symbol can only be used in the absence of all confusion regarding the appearance of a sign, symbol or official label on the subject.
12 The choice of signs or terms used in publicity, as well as the colours which could be associated with them, must not suggest ecological virtues that the product does not possess.
13 In the event that it is impossible to justify global expressions, taking into account difficulties encountered on the subject, publicity will use instead expressions such as 'contributes to the protection of your environment by...', 'contributes in protecting your environment by...', 'contributes to the environment by...', adding the necessary details relating to the elements in question.
14 Absolutely no publicity can represent behaviour, either contrary to the protection of the environment or inciting behaviour contrary to the protection of the environment without a positive corrective statement.

Fig. 13.1 France's Environmental Advertising Code
(adapting from Bureau de Vérification de la Publicité (1990) by North (1990))

conflicting information, consumers are looking for simple clues about the eco-performance of products. According to The Roper Organization, by 1992, 54 per cent of Americans read labels to see if products were environmentally acceptable, but that 36 per cent of them 'do not really believe the labels claiming that a product is environmentally safe'. In their investigations into green labelling the Consumers' Association (1990) found five grounds for criticism of current marketing practice.

1 *Excessive claims.* The Consumers' Association proposed the banning of very general claims such as 'environmentally friendly'.

2 *Multiple claims.* Scrutiny of aerosol cans revealed ten different forms of wording relating to CFCs and the ozone layer. The differences in wording had no relationship with the environmental performance of the product, but did produce different consumer perceptions of environmental performance. For example, consumer discussion groups identified aerosols labelled 'ozone-safe' as 'greener' in some way than those labelled 'ozone-friendly'.

3 *Unexplained claims.* A number of environmental claims such as 'biodegradable', 'phosphate-free', 'enzyme-free' or 'environmentally friendly pulp' were poorly understood by consumers and considered unhelpful. Other claims such as 'contains no NTA' will mean nothing to consumers, unless they happen to know that NTA is a phosphate alternative used in some detergents.

4 *Meaningless claims.* The marketing of washing-up liquids has involved companies using 'phosphate-free' labels on products which have never contained phosphates (since phosphates are used as whiteners in detergents for clothes).

5 *Unrealistic claims.* A wide range of products and packages are supplied labelled as 'recyclable'. This is fine in acting as a reminder to consumers to recycle, but if suitable recycling facilities do not exist in the area in which the product is sold, the manufacturer is implying a product benefit to consumers that the consumer cannot realise.

Sales promotions

The greenness of sales promotions is difficult to interpret. On the one hand, sales promotions increase the value of the product offering to benefit consumers in a way that advertising does not. On the other hand, sales promotions all aim to increase sales and consumption, and they often do this through extra packaging (for multipacks) or 'free' gifts which may not really be needed by consumers. Sales promotions can be a very cost-effective way for companies to put a green

message across. They can be particularly useful as a complement or an alternative to advertising in raising awareness of and encouraging trial of new green products. Examples include:

● *Free trials and samples.* Church and Dwight's 'Arm and Hammer' baking-powder toothpaste relied on an intensive free-sampling programme to penetrate the European market.

● *Coupons.* In the USA the 'Friends of The Environment' coupon redemption programme involves 5 per cent of the value of redeemed coupons going to environmental charities relating to one of five themes that can be nominated by the consumer.

● *Competitions.* Famous Grouse Whisky ran a 'Naturefund' competition where consumers had to complete the slogan 'The Famous Grouse Scotch Whisky and the RSPB can work together to protect British birds by ...'. Tesco linked its 'Greener Grocer' advertising theme into a prize draw featuring 42 Vauxhall cars and £250 000 (188 000 ECUs) worth of lead -free petrol.

● *Free gifts.* International Paper gave away over 10 million pine seedlings at a festival held at the White House. This was a very clever and cost-effective move given that the company routinely grows more seedlings than it needs and must dispose of the excess (Penzer 1990). The use of the gift communicated a concern for reafforestation and sustaining tree supplies.

● *Product warranties.* Tupperware products' claim to greenness emphasises the products' durability backed up by a lifetime guarantee.

● *Winning or sponsoring green awards.* Rolls-Royce's awards for the RB211-535E4 turbofan engine provided useful PR which helped the product to gain a major share of the £15 billion (11.3 billion ECUs) engine market. ICI has managed to negate some of the negative environmental publicity it has had by stressing its award-winning green technology including its clean ammonia synthesis process, its water-based resins, and its 'Hydecat' chlorine waste catalyst.

One of the most ambitious green promotions run so far came from Lever Brothers in the USA. Fifty million free-standing insert coupons (FSI) for money off Lever products were distributed. For each coupon redeemed, Lever pledged to donate five cents towards the construction of playgrounds made using 100 per cent post-consumer recycled plastics and other green building materials. The FSI also involved a children's essay competition on 'How Recycling Helps My Community' with a prize of savings bonds for the winner plus a playground for his or her community. The FSI also contained details of a self-liquidating premium whereby children could send for school kits made of recycled materials.

This promotion contains a wide array of green themes including recycling and the use of recycled materials, community resources, local entrepreneurial initiatives and providing entertainment, exercise and education for children. The targeting of children recognises the 'trickle-up' effect in which children influence parents' purchasing decisions. Lever's Director of Environmental Affairs commented, 'Whether it is cigarettes or the environment, children are great behaviour modifiers.'

Sales promotions create many opportunities for creativity. A promotional scheme run by Environmental Preservation Inc. in the USA takes a novel approach to preserving the 150 000 acres of virgin rainforest in Costa Rica's Talamancan Corridor. The land is to be turned into 'the world's first consumer-interactive corporate natural theme park'. Corporate sponsors such as Kellogg's, Benetton and Quaker Oats will purchase sections of the land. These are then sold to consumers in small (three metre square) deeded parcels. The advantage to the company is that the return of sale registration cards will allow them to build a database of environmentally concerned consumers, and also to build brand loyalty among such consumers who will become part owners of the 'Company X nature preserve' (Green Market Alert 1993).

Direct mail

Faced with concern about the waste involved in junk mail, direct mail users and agencies are enthusiastic about going green in principle, while expressing reservations about cost and quality problems associated with recycled paper in prac-

tice. However, improvements in recycled paper manufacture are rapidly closing both the cost and quality gap with virgin paper. The Body Shop showed that the quality problems of recycled paper are not insurmountable, by developing an award-winning catalogue from very low-grade recycled paper. In industrial markets there is an increasing shift towards on-disk catalogues. Pioneering companies such as SKF, RS Components and Universal Stationery are now providing corporate buyers with catalogues on disk. These feature in-built order processing software, automatic key customer discounts and they offer considerable scope for reducing the amount of paper consumed by catalogues and for allowing more frequent updates.

Point-of-sale promotional materials

Although technically an advertising medium, point-of-sale promotions (POS) is frequently closely linked to retail promotions and is therefore placed under the sales promotion umbrella. POS includes anything which is not part of the product and which is designed to communicate with the customer at the point of sale. POS materials include posters and mobiles, leaflets, dispensing bins, cartons and racks, display stands, shop signs and illuminated displays. Given that research from the Point of Purchase Institute suggests that up to 80 per cent of consumer purchase decisions are made or finalised in-store, there is considerable opportunity to influence consumers effectively. The rise in green POS materials is reflected in the emergence of specialist agencies such as New York-based Thomson–Leeds. In the USA, Wal-Mart introduced a green 'shelftalker' programme in 1989 to highlight the environmental benefits of specific products and packaging to respond to increasing consumer interest in environmental information.

There is also a growing trend in 'take-away' POS promotional literature in the form of newsletters and magazines, particularly among retailers. Such magazines regularly carry environmental features and offer considerable opportunities to combine promotion with consumer education on environmental issues. Even service providers have become involved in such initiatives. In 1990 Barclay's Bank produced a Barclayloan *Environmental Special* magazine including details of corporate environmental sponsorship, articles about recycled paper and a competition linked to a tree-planting initiative.

Selling

In industrial marketing the sales-force is the key channel of communications with customers. To support a successful green industrial marketing strategy, the sales-force needs to be able to answer the questions customers might have concerning environmental performance. Salespeople also need to know the right questions to ask customers, to evaluate their likely interest in greening now and in the future. At a practical level, the sales-force of a green company should also be working with the guidance of an ethical code, and driving cars fitted with catalytic converters and running on lead-free petrol. The marketer should ensure that the sales-force is aware of:

● the environmental strategy at a marketing and corporate level;

● the environmental performance of the product range;

● the environmental performance of the company in terms of its processes, policies and practices;

● the need to evaluate the customer's interest in green issues, and to find out from the customer whether or not the end-consumer is likely to demand greener products.

Public relations

Public relations (PR) has grown in importance in recent years as an element of the marketing mix. Much of the emphasis in PR is related to corporate image (*see* Chapter 12) but it is also an important means for a company to promote itself and its products to its various external markets. This can be achieved through a number of activities including:

● corporate image and corporate communications management;

● managing media relations;

● participation and sponsorship of major events such as Earth Day in the USA or Green Shopping Day in the UK;

● trade fairs and exhibitions;

● product publicity.

Media relations has been an important aspect of green communications because of the newsworthiness of green issues. This has created a wide range of opportunities for companies to generate competitive advantage through PR. Companies' environmental performance has also become a subject for debate on prime-time TV. When the chairmen of the top three American car makers appeared on ABC's *Nightline* show to explain and answer questions on their companies' positions on a range of issues, environmental concerns dominated proceedings. Favourable news coverage can meet many of the communications objectives set for green advertising campaigns at a greatly reduced cost. Dependence on the use of media which is not being paid for makes PR a far less controllable form of communication than advertising, however, in terms of message content, timing and frequency.

INFORMING AND EDUCATING CONSUMERS

Informative advertising

Marketing communications, and advertising in particular, is often criticised for the degree to which it attempts to persuade and manipulate rather than to inform. An informative communications strategy might seem an obvious choice for the environmental marketer, but it has its difficulties. Advertising's effectiveness is usually based on short bursts of information containing a simple message which demonstrates the product and its benefits. It is less adept at providing explanations, and the more complex the explanation becomes, the harder it becomes to integrate it within an advertisement. Well designed advertising can succeed in informing consumers about environmental issues, however, and can help to raise awareness and improve understanding. Faced with the relatively slow uptake of unleaded petrol in the wake of the 1987 budget price reduction, Esso's market research showed that UK consumers were confused by conflicting messages from the motor trade concerning a range of issues including the suitability of unleaded fuel for different cars, the costs of conversion and the availability and performance of unleaded. Esso then launched an informative press advertising campaign with the theme 'Esso explodes a few myths about unleaded'. The campaign, combined with further price cuts in 1988, helped to secure mass-market acceptance for the product.

An important communications challenge for green advertisers is to help their customers to make the links between the causes and effects of environmental and social problems, their potential solution and products and providers. The Co-operative Bank's advertising campaign to promote its environmentally and socially responsible investment policy used several adverts each with a series of pictures linked to a sentence that formed a small 'story'. One such story line was

> 'This is the daughter – The Hills sent to law school – Using savings they kept in a bank – Which their bank had invested – Abroad in a country – That denies most of its people – legal rights.'

This was followed by a reassurance that 'It happens. But not at the Co-operative Bank.' The implications of the advert's message are interesting: that your life choices have funding implications, and that your choice of financial services to fund your own life choices, through the operation of international banking, can help to determine the life choices available to people on the other side of the world. Walking into the branch of the bank in the village where you live may seem like a local affair, but in the delocalised world, the decision that you make there can have global implications.

Informative booklets and guides

In the USA the swing back towards more traditional cleaners created a new communications opportunity as customers began to request more information from companies such as Church and Dwight and Heinz. They quickly responded by producing booklets containing hints for using non-toxic cleaning agents effectively (Scerbinski 1991). Providing such booklets has the potential to deal with the problems of covering complex green issues more comprehensively than in a 30 second television advertisement, or on a two inch square label. Rank Xerox produced an eight-page A4 brochure entitled *Xerox Paper and the Environment*; Sainsbury's produced *Living Today*, a 20-page booklet explaining environmental issues in simple terms together with advice on the contribution that consumers can make and details of the steps the company is taking. One of the most ambitious attempts to educate consumers came from paper manufacturer, Eka Nobel. It produced *The White Book on White Paper* to inform consumers that its paper, although pure white, was produced using its 'Elemental Chlorine Free' and 'Totally Chlorine Free' bleaching processes. The fact that consumers were in danger of discriminating against a brilliant white product on the basis of assumed environmental damage is in itself an interesting sign of the times after decades of 'whiter than white' promotion in paper and many other markets. The book was direct mailed to around 2000 targets and was requested by another 1000. In the follow-up research 98 per cent of respondents were positive about the book, and 72 per cent thought that the book's message and sender could be trusted.

The importance of communication and the provision of information in relation to environmental improvement is underlined by the experience of Migros when it switched to selling toothpaste presented as tubes rather than tubes inside boxes. Initially sales fell, which seemed to confirm the gloomier predictions of those who cautioned against responding to environmental concern. However, once Migros explained the reasons for the change, sales recovered to their previous levels.

1 Before advertising planning begins, consider concept testing the proposed environmental benefit to make certain that, *from the consumer's perspective:*
- the product is seen as providing a real and meaningful environmental benefit;
- the benefit is seen as an improvement over competitive products.

2 The environmental advertising claim should be written to provide specific and detailed information on the product's environmental benefit. Then, consider pretesting the claim to make certain that, *from the consumer's perspective* the claim:
- states the specific aspect of the product in which the environmental benefit lies;
- provides specific data to permit the consumer to believe that the environmental product benefit is real;
- provides a context for evaluating the promoted environmental benefit;
- provides definitional support for all technical terminology;
- explains why the promoted environmental product attribute will result in an environmental benefit.

3 When determining how much emphasis to give the environmental claim in the advertising examine the relationship between the source of environmental improvement and consumer attitudes toward the product:
- First make certain that consumers understand that the product delivers (or continues to deliver) expected levels of traditionally important category benefits.
- Then promote the product's environmental benefit.

4 When thinking about the context in which to place the product's environmental claim keep the advertising personal:
- Stress the contribution to the environment which *each individual* makes by purchasing environmentally better alternatives.
- Reinforce the target's environmentally conscious/responsible behaviours.

Fig. 13.2 A summary of environmental advertising recommendations
(Source: Davis (1993))

RAISING ENVIRONMENTAL AWARENESS

Involvement in education

Another important element of consumer education is raising the awareness about, and understanding of, environmental issues and their potential solutions. If a company can present itself as part of the solution, there can be valuable promotional benefits. A key area where companies are getting involved is in sponsoring and facilitating environmental education in schools. This has the benefit of targeting an important audience – children – and simultaneously demonstrating environmental and social responsibility. David Buzzelli, Vice President of Environment, Health and Safety for Dow Chemical, a company with considerable involvement in sponsoring environmental education states:

'Our interest is not altruistic. Business needs a voting public that is environmentally literate, that is able to prioritize issues and make intelligent decisions.'

Dow's educational sponsorship has included funding a recycling roadshow, funding a pilot programme for environmental curriculum development and co-sponsoring a 'teach the teachers' environmental issues training initiative.

In-store education

At an in-store rather than in-school level, Bonjour Jeans developed an unusual multimillion dollar environmental awareness campaign under the banner 'Let's Save Our World ... We Have Nowhere Else To Go.' The campaign involved two-page advertisements in magazines such as *Seventeen*, *Mademoiselle*, *Cosmopolitan* and

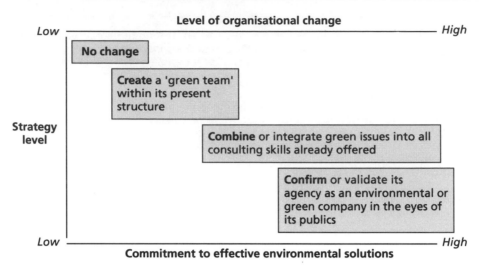

Fig. 13.3 Advertising agency response to the green challenge
(Source: McDonagh (1994))

Rolling Stone. The advertisements featured a message from company President Charles Dayan about the urgency of saving the environment, followed by pictures of top models wearing Bonjour Jeans. All Bonjour products were then tagged with special environmental tags, focusing on one of five key green themes – water, energy, recycling, pollution and food. The tags provided consumers with environmental information along with practical tips such as 'Take showers, not baths, to cut water consumption'. Bonjour's campaign shows that a business does not need to be in the front line of environmental issues to be able to benefit from environmental marketing. However, there is always the danger that the environmental lobby will see this as 'bandwagon jumping' unless the company involved ensures that it is putting its own house in order as well as giving out free advice to customers (*Marketing News* 1990).

MANAGING GREEN PROMOTIONS

The process of developing green advertisements is the same as in conventional advertising. Davis (1993) provides a checklist of factors to be considered during the process (*see* Fig. 13.2). A key player in the process of developing any advertis-

ing campaign is the advertising or marketing communications agency. An agency's account managers and planners will work with the product or brand managers from a client company to produce a plan including an advertising strategy, a set of objectives and a target audience. Briefs will be produced for the agency's creative teams and media buyers. Agencies vary in terms of the degree to which they are willing to commit themselves to contributing to the development of environmental solutions, and in the degree to which they are willing to restructure their operations to pursue clients with a green brief. One explanation for the poor quality of much of the early environmental advertising was a lack of environmental understanding among advertisers and advertising agencies. Green issues emerged with a suddenness that caught many companies by surprise and launched them into an advertising territory that was unfamiliar to them. Advertising agencies are now becoming increasingly geared up to help potential clients to develop green advertising campaigns. Small specialist green agencies such as MediaNatura have emerged, and large agencies like Saatchi & Saatchi, mostly now contain specialist green teams. McDonagh (1994) outlines four strategies for agencies which are summarised in Fig. 13.3.

Bernstein (1992) suggests two acronyms for advertising campaigns. One to check the effectiveness of an advertisement in traditional terms, the second to act as a 'green screen'. The fundamentals of the advertisement can be checked with reference to VIPS:

● Is the advertisement *Visible* in getting its message noticed?

● Is the advertisement distinctive in its *Identity*, through branding and links to corporate identity?

● Is the advertisement making a *Promise* of future satisfaction of customer needs?

● Is the advertisement *Simple*?

In addition to this, the greenness of an advertisement can be screened by reference to SHARE. Is the advertisement acceptable in its portrayal of and relationship to:

● sex;
● health and safety;
● age;
● race;
● environment.

The elegant part about the SHARE acronym is that as well as suggesting social concern, share is one meaning of the Latin word 'communicare'.

CASE STUDY

Schering Agriculture's Green Science

The agrochemicals business has been high on the campaigning priorities for environmental groups, and is one of the industries viewed with deepest suspicion by the general public. It therefore takes both courage and conviction for an agrochemicals business to promote itself as green. The Schering Group is a German multinational with over 100 subsidiary companies spread across Europe and beyond. Its growth has been both organic and by acquisition, and in 1983 one of the acquisitions was the British agrochemical businesses FBC. The company was underperforming at the time, and the change of ownership presented an opportunity to change the company's strategy, name and positioning. According to Schering Agriculture's Marketing Director, David Morgan:

'There was a significant risk, but we believe corporate identity is of fundamental importance to the company's success. Our image in the past was somewhat nebulous, so we felt confident to start effectively from scratch.'

Customer needs were researched as part of the company's marketing review. The research showed that the farmers and agricultural distributors who bought FBC products wanted

suppliers to be international, research-based, innovative, ethical, responsible and professional.

In 1986 the company was relaunched as Schering Agriculture amid a blaze of marketing communications under a campaign theme of 'Green Science'. As the company's Marketing Services Manager, Frances McKim commented:

'We didn't go Green in the sense that we sat down and said "What can we do? Let's go Green." As part of our marketing review for the launch of the new company we looked at our objectives as a business, the way we conducted our business and what our philosophy was. The Green approach wasn't new but it was something we really identified for the first time in our review. From there, we needed a way of putting this message over to farmers and distributors and that is where Green Science came from. It was a statement of our philosophy, scientific effort and care for the environment.'

The rebirth of the company as Schering Agriculture was implemented in a 'Big Bang' during September 1986. Over a 48-hour period all the company depots' nameboards were changed along with business cards and stationery. The company's 1000 crop sprayers were repainted

▶

and distribution was switched to newly painted vehicles, brought into service to replace the contract fleet used while repainting took place. Within four days every vestige of FBC had been removed. Although this involved an enormous upheaval, in one sense the emphasis on the new colour was convenient – green had coincidentally been the colour of Schering's company livery since 1851.

To support the new name and identity an advertising barrage was unleashed consisting of over 100 advertising insertions in trade, national and local press, and in an unusual departure for an industrial firm, television advertising as well. This was supported by 50 000 direct mailshots including a high quality brochure and video aimed at all customers and technical contacts. This communication effort succeeded in generating both awareness and interest, and in forging a link between 'Green Science' and Schering Agriculture. To turn awareness of Schering and Green Science into better understanding of the two, in March 1987 a range of below-the-line sales promotions were launched. A series of pocket educational guides and information packs were produced to help farmers with problems such as pinpointing disease, identifying weeds and coping with legislative change. The Green Science Disease Alert service was set up to give farmers advanced warning of disease outbreaks in their area. The company also developed a guide to farm conservation in conjunction with the Farming Wildlife Trust.

The effect of the campaign was remarkable. In a mature, competitive and static market the campaign was responsible for an increase in sales of 23.7 per cent, representing a 2.5 per cent growth in marke share. In the month during which the campaign was launched, spontaneous awareness of the company within the industry jumped from 22 per cent for FBC to

41 per cent for Schering Agriculture. During the first two years under the Green Science banner, profits increased by 24.4 per cent. The Green Science campaign had a wide range of further benefits for Schering. Market research revealed that in the wake of the campaign the perception of customers was that the company was more international, more efficient, better managed and more R&D based. Sales staff were also perceived as being of higher calibre and as calling more frequently.

The campaign was not only targetted externally. 'Staff were a key target audience,' says David Morgan. In a campaign that was as much about creating a new corporate culture and identity internally as a new market position externally, Frances McKim commented:

'Green is not just a colour that can be put on your products as an afterthought. It has to be a company philosophy that the whole staff can get behind.'

On the day of the launch, the company gathered together its 430 UK staff for a spectacular laser show introducing them to the Green Science concept. Under the new identity, staff turnover has dropped dramatically, and morale is claimed to be much improved. In an industry with such a negative image, it appears much more motivating to work for a company with a positive message.

The cumulative success of the campaign was such that it was one of the Chartered Institute of Marketing's 1989 National Marketing Award winners. As David Morgan commented:

'We've dramatically improved perceptions of the company as well as the industry as a whole. When we first launched the Green Science campaign we thought the theme would be relevant for two years. But now we see it as valid for many years to come.'

(Adapted from Homer, S. (1989) 'How "Going Green" Can Change Customer Perceptions', *Industrial Marketing Digest*, Vol 14 (4), pp 67–74 and other sources.)

CHAPTER 14

Getting it there – channels of distribution

'A distribution system ... is a key external resource. Normally it takes years to build and is not easily changed. It ranks in importance with key external resources such as manufacturing, research, engineering, and field personnel and facilities.'
(Corey 1976)

INTRODUCTION

When the environmental impact of products is discussed, it is usually in terms of their manufacture, use or disposal. An important dimension of a product's eco-performance relates to the energy consumption and other socio-environmental impacts involved in getting a product safely from the place of manufacture to the place of consumption. The channels of distribution that a company uses can be viewed from a physical and from an economic perspective. In physical terms, distribution deals with the logistical challenge of getting the product to the consumer. In economic terms, distribution is concerned with developing and managing a channel structure which in addition to supporting the physical distribution of goods, is capable of handling the exchanges of information, money and ownership that marketing relies upon. For companies that view it in terms of physical 'place' issues, distribution can become relegated to an essentially tactical marketing practicality, which only needs to be tackled after more 'strategic' mix decisions about the product, its price and promotion have been planned. In reality, effective channel structure management is of strategic importance to the success of almost any product. Given that distribution costs typically account for between 30 and 40 per cent of the selling cost of manufactured goods, it is surprising that distribution remains so often neglected as an element of marketing strategy.

For the environmental marketer, distribution is clearly an issue of strategic importance. As the Exxon Valdez disaster or the outcry over the cruelty involved in the transport of livestock to the slaughterhouses of southern Europe vividly illustrated, how a product is distributed can be even more important for a product's eco-performance than how it is made. Both the physical and economic dimensions of distribution have implications for the green agenda. In physical terms, few of us live in such remote locations that we do not daily witness the movement of goods by road, or see the physical impact of distribution in terms of the shops, warehouses and car parks that dot the landscape. In terms of channel development, an important strategic challenge in the early development of green products has been gaining access to conventional distribution channels. Even for marketers not taking an interest in the environment, the green challenge can have impacts which resound through entire channel structures. The publication of the *Good Wood Guide*, which highlighted the eco-performance of companies involved in the supply of wood products from forestry through to retail, sent shockwaves through the entire industry overnight.

The development of distribution systems and the transport infrastructure that supports them is also an important driving force behind the delocalisation of markets. This in turn can have significant environmental impacts. Transport infrastructure projects such as the M3 link over Twyford Down or the Channel Tunnel rail links have often been violently opposed due to their impact on local residents, landscapes and wildlife habitats. The Trans-Amazonian Highway, providing a distribution link into the heart of Amazonia and financed by the World Bank, has proved an environmental disaster and greatly accelerated the liquidation of the rainforest. In Europe, according to OECD figures, in the years 1970 to 1988 the amount of motorway tripled in France, while in Italy the number of vehicles increased by over 150 per cent, with the amount of traffic on the road being doubled.

THE DISTRIBUTION PROCESS

In physical distribution there are effectively three ways in which products and customers can be brought together to effect the delivery of a product or a service. The first is to bring the customer to the product. Factory shops and farm shops attract customers on the basis of the relatively low prices possible for goods freed from the cost burden of distribution and retail. By contrast, industrial marketing, direct marketing and door to-door marketing bring the product all the way to the customer. In between are a variety of channel structures which allow the customer and the product to meet halfway, at a location where a convenient variety of products is available at a location within easy reach of the customer's home. Since services cannot be stored, in the service sector the choice is a simpler one between the customer going to the service provider or the customer having the service delivered to his or her door. Therefore a customer can visit a bank or indulge in home banking and can visit a hairdressing salon or be visited by a hairdresser. The geographical relationship between the point of manufacture, the point of purchase and the point of use will affect the eco-performance of prod-

ucts. In the increasingly international economy, as the average distances travelled by products and the energy consumed to transport them increases, so their eco-performance declines.

DEVELOPING A DISTRIBUTION STRATEGY

Figure 14.1 demonstrates the key issues that need to be resolved in developing and implementing a logistics strategy (within which distribution represents the downstream part of the total logistics process). The green challenges that confront the logistics process within companies were investigated by Szymankiewicz (1993) with a study of 250 companies. The key green issues were found to be packaging and waste creation, the disposal of waste, noise and emission levels and the consumption of fuel resources.

The conventional approach to distribution management encompasses a number of elements including the speed and timeliness with which products are delivered, the distance and means by which they travel, the locations that they travel to and from, and the costs and risks involved in their movement. Green distribution adds another important dimension to these issues – that of eco-efficiency. As Wasik (1991) notes, society is becoming far less tolerant of supply-chain inefficiencies, and this has acted to put the physical impact of the distribution process much more in the spotlight. The artificially low cost of transportation due to its treatment of the environment as an 'externality' has led to some very inefficient patterns of consumption and production. Schumacher pointed out that it seems bizarrely inefficient to transport biscuits baked in the South of England for sale in Scotland, when other biscuits baked in Scotland are being transported for sale in the South of England. Creating more efficient distribution systems which produce less pollution and waste per product moved can be tackled in several ways.

Facility location

Companies can attempt to optimise the number and location of retail outlets and distribution

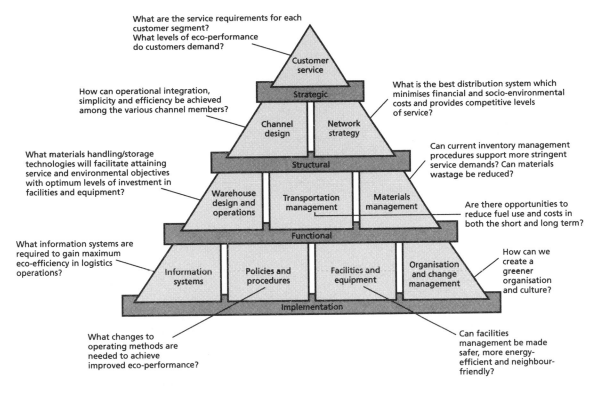

Fig. 14.1 Key issues in logistics strategy
(adapted from *Anderson Consulting*, Arthur Anderson & Co)

depots to create a more efficient pattern of product and customer journeys. There is no shortage of economically based models and computer packages available to help companies to decide how many outlets and depots they need, and how to locate them. These are typically based on profit maximisation, however, which, given the existence of the transportation eco-subsidy, will tend to be different from the most eco-efficient pattern. Figure 14.2 suggests a trade-off between the number of depots and the number of vehicles required that will combine to produce an ecologically optimum number of depots required. It is better for the environment, and usually for the supplier's business prospects, to locate depots and outlets close to customers. Many products can share one journey from producer to a retail outlet, but fewer products will be likely to travel together with individual customers making their homeward journey. However, the availability of

relatively cheap fuel and the pursuit of economies of scale has led to increasing centralisation of both production and distribution. Large superstores covering a larger catchment area than the smaller local stores that they supersede are very much a function of 'the great car economy'.

Facility design

Companies can site and design facilities to minimise their environmental impact. Many new grocery superstores have replaced or augmented conventional boilers by circulating waste heat from refrigeration units. ASDA used a relatively derelict site for the development of a distribution centre, business park and store at its Magna Park site. It spent over £500 000 (375 000 ECUs) on landscaping, planting trees and shrubs and stocking water bodies with fish and other aquatic life. An adjacent area of woodland is also planned.

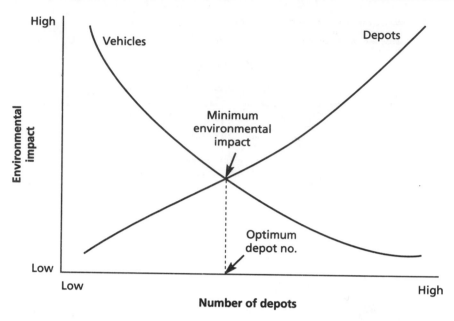

Fig. 14.2 Minimising environmental impact of logistic operations through optimal depot numbers
(Source: Institute of Logistics and Distribution Management)

This major environmental investment gained the company awards and considerable public relations benefits.

Vehicle policy

Most goods are distributed by road, and most large businesses have fleets of distribution vehicles and/or company cars. The internal combustion engine is one of the most serious contributors to the problems of pollution and environmental degradation. Minimising the environmental impact of company vehicles needs to be a key agenda item for any environmental marketer. Companies can introduce a vehicle purchase policy adapted to give a priority to fuel-efficient, aerodynamic and low-emission vehicles. Larger heavy goods vehicles (HGVs) produce less environmental impact per unit than smaller trucks, but the prospect of even larger trucks driving through our urban streets still seems a daunting prospect, even if they bring some eco-efficiencies of scale. Driver training is another important factor in determining the efficiency of vehicles. BRS has five driver training schools at which fuel

economy is the most popular course. Trained drivers are said to achieve around 20 per cent efficiency improvements. Noise is an emission which is often ignored, partly because it is generally viewed by people as 'less controllable' than others. Jolly and Charter (1992) cite the example of Austria whose pioneering introduction of a 90 decibel limit for night traffic noise (to be emulated by the EU) led to the German truck manufacturer MAN selling 4000 new 'silent' trucks into Austria in just over two years.

Choice of transport mode

Road and rail are the two major forms of freight transport. Economic criteria have dominated the choice between them in the past, and the flexibility, speed and low cost of road has accounted for a gradual flow of freight away from rail. Both transport modes have considerable environmental impacts in their operation and in the construction of their infrastructure. These impacts have not yet been reflected in the costs paid by the transport user or final customer. According to figures from The Netherlands Road Transport Institute, rail transport uses only one third as much energy per freight unit than road. Heavy goods vehicles (HGVs) also contribute more to aesthetic pollution, noise, congestion and transport-related deaths. With regard to the construction of infrastructure, rail track is estimated to need 80 per cent less land, 90 per cent less aggregate for construction and would use only one third as much energy in construction and maintenance compared to a motorway capable of handling the same level of freight (TEST 1991). For green companies, such as Migros, moving freight on to rail has become an important part of their green strategy. During 1986 around 36 per cent of Migros goods were moved by rail.

While the road network continues to benefit from the eco-subsidy, and while road infrastructure projects are preferred to rail investment, road transport will remain more cost effective for companies despite rail's eco-efficiency. When Carel Van Miert was appointed EU Environment Commissioner in 1992 he proposed that transportation development and environmental objectives must be integrated, which would mean increasing the price of road transport as well as promoting rail and waterborne transport. If these proposals can ever overcome the considerable combined might of the road lobby, the eco-subsidy currently enjoyed by road transport may be reduced in the near future.

Other forms of transport also have their environmental problems. In the case of the pipelines used to transport commodities such as gas, oil and water, the environmental impacts generally relate to their construction and their losses during operation. These can be gradual, such as the 5 per cent losses of natural gas within the UK's gas distribution network claimed by Friends of the Earth, or sudden as in the oil spill in Russia's Komi Province in 1994. Air transport is used for a relatively small proportion of all products, but the atmospheric impact of the operation of aeroplanes, and the human impact of the operation of airports are both causes of concern. The issue of the risks posed by seaborne freight is largely focused on oil tankers in the wake of disasters such as the Exxon Valdez and the Braer, or shipments of toxic waste such as that carried aboard the Karin B.

Choice of transport services provider

With the internationalisation and Europeanisation of markets, companies are becoming increasingly reliant on third parties for distribution services. This provides an opportunity to seek out relatively green providers. Some distribution services such as British Road Services, Peter Lane Transport and Excel Logistics have implemented environmental programmes covering issues such as driver training, vehicle maintenance and vehicle design. Excel has taken a range of steps to improve its eco-performance (Penman 1994):

● It is pioneering new aerodynamic vehicle forms which together with the application of speed limiters and good driving practice have the potential to save 15 per cent, or £2 million (1.5 million ECUs), on fuel bills. If similar practices were applied to the entire UK distribution industry it would save up to £400 million (300 million ECUs) on fuel costs.

● It is switching over 90 per cent of its refrigerated vehicle fleet to non-CFC coolants.

● It is introducing reductions in noise pollution through use of brake silencers and plug-in-power points for refrigeration vehicles at depots.

● It is recycling all used engine oil.

● It is introducing recycled water use in all new (and some existing) vehicle washes.

● It is conserving energy through heat recycling from refrigeration units, electrically operated doors to minimise unwanted heat gains or losses, the application of energy audits for facilities and a high priority for energy efficiency in new facilities.

Materials handling

The materials handling process can create a range of environmental impacts including energy use by mechanised handling equipment, noise produced from the operation of a goods depot and the release of CFCs from refrigeration equipment. Although it is the movement of goods on the road that we associate with pollution, their movement in and around a depot can also cause pollution. According to figures from America's Environmental Protection Agency, the operation of a fork-lift truck for an hour will produce the same level of air pollution caused by driving 250 miles in a typical car. Just-In-Time (JIT) initiatives can increase the efficiency of the distribution process by reducing the need for product storage and the associated additional materials handling requirements. The environmental downside of JIT is that it often requires suppliers to make smaller but more frequent deliveries of materials which is ecologically inefficient. In Japan JIT systems are increasingly being abandoned in the face of the growing dysfunction of the transportation system (Nieuwenhuis 1994). For the Japanese vehicle manufacturers that pioneered JIT this is particularly ironic, as the technical and economic excellence of their own production system is effectively being strangled by the environmental consequences of their own products.

Shipping packaging

Packaging is generally associated with the material which contains and presents the product on the retailer's shelf. However, a good deal of packaging material will be used to get the product from the manufacturer to the retailer, and this is commonly called 'shipping packaging'. It includes wooden pallets, shrink wrap and large cartons or crates which contain the individual products, together with labelling instructions concerning the handling and storage of the products. Packaging is an important area for the improvement of eco-performance (*see* Chapter 15) and many companies are seeking to reduce, reuse or recycle as much of their packaging materials as possible. This has moved shipping packaging away from its usual technical and tactical role to become an area for innovation and the generation of competitive advantage. Design skills once only applied to products and product packaging are now being applied to shipping packaging. In the USA Rehrig Pacific now offer a reusable crate for transporting 2-litre soft drink bottles with a 7- to 12-year lifespan, which doubles as an in-store display unit.

Creating a greener distribution strategy

Developing a credible green distribution strategy goes beyond improving the practicalities of fuel efficiency, shipping packaging and the noise produced by depots. Contemporary channel structures are often complex in nature and involve some delicate balances of power. Relationship building and management are important in distribution management, and also in the greening of distribution. At B&Q, logistics has formed a key component of a greening strategy which has been backed up by a thorough environmental review and the development of environmental policies. Their 1993 Environmental Review included:

- the development of 'Centralised Distribution' at B&Q bringing environmental benefits such as reduced vehicle movements and a reduction in transit packaging;
- the establishment of a policy and targets aimed at reducing vehicle emission impacts;
- the reduction of transit packaging in conjunction with suppliers, aiming for a 30 per cent reduction in the total corrugated board used by UK suppliers within the first year;
- a cost and benefit analysis undertaken into the practicalities of store-based collection and recycling systems for packaging materials;
- insistence that logistics subcontractors operate an environmental policy consistent with B&Q's and commission their own comprehensive environmental audit;
- the promotion of environmental awareness both within B&Q's Logistics Department and its subcontractors.

Funding improved distribution eco-performance is not necessarily difficult since fuel reduction and improved eco-efficiency is likely to form a major component of the strategy. Other elements, such as using cleaner and quieter vehicles or non-CFC refrigerants can be expensive.

Distribution and availability

Availability is an important facet of a company's channel structure and distribution arrangements. Baker (1992) puts forward the argument that 'Consumption is a function of availability' and that to an extent, brand shares become a self-ful-filling prophecy. This occurs because the most available (as opposed to the best) product will be the easiest to purchase; its sales volume will therefore be high, and this success will ensure that retailers will continue to make it widely available.

One of the questions posed by current trends in retailing is the social acceptability of the pattern of availability that our channel structures are creating. Out-of-town shopping complexes reflect the dominance of the car within western Europe. The location of such complexes near major road networks helps to minimise distribution costs. However, it poses the question of whether it is acceptable that those without the use of a car are being denied access to the goods that they need at competitive prices. Those without access to a car will include many on low incomes, and many who are elderly and disabled. Some 25 per cent of the UK population does not have access to a car, and it was in response to concern over the relegation of the carless to 'second-class shoppers' that led Asda to lay on free bus services to many of its large stores. The physical layout of stores can also limit access for certain types of customer. Groups representing the disabled have campaigned for many years for better access to commercial buildings, while parents with pushchairs are frequently confronted with children's departments in stores which are not at ground level.

CHANNEL CHOICE

Channels vary in a variety of respects including their geographic coverage, the nature, number and variety of the intermediaries used, the degree of independence that intermediaries have from suppliers and the degree of specialism among intermediaries. The style of channel that a particular manufacturer or product will use, will be determined by the nature of the product and its market. If a product is heavy, technologically complex and innovative it will tend to be sold by small specialist dealers or, if it is an industrial product, directly by the company sales-force. Small, mature consumer goods will tend to be sold through large department stores and super-markets or by mail order. Green consumer goods took a considerable time to move beyond specialist and often 'alternative' channels to break into conventional retail channels. The initial growth of Ecover cleaning products in the UK was achieved through the rather unusual route (for a domestic cleaning range) of selling through health food shops before gaining access to the shelves of the major multiple retailers.

There are a wide variety of channels through which a product can be physically delivered to the customer, from hypermarkets to vending machines. The environmental and social impact of different types of channel varies. The rise of hypermarkets and superstores has provoked environmentalist criticism due to the amount of land they occupy for their buildings and car parks, the new road construction that has serviced them and their promotion of a car-based economy. Socially there are also concerns about the decline of super-markets and independent retailers in small towns and villages as trade switches to superstores and hypermarkets. In the USA the rise of 'no-frills' discount houses has created a resource-conservative approach to retailing, albeit one that is still heavily car-orientated. Mail order home shopping has been an increasing phenomenon in recent years. This involves significant resource savings over conventional retailing, although these are partly offset by the level of resources consumed by catalogues, packaging and individual product deliveries.

Distribution systems have tended to be relatively fragmented, involving a number of independent parties. Each has sought to maximise its own profit, even if this was at the expense of the profitability of the channel as a whole. This meant that in the past the development of a distribution strategy has often been a confrontational affair with retailers and manufacturers locked in a battle of wills and bargaining power which focused on price and individual self-interest. During the 1980s a longer-term partnership approach has been adopted by an increasing number of companies in the search for strategic stability and competitive advantage. There is also a trend towards integration within channels in which one party purchases other links in the supply chain, or uses its power to influence or contractually bind other parties. In many industries green progress will be made easier by the emergence of such vertical marketing systems (VMS) which provide opportunities to reduce fragmentation and inefficiencies. The corollary to this may be a concentration of power among a few large companies, and a reduction of consumer choice and channel-based employment, which may be considered less desirable.

The more parties that exist within a supply chain, the greater the number of journeys and loadings/unloadings that a product will undergo. As the economics of physical distribution are corrected to take the costs of environmental damage into consideration, so the incentive to streamline distribution channels will increase. Channel simplification has been an important element of The Body Shop's success. Here the manufacturer-come-retailer has sought out direct suppliers at a 'grass-roots' level, often in less industrialised countries. This allows the money generated by final sales to be invested in ways which can sustain the supplying community and environment rather than being dissipated among the middlemen of a long supply chain.

THE ROLE OF RETAILERS

The power of retailers

The traditional view of marketing is that the decision-making power within supply channels rests with the producer, with retailers acting as relatively passive intermediaries. This situation has altered radically during the 1980s, with power moving increasingly towards the retailer. Shultz (1987) sees the increasing size of retailers through acquisition and merger, and the informational power given to retailers by their electronic point of sale (EPOS) systems as key driving forces behind this shifting power balance.

To be successful any new green product has to gain access to potential customers through a suitable distribution channel. For food and grocery items and many categories of consumer durables, this means gaining shelf space in supermarkets and high street retailers. As Hopfenbeck (1993) notes, retailers have an important role as gatekeepers controlling the flow of products and information between producers and consumers. He goes on to illustrate how some retailers have grasped the significance of this 'mediating role' with the following extract from the environmental principles of German retailer Otto Versand:

'We play a significant mediating role between production and the consumer, and it is our intention to use this function in the service of environmental protection.

Eco-friendliness is an important criterion in purchasing the products we offer. Our customers are reminded of this in the catalogue, because we feel that only when demand for eco-friendly products rises will manufacturers be able to respond effectively. Environmental protection should not be seen as an added extra. It is a basic purchasing principle.

It is our goal to bring about changes in manufacturers' behaviour, but also in that of our many millions of customers. Nobody can achieve this alone. Competence and authority are called for, but above all credibility.'

The gatekeeping role can also be used by retailers to prevent particularly grey products from reaching the market. German retailers Hertie withdrew, changed or introduced around 2000 products on environmental grounds during 1989 alone. An effective gatekeeping role depends upon retailers agreeing and policing eco-performance standards with suppliers. A purchasing manager for Sainsbury's was quoted in Tyler (1992) as saying:

'We produce a detailed specification and carefully check the chain of supply of ingredients to be used. We insist that each of our suppliers establish that no animal tests ... are conducted on any ingredient ... indeed that no such tests have been conducted for at least five years.'

Swindley (1991) found that over half of a sample of retail buyers felt that ecological considerations were important in their buying decisions. However, Strong (1994) in a study of the role of buyers within major UK supermarkets found that 43 per cent of buyers did not set performance standards for suppliers and less than half conducted any research to evaluate the environmental impacts of products, materials and production processes.

The greening of traditional retailers

Throughout the industrialised world, leading retailers have adopted a strategy of environmental improvement as part of their corporate and marketing strategy. Firms such as Wal-Mart in the USA, Loblaw in Canada, Migros in Switzerland and Tengelmann in Germany have responded to the concerns of customers and society by introducing a range of environmental initiatives and placing pressure on their suppliers to improve their 'upstream' eco-performance. In their role as the channel between manufacturer and the final consumers, retailers are often the first to feel the effects of any green consumer reaction. This was the case with the campaign against CFC-driven aerosols. As John Elkington commented (in Rock 1989):

> 'eight years ago the only environmental thing the supermarkets could think of was returnable bottles ... But the issue of CFCs in aerosols caused a profound change. It affected stocking policies in all chains.'

It was during 1987, in the face of mounting environmentalist pressure and consumer concern, that leading UK retailers including Sainsbury's, Safeway, Tesco and the Co-op pledged to phase out CFC-propelled aerosols. It was not until early 1989, however, that the UK aerosol industry made a similar response. In response to green concern many retailers' initial reaction was the delisting of environmentally damaging products and the introduction of green brands. This was followed by the development of green own-brands, particularly in household goods such as cleaners and toilet tissue.

The people who hold the key in the retailers' gatekeeping role are the buyers within the major retail chains. In a survey of supermarket grocery buyers, their purchase decisions in response to the pressure to adopt more green products, were found to be influenced by the following factors (Strong 1994):

- *Product range being purchased*. Buyers responsible for detergents, household cleaners, toiletries and paper products gave the most consideration to environmental issues.

- *Visibility of the issues to consumers*. Recycled content and recyclability of packaging, as an element of eco-performance which is relatively visible to consumers, was seen as important among buyers.

- *Ability of supplier to improve eco-performance cost effectively*.

- *Promotability of environmental benefits*. While recycled content in packaging is simple to promote to consumers through on-pack information, complex issues relating to manufacturing processes can be difficult to promote to the final consumer.

- *Media interest in related green issues*.

- *Pressure group influence*.

In the UK retail sector the late 1980s produced a flurry of activity, much of it prompted by the publication of *The Green Consumer Guide* and the publicity surrounding Green Shopping Day. While Tesco advertised itself as the 'Greener Grocer', Sainsbury's responded by claiming to be the 'Greenest Grocer'. Although Bernstein (1992) is rather disparaging about such claims and counter-claims, in Tesco's case it was a central component of a communication campaign which won it *Campaign*'s 1989 Advertiser of The Year award. Meanwhile, Safeway held the high ground on organic produce, Asda topped the recycling charts and the Co-operative Society introduced a wide ranging environmentally orientated strategy. The initial flurry of green product introductions and environmental marketing communications campaigns has been followed by a less public, and less public relations orientated, approach to the environment among UK retailers. Faced with consumer confusion and cynicism and conflicting information from suppliers and environmental groups, some retailers have chosen to consolidate their green position on their shelves and concentrate on environmental improvement by responding to the increasing range of European legislation. A combination of conservatism in the face of the complexities of the green agenda and a lack of organisational commitment and control has prevented any very radical changes among Britain's retailers (Simms 1992).

The emergence of green retailers

In addition to the greening of existing channels, there is an emergence of specialist green channels, of which one of the first, and probably the best known, is The Body Shop. Since 1990 in the USA, retailers such as Earth General, Earth Mercantile, Restore, The Earth Store, Eco-wise and Terre Verde have opened in nearly every region. Within Europe, the concept of 'Fair Trade' channels which aim to help spring the economies of developing countries from the 'commodity trap' and the influence of the powerful multinationals whose cartels control most commodity trades. Vidal (1993) reporting on green trends within retailing remarked that:

'Slick German and Dutch fair trade companies are expanding rapidly and continental supermarkets have been quicker to see the financial possibilities. In Britain, the success of Café Direct, set up last year by Oxfam, Traidcraft and others, is illuminating. The coffee, bought from co-operatives and small producers, is now sold by eight supermarket chains and is improving its market share monthly. The possibilities of supermarkets taking a wider range of fair trade goods – chocolate, honey and nuts, for instance – has never been greater.'

Green direct marketing

Direct mail can be used as a distribution channel as well as a means of promotion. Manufacturers may opt to supply a customer directly via mail order, or through a mail order house, as opposed to a conventional retailer. An alternative direct channel is teleshopping, which emerged as a competitive force in some markets during the 1980s with organisations such as the Shopping Channel in the USA or Minitel in France meeting with considerable success. The use of direct channels can reduce the human, physical and financial resources consumed within the marketing channel by the ordering, handling, storing, displaying, promoting, selling and delivery of the tangible product among different links in the supply chain. Conversely such channel simplifications may also increase environmental costs if product distribution involves a more fragmented and less efficient pattern of journeys for individual products. In services such as home banking, where it is the customer's journey to the service provider that is eliminated, the environmental advantages of home purchasing are more clear-cut. Although the use of home shopping has frequently been cited as a retail revolution waiting to happen, in the short term it is likely to continue as a complementary means of distributing products rather than a serious alternative to conventional retailing. Teleshopping, for example, continues to be of greatest interest to customers who are housebound, geographically remote or too 'time-poor' to engage in much conventional shopping activity.

During the early phase of green consumer concern, direct marketing has been important as a means of serving customers who may be too widely dispersed to justify the establishment of specialist green retail outlets. One of the most successful green direct mail retailers is the American company, Seventh Generation. It sells around 200 different green products including recycled toilet paper, beeswax crayons, cruelty-free toiletries and string bags for shopping. The company donates 1 per cent of gross sales to green charities, uses its catalogues to educate potential customers about the environment and operates with social responsibility and employee participation as its fundamental principles. Launched in 1988 on a shoestring, it generated sales in excess of $1 million (467 000 ECUs) in its first full year of operation.

Within mainstream direct selling there is also an increasing use of environmental and social criteria to generate competitive advantage. Betterware, the direct shopping housewear retailer, highlights a variety of green dimensions in its 'Home Shopping System' catalogue, underpinned by a statement of environmental principles:

'Betterware recognises its future responsibilities in the community beyond the immediate concern of its shareholders and employees and is therefore working towards improvements in the conservation of energy and natural resources and the minimisation of waste.

Environmental considerations will play a significant part in our choice of services and products; those products which achieve higher standards of environmental performance based on "fitness for purpose" will be given preference over less friendly products.

Betterware will also support social and environmental causes with annual donations.'

This policy is backed up by:

1 a 'tree for a tree' replanting policy for paper consumed for its catalogues;

2 a reuse of catalogues at least five times to reduce the number of trees needed for catalogue production from 35 000 to 7000;

3 sustainable sourcing for wooden products;

4 CFC-free products;

5 child-resistant caps;

6 measure strips on bottles;

7 a minimal packaging policy;

8 a spare parts availability policy;

9 the donation of 1 per cent of all profits through the Betterware Foundation.

FROM ONE-WAY TO TWO-WAY CHANNELS

Reverse logistics

A grey vision of distribution is as a pair of one-way processes. Goods and information move down the supply chain, and money, and perhaps information, flow back up it. The green challenge, like the law of gravity, is introducing the inevitable logic of 'what goes up must come back down' into distribution management. The recovery and reuse of pallets has been a big business in itself for many years. This has now been extended to include the reclamation of cardboard boxes, stretch wrap, strapping bands, and dunnage in a process that has become known as reverse logistics. It is now also beginning to be extended to include consumer packaging and obsolete products. The German Packaging Ordinances mean that both manufacturers and retailers have a responsibility to take back consumer packaging.

In industrial marketing reverse logistics has given several important markets a whole new direction. Dutch packaging giant Van Leer has set up a collection system for used steel drums in Europe and North America. When the system was introduced in the USA large-volume customers were given a code and a freephone number to call to arrange to have their used drums collected. Van Leer had arrangements with a network of drum reconditioners who would either recondition, shred or crush each used drum depending on its condition. Major customers such as Dow Corning and Johnson Wax highlighted their involvement in the drum collection system in their own environmental marketing communications strategies. In Germany the company's decision to introduce a similar system was spurred on by the introduction of the Packaging Ordinance. Van Leer appointed four regionally based reconditioning firms who set up a partnership and funded 18 strategic collection points to collect Van Leer drums from customers all over Germany (Miller and Szekely 1994).

Closing the loop

The ultimate aim of greener distribution is to help to 'close the loop' so that products are reused instead of travelling from cradle to grave. Although the concept of a closed-loop system may sound ambitious, it ranks alongside total quality as something to strive towards, and something that many companies are pursuing. In the future, the supply loop may be closed by legislative force rather than by its economic appeal to companies, in response to rising prices for virgin material. Hopfenbeck cites the case of personal computers in Germany where there is an annual 10 000 tonnes of computer waste, growing at 10 to 15 per cent annually. Only some 5 to 10 per cent of this currently finds its way back into the supply chain, and very few suppliers offer a return service for old product. This has led to discussions about obliging companies to accept their old product waste, as well as its discarded packaging waste.

IBM has responded to this by offering a disposal service to its German customers since June 1990. They have achieved a recycling quota of 83 per cent, with rates for some components reaching 90 per cent, the remainder being disposed of elsewhere. Some components such as cathode ray tubes and some plastics have caused problems in recycling. This has led companies such as IBM and Fiat to reduce the variety of plastics used in product design, and

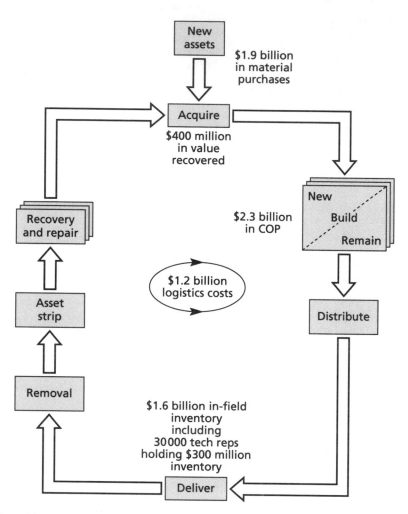

Fig. 14.3 Xerox's closed-loop supply chain
(Source: Stenross and Sweet (1992))

CASE STUDY

Xerox

The document processing business of Xerox is a truly global enterprise. In 1990 it generated sales across 130 countries of over $13.6 billion (6.4 billion ECUs). The company operates a sales-force of 15 000 backed up by 30 000 technicians providing after-sales service and a network of distributors, dealers and agents. Xerox is a leading example of two important trends in the management of the logistics and distribution process. First, its supply chain is one of the largest 'closed loops' in operation, and is illustrated in Fig. 14.3. In 1990 some $400 million (187 million ECUs) worth of parts were recovered from old machines and used in the production of new products. Although this is relatively small in comparison to the $1.9 billion (890 million ECUs) spent on new materials, in response to the economic, ecological and corporate image benefits of recycling components, the resource recovery effort is to be an increasing feature of its future strategy. Second, Xerox is a leading example of a company which has changed its entire logistics and distribution process to create an integrated supply chain. Following a benchmarking review which showed Xerox's logistics operations to be underperforming compared to other diversified electronics companies, in 1989 a Central Logistics and Asset Management Group was established. Its goals were to create an integrated global supply chain and improve customer satisfaction while cutting inventory requirements and expenditure. To do this required a complete re-engineering of Xerox's supply chain and channel structure involving changes to the organisation's culture, performance measurements, reward systems, relationships and working practices. The central logistics group were given the power to cut across functions, divisions and hierarchical lines in search of its new 'Inventory Management and Logistics Process Vision'.

The new vision was not explicitly about environmental marketing, but the two elements defined as the keys to its success were 'customer satisfaction' and 'recycling'. Xerox's efforts in pursuit of this vision were certainly a success. By 1991 customer satisfaction had increased by 7 per cent as a result of improved distribution performance, and the logistics costs in the Profit and Loss account had been cut by $100 million (47 million ECUs). These technical and economic benefits were accompanied by a major saving in materials, as inventory worth over $700 million (327 million ECUs) was removed from the supply chain. Xerox proved that environmental improvements can go hand-in-hand with improving customer services and reducing costs, and that considerable eco-efficiencies are available from re-engineering more than just the production process.

(Adapted from Stenross, M. and Sweet, G. (1992) 'Implementing an Integrated Supply Chain: The Xerox Example', *in* Christopher, M., *Logistics and Supply Chain Management*, Pitman Publishing.)

CHAPTER 15

Green packaging unwrapped

'In the throwaway economy, packaging becomes an end in itself. Hardware supplies, children's toys, cosmetics, toiletries, pharmaceuticals, music recordings, food and drinks, and every other conceivable consumable is mounted on cardboard, wrapped in paper, sealed with plastic, or subjected to all three.'
(Alan Thein Durning)

INTRODUCTION

Packaging is one of the 'Cinderella' fields of the marketing discipline which has received comparatively little coverage in the marketing literature, yet which can play a vital part in the success or failure of products in practice. It is also a major industry in its own right, with a global market for consumer goods packaging worth over £55 billion (41 billion ECUs) annually, with a smaller but still significant £32 billion (24 billion ECUs) spent on packaging industrial products (Izatt 1992). Within consumer goods markets, packaged foods account for almost half of all packaging, beverages account for fractionally under a quarter, while cosmetics and health care account for a further 12 per cent.

Packaging offers considerable scope for marketers to differentiate their products and inject some creativity into the marketing mix. Advances in packaging technology have created many new marketing opportunities from wine-in-a-box to freezer-to-microwave ready meals. The design of packaging also plays a vital role as a branding tool. The Jif lemon, Matheus Rosé and Toblerone are all brands made distinctive by their packaging. Even supermarket own-label products (previously considered as unbranded) now appear in increasingly stylish and attractive packaging in an attempt by the supermarkets to raise their own-label products to branded good status.

Despite its potential importance as a strategic marketing mix variable, packaging is more usually discussed in technical terms. Briston and Neill (1972) propose three definitions which emphasise this technical role.

1 Packaging is the art, science and technology of preparing goods for transport and sale.

2 Packaging may be defined as the means of ensuring the safe delivery of a product to the ultimate consumer in sound condition, at a minimum overall cost.

3 Packaging must protect what it sells, and sell what it protects.

These definitions only incorporate the environment if we take the word 'overall' in the second definition to mean 'economic and environmental'. A more comprehensive breakdown of the functions of packaging, which explicitly includes eco-performance based on the ideas of Roder and defines eight main functions for packaging, is shown in Fig. 15.1.

Few industries have felt the impact of the green challenge as profoundly as the packaging industry. For many years there were two 'E' factors that determined the success of any given form of packaging: consumers wanted packages that were *economical* to buy and *ergonomic* in use. The green challenge has added a third 'E' with consumers demanding that packaging is also *environ-*

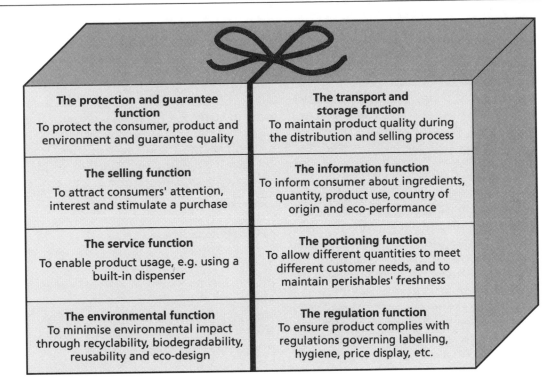

The protection and guarantee function
To protect the consumer, product and environment and guarantee quality

The transport and storage function
To maintain product quality during the distribution and selling process

The selling function
To attract consumers' attention, interest and stimulate a purchase

The information function
To inform consumer about ingredients, quantity, product use, country of origin and eco-performance

The service function
To enable product usage, e.g. using a built-in dispenser

The portioning function
To allow different quantities to meet different customer needs, and to maintain perishables' freshness

The environmental function
To minimise environmental impact through recyclability, biodegradability, reusability and eco-design

The regulation function
To ensure product complies with regulations governing labelling, hygiene, price display, etc.

Fig. 15.1 The main functions of packaging

mentally sensitive in disposal. A survey by the US journal *Packaging* found that concern about waste is making recyclability an increasingly important package attribute in terms of its effect on consumers' purchase decisions.

The experience of McDonald's and its polystyrene clamshells (*see* page 167) has shown the packaging industry and its customers the potential damage that can be done if a particular form of packaging comes under attack on environmental grounds. In the light of the McDonald's experience, TetraPak launched an environmental initiative including recycling schemes and advertising campaigns backed up by life-cycle analyses aiming to demonstrate the environmental soundness of its asceptic 'beverage bricks'. As Izatt (1992) puts it:

'Designers must strike a balance – creating environmentally responsible packaging that also protects and promotes the product.'

It is the perceived lack of environmental responsibility in the design and use of packaging that has made packaging a key focal point of environmen-

talist pressure. Buzelli (1991) suggests that McDonald's problems stemmed not from the actual eco-performance of its packaging, but from the fact that the polystyrene clamshell had become a symbol of a wasteful society. Around 50 million tonnes of packaging is thrown away as waste each year within the EU alone.

THE ROLE OF PACKAGING

The packaging of a product has both a physical and a psychological dimension. Physically the packaging contains and protects the product while allowing it to be stored and displayed safely and effectively. Psychologically packaging contributes to the differentiation, identification and promotion of a product by ensuring that it is distinctive and attractive and has shelf 'presence'. A typical large supermarket may contain over 35 000 different items. This makes it very important that packaging identifies and distinguishes a company's products and attracts customers to them.

The package has to satisfy a variety of stakeholders. Production managers want ease of filling; retailers want ease of display and storage; consumers want convenience, safety and value; environmentalists want minimal use of materials and maximum recycling; while the marketer wants ease of distribution, protection and shelf presence.

TYPES OF PACKAGING

We tend to associate packaging with the materials that the consumer discards before or after using the product. However, there are four elements of packaging which combine to form the total packaging content. *Primary packaging* comes into contact with the core product, keeping it safe and (where appropriate) fresh. In many cases changes to the nature of the primary product will influence the primary packaging. For example, where a drink is switched to a concentrated formulation for consumer dilution, the packaging material needed (for the same level of consumer benefit) drops by 85 per cent and the shelf space required drops by 90 per cent. *Secondary packaging* contains and presents the wrapped or contained core product. *Shipping packaging* helps in the storage and transportation of the product, and is often discarded before the product reaches the consumer (*see* Chapter 14). The final element of packaging is the *labelling*. This is the information printed on or with the packaging.

The labelling of a product can communicate a great deal of information which will be of interest to the consumer. Green consumers like any others will be interested in information which indicates price and ingredients, aids identification and provides technical product information or guarantees. Labelling also provides an opportunity to inform the consumer about the environmental performance of the product and the company that provides it. Information relating to the packaging itself is also an increasing feature of product labelling. The EU Ecolabelling criteria being developed for products such as detergents include consideration of the total amount of packaging material used, and the proportion of virgin mater-

ial it contains. Labelling is also used to encourage consumers to dispose of used packaging in a responsible way: for example, the 'Keep Your Country Tidy' slogan and 'Tidyman' logo on disposable packaging can be used to prompt consumers to avoid littering. Labelling is also important to encourage and aid recycling efforts. Cans can be grouped for recycling according to whether they are aluminium or steel. America and Sweden have introduced labelling to identify the six major packaging plastics to aid recycling.

PACKAGING MATERIALS

There are a wide range of physical resources involved in packaging. The most commonly used are:

- *Glass*. This is mainly used for bottles and jars, over 6 billion of which are used in the UK alone each year. Glass containers can be reused or recycled, and despite the energy-intensive nature of glass production, its natural image and the environmental backlash against the plastics industry have given a new lease of life to glass in many markets.

- *Metal*. A wide range of food and drink products come packaged in cans made either from tin-plated steel or aluminium. Both of these can be recycled, and in countries like Sweden some 95 per cent of all aluminium cans are recycled. Metal foil is also used to package foodstuffs and confectionary and small vulnerable consumer goods such as photographic films and condoms.

- *Plastics*. This is widely used for packaging food and drink, consumer goods and as wrapping for product shipping. It accounts for over 30 per cent of all European packaging by weight, with the average European household disposing of 40 kg of waste plastic each year. Polystyrene foam is widely used as protective secondary packaging for a wide range of fragile products. Problems of quality reduction limit the opportunities for plastic recycling, and the major opportunity for reusing plastic packaging is for it to be incinerated for its energy value.

● *Paper and cardboard.* Paper is one of the most important packaging materials, particularly for food products where the increase in demand for convenience foods and individually portioned products is leading to a growth in paper usage for packaging. The majority of large consumer goods come in some form of protective secondary cardboard packaging. Paper is commonly used in retailing for bags and for wrapping light consumer goods such as stationery. Powdered and granulated products such as cement and animal feed come in heavy-duty paper sacks.

● *Wood.* Relatively few products are packaged in wood, but it is widely used to provide shipping packaging in the form of pallets or crates.

CONCERN ABOUT PACKAGING

Green concerns

Packaging has become a particular focus of green concern. This is partly because the packaging of a product offers opportunities for improving the environmental performance of the tangible product without altering the core product. There are several important green packaging issues:

1 *Resource consumption.* Packaging accounts for almost 5 per cent of total UK energy consumption, 40 per cent of German paper consumption and nearly 25 per cent of American plastic consumption (Durning 1992).

2 *Low recycling rates.* Only a relatively small proportion of recyclable packaging material is recycled. According to data from the Environmental Protection Agency, some 99 per cent of all discarded plastic in the USA is not recycled, even though it is standard practice to now label plastic packaging as 'recyclable' (Larson 1990).

3 *Information and labelling.* In countries like the UK there is little control over the labelling of supposedly green products. This has led to concern among environmental and consumer groups about the claims made about the packaging of products as well as the products themselves.

4 *Waste.* According to figures from Eurostat, at the beginning of the 1980s, discarded packaging material accounted for more than 40 per cent of municipal waste for some European countries. Overpackaging, inefficient packaging design, a failure to use recyclable materials, and an emphasis on disposability are all criticisms levelled at the packaging industry as contributing to waste. Insufficient packaging of products can also lead to waste, however. If a product becomes damaged or impaired during transportation, handling, storage or display, then the resources which went into manufacturing and distributing the product are wasted. In the UK, food packaging reduces waste down to 2 per cent. In some less industrialised and East European countries, wastage rates run at between 30 and 50 per cent.

5 *Litter.* A great deal of litter is the result of discarded packaging from fast food, cigarettes, canned drinks and confectionary. Litter is often a major environmental concern at the local level, and a company must consider the effect that repeated exposure to a company's cherished brand name in the form of litter has on consumer perceptions of that brand.

Consumerist concerns

There has also been concern expressed by consumer groups over the social acceptability of some elements of packaging and packaging techniques. The main concerns are:

● *The use of half-empty packages.* A large food box which contains a much smaller bag of produce inside is a good examples of this. This is often caused by the use of standard-sized packs for different weights and densities of product.

● *The use of containers with double-skins, rounded bottoms, or internal packing* presents an optical illusion to consumers in terms of the quantity of produce that they are purchasing.

● *The use of packaging which is close in colour, shape or image to a market-leading brand.* Such 'copy-cat' packaging can confuse customers without infringing copyrights or patents.

● *The failure of packages to be user-friendly to elderly or disabled people.*

● *The price of packaging*, which for some products is disproportionately large. A 1976 study by the UK's Price Commission entitled *The Unit Prices of Small Packs* found that for a product like liquid antiseptic the packaging accounts for 83 per cent of the selling price.

Overpackaging

A variety of products have been criticised for being overpackaged, often defined as using packaging which accounts for more than 10 per cent of product volume. Consumer groups have campaigned against overpackaging because it represents poor value for customers, and environmentalists have campaigned against its wasteful use of resources. If a product is overpackaged it is unnecessarily using scarce natural resources, consuming energy and creating unnecessary waste and litter. There are several ways in which a product may become overpackaged.

1 *Using unnecessary multiple layers of packaging.* This could be subtitled the 'Ferrero Rocher syndrome', where in pursuit of a luxurious image, chocolates are packaged in paper-labelled foil, nestled in a paper cup, sat in a large plastic box and/or shrink-wrapped in plastic.

2 *Putting sturdy plastic containers inside cardboard boxes.* Shampoos and toothpastes are among the products where secondary cardboard 'outers' are being removed and the primary packaging being used to present the product on the shelves or from a dispensing rack.

3 *Using larger containers than necessary to occupy shelf space.* This improves products' shelf visibility and can 'squeeze' competitor brands from the shelf. One interesting example of a controversy involving an oversized package is the case of CD packaging. In Europe the standard package is the 125 mm by 142 mm plastic case. In the USA the plastic cases are housed within a 152 mm by 305 mm cardboard 'long box'. It was only after combined pressure from environmentalists, musicians and legislators that the record industry was finally forced to get together and agree upon a new set of packaging standards. The record companies were reluctant to abandon the old packages because they offered more of a platform from which to visually promote the product, and because they felt the long box made theft more difficult. Despite the complaints of record companies and retailers about increased security costs, the reduction in packaging will create significant savings. Since it will allow retailers to stock many more CDs in the same space it will also increase consumer choice and boost sales volume (Casey 1992).

4 *Multipacking individual items which are already packaged to form 'value packs'.* Cassette tapes frequently come individually wrapped and then rewrapped as a multipack. Many small items are generally available only in multipacks (for example, a dozen cup hooks or a pair of bicycle pedals) which can force the consumer to buy more than he or she requires.

5 *Packaging highly durable products which could be sold equally well unpackaged.* The use of blister packs for small durable items like ballpoint pens, combs and screwdrivers is now widespread. Such packs are useful to retailers for displaying the products and for carrying barcodes to activate computerised tills and stock systems. However, blister packs are wasteful of resources and difficult to recycle being a paper/plastic mix. Such items could be sold from dump bins or other dispensers.

PACKAGING AND THE CONSUMER

Packages as promoters

Marketers have often been resistant to the idea of developing greener packaging, and have focused on the benefits claimed for packaging in terms of attracting consumers and as a signal of product quality. These benefits may have been overemphasised in the past. A large and representative survey by the Consumers' Association found that 60 per cent of consumers claimed that packaging did not influence their consumption decisions, and 58 per cent felt there was no link between packaging quality and product quality. As

Wheeler (1992) puts it, in an era of increasing environmental concern 'packaging glitz, now tantamount to waste, will no longer sell'. Despite the enthusiasm for environmental protection among supermarkets, it is generally accepted in the packaging industry that they would not give shelf space to green products whose environmentally sound packaging was visually less attractive than grey alternatives.

The development of green packaging has a tendency to increase the degree of uniformity among packaging designs. If refilling systems are to accept bottles, or if reverse-vending systems are to accept cans for recycling, the sizes and shapes have to become relatively uniform. This places an additional communication burden on other aspects of the package such as the graphics and branding. As Sharon North of design consultancy, Fischer Ling and Bennion, says:

'Product differentiation, size impression, strength of branding and on-shelf presence are increasingly communicated only through the graphics. For example, in the detergents market, increasingly Tetrapak refills are all the same shape and size and could hold anything from milk to detergents. The only way of communicating product and manufacturer is through the branding.'

Some may see the trend towards more uniform packaging for improved eco-performance as a loss in terms of freedom of choice, variety, fun and opportunity for creativity. However, if the quality of the contents is differentiated and excellent enough, and is communicated through the graphic design of the packaging, does it really matter if all the products come in the same functionally shaped pack? Environmentalists might argue that if legislation enforcing eco-efficient packaging deprived manufacturers of the opportunity to create differentiation on the basis of pack design, it would force companies to address real customer benefits of product performance and value for money. Certainly one could look at the markets for CDs or burgundies and see (with a few exceptions) products with identical packages which are highly differentiated, satisfying to consume and relatively fun to market.

The demand for eco-efficient packaging

Although consumers may not discriminate in favour of particularly good packaging, poor packaging can be an important source of competitive disadvantage (most of us at some point in our lives will be driven to the brink of insanity by the failure of a package to release its contents). A 1982 survey of American consumers by A.C. Nielsen revealed that 46 per cent of them had discarded or returned a product due to defective packaging in the previous year, of whom 19 per cent intended to avoid the brand in future. It is now the eco-performance, as well as the technical performance of packaging that is of interest to consumers. According to Achenbaum (1991) the proportion of consumers who answered 'yes' when asked if they would switch brands to choose a product in an environmentally safe package were as follows:

USA	67%
West Germany	88%
Former East Germany	90%
Italy	84%
Spain	82%

For the environmental marketer, the green packaging challenge consists of improving the eco-performance of packaging, communicating the eco-efficiency of improved packaging to consumers, and persuading them to meet any price increases which packaging improvements involve.

Early indications suggest that marketers are meeting this packaging challenge. A 1990 Teague/Gallup survey of packaging executives within *Fortune 500* companies revealed that 58 per cent believed that consumers would accept higher prices for environmentally friendly packaging, and 47 per cent had already made environmental improvements to their packaging. There is some evidence that their faith in the greenness of consumers is not misplaced.

● A survey by *Packaging* magazine among US consumers revealed that although there was enthusiasm for recycling of packaging and for more biodegradable packaging (despite the difficulties) they did not favour the banning of environmentally unfriendly packaging (Larson 1990).

● Research by Gerstman and Meyers in 1990 revealed that American consumers were willing to pay a premium of around 5 per cent for environmentally improved packaging.

● A UK Gallup survey on behalf of Crown Berger paints found that half of all consumers would pay at least 10 per cent more for products in recycled packaging.

Whether consumer interest is matched by consumer understanding of the issues involved in green packaging is less clear. Research by Lawson and Wall (1993) into the attitudes of New Zealand consumers towards different types of packaging materials, found that consumer knowledge in relation to eco-performance was poor and confused, and that 'consumers perception of packaging materials are best reflected in other attributes related to the specific performance benefits to the consumer ... and that environmental aspects are not a dominant feature.' The difference between their results and the other studies may relate to cultural differences, or it may be a consequence of the environmental marketing strategies of different sectors of the packaging industry. Gillespie (1992) identifies the wrangling between the glass and plastics industry about relative eco-performance of different packaging materials as counter-productive in creating consumer distrust of all packaging.

PACKAGING AND HEALTH AND SAFETY

Any packaging must protect the contents against a range of potential contaminants and sources of damage including heat, light, impact, compression, pests, bacteria, pilferage, air, water and harmful vapours or liquids. This is particularly important in products such as food and medical products. Concerns that product protection should be the number one priority for medical product packaging led to it being specifically excluded from the new EU Packaging Directive.

In terms of food products, hygiene and safety issues can also limit the opportunities for using recycled materials. Glass and metal are both recycled at a high enough temperature to make it as safe as virgin materials. Paper and plastic pose more of a problem. Paper becomes physically downgraded by recycling, and fibres can normally be recycled only four or five times. Recycled paper is not normally used for food containment, although it may form part of the overall packaging. Plastic recycling involves temperatures too low to remove contaminants that can be absorbed into the porous molecular structure of the plastic. Recycled plastic is again not normally used for food containment, the exception is PET which can be cleanly chemically recycled, although this process makes the recycled material some 25 per cent more expensive using current technology.

Health and safety has also become an important issue in packaging following poisoning incidents such as the fatal incidents involving Tylenol in the USA and the hospitalisation of two people after drinking poisoned tonic water in the UK during 1994. The demand for tamper-proof seals has led to an increase in the total amount of packaging used, and to the increased use of mixed plastic and glass packages which pose problems for recycling. In such cases the environmental and the societal benefits have to be traded off to some degree.

GREEN PACKAGING STRATEGIES

Removal

An obvious answer to the problem of overpackaging is to remove unnecessary layers. Kraft General Foods, Europe's largest packaging buyer, replaced the traditional bag-in-a-box package for its Kenco coffee with a simpler vacuum-packed foil pouch (although in this case the design brief was based around improved customer convenience with eco-improvements described as 'a pleasant bonus'). Kenco's changes, although not environmentally motivated, may prove fortuitous if it wants to sell through Migros, the Swiss retailing giant, which has insisted that suppliers eliminate all superfluous packaging. In Germany SmithKline Beecham were the first company to switch to selling toothpaste in carton-free tubes. This saved money and the packaging costs associated with the 'Green Dot' scheme. It was also appreciated by consumers, with the improved environmental performance of the product leading to increased sales and helping to establish the company as the leading oral health care company in Germany.

Removing one layer of packaging from a product may not sound the sort of initiative with world-saving potential, but the cumulative savings can be surprisingly large. Removing one layer of packaging (a plastic bag) from one product type (T-shirts) sold through one retailer (German green retailer Hertie) during one year (1989) removed 2.7 million plastic bags from the European waste stream.

Reduction

There are a number of ways in which a marketer can reduce the resources for packaging consumed by a product without compromising the primary performance of the product or the packaging.

● *Sell in larger unit sizes*, which uses proportionally less packaging materials.

● *Sell refills.* Fabric softeners, sweeteners, moistened wipes, spices and cosmetics are just a few of the products available as refills for existing dispensers. This removes the need to buy a built-in dispenser each time the core product is purchased. Procter and Gamble introduced a concentrated refill carton for its Lenor fabric softener which uses 65 per cent less packaging than the conventional bottle and 90 per cent less plastic. They have also introduced a plastic pouch refill for products such as Ariel and Lenor fabric softeners which uses 70 per cent less material than a conventional bottle. The product provides a cash benefit to consumers in the form of a lower price, and savings for the manufacturer since the pouches provide higher profit margins than the conventional bottles.

● *Use efficient design forms.* In terms of the ratio of content to packaging material, the most eco-efficient packaging design would be a sphere (although imagining its widespread use conjures up images of supermarket chaos while shoppers chase rolling products up and down the aisles!). It is also not necessarily eco-efficient overall, because of the volume of off-cut waste that would be created in packaging production. The eco-efficiency of a package design relates to a number of factors. In 1974 the International Paper Company introduced a new carton for individual milk servings in America. Taller and more slender than the traditional half-pint carton, the new 'Eco-Pak' used 16 per cent less paperboard. With a market of nine billion units, a switch by the entire industry had the potential to save over $10 million (47 million ECUs). Ecologically speaking the change would eliminate 1000 rail truck loads of paperboard going from paper mills to converting plants, save over 4000 truck journeys between the processing plants and the dairies and allow delivery trucks to each handle up to 70 per cent more units of finished product (Russell 1976).

● *Reduce the thickness of the packaging material.* Steel cans are now 40 per cent thinner and lighter than 20 years ago, while the amount of plastic required to make a drinks bottle has declined by 70 per cent according to the Paper Industry Research Association.

● *Switch the packaging to a material of which less is needed.* Fewer resources are required to use PET plastic to make a viable drinks container instead of glass. A lorry carrying glass bottles will use six times as much space for packaging material and 66 per cent more fuel due to extra packaging weight, compared to one carrying similar bottles made of PET.

● *Improve the resource efficiency of packaging processes.* For example, steel cans now require 39 per cent less energy for manufacture than in 1977.

Successful packaging reductions programmes can make a significant contribution to reducing total costs. DuPont in the USA created savings from reduced packaging waste of over $15 million (7 million ECUs) for 1992 alone.

Reuse

Glass bottles for milk and other beverages are the most traditional reusable packaging. A bottle needs to make ten trips to become cost effective in energy savings, and for the British dairy trade milk bottles make an average of 12 trips (although in some areas the average is as high as 40). In the UK, the use of returnable bottles has fallen steadily since the abandoning of money-back deposits. Between 1977 and 1987 the use of returnable bottles fell from 60 per cent of carbonated drinks to 19 per cent and from 60 per cent of beers to 23 per cent. This is despite the fact that in a Friends of the Earth survey of 35 000 UK shoppers, 84 per cent said they would be willing to return empty bottles for recycling. The demise of returnable bottles happened because they call for either increased transportation costs, or smaller localised bottling plants (which reduce economies of scale). In other parts of Europe reusing bottles is on the increase. In Denmark all carbonated drinks, 99 per cent of beers and 86 per cent of mineral water comes in returnable bottles. Migros, the Swiss supermarket chain, abandoned one-trip disposable packaging for its drinks products. Having designed the bottles, and a returns system based around universal bottle sizes, they installed collection machines which exchange cash vouchers for returned bottles. Each Migros bottle now completes an average of 20 trips.

Glass is not the only packaging material that can be reused. The Body Shop provides a refill service for customers returning their plastic bottles. Packaging consumption can also be reduced if consumers are encouraged to reuse packaging. Supermarkets are encouraging consumers to use less plastic shopping bags by selling sturdy reusable bags or offering a penny refund for consumers that reuse plastic bags.

Recycling

About one third of all domestic solid waste, by weight, is packaging. Countries vary in terms of the proportion of waste that is recycled, although for Europe as a whole only some 19 per cent of all packaging is recycled. The current situation regarding recycling of packaging materials within the EU varies widely. Table 15.1 shows the relative proportion of key materials recycled during the early 1990s in five European countries.

Table 15.1 Proportion of materials recycled

Country	Glass recycling rate (%)	Tin plated steel can recycling rate (%)	Proportion of recycled fibre in paper and board (%)
Belgium	46	33	26.6
Holland	55	48	69
Germany	40	53	48
France	31	22	44.7
UK	18	12	53

Recycling can produce major savings in raw materials and energy. Packaging materials that cannot be directly recycled can be indirectly recycled by transformation into another useful material. Waste glass from bottles and jars can be recycled as glass fibre for insulation. Packaging materials can also be created from the recycling of other materials. Shredded waste paper and cryogenically fragmented old car tyres are both used to create protective packing materials used in product distribution.

A desire to move to recycled packaging can have a variety of implications for a marketer. Technically a desire to use recycled paper fibres can require adjustments to package design and printing. Economically, pricing changes may be required, and, psychologically, consumer response to the use of recycled materials will need to be considered. For liquids, packaging them in recycled glass bottles may be a preferred option, in which case it will be far cheaper to use recycled green glass, of which there is a glut in Europe, rather than clear glass. This may make economic sense, but could cause problems in terms of consumer expectations. While everyone identifies champagne with green bottles, it is somehow difficult to imagine pouring milk or whisky from a green bottle.

Although recycled packaging is generally assumed to have a superior eco-performance, the differences in performance can be less than expected. Gillespie (1992) relates the experiences of the Best Foods division of CPC International. It commissioned a study looking at the feasibility of converting the cartons of its Mueller's brand of pasta to recycled materials. The study revealed that, for this particular product, the switch to recycled materials would add about 20 per cent to the weight of the packaging and increase the fuel consumption involved in distribution. This left the company with a dilemma. To introduce a package that was ostensibly greener, with all the accompanying opportunities for generating positive PR coverage and consumer approval, or to resist this opportunity and stay with a package which on balance it considered to be economically and environmentally superior. In the end, it kept faith with the existing package, which (providing its calculations were accurate) presents a reassuring example of a victory of substance over superficial style.

The recycling of redundant packaging can create a whole range of business opportunities. A good example of a collection-orientated opportunity is the 'Lucky Can' unit developed by Egapro Management AG of Switzerland. It operates on the same principle as a 'fruit machine', with can depositors who dial up the right symbols being rewarded with coupons, prizes or maybe just an environmentally based message. During test marketing in Austria the units averaged over 1000 cans per day each and if distributed nationally they are expected to boost collection rates from around 10 per cent to over 50 per cent.

Biodegradability

Packaging magazine's survey of US consumers showed that the concept of biodegradable packaging continues to appeal to consumers despite mounting research evidence suggesting that worthwhile degradation of such materials generally does not occur within landfills (Larson 1990). Plastic containers which cannot be reused survive almost indefinitely in landfill sites. 'Biodegradable' plastics which can break down after use, have been developed and used for packaging materials such as shampoo bottles and supermarket carrier bags. Biodegradable plastic comes in two types: each is only capable of breaking down under the right conditions, and both leave residual polymers as a less visible pollutant. One type is ecolyte, which breaks down when exposed to sunlight; the other is bioplastic, which breaks down when buried in soil. Truly biodegradable plastics based on sugar and corn starch (rather than oil) have recently been developed, and Ottman (1992a) quotes the use of corn starch based materials to produce edible packaging.

Technology developments

Innovations in packaging technology can allow for improvements in the eco-performance of products. For example, in the USA Sanyo developed a package for its rechargeable batteries which doubles as a mail-back pack to allow the product to be recycled. Such a concept allows the package, which is usually viewed as an environmental liability which must be reduced or removed, to become a positive provider of ecological benefits. Sometimes packaging improvements are a question of transferring a successful packaging technology from one market to another. Lever Brothers have experimented with the 'bag-in-box' technology used extensively in wine marketing, for liquid detergents and fabric softeners.

POLITICAL DEVELOPMENTS

Packaging has become an important item on the political agenda. Perhaps politicians sense that to attack on environmental grounds the products that people consume is likely to be a source of lost votes. In contrast, attacking the disposable packaging that products come in allows them to appear environmentally proactive without losing votes. Political action comes in a variety of forms. Some countries have gone as far as banning particular packaging types. Denmark banned aluminium cans for drinks and is considering a ban on PVC, while Sweden plans to ban non-refillable PET bottles. Another popular form of initiative is

Table 15.2 Examples of financial and legislative measures to reduce the packaging volume in municipal solid waste (MSW)

(a) Examples of the regulatory approach to waste recycling

Country	Regulatory standard (target)
Austria	Has passed a regulation which mandates the following refilling/recycling rates for glass and cans: Beer: glass 70% by 1992; cans 90% by 1994; Carbonates: glass 60% by 1992; cans 80% by 1994; Juices: glass 25% by 1992; cans 40% by 1994.
Belgium	Target level of 30% of waste to be recycled by 1995; the balance to be incinerated; landfill to be used only as a last resort.
Canada	National Packaging Protocol adopted in 1990, aims to reduce packaging in the MSW by 20% (from 1998 levels) by 1992 and by 50% by the year 2000.
Italy	Legislation has laid down a 50% recycling target for both glass and cans, to be achieved by the end of 1992. From April 1993, containers which have not met this target will have a penalty tax imposed on them.
UK	50% of recyclables (25% of total MSW) to be recycled by the year 2000.
US	1988, EPA National goal of reducing waste disposal by 25% by 1992 via recycling and source separation.

(b) Examples of the use of economic instruments in the management of packaging waste

Country[1]	Type of economic instrument[2]	Application: in use under study/proposed
Austria	• deposit-refund • product charge	refillable plastic beverage containers subject to mandatory deposit of ÖS 4 non-returnable beverage containers: ÖS 0.5 to 1 per container
Belgium	• waste charges (incentives)	MSW
Canada	• deposit-refund • waste charge	beer and soft drinks containers non-refillable containers
Italy	• product charge	non-biodegradable plastic bags
UK	• recycling credits	MSW
USA	• deposit-refund • marketable permits • waste charges	beverage containers newsprint unseparated waste

1 Some instruments apply at state, province or regional levels only.
2 User charges for collection and treatment of MSW are applied in almost all industrialised countries; taxes on the use of virgin materials have been implemented in Denmark.
Source: Turner (1992)

taxation. Denmark has levied general taxes on packaging, while Italy has considered imposing taxes on materials that do not reach its targets of 50 per cent for glass and metals and 40 per cent for plastics. A summary of key European regulations and fiscal measures relating to packaging is presented in Table 15.2.

The most significant political initiative is the EU Directive on Packaging and Packaging Waste which aims to reduce the waste created and the resources consumed by packaging. It seeks to harmonise the rules regarding packaging across Europe and achieve the recovery of 90 per cent of packaging (by weight) and the recycling of

60 per cent by 2003. This would compare with a 1993 situation in which around 40 per cent is recovered and only 10 per cent is recycled. The directive also places limits on the allowable concentrations of heavy metals within packaging. Marking schemes will be used to indicate where packaging is reusable, what the materials used are and what the recycled content is. To implement the directive, member states will need to set up effective packaging waste management and waste material recovery systems and to set targets for collection and recycling.

By 1 January in the year 2000 no packaging will be sold in the EU that is not refillable, reusable or recoverable. Consumers must be fully informed about the environmental implications of packaging and the marketing of unnecessary packaging will be prohibited. So presumably the Ferrero Rocher chocolate will be a very different looking product in the new millennium.

RECYCLING SCHEMES AND SYSTEMS

Where packaging is designed to be recyclable, there will be no environmental benefits if the systems to recycle the packaging are not available and accessible to consumers. Resource banks and household collection services are the most common method of reclaiming used packaging for recycling. There are a variety of types of recycling schemes that operate:

● *National initiatives.* The German packaging ordinances make it mandatory for suppliers to take back their packaging materials and makes them responsible for their fate. Consumers are also now entitled to leave packaging at the supermarket. This represents the institutionalisation of an old green protest tactic of abandoning excess packaging materials at the supermarket check-out. The regulations originally aimed to prompt the recycling of some 100 000 tonnes of synthetic packaging materials annually; but within a few months over 400 000 tonnes had been collected. The German recycling industry's infrastructure was engulfed, leading to a twelvefold increase in exports to foreign landfills. The system has been

criticised on the basis that it is costly to run, it presents a barrier to trade, is impossible to implement fully due to the ban on incineration, and its environmental benefits have been questioned by critics.

The German Green Dot system has certainly made an impact, although not always in ways which were foreseen. It may only operate at a national level, but the impact on packaging users and manufacturers has had international and even global repercussions. The German ordinances resulted in Hewlett Packard embarking on a redesign of its office-machine packaging worldwide. Other consequences have been less beneficial. The Green Dot system has acted to confuse the previously environmentally confident German consumers, many of whom have misinterpreted the symbol as analogous to the Blue Angel mark (Kulik 1993).

● *Local initiatives.* Local government has long had the responsibility for waste collection and so is the logical agent to organise recycling programmes. In the UK, two of the largest recycling schemes are run by the Adur District and Sheffield City Councils. However, such schemes have been threatened by the flood of recycled plastics and paper on the market as a result of the French and German collection schemes.

● *Manufacturer initiatives.* Recycling schemes can often bring economic benefits for manufacturers, and providing or supporting recycling collections can do much to enhance their green credentials. Companies such as Coca-Cola have regularly sponsored local recycling schemes. Large companies' in-house schemes can do a great deal to recycle waste. DEC's Waste Management Programme was instituted in 1988 with a wide brief aimed at reducing the $54 million (25 million ECUs) spent annually on packaging (equating to some 27 000 tonnes of material). Recycling schemes for paper, plastics and components were a central element of the programme together with initiatives involving packaging redesign, CFC elimination and the disposal of excess and obsolete equipment. The packaging element of the programme had an initial brief of reducing DEC's packaging usage by 5400 tonnes and the accompanying bill by $30 million (14 million ECUs) by 1993.

● *Retailer initiatives*. Retailers represent the central point through which consumers pass to buy their new packaged goods, and therefore they represent the most obvious point for consumers to deposit their used packaging for recycling. Retailers have made the provision of recycling facilities a key element in their environmental strategies.

The operation of recycling schemes

Depending on the influence of local government, German households mostly have between four and nine different types of bins or collection bags covering categories such as biodegradable waste, washed tins, waxed cartons, clear glass, coloured glass, cooking oils and fats, and clean card and paper. The waste needs to be sorted and cleaned, requiring considerable input from the consumer. Gedye (1993) comments:

'Washing up the rubbish has become the most trying task of the day for the German Hausfrau as she copes with a fresh array of colour-coded dustbins for recyclable household waste ... Letters are written to newspapers by housewives agonising over what to do about cleaning the insides of mustard tubes. Should they be split open? Do you run the contents of your rubbish through the dishwasher? Do you use washing-up liquid or merely pass them under the hot tap?... You need a double whisky after the washing up in Germany. With all the different containers, the kitchen has become an obstacle course.'

For the German consumer the recycling system provides no direct personal benefit in economic terms, but it is being widely supported by them despite the inconveniences that it involves. Although it may presently seem excessive to consumers in other countries, the German system could well be a glimpse into the future. One of the curiosities about Gedye's report is the way it highlights how ease of cleaning after use has become important in German consumers' eyes. This is something that the designers of mustard tubes and many other forms of package will have never given serious thought to.

GREEN PACKAGING DESIGN

Packaging redesign is important in eliminating waste rather than dealing with it post-consumption. Redesign was a key element of DEC's waste reduction initiative. For example, it used to pack its computer mice in three layers of material: blister pack wrapping, polystyrene reinforcers, and finally a cardboard box. Now it has reduced all that to a single, redesigned cardboard carton. In addition to providing the production information on the outside, this also furnishes the necessary strength and protection previously given by the original three packaging layers (Nielsen 1991). Table 15.3 quantitively illustrates what DEC has achieved in packaging design for four of its computer products: mouse, software (including documentation), computer modules, and computer cabinets. Chick (1992) provides a useful checklist of issues to be considered when designing or selecting eco-efficient packaging (see Fig. 15.2).

The issues involved in assessing the relative merits of different forms of packaging and their acceptability in the eyes of consumers can be rather complex. Conventional plastic as a packaging material has come under attack because of its bulkiness and durability within landfill sites, where it accounts for 20 per cent of municipal waste. In

Table 15.3 Reduction in packaging volume at DEC

| Computer product | Product vol. (cm3) | Packaging vol./Product vol. | | Reduction (%) |
		Before	After	
Mouse	216.96	8.62	0.94	89.1
Module	791.98	2.79	0.72	74.3
Software	181.90	15.17	1.79	88.2
Cabinet	900,472	0.36	0.25	31.0

Source: Nielsen (1991)

- Does the production of the packaging material have an adverse effect on the environment? For example:
  –Does the material come from a scarce or seriously declining source?
  –Is production of the material energy-intensive?
- Design or choose packaging where the materials can be easily reused or recycled. Does the combination of materials create difficulty for recycling?
- Avoid *coloured* polyethylene terephthalate (PET).
- Ensure the chemicals used in a pack do not cause environmental damage (e.g. CFCs), or choose a chemical-free alternative pack (e.g. pump-action sprays).
- Do environmental protection laws in any proposed market either constrain the use of chosen materials or increase their production or disposal costs?
- Can concentrated products that fit into smaller packages be developed?
- Avoid excess packaging: only use what is necessary.
- Use reclaimed (secondary) materials wherever possible, which encourages the development of the recycling industry.
- Support resource-efficient reclamation schemes; consider whether material identification would help. It is vital that any collection system coincides with the development of markets and that companies start to 'sell' the reusability or recyclability of their product.
- Give proper consideration to pollution that may be caused during manufacture or as post-consumer waste, e.g. pigments formulated with cadmium, lead or chromium.
- Ensure the pack, the information and the overall appearance encourage the efficient use, reuse and disposal of the contents and the pack.
- Consumer education material and advertising should be considered as an accompanying option to the pack.
- Establish a system for checking and collating information about the environmental implications of different materials, processes, etc.
- Ensure appropriate training has been given to designers, marketers, advertisers, packaging engineers, etc.

Fig. 15.2 Checklist for designing or choosing a green package
(Source: Chick (1992))

1990 30 million tonnes of plastic packaging were disposed of globally, 14 million tonnes in western Europe. Biodegradable plastics have been developed, but some of these can take over 200 years to decompose under favourable conditions and then form plastic dust which, although more compact, is far from environmentally safe. Recycling of plastic is currently growing in popularity, but it requires effective streaming of different plastic types within the waste collection process. The logistical challenges of plastics recycling added to the capital cost of equipment helps to explain why under 10 per cent of waste plastic is recycled. The final option is to incinerate used plastics as an alternative fuel, but this requires careful emission control to minimise the resulting air pollution.

Ecobalance research

One method of gathering information on environmental performance which has been applied to aid the design of green packaging, among

Table 15.4 Example of an eco-balance comparison: environmental aspects of Van Leer's Probit™ Pack compared to a Tetra-Pak (for an individually packaged drink)

	Probit-Pack/200ml	Tetra-Pak/200ml
Choice of raw material	Negative image of plastic	For greater part renewable material, but also negative image of plastic – additional environmental negatives for aluminium
Reduction at source	Uses less raw material	Uses more materials and uses in particular aluminium
Production process – energy consumption and pollution	Comparable	Comparable
Waste of contents due to leakage	Pack very reliable	More vulnerable
Reuse of product	Single trip pack	Single trip pack
Reuse of materials	Not possible; laminate	Not economically feasible
Thermal recycling	Possible • minimal energy contents • hardly any residue	Possible • more residue (aluminium)
Degradability as litter	Does not degrade	Partly degrades
Degradability in landfill	Does not degrade	Dos not degrade
Volume in waste stream	Minimal space in landfill	Takes more space

Source: Miller and Szekely (1994)

other things, is ecobalance research. Pioneered in Germany, The Netherlands and Denmark, this technique uses an environmental cost/benefit approach to study each phase of the cradle-to-grave product lifespan. An example of an ecobalance comparison between two forms of packaging is shown in Table 15.4. Such an approach can yield unexpected results. Plastic shopping bags were an early packaging target for environmentalists. Ecobalance research by the German Environment Ministry found that sparingly used (and reused) plastic shopping bags were better than recycled paper bags once energy efficiency differences, pollution during manufacture and opportunities for recycling were taken into account. However, environmentalists typically view such contests as irrelevant, because neither product can ecologically outperform durable shopping bags used repeatedly.

CASE STUDY

Suchard's Milka cow

Tree planting and chocolate may not seem to have any obvious connection. Yet Jacobs Suchard, the Zurich-based chocolate and coffee group, was delighted three years ago to accept sponsorship of reforestation projects in the Alps. 'The idea could have been invented for us,' says Walter Anderau, head of corporate affairs.

The connection is supplied by the lilac Milka cow, a symbol of one of Jacobs Suchard's most popular chocolate brands. By protecting the habitat of the Milka cow – a Simmental cow painted lilac for Suchard's packaging – the message that the chocolate is made from healthy Alpine milk is made more credible. Jacobs Suchard's main markets are Germany, France, Switzerland and Austria, all with Alpine regions. Since 1991, Jacobs Suchard (part of US products conglomerate Philip Morris) has sponsored the planting of 300 000 trees in five countries as part of its collaboration with Alp Action in the 'Green Roof for Europe' campaign. This is the biggest of the 30 projects launched by Alp Action, founded by Prince Sadruddin Aga Khan to mobilise corporate funding for environmental protection in the Alps. The project, which has cost Jacobs Suchard more than one million Swiss francs (£444 000), has involved thousands of children and plays a key role in its marketing strategy. Reforestation projects are scheduled for Austria, France, Germany, Italy, Slovenia and Switzerland in the coming years.

Jacobs Suchard's concern for the environment does not stop with tree planting. Since 1986, it has sought to 'green' its activities across the board. It started with a rethink of packaging requirements, necessitated by the need to streamline packaging inherited from acquired companies. The group has since extended its environmental concerns to production, transport and its housekeeping. Jacobs Suchard uses a recyclable plastic monofoil for its Milka Lila Pause chocolate bar which is cheaper, 'greener' and attractive to consumers. Its redesigned chocolate boxes have saved up to 50 per cent on packaging and dispensed with polyvinyl chloride. Similarly, coffee in Germany is sold in vacuum packs containing practically no aluminium. With the same product protection, Jacobs Suchard claims to have reduced waste by 47 per cent, energy use by 37 per cent and water consumption by 48 per cent. The company plans to extend monopacks to all markets. Further down the chain, the group uses multi-entry pallets of recyclable materials for shop deliveries. These pallets are later collected and reused. In this way, Jacobs Suchard has cut the total amount of primary and secondary packaging by 5 per cent – 10 000 tonnes – in three years. Fuel use per cubic metre transported by the company has been more than halved from 1987 levels. Packaging has been redesigned and standardised with efficient packing and transport in mind. Cocoa and coffee beans are increasingly shifted by rail in special bulk containers; half the tonnage moved by Jacobs Suchard last year went by train against 5 per cent in 1987. 'All this greenery is,' says Anderau, 'more a "feel-good" factor than a big money saver.' Financial costs and benefits are often difficult to identify.

Environmental objectives are just one factor in the investment in new packaging or factory modernisation. The company has invested about $23 million (£15 million) directly since 1977 on environmental protection measures. This includes $4 million on its new chocolate factory in Berlin and $3 million (with another $10 million planned) on its Lorrach facility near Basle. Anderau believes these costs probably offset a large part of the savings from pro-environment activities. However, the 'feel-good' factor counts for Jacobs Suchard's workers and its consumers. At Lenk, home of the Milka cow, Jacobs Suchard launched a programme to plant a tree for every baby born to an employee's family, an Alpine farming tradition.

Source: Williams, F. (1993) 'Suchard Grazes on Green Pastures', *Financial Times*, 25 June, p 10.

CHAPTER 16

The price of environmental excellence

'What is a cynic? . . . A man who knows the price of everything and the value of nothing . . . And a sentimentalist . . . is a man who sees an absurd value in everything, and doesn't know the market price of any single thing.'
(Oscar Wilde, *Lady Windermere's Fan*)

INTRODUCTION

If the discipline of marketing were a child, then, although a variety of older disciplines could make a claim to have contributed to its gene pool, the most likely candidates for parenthood would be the fields of economics and psychology. Nowhere is the inheritance of these two disciplines more obvious in marketing than in the setting and management of pricing. When a price for a product is set, the forces of economics and psychology collide. Economic approaches to pricing emphasise the role of supply and demand, and the relationship between costs and price in determining profit. Psychological approaches involve analysing the potential customer reaction to prices, and what a particular price communicates to the customer. However good the rational economics behind the pricing strategy of a product, it is the customer's perception of the product's value that determines whether or not a purchase will be made.

In pre-industrial times pricing was a simple matter. The commandment of Christ 'Whatsoever ye would that men should do unto you, do ye also unto them' was interpreted as meaning that everything had its correct 'just' price. Therefore all goods had a single inherently correct price that was not influenced by supply and demand. Although the merchants of the day did their best to overcome this barrier, the Church ensured that they had little opportunity to charge a price

which was not a socially responsible one (Luthans *et al* 1990). Today, setting a price for a product is a fundamental component of marketing management, and involves a range of techniques which vary from the simple and intuitive to the formal and highly complex. Table 16.1 provides a simple classification of contemporary pricing strategies devised by Tellis (1986).

The green challenge has the potential to affect any company's objectives, cost structure, its profit margins and its customers' perceptions about the worth of its products. It can therefore impact on prices in a number of different ways. Conversely, the prices that are asked for the products that we buy will have a profound effect on the environment. For those who believe that the path towards sustainability depends on the use of market mechanisms, the integration of environmental costs into product costings and prices is a vital step. While consumption continues to expand, taking advantage of prices which do not reflect the environmental costs of products, the environment will continue to be unsustainably consumed.

The issue of prices has certainly been one of the most contentious in the early development of environmental marketing, with a range of questions occupying the minds of managers, customers, politicians and pundits. Should the environment be protected through price-based market mechanisms, or through government

Table 16.1 A classification of pricing strategies

Vary prices among consumer segments	Objective of firm	
	Exploit competitive position	Balance pricing over product line
Random discounting	Price signalling	Image pricing
Periodic discounting	Penetration pricing Experience curve pricing	Price bundling Premium pricing
Second market discounting	Geographic pricing	Complementary pricing

Source: Tellis (1986)

intervention on a command and control basis? Must protecting the environment inevitably mean higher prices? Who will have to meet any additional costs that protecting the environment entails? How will consumers respond to any green premiums for more sustainable products?

PRICES AND THE ENVIRONMENT

Taking a global perspective on pricing reveals the extent to which pricing is skewed in favour of destroying the environment. In some of the most populous countries on earth, energy in particular is heavily subsidised. Coal prices in China and India are kept lower than marginal costs, while during 1993 the weakness of the rouble meant that the price of oil within the former Soviet Union fluctuated between 33 and 4 per cent of world market prices. An OECD study estimates that global energy subsidies (at 1985 prices, net of the taxes imposed in industrialised countries) amounted to £152 billion (114 billion ECUs). This amounts to a $45 (21 ECUs) subsidy for each tonne of carbon being pumped into the atmosphere (Norman 1993). Eliminating such subsidies would produce an estimated reduction in the growth of carbon emissions of around 20 per cent over the next 60 years, while raising the real incomes of many less industrialised countries through improved energy efficiency.

A similar situation exists for water. A study by the World Resources Institute in seven Asian countries found that receipts for water supplied by government irrigation projects averaged under 10 per cent of the cost of supplying the water. Farmers will clearly be far more wasteful of water which is over 90 per cent subsidised. Changes to the way in which the use of natural resources are priced will be central in progressing towards a sustainable society. Increasing evidence of environmental degradation is bringing home to consumers that the price of consumption is not simply a monetary one. Industrialisation, development and overconsumption can extract a price in terms of health, freedom and spiritual well-being.

Abandoning the eco-subsidy in many markets would have effects that would be profound to say the least. Hopfenbeck (1993) quotes research conducted by Frederic Vester aiming to quantify the 'full value' of a tree, including its environmental benefits (although excluding any social benefits such as aesthetic value or contribution to leisure). He calculated that for a typical 100-year-old beech tree, the current market price would value the wood at around £9 (7 ECUs). Taking into account the environmental benefits of a tree (particularly if it was part of a forest), the value would be some £180 000 (135 000 ECUs). Although the assumptions used in the calculations might be challenged by others, this simple exercise showed the extent to which the challenge of reflecting environmental values in the prices we pay is a considerable challenge.

PERSPECTIVES ON PRICES

It is a cliché that everything and everyone has their own particular price. The concept of whether or not we should attempt to put price tags on everything within the natural environment has divided economists, environmentalists, accountants and politicians. The Pearce Report (Pearce 1990) puts forward the pro-price argument:

'The market is a powerful means of modifying consumption and production patterns to make them environmentally benign. To do this it is necessary to ensure that prices reflect the value of the environment used in the production of goods and services.'

Such an argument hinges on what exactly the term 'used' means in this context. Elements of the environment can be consumed by the production process without being used in it. Hines (1991) expresses concern about the attempt to bring natural resources on to the corporate balance sheet and into the world of rational economics by attaching prices to nature. She argues:

'Nature can be given prominence in accounting reports without reducing it to a number. Quantifying our environment must inevitably further alienate people from nature.'

Perhaps because we live in a world which is increasingly governed by prices, it is easy to take the concept of price for granted. However, it can be viewed from several perspectives. A price can be considered as:

● *A reflection of the cost of production,* particularly when companies price their products by standard cost or cost-plus-profit methods. At present prices only reflect the market costs of production, and exclude the many environmental costs of production. Initiatives aimed at encouraging the use of 'full cost pricing', which reflects and covers all the environmental costs are underway within several organisations. In 1992 the concept crossed over from the environmentalist to the business arena when Frank Popoff, President of Dow Corning, called upon the business community to adopt full cost accounting.

● *A key variable in the pursuit of profit.* By estimating demand and cost, prices can be set to generate specific levels of profit. Prices may be set to maximise profits, to provide a target rate of return for investors or to generate a specific level of cash flow.

● *A signal of quality to consumers* as shown by the research findings of Tellis and Gaeth (1990) among others.

● *A basis for market segmentation,* with different prices paid for the same product in different market segments.

● *A measure of a product's worth* which allows different forms of product to be compared and considered. A customer might try to decide between a bottle of wine and a box of chocolates each costing £5 to buy as a gift.

● *A reflection of the demand that exists for a product and the available supply.* Economic theory states that as supply expands or as demand falls, so the price will drop. Conversely a reduction in supply or an increase in demand will push prices up.

● *An important basis for competition.* The logic of Porter's model of competitive advantage (*see* page 146) dictates that companies should either pursue competitive advantage through some form of differentiation or by being a low-cost (and usually by implication also a low-price) supplier.

● *A key marketing variable* that can be manipulated to achieve a wide variety of marketing objectives. Low promotional pricing can be used to fill up slack demand, while psychological pricing can be used to place the price below key perceived price barriers.

PRICING AND COSTS

The relationship between costs and prices is an important issue within the evolving green management agenda. It is also one of the most controversial. Environmentalists want products and their prices to bear the full costs of the environmental damage that they create. The business community insists that its customers would not bear such costs, or that without legislation, the environmentally responsible company will simply be undercut by its irresponsible competitors.

The perceived additional costs of adopting a greener strategy is certainly an important psychological barrier to greening for many marketers and other managers. However, in some cases this may be based more on assumptions about the costs involved than knowledge. In a survey of major chemical manufacturers and users, more than half did not know what the future cost implications of environmental improvement would be, or what the company had spent or planned to spend on environmental protection (Peat Marwick Mitchell 1990). Many investments in clean technology have proved to be cost effective, even though they involved a fundamental re-engineering of the entire production system (*see* page 204). Concern about cost has been enshrined within European environmental legislation in the BATNEEC principle (Best Available Technology Not Entailing Excessive Cost). Many environmentalists view the BATNEEC provision as a 'Get Out of Jail Free' card dealt to businesses, which is used to minimise environmental expenditure. This has earned it the nickname of the CATNIP principle (Cheapest Available Technology Not Involving Prosecution).

For many companies, developing and implementing an environmental marketing strategy will involve new or increased costs which will need to be reflected in increased prices, particularly where cost-based pricing is used. For manufacturers facing increased costs due to tightening environmental legislation or customer pressure, part of the cost burden comes from the fact that their response has been to add 'end-of-pipe' technologies to clean up their products or production process. A catalytic converter or a sulphur scrubbing system for a coal-fired power station are obvious examples of 'end-of-pipe' technologies. Since these are added on to the existing products or production systems they inevitably involve additional cost.

The alternative approach is to design products and production systems that avoid pollution and environmental damage. Although there is obviously a high initial capital cost for such redesigns, such changes can reduce costs by minimising waste and possibly creating saleable by-products. The entire 3M's philosophy that 'Pollution Prevention Pays' underlines the fact that environmental improvement done as part of a fundamental rethink of products and processes can increase, rather than reduce, profits. In 3M's case the global savings from the '3 Ps' programme is often quoted as being $500 million (234 million ECUs) between 1975 and 1990. This figure was produced using a very conservative accounting convention, and the 'real' savings have been estimated at over a billion dollars. Weissman and Sekutowski (1992) put forward a detailed case that fundamental change of production systems can be economically, as well as environmentally, beneficial, backed up by a range of examples.

The sort of cost increases that companies can experience in relation to the green challenge include:

• Primary products may become more expensive as producers are increasingly required to restore the sites of extraction, or manage stocks of renewable resources more sustainably.

• Capital expenditure may increase on cleaner processes and technology. In the US alone over $135 billion (63 billion ECUs) worth of equipment relies on CFCs. The equipment write-off costs of eliminating all CFCs by 2000 is estimated at up to $34 billion (16 billion ECUs) (Blackburn 1989).

• Costs may be incurred by complying with new green legislation. European car manufacturers have spent an estimated extra $7 billion (3.3 billion ECUs) on mandatory new pollution control equipment for cars in Europe between 1990 and 1993. Walley and Whitehead (1994) point out that Texaco's five-year environmental plan to reduce emissions and comply with tougher environmental laws will cost a total of over $7 billion – equivalent to three times the book value of the entire company.

• Transport costs for finished products and raw materials are likely to rise in future as the eco-subsidy enjoyed by fossil fuels is eroded by carbon taxes or other means.

• Costs of preparing for ecological disasters or clean ups in terms of insurance premiums and clean-up equipment and procedures may increase. Figures from the US suggest that $70 million (33 million ECUs) has to be set aside to cover the average clean-up cost of a hazardous waste site, with the largest megasites costing up to $169 million (79 million ECUs) to restore.

● Green overheads will be incurred associated with changing the management and marketing of the company. This includes changing policies, systems, practices and culture to become greener.

● Costs associated with green taxation will be incurred. In countries like Denmark there are taxes on scarce raw materials, polluting processes and the disposal of wastes. In Sweden companies are charged around £2.50 (1.88 ECUs) for each kilo of sulphur they emit.

● There will be an increasing cost of finance and insurance. The requirement to conduct environmental audits on the part of lenders, and the increasing environmental insurance risks to be borne are likely to drive up the costs of business finance (Bebbington and Gray 1992).

Although it is the additional costs of creating green products and production processes that are often emphasised by companies, there are also a range of potential green savings which can offset these additional costs.

● Savings can be made by reducing product inputs of raw materials and energy. The prices that companies pay for their inputs are often negotiated on the basis of the volume of business being placed. A green strategy may therefore significantly reduce the cost of a key resource going into the production system, but may also have the effect of raising its unit price.

● Savings can be made in company overheads in terms of reduced use of office supplies, heating and lighting. Marks and Spencers' 'Turn-it-off' campaign which has been running in its offices since 1974 (when it was inspired by the oil price shocks) saved an average of £3 million (2.25 million ECUs) per annum over its first 15 years of operation.

● Savings can be made from reducing unnecessary packaging.

● Switching to cheaper lead-free fuel for distribution and company vehicles can bring savings.

● Savings can be made from reduced waste disposal costs.

● Savings can be made from the contributions from the sale of by-products.

As the polluter is increasingly made to pay, and as the costs of poor environmental performance become more significant, so investments in improved eco-performance will appear more attractive to companies. In the aftermath of Bhopal and the Love Canal disasters Union Carbide and Hooker's parent each faced total costs of over $3 billion (1.4 billion ECUs) (Mahon and Kelly 1987). Even companies who do not adopt a greening stategy may still find their product costs changing to reflect the costs of insuring against any environmental damage that the company may have to clean up. As the technical performance and price competitiveness of maturing green brands improves, so grey products will also incur additonal marketing costs needed to differentiate them from their green rivals.

As green products mature and can take advantage of economies of scale and learning curve effects, they have a better opportunity to achieve price parity with entrenched conventional products. Recycled paper products accounted for 4 per cent of total American office paper products demand in 1992 at a price premium of around 10 per cent. By 1997 recycled products are expected to account for 7.4 per cent of the market with a price premium of only one per cent.

PRICING AND SUPPLY

Environmental concerns can have a very profound effect on the pricing of almost any product by altering its level of supply or demand (Leaming 1990). For some natural resources their prices will increasingly be determined by their scarcity. As natural resources become scarce, the costs of collecting them typically increase, and demand will begin to exceed supply. Both these factors will push prices up. This effect has been demonstrated in areas like the fish market, where scarcity has pushed the price of North Sea cod above that of salmon. Economists argue that in this way market mechanisms will prevent environmental resources from becoming exhausted (Cairncross 1991). This argument, although comforting, suffers from several flaws:

● Market economics assumes that the buyers of a resource will be willing to compete for the resource and to pay the resulting increase in price. Where there is only one buyer for a resource, or where a group of buyers can act in concert to dictate prices, the supplier will continue to use up the resource at the best price that it can negotiate.

● Economic theory dictates that as the supply of a resource dwindles, so its price will rise. This will encourage companies to develop a substitute product instead. However, once the cheaper substitute has been developed, what is the likely response of the owners of the original natural resource? They will drop their own price to enable the natural resource to remain marketable, leading to its eventual elimination.

● In the case of wild animals, a rising price due to scarcity is more of a death sentence than a salvation. The African elephant would have been extinct in the wild many years ago if international governmental action had not attempted to control the market for ivory.

● Natural systems, such as the breeding population of a certain species, can cross their threshold of stability and become doomed to extinction long before the numbers have become small enough to suggest a crisis in economic terms.

Supply restrictions and increasing prices can occur as a result of environmental considerations other than resource depletion. Supply restriction can result from:

● legal restrictions, as is the case with nuclear fuels;

● fear of product liability among suppliers;

● the restriction of environmentally acceptable alternative technologies to a limited number of suppliers due to patent protection or developmental time lags (this applies to products such as CFC substitutes).

The interaction of supply and prices in the green challenge is not simply an issue of managing resource depletion. For some products the challenge involves coping with supply expansion linked to environmentally based activities. The 'scrubbing' of industrial gases produces vast quantities of sulphuric acid as a by-product, depressing the market price. For natural mineral resources, an increase in the market price will typically appear to increase the supply. This is because from an economic perspective, resources are not counted as part of the available supply unless they are economically extractable.

PRICING AND DEMAND

Where the expansion in demand for a green product outstrips the growth in supply, prices may rise. This is not a widely observable phenomenon, since most green products enter the market with a premium price with little room for future increases, although some examples exist (green investment products being a simple example). More significant and commonplace has been a drop in demand and price for products which are identified as environmentally harmful. An extreme example is the asbestos market in which health and safety concerns are creating a negative price, as previous buyers of the product pay large sums of money to have it removed again (Leaming 1990).

Pricing is also used to change the level of demand and to increase consumption through the use of volume discounts and rate structures based on a reduced unit price for increasing the number of units purchased. In areas such as energy pricing some economists have argued in favour of flat or inverted rate structures to encourage heavy users to be more frugal.

Demand factors

For many products, cost factors are not important in the setting of prices, except in determining a minimum level for prices which still achieve an acceptable level of profit. The price set for green products has to reflect demand factors as well as any short-term cost changes. For the environmental marketer a key question is 'How much of a premium is my customer willing to pay for improved eco-performance?' The answer to this question is influenced by a variety of factors including:

- *The nature of the product and the level of differentiation operating in the market.*

- *The credibility of the company as a green producer.* A company which has had little, or previously damaging, contact with the environment will have problems convincing consumers to pay a green price premium.

- *The profile of the green issues to which the product is linked.* For example, free-range eggs and dolphin-friendly (rod-and-line caught) tuna both command premium prices due to the high profile and emotive nature of battery farming and drift net fishing on the green agenda.

- *The perceived value of green products.* This can pose problems for the environmental marketer if a green product has a lower perceived value than traditional alternatives. HCFC aerosol propellants are lighter than CFCs, making the aerosol cans appear less full and therefore poorer value. Organic vegetable strains are usually selected to achieve an attractive taste and texture. Many non-organic growers select plant strains and use pesticides with the aim of creating a more attractive shelf appearance. The shelf appearance can attract the consumer to the non-organic produce, even when its taste is inferior to organic varieties. Perceived-value pricing involves matching the price of a product to its perceived value in the eyes of the customer. This perceived value is the result of the effect of the other marketing mix variables on the customer. Such an approach can only work if the company can assess accurately how the customer values its offerings.

- *The nature of the customer*, in terms of their price sensitivity and their awareness of, and interest in, the environmental issues that relate to the product. Where a green premium pricing strategy is being used, it should be linked to marketing communications efforts to inform and educate the consumer. This can help to overcome the perceived value problems associated with some green products.

CUSTOMER RESPONSE TO PRICING

The most important issue in the pricing of a product, green or otherwise, is how customers respond. Consumer affluence and the closely (and usually inversely) related concept of price consciousness are important influences on this response. So too are the relative importance of prices and price differences within a given market and the degree to which the market involves 'standard' or generally accepted price levels and ranges.

The green premium

Green products are usually presented to the market at premium prices, either to reflect higher costs or to take advantage of strong green demand. However, the idea that green products are in some way unusually expensive is perhaps something of an illusion. The reality is that grey products are unrealistically inexpensive. The costs associated with environmental degradation in grey products are largely not reflected in their prices, so that the environment is effectively providing a subsidy.

The unquestioning acceptance of the eco-subsidy enjoyed by grey products is reflected in a fundamental bias in much of the research that has been conducted on consumers' willingness to pay for green product and process improvements. The choice is always presented to consumers as 'Would you be willing to pay more to protect the environment?' the emphasis being on the environment as an additional expense. It would be more interesting to ask people whether they would prefer to buy products that cost, say, 10 per cent less, but damage the environment more. This is the current situation where the environment is subsidising the consumer and the manufacturer. As long as this fact is disguised by the presentation of the environment as an additional cost burden, progress towards sustainability is likely to be slow.

Even when presented with the environment as an additional cost burden, a number of surveys have shown a professed willingness among consumers to accept higher prices in return for better environmental protection. Taking the UK as an example, the Department of Environment's 1986 Consumer Attitudes survey revealed that 68 per cent of adults would support an extra 16 pence on petrol prices and 59 per cent would support 50 pence per week on electricity bills to reduce pollution. In *The Guardian* newspaper's 1993 'State of the Nation' survey, 71 per cent of those surveyed agreed that 'the government should give a higher priority to environmental policy, even if this means higher prices for some goods'. This was an increase from 65 per cent in 1992 and 69 per cent in 1991, showing consumer support for green pricing growing despite a lengthy recession. It is not just industrialised countries such as the UK which show a willingness to pay a green premium. Table 16.2 shows the results of a 1992 Gallup Poll investigating consumers' willingness to pay for environmental protection.

Table 16.2 Are people willing to pay for environmental protection?

Country	Percentage of people expressing a willingness to pay higher prices to protect the environment
India	56
Philippines	30
Turkey	44
Chile	64
Poland	49
Mexico	59
Brazil	53
Hungary	49
Uruguay	55
Russia	39
Republic of Korea	71
Ireland	60
Great Britain	70
Netherlands	65
Canada	61
West Germany	59
Denmark	78
USA	65
Finland	53
Norway	73
Japan	31
Switzerland	70

In practice a discrepancy between reported willingness to pay extra for green products and actual sales levels is often observed. Usually this is explained as consumers wishing to appear socially responsible and over-reporting their concern to market researchers. McDougall (1994) reported:

'Because there is a high degree of social acceptability connected to being environmentally responsible, consumers will often overstate their concern. Stated or reported behaviours (e.g. willingness to pay a premium for products that are environmentally safe) usually are much higher than actual behaviours (e.g. actually paying a premium).'

Wilson and Rathje (1990) also focus on 'over-reporting' socially acceptable behaviour in relation to the environment. There is an alternative explanation for this, that the products marketed as 'green' lack sufficient credibility in consumers' eyes to justify paying extra. BRMB/Mintel found that 71 per cent of British consumers thought that companies were using green issues as an excuse to charge higher prices. Just as customers will not pay more unless they are convinced that they are getting added value in a techno-economic sense, they will not pay more for added socio-environmental virtue unless they find it convincing.

The market research conducted by MORI on behalf of Welsh Water suggests that consumers are not simply interested in the appearance they give to market researchers. Welsh households were surveyed using a questionnaire attached to consumers' water bills. These were returned directly to the company. The company was shocked that over 77 per cent of the 1.2 million households they serve expressed a desire to pay higher prices for better water quality and environmental protection. This came in a market where consumers have little choice but to pay any price increases since they cannot easily switch suppliers. The chief executive of the company commented that it would be 'foolish' to ignore such customer pressure and allocated an additional £100 million (75 million ECUs) for cleaning up rivers and coasts.

Other examples of customers' willingness to pay the green premium in practice are also emerging. When Universal Office Supplies tried to develop a green version of its shorthand note-books, as part of a portfolio of 30 green products, it was unable to find a large supplier capable of producing the sort of volumes that would allow the product to become cost competitive. Instead they used a small Scottish supplier and launched the product at more than double the conventional price. Despite this, sales rapidly reached 25 per cent of those for conventional pads, despite the general cost competitiveness of the office stationery market (Barry 1990).

Price and usage

The price, and the method of pricing, can also determine the extent and nature of product usage and can influence other purchase decisions. For example, the price of petrol can influence the size of car that a consumer will buy, and how often he or she will use it in preference to other means of transport. Certain products are charged at a fixed rate, which provides consumers with no incentive to be economical. In fact, the more they use, the less they are paying on unit basis. Certain basic domestic services such as the supply of water and sewerage services, or the collection of domestic refuse have traditionally been charged on a fixed annual charge in many countries. Metering the supply of water and charging households for refuse disposal on a number of rubbish bags collected basis would appear to be more environmentally sound solutions. However, in practice such solutions can run into difficulties. In many areas where water metering has been introduced in the UK, families on low incomes have been presented with water bills they cannot afford to pay. The response of many such families has been to reduce their usage of water to such an extent that their health has become endangered. The increasing incidence of sickness related to low water usage has led the Association of Environmental Health Officers to lobby against water metering. In the case of charging for refuse disposal, using a cost per bag basis would appear to be very effective green pricing. It would encourage households to recycle more materials, and to compress their waste to fill a minimum number of bags thereby reducing the amount of landfill space used for disposal. In practice, however, such a change in pricing would probably encourage some people to engage in 'fly-tipping' to dispose of their excess waste illegally.

SOCIALLY RESPONSIBLE PRICING

The impact of pricing on natural resources and the environment is not the only green dimension of pricing. The fairness of pricing has been a key issue for the consumer movement since its inception. Prices play a large part in determining which consumers will be able to gain access to a particular product or service. The pricing of the basic necessities of life, including food, drink, clothing, shelter, heating, water for cleaning and health care, is an important item on the social agenda. In many countries, the consumption of the majority of the population rarely gets beyond these essentials.

Pricing, when approached from a purely economic perspective of maximising profits according to the supply and demand situation, can lead to some very socially irresponsible practices. Anderson (1992) highlights the fact that in the aftermath of Hurricane Hugo, ice was being sold at $10 (4.67 ECUs) a bag and plywood at $200 (97 ECUs) a sheet. This price gouging was defended by the economist LaBand (1989) on the basis that it was necessary to 'guarantee that scarce goods are allocated to those buyers who place the highest value on them' and that price gouging was 'the free market's mechanism for ensuring that economic resources flow to their most highly valued uses'. LaBand suggests that politicians who legislate against price gouging deserve an 'F in Economics' – we can only speculate on the grade he would achieve on a course in business ethics.

Promotional pricing has also been a cause of social concern where misleading price comparisons, spurious discounts and misleading credit terms have been used to persuade consumers to make a purchase. In most countries promotional pricing is now tightly controlled by law. There are also a variety of markets including petrol, currency, restaurants and bars where the display of pricing information is regulated to protect the customer.

Profiteering and 'overpricing'

Where imperfections in a market exist, such as supply restrictions, cartels or a lack of information for consumers, they provide producers with an opportunity to exploit these imperfections in pursuit of higher profits. In a market such as pharmaceuticals there has been considerable concern expressed by consumer groups and governments about the power of producers and the prices they charge, particularly following the revelations of 'whistle-blower' Stanley Adams at Hoffman La Roche.

Many companies have adopted a demand-based approach to the pricing of green products. Regardless of costs, they set prices according to the levels of demand and the perceived value of green products to consumers. This can lead companies into difficulties if environmentalist or consumer groups highlight a green product as exploiting the consumer rather than benefiting the environment. Premium pricing of healthier products such as unsliced wholemeal bread has been a target for complaints by groups such as the Food Commission; since it is cheaper to manufacture than its white-sliced competitors. The cheapest food on the market are often products that are high in fat and carbohydrate but low in terms of fibre, vitamins and minerals. This has created a situation where people on low incomes find it difficult to feed their families a healthy diet since the healthy options in the stores are only available at premium prices. Despite the attractiveness of adding a significant demand-led green premium to products, negative publicity on pricing can create a consumer backlash. Marks and Spencer, despite its image for value and as a responsible company, ran into criticism for pricing six free-range eggs in its Newcastle store at a 34 pence price premium over a local wholefood shop using the same source of supply.

PRICE AND STRATEGY

A common approach to pricing strategy is to see it as a balancing act between product price and product quality to create a value level. A company may have a reputation for producing the highest quality/highest price products, or the lowest price/highest value products. Either way, price may be set to ensure that such an image is not compromised. For environmental marketers pricing involves a three-way balance between price, eco-performance and primary performance, to create a green-value strategy. The green-value position which a company chooses to occupy will reflect:

- pricing objectives
- demand factors
- cost factors
- competitor offerings
- the pricing method used
- the overall marketing strategy.

The strategic element of pricing may be an important factor in creating the green premiums which have been prevalent in the early phase of environmental marketing. Where a producer is offering both a grey product and an alternative green product, there is an inherent logic that the green product must be marketed at a premium. If all other factors, including price, were roughly equal between a grey and a green product, then few consumers are likely to discriminate in favour of the grey product. The producer therefore has the choice between replacing the grey product variant with the green one, or introducing the green product as a higher priced alternative to the grey one. Replacement involves the risk that not all consumers would stay with the brand in its switch from grey to green, since some may not believe in the effectiveness of green brands. If the green product is presented as a complementary brand, this reduces the risk of losing any of the existing customers while allowing existing and new green customers to buy the green alternative. The premium price also allows the generation of increased profit by skimming off those consumers who are willing to pay a premium.

TOWARDS SUSTAINABLE PRICING

In the short term, costs and prices will generally prevent the emergence of totally green, sustainable products. Since grey products are effectively subsidised by the environment, they are unrealistically cheap. A product priced to cover the costs of being truly sustainable would be unable to compete unless customer price sensitivity was very low. As the urgency behind environmental protection rises, so the environmental subsidy given to grey products will be whittled away. In the meantime, those wishing to develop green products will have to concentrate on making gradual improvements towards sustainability, funded by the savings that come from a reduction in waste and the revenue generated by any available green premiums. As Bebbington and Gray (1992) note, for some products a sustainable price will be impossible to achieve because it is infinitely high. A CFC-driven aerosol damages the ozone layer, an irreplaceable and therefore priceless asset. This makes a sustainable price for the aerosol infinity.

A key barrier in developing sustainable products is the emphasis on price as opposed to cost. Many consumers and many companies make purchases on the basis of a product's price, as opposed to the total cost of owning and using the product. The emphasis on unit price has led to the sale of inefficient light-bulbs with short lives and cars and buildings which cost a great deal more to operate than they need to. Davis (1991) in considering buildings suggests that 'had total cost of construction, maintenance and operation over a 50 year period been used as an alternative criterion for minimization a very different stock of buildings would be in existence.' One choice that the green consumer is increasingly likely to be faced with is whether or not to buy a product which costs more but will last longer or is cheaper to run. This could be a low-energy light-bulb, a house insulated to Scandinavian standards or a £20 (15 ECUs) bath towel designed to last a lifetime.

Pricing will be an important tool in the search for a sustainable economy among marketing managers and public policy makers. Conventionally the market price of mineral deposits determines the supply of economically extractable reserves. The costs of exploiting a particular mineral deposit rise as it becomes depleted. Eventually costs reach a point where, at prevailing market prices, the deposit cannot be exploited profitably enough to meet corporate objectives and is closed down. Mineral deposits such as oilfields and coal faces can be very difficult and expensive to reopen once closed. Market fluctuations can therefore lead to potentially valuable reserves being wasted when oilfields are capped during times of a market glut and a low price.

Pricing can also be used as a tool to demarket particular products to conserve their supplies or to prevent overexploitation. Before the privatisation of British Gas, the UK government frequently cited gas price rises as a contribution to energy saving. In certain circumstances a company may elect to raise prices to discourage demand or 'demarket' a product. For example Cyprus successfully raised the costs of its holidays to attract a smaller number of more affluent tourists.

Readers might be tempted to think that the voluntary use of pricing to protect the environment is unlikely to materialise in practice since oil companies will not agree to tap an oil reserve until they reach break-even point, and few products are likely to be volunteered for demarketing. Although some holiday destinations have adopted a demarketing strategy based around raising prices and reducing the supply, most demarketing is achieved by the imposition of taxes on environmentally hostile products. However, a simple practical example which proves that a pricing strategy can reduce waste, protect the environment and increase customer satisfaction, comes from some of Singapore's most popular 'steamboat' restaurants. (Steamboat involves groups sharing a cooking pot full of boiling stock. Each person then helps themselves to a wide variety of raw ingredients which are simmered and eaten one at a time in the communal pot – rather like a fondue without the cheese.) Diners can help themselves to as much as they like, and there is a set price, with one small traditional proviso; each person hands back their plate when they come to pay, allowing the leftovers to be weighed, and diners who exceed a 50g maximum must pay double. This pricing policy both discourages and covers the costs of wastage, and encourages diners not to risk overindulging because their 'eyes were larger than their stomachs'. The policy also appears to do nothing to impair customer satisfaction, since the restaurants are invariably packed. Diners are generally in favour of the double pay rule, on the basis that wastage would otherwise push the prices up for all.

If, in the long term, environmental degradation proves to be the death of conventional economics, could we see the development of new greener economic systems in which very different forms of price are used? Although this may sound far fetched, the development of alternative local economies in which barter plays an important part are gaining in strength in some areas. Places such as Vancouver Island in Canada, and Gloucester in the UK, have well established Local Economy and Trade Systems (LETS). Some LETS use an alternative local currency as a medium of exchange, while others such as the Vancouver Island system, use a computer system to record purchases and sales. Such systems encourage a new local focus on business and a more human and less economic approach to marketing exchanges. On a more international scale, the phenomenon of countertrade as a means of overcoming trade barriers and some of the problems within the international financial environment is also becoming increasingly important. Estimates put the total value of countertrade at between 25 and 40 per cent of the world's total exports (El Kahal 1994).

EPILOGUE – WHICH PRICE ARE WE GOING TO PAY?

Ending a discussion about the potential contribution of environmental marketing with a discussion of pricing is highly appropriate. Societies and consumers pay two prices for the goods and services that are consumed. The economic price is clearly defined, must be paid today or soon after, and any debt that is incurred can be paid later. The socio-environmental price is unclear, can be deferred today (even if it must be paid eventually) and any debts incurred are unlikely to be repaid. Until the monetary price reflects the socio-environmental price, or unless consumers and companies can be educated and persuaded to purchase less environmentally damaging goods and services, even at higher prices, we will continue to degrade and exhaust the environment that we all depend upon. By ending on the issue of pricing and the economics of the market, the discussion has also come full circle. It is the flaws in economic theory that have driven the industrial development and stimulation of overconsumption that has allowed the environment to reach crisis point. Unless economic theory, like our production systems, is 're-engineered' to bring it into harmony with the physical environment, the desires of the consumer and the intentions of marketers will not be sufficient to avoid environmental catastrophe. Davis (1991) builds on Schumacher's critique of conventional economics to summarise the six key changes needed to achieve the transformation from unsustainable (grey) development to sustainable (green) development.

1 To replace the indiscriminate development of the free market, we need discriminating development. This will involve all who are able to, joining in the creation of 'real wealth' both financial and non-financial. The emphasis will be on appropriate technology, equity of distribution, and minimum waste and environmental impact.

2 The environment needs to be viewed as a limited resource which must be managed and conserved instead of as a limitless supply of environmental capital to be exploited.

3 Instead of maximising the growth of manufacturing, maximum use will be made of the 4 Rs of repair, recondition, reuse and recycling.

4 Creative work which makes the fullest possible use of human abilities and energies will replace the grey unskilled work of our mass production systems.

5 The maximisation of material growth will be superseded by an emphasis on growth in forms of satisfaction that do not rely on large quantities of energy and materials.

6 A switch from a tendency for investment to be impersonal and managed by financial institutions, towards self-directed personal investment in which investments are chosen to support sustainability.

Achieving sustainability as a key objective has now been embraced by a wide range of governments, industries and companies. However, implementing the strategies that will allow any form of objective to be attained always involve costs. Organisations will often embrace a new objective, whether it is total quality, equal opportunities, improved customer service or sustainability, only to see progress towards it founder on the twin reefs of cost and managerial conservatism.

FINAL QUESTIONS

So how will the story end? Will marketers lead the way to a better world of sustainable products and companies? Will consumers simply revolt and become conservers? Will the marketing machine continue stimulating demand and consumption until we reach the brink of environmental collapse? At the brink, will the technologists rush forward to provide a dramatic reprieve; or is the drama in the tradition of the best French movies in which the ultimate tragedy seems somehow inevitable? The green challenge and the emergence of environmental marketing raise many questions which, during the 1990s, are unlikely to meet with conclusive answers.

How will grey marketing be remembered?

According to the head of a Swedish engineering firm, quoted in the *Brundtland Report* (WCED 1987):

'We treat nature like we treated workers a hundred years ago. We included then no cost for health and social security of workers in our calculations, and today we include no cost for the health and safety of nature.'

In another hundred years' time, the unsustainable business practices of the twentieth century will probably (or should that be hopefully?) be regarded much as we view Victorian working practices such as forcing children down mines, dismissing workers for becoming ill or pregnant and allowing poverty and starvation to keep wages low. If we could travel back and confront the leading Victorian industrialists of the day, they would have argued convincingly and sincerely that this was the way it had to be. To treat workers any better would have led to the collapse of the economic and technical order. The arguments they would have used against protecting workers from the worst excesses of socially irresponsible industrialisation would undoubtedly bear a striking resemblance to the arguments currently being used against better protecting the planet against the excesses of environmentally irresponsible industrialisation.

Can we escape the prisoners' dilemma?

The problem for businesses in responding to the green challenge is often discussed in terms of the famous 'Prisoners' Dilemma' analogy. The analogy works as follows: two or more members of a gang of criminals are taken to the police and are subjected to individual interrogations. Each prisoner is confident that there is not enough evidence for the police to secure a conviction, and that if all the gang members remain silent, no charges will be brought. However, each prisoner still faces a dilemma. If one of the other gang members confesses and incriminates the others in return for a reduced sentence, then the other prisoners will all face a severe sentence. Each prisoner will have to choose between a silence which will mean either freedom or a long prison sentence, or confessing and facing the certainty of a light sentence. This analogy is often used in situations where all businesses will benefit by sharing a responsible approach, but where short-term advantage can be accrued by companies who are willing to 'break ranks'.

This analogy is rather back-to-front in relation to the green challenge facing businesses, in that, for the prisoners, it is in all of their long-term interests to act in a socially irresponsible way and not co-operate with the police. Furthermore, for the prisoners, it is sticking to their original plan of non-co-operation which yields the highest gain, while for businesses, it is a question of responding to change and abandoning or amending existing plans that provides the best hope for long-term success.

A better analogy for the situation facing businesses might be the following *Castaways' Conundrum*:

> Two sailors are shipwrecked on a desert island. It contains enough fresh water for them, a small supply of edible plants, and a large flock of fat, tasty, stupid and flightless birds – distant cousins of the dodo. For a time the sailors live well, with roast fowl forming their staple diet. However, the flock gradually dwindles until there is only one pair of birds left. The sailors discuss what they should do next, and agree not to kill the birds but to rely instead upon the one rather large egg per day that the female produces. This provides just enough food for the two of them to survive, and this situation continues for almost a year. They then sit down to discuss again what they should do. They know that their pair of birds will not survive indefinitely, and they know from their original observations that allowing the female to incubate her eggs would halt egg production for twenty days once the clutch reached four. They could kill and slowly consume the male bird in the meantime, but they have no idea what effect this would have upon the ability of the female to rear her brood. And what if the brood didn't hatch successfully? What should they do?

This analogy contains the essentials of the green challenge:

1 an environment with limited resources;

2 a careless use of resources in the past because they appeared to be plentiful;

3 a realisation that the environment cannot indefinitely sustain a particular pattern of activity, and must be conserved;

4 an attempt to halt the rate of environmental damage which will postpone, but not ultimately solve the problem of creating sustainability;

5 the eventual need for painful decisions to be made to bring about sustainability.

Will greening take all of the fun out of marketing?

Marketing during most of the 1980s was undoubtedly fun. Economic growth, exciting new technologies, and generous marketing budgets all made it an exciting field to work in. The technologies of the products and the technical accomplishment and sheer hyperbole of much of the marketing communications that promoted them were often irresistible and enjoyable. Marketing in the 1980s brought a lot of pleasure to a lot of people, and this is something positive. However, the price of unsustainable growth cannot be deferred for ever. In this way, industrialised economies resemble companies that are overtrading, where expansion and activity mask the underlying flaws in the basics of the business.

The emphasis on prices brings us back into the techno-economic paradigm, however, which is perhaps not an appropriate way to end. A more positive view of the shift from the unsustainable to the sustainable comes from Bernstein (1992), who views it as a positive progression away from a society based around pleasure to one based around happiness. Instead of an emphasis on pleasure which is short-term, self-centred, oblivious and carefree, we will move towards an emphasis on happiness which is long-term, shared, aware and caring. This may be rather utopian, but it was the ever quotable Oscar Wilde, who pointed out that there is little value in a map which does not have Utopia marked upon it. If we can learn to pay a price for the goods and services that we consume, that strikes a balance between the cynical and the sentimental, then perhaps marketing can help to guide society towards a happy and sustainable future. If the wider changes that are proposed in the likes of the *Brundtland Report* can be marketed successfully to the governments and electorates of the world, then the benefits of true global sustainability may become a reality. A pleasant thought on which to end any book, and one which suggests that the quest for sustainable marketing as we move towards a new milennium might be fun after all.

REFERENCES

Aaker, D.A. and Myers, J.G. (1987) *Advertising Management* (3rd edn), Prentice-Hall.

Abt Associates Inc. (1990) *Environmental Consumerism in the US.*

Achenbaum, A. (1991) *A Global View of Consumer Environmental Trends and the Advertising Community's Response*, paper presented at the AMA's Environmental Conference, Green Marketing from a Marketer's Perspective.

Allen, D.M. (1994) 'Waste Minimisation and Treatment: An Overview of Technologies', *Greener Management International*, 5, pp 22–8.

Alvord, J. B. (1991) *Update on Environmental Labelling and Packaging Regulations: Domestic and Internationally*, paper presented to the AMA's Environmental Conference, Green Marketing from a Marketer's Perspective.

Ames, B.C. (1970) 'Trappings Versus Substance In Industrial Marketing', *Harvard Business Review*, Vol 48(4), pp 93–102.

Amyx, D.A., DeJong, P.F., Lin, X., Chakraborty, G. and Wiener, J.L. (1994) 'Influencers of Purchase Intentions For Ecologically Safe Products: A Exploratory Study', *in* Park, C.W. and Smith, D.C. (eds) *Marketing Theory and Applications, Proceedings of the 1994 AMA Winter Educators' Conference*, pp 341–7.

Anderson, L.M. (1992) 'The Dismal Science Revisited', *Business Horizons*, Vol 35(3), pp 3–5.

Anderson W.T. and Cunningham W.H. (1972) 'The Socially Conscious Consumer', *Journal of Marketing*, Vol 36(4), pp 23–31.

Ansoff, H.I. (1984) *Implanting Strategic Management*, Prentice Hall.

Argyle, M. (1987) *The Psychology of Happiness*, Methuen.

Ashley, S. (1993) 'Designing for the Environment', *Mechanical Engineering*, Mar, pp 52–5.

Associated Press, 'Presbyterians Ratify Teaching on Sex, Ecology', *The Boston Globe*, 9 June 1991, p 4.

Avernous, C. (1991) 'An Uneven Track Record on the Environment', *The OECD Observer*, No 168, pp 9–13.

Baden, J.A. (1992) 'Business, Science and Environmental Politics: Towards a Political Economy of Hope', *Columbia Journal of World Business*, Vol 27(3/4), pp 27–35.

Balderjahn, I. (1986) *Das Umweitbewusste Konsumerstenverhalten*, Duncker and Humbolt.

Balderjahn, I. (1988) 'Personality Variables and Environmental Attitudes as Predictors of Ecologically Responsible Consumption Patterns', *Journal of Business Research*, 17, pp 51–6.

Baker, M.J. (1991) 'One More Time – What Is Marketing?', *in* Baker, M.J. (ed) *The Marketing Book* (2nd ed), Butterworth–Heinemann.

Baker, M.J. (1992) *Marketing Strategy and Management* (2nd edn), Macmillan.

Barnard, J. (1990) 'Exxon Collides With the "Valdez Principles"', *Business and Society Review*, 74, pp 32–5.

Barry, T. (1990) 'Are Buyers Going Green?', *Purchasing and Supply Management*, May, pp 27–9.

Baudrillard, J. (1988) *Selected Writings*, Polity Press.

Bebbington, J. and Gray, R. (1992) 'Greener Pricing', *in* Charter, M. (ed) *Greener Marketing*, Greenleaf.

Beck, U. (1992) *Risk Society: Towards a New Modernity*, Sage.

Bell, M.L. and Emory, C.W. (1971) 'The Faltering Marketing Concept', *Journal of Marketing*, Vol 35(5), pp 37–42.

Bennett, R.C. and Cooper, R.G. (1981) 'The Misuse of Marketing: An American Tragedy', *Business Horizons*, Vol 24(6), pp 51–61.

Bernstein, D. (1992) *In The Company of Green: Corporate Communication for the New Environment*, ISBA.

Blackburn, V. (1990) 'Who Pays The Costs Of Going Green?', *Investors Chronicle*, 4 May.

Bocock, R. (1993) *Consumption*, Routledge.

Bond, C. (1989) 'Green Beanfeast', *Marketing*, 28 Sept, pp 45–7.

Boorstin, D. (1962) *The Image*, Weidenfield and Nicholson.

Bowen, D. 'Streets Ahead', *The Independent on Sunday*, 11 Apr 1993.

Brake, D. (1993) '486 Processing Power is Wasted on the Average User', *Personal Computer World*, Dec, p 250.

Bringer, R.P. and Benforado, D.M. (1989) 'Pollution Prevention as Corporate Policy: A Look at the 3M Experience', *The Environmental Professional*, Vol 11.

Briston, J.H. and Neill, T.J. (1972) *Packaging Management*, Gower Press.

Brookes, R. (1988) 'Breaking the Rules', *Marketing*, 7 July, pp 22–3.

Brookes, S.K., Jordan, A.C., Kimber, R.H. and Richardson, J.J. (1976) 'The Growth of the Environment as a Political Issue in Britain', *British Journal of Political Science*, 6, pp 245–55.

Brown, L. (1992) *State of The World*, WW Norton.

Brown, M. (1992) 'Science, Technology and the Environment', *The OECD Observer*, No 174, pp 11–15.

Brown, S. (1993) 'Postmodern Marketing?', *European Journal of Marketing*, Vol 27(4), pp 19–34.

Buckholz, R.A. (1991) 'Corporate Responsibility and the Good Society: From Economics to Ecology', *Business Horizons*, Vol 34(4), pp 19–31.

Buckholz, R.A. (1992) 'The Big Spill: Oil and Water Still Don't Mix', *in* Buckholz, R.A. *et al* (eds) *Managing Environmental Issues: A Casebook*, Prentice Hall.

Buckholz, R.A., Marcus, A.A. and Post, J.E. (1992) *Managing Environmental Issues*, Prentice Hall.

Burke, T. and Hill, J. (1990) *Ethics, Environment and the Company*, Institute of Business Ethics.

Buttle, F. (1989) 'Marketing Communication Theory: Review and Critique', *in* Pendlebury, A. and Watkins, T. (eds) *Proceedings of the 1989 Marketing Education Group Conference*.

Buzelli, D.T. (1991) 'Time to Structure an Environmental Policy Strategy', *Journal of Business Strategy*, Vol 12(2), pp 17–21.

Cairncross, F. (1991) *Costing The Earth*, Economist Books.

Capra, F. (1983) *The Turning Point*, Bantam.

Carlson, L., Grove, S.J. and Kangun, N. (1993) 'A Content Analysis of Environmental Advertising Claims: A Matrix Method Approach', *Journal of Advertising*, Vol 22(3), pp 27–39.

Carroll, A.B. (1979) 'A Three-Dimensional Conceptual Model of Corporate Performance', *Academy of Management Review*, Vol 4 (4), pp. 497-505.

Carson, D. (1968) 'Marketing Organisation in British Manufacturing Firms', *Journal of Marketing*, Vol 32(2), pp 268–325.

Carson, P. and Moulden J. (1991) *Green is Gold*, Harper Business.

Carvioner, B. (1977) *The Poverty of Power*, Cape.

Casey, E.J. (1992) 'A Plan For Environmental Packaging', *Journal of Business Strategy*, Vol 13(4), pp 18–20.

Charter, M. (1990a) *The Greener Employee*, KPH Marketing.

Charter, M. (1990b) *Graduates: Fewer and Greener*, KPH Marketing.

Charter, M. (1992) *Greener Marketing*, Greenleaf.

Chase, D. (1991) 'The Green Revolution: P&G Gets Top Marks in AA Survey', *Advertising Age*, Vol 62(5), pp 8–10.

Chick, A. (1991) 'Greener Packaging', *in* Charter, M. (ed) *Greener Marketing*, Greenleaf.

Christensen, K. (1991) 'Don't Call Me a Green Consumer', *Resurgence*, 145, pp 4–6.

Clairmonte, F. and Cavanagh, J. (1992) *Merchants of Drink: Transnational Control of World Beverages*, Third World Network.

Clements, M.A. (1989) 'Selecting Tourist Traffic by Demarketing', *Tourism Management*, Vol 10(2), pp 89–95.

Clifton, R. and Buss, N. (1992) 'Greener Communications', *in* Charter, M. (ed) *Greener Marketing*, Greenleaf.

Cobb, R. (1989) 'Toeing the Green Line', *Campaign*, 15 September, pp 60–2.

Coddington, W. (1993) *Environmental Marketing*, McGraw-Hill.

Commoner, B. (1972) *The Closing Circle: Confronting The Environmental Crisis*, Cape.

Commoner, B. (1990) 'Can Capitalists Be Environmentalists?' *Business and Society Review*, 75, pp 31–5.

Consumers' Association (1990) 'Green Labelling', *Which?*, Jan, pp 10–12.

Converse, P.D. and Huegy, H.W. (1946) *The Elements of Marketing*, Prentice Hall.

Cooper, T. (1994) 'The Durability of Consumer Durables', *Business Strategy and the Environment*, Vol 1(4), pp 23–30.

Corbett, C.J. and Wassenhove, L.N. (1993) 'The Green Fee: Internalising and Operationalising Environmental Issues', *California Management Review*, Vol 36(1), pp 116–35.

Corey, R.E. (1976) *Industrial Marketing: Cases and Concepts*, Prentice Hall.

Cotgrove, S. (1982) *Catastrophe or Cornucopia: Environment, Politics and the Future*, John Wiley and Sons.

Cottam, N. (1993) 'Coming Clean with a Clear Message', *Greener Management International*, 1, pp 35–40.

Cox, W.E. (1967) 'Product Life Cycles as Marketing Models', *Journal of Business*, Vol 40(4).

Crittenden, B.D. and Kolaczkowski, S.T. (1992) *Waste Minimisation Guide*, Institute of Chemical Engineers.

Daly, H. (1990) 'Towards Some Operational Principles of Sustainable Development', *Ecological Economics*, 2, pp 1–6.

Dasgupta, P.S. (1982) *The Control of Resources*, Basil Blackwell.

Davis, J. (1991) *Greening Business: Managing for Sustainable Development*, Basil Blackwell.

Davis, J. (1993) 'Strategies for Environmental Advertising', *Journal of Consumer Marketing*, Vol 10(2), pp 19–36.

Davidson, A. (1992) 'Consumer Magazines and the Environment', *in Proceedings of Seminar on Environmental Aspects of Comparative Testing*, IOCU, The Hague.

Derrick, M. 'Fiat proves Beautiful doesn't have to be Big', *The Independent: Special Report on Fleet and Executive Cars*, 30 June 1993.

Develter, D. (1992) *Ecover – The Ecological Factory Manual*, Ecover Publications.

Diamantopoulos, A., Bohlen, G.M. and Schlegelmilch, B.B. (1994) 'Predicting Green Purchasing Decisions From Measures of Environmental Consciousness: A Two Sample Comparison', *in* Bell, J. *et al* (eds) *Proceedings of 1994 Marketing Educators' Group Conference*.

Diffenbach, J. (1983) 'Corporate Environmental Analysis in Large US Corporations', *Long Range Planning*, Vol 16(3), pp 107–16.

Donaton, S. and Fitzgerald, K. (1992) 'Polls Show Ecological Concern is Strong', *Advertising Age*, Vol 63(24), 15 June, p 49.

Dossi, P. (1992) 'One Half of the Sky', *in* Koechlin, D. and Muller, K. (eds) *Green Business Opportunities: The Profit Potential*, Pitman.

Douthwaite, R. (1992) *The Growth Illusion*, Green Books.

Downes, A. (1972) 'Up and Down With Ecology – the Issue Attention Lifecycle', *Public Interest*, 28, pp 38–50.

Drucker, P. (1960) 'The Shame of Marketing', *Marketing Communications*, Aug, p 60.

Drucker, P.F. (1973) *Top Management*, Heinemann.

Drucker, P. (1989) *The New Realities*, Harper & Row.

Drumwright, M.E. (1994) 'Socially Responsible Organizational Buying: Environmental Concern as a Non-economic Buying Criterion', *Journal of Marketing*, Vol 58(3), pp 1–19.

Duck, J. (1993) 'When Simplification Doesn't Work', *Across the Board*, Vol 30(3), p 163.

Duff, C. (1992) 'Norsk Hydro's Environmental Report', *Long Range Planning*, Vol 25(4), pp 25–31.

Dunlap, R.E. and Van Liere, K.D. (1984) 'Commitment to the Dominant Social Paradigm and Concern for Environmental Quality', *Social Science Quarterly*, Vol 65(4), 1013–28.

Dunne, N. 'Eco-tourism Gets a Collective Voice', *Financial Times*, 14 Oct 1992, p 18.

Durning, A.T. (1992) *How Much is Enough?*, Earthscan.

Dwek, R. (1993) 'Green Info. Overload Baffles Consumers', *Marketing*, 27 May, p. 8.

Eckberg, D.L. and Blocker, T.J. (1989) 'Varieties of Religious Involvement and Concerns: Testing the Lynn White Thesis', *Journal for Scientific Study of Religion*, Vol 28, pp 509–17.

Ecotech (1992) 'The Development of Cleaner Technologies: A Strategic Overview', *Business Strategy and the Environment*, Vol 1 (2), pp 51–8.

Ehrlich, P.R. (1968) *The Population Bomb*, Ballantine.

Ehrlich, P.R. and Ehrlich, A.H. (1990), *The Population Explosion*, Simon and Schuster.

Einsmann, H. (1992) 'The Environment: an Entrepreneurial Approach', *Long Range Planning*, Vol 25(4), pp 22–4.

Elgie, S.S. (1990) *Travel Problems and Opportunities – Turning Adversity to Advantage in the 1990s*, Elgie Stewart Smith.

El Kahal, S. (1994) *An Introduction to International Business*, Pitman.

Elkington, J. (1994) 'Toward the Sustainable Corporation: Win-Win-Win Business Strategies for Sustainable Development', *California Management Review*, Vol 36(2), pp 90–100.

Elkington, J. and Hailes, J. (1988) *The Green Consumer Guide*, Victor Gollanz.

Elkington, J., Knight, P. and Hailes, J. (1991) *The Green Business Guide*, Victor Gollanz.

Etzioni, A. (1988) *The Moral Dimension, Towards a New Economics*, Free Press.

Evans, J.R. and Berman, B. (1982) *Marketing Management*, Macmillan.

Farmer, R.N. (1967) 'Would You Want Your Daughter to Marry a Marketing Man?', *Journal of Marketing*, Vol 31(1), p 1.

Feldman, S. (1988) 'Structure and Consistency in Public Opinion: The Role of Core Beliefs and Values', *American Journal of Political Science*, Vol 32, pp 416–40.

Field, R. and Phillips, N. (1992) 'The Environmental Crisis in the Office: Why Aren't Managers Managing the Office Environment?', *Journal of General Management*, Vol 18(1), pp 35–50.

Fiori, J. (1989) 'How Green Are Europe's Consumers?', *Campaign*, 22 Sept, pp 39–40.

Fisk, G. (1973) 'Criteria for a Theory of Responsible Consumption', *Journal of Marketing*, Vol 37(2), pp 24–31.

Flodhammar, H. (1994) 'Ecologically Conscious Consumer Behaviour In A Comparative Study Between Great Britain and Sweden', *in* Bell, J. *et al* (eds) *Proceedings of the 1994 Marketing Education Group Conference*.

Ford, R. (1992a) 'Green Marketing', *in* Koechlin, D. and Muller, K. (eds) *Green Business Opportunities: The Profit Potential*, Pitman.

Ford, R. (1992b) 'The Green Organisation', *in* Koechlin, D. and Muller, K. (eds) *Green Business Opportunities: The Profit Potential*, Pitman.

Foote, E. (1981) 'Advertising and Tobacco', *Journal of the American Medical Association*, 245, pp 1667–8.

Friedman, J., 'Bulgaria's Deadly Secret', *Newsday*, 22 Apr 1990.

Gedye, R., 'Many Bins Make Hard Work in the Colour-Coded Eco-Kitchen', *Daily Telegraph*, 4 Mar 1993.

Gerstman and Meyers Inc. (1989) *Consumer Solid Waste Management: Awareness, Attitude and Behaviour Study*.

Gillespie, R.J. (1992) 'Pitfalls and Opportunities for Environmental Marketers', *Journal of Business Strategy*, Vol 13(4), pp 14–17.

Gist, R.R. (1971) *Marketing & Society: A Conceptual Introduction*, Hall, Rinehart & Winston.

Goldman, R. (1992) *Reading Ads Socially*, Routledge.

Goldsmith, E. (1993) 'A Strategy for Ensuring the Habitability of Our Planet', *RSA Journal*, Jan/Feb, pp 23–31.

Goldthorpe, J.H. *et al* (1969) *The Affluent Worker in the Class Structure*, Cambridge University Press.

Gray, R. (1990) 'The Accountant's Task As A Friend To The Earth', *Accountancy*, Vol 105(1162), pp 65–9.

Grayson, L. (1992) *BS 7750: What the New Environmental Management Standard Means for Your Business*, Technical Communications Publications.

Greenley, G.E. (1986) *The Strategic and Operational Planning of Marketing*, McGraw-Hill.

Green MarketAlert (1993) 'Environmental Promotions: Alive, Well and Ambitious', *Green MarketAlert*, Sept, p 8.

Greeno, J.L. and Robinson, S.N. (1992) 'Rethinking Corporate Environmental Management', *Columbia Journal of World Business*, Vol 27(3/4), pp 222–32.

Grieshop, J.I. and Stiles, M.C. (1989) 'Risk and Home-Pesticide Users', *Environment and Behaviour*, Vol 21, pp 699–716.

Grunert, S.C. (1993) 'Green Consumerism in Denmark: Some Evidence From the OKO Foods Project', *Der Markt*, 3, pp 140–51.

Gummesson, E. (1987) 'The New Marketing', *Long Range Planning*, Vol 20(4), pp 10–20.

Gunter, V.J. and Finlay, B. (1988) 'Influences in Group Participation in Environmental Conflicts', *Rural Sociology*, Vol 53, pp 498–505.

Halal, W.E. (1986) 'The New Management: Business and Social Institutions for the Information Age', *Business in the Contemporary World*, Vol 2(2), pp 41–54.

Harrison, B. (1990), 'The American Experience', Public Relations special issue, *The Greening of PR*, Vol 8 (5), pp. 8–9.

Harrison, E.B. (1992) 'Achieving Sustainable Communications', *Columbia Journal of World Business*, Vol 27(3/4), pp 242–7.

Hay, R. and Gray, E.R. (1974) 'Social Responsibilities of Managers', *Academy of Management Journal*, Vol 17(1), pp 135–43.

Heeg, F.J. (1984) 'Recycling Management', *Management-Zeitschrift io*, Vol 53(11).

Henderson, H. (1991) 'New Markets, New Commons, New Ethics: A Guest Essay', *Accountancy, Auditing and Accountability Journal*, Vol 4(3), pp 73–80.

Henion, K.E. (1972) 'The Effect of Ecologically Relevant Information on Detergent Sales', *Journal of Marketing Research*, Vol 9(1), pp 10–14.

Henion, K.E. and Kinnear, T.C. (1976) *Ecological Marketing*, American Marketing Association's First National Workshop on Ecological Marketing.

Hindle, P., White, P. and Minion, K. (1993) 'Achieving Real Environmental Improvements Using Value-Impact Assessment', *Long Range Planning*, Vol 26(3), pp 36–48.

Hinds, M.D.C., 'In Sorting Trash, Households Get Little Help From Industry', *New York Times*, 29 July 1989.

Hines, J.M., Hungerford, H.R. and Tomera, A.N. (1987) 'Analysis and Synthesis of Research on Responsible Behaviour: A Meta Analysis', *Journal of Environmental Education*, 18, pp 1–8.

Hines, R. (1991) 'On Valuing Nature', *Accounting Auditing and Accountability Journal*, Vol 4(3), pp 27–9.

Hochman, D., Wells, R.P., O'Connell, P.A. and Hochman, M.N. (1993) 'Total Quality Management: A Tool to Move from Compliance to Strategy', *Greener Management International*, 1, pp 59–70.

Hocking, R.W.D. and Power, S. (1993) 'Environmental Performance: Quality, Measurement and Improvement', *Business Strategy and Environment*, Vol 2(4), pp 19–24.

Hoffman, A.J. (1993) 'The Importance of Fit Between Individual Values and Organizational Culture in the Greening of Industry', *Business Strategy and the Environment*, Vol 2(4), pp 10–17.

Hofstede, G. (1983) 'The Cultural Relativity of Organizational Practices and Theories', *Journal of International Business Studies*, Fall, pp 75–89.

Holcombe, J. (1990) 'How The Greens Have Grown', *Business and Society Review*, Fall, pp 20–5.

Holliman, J. (1971) *Consumer's Guide to the Protection of the Environment*, Pan/Ballantine.

Holloway, M. and Wallich, P. (1994) 'How Green Is My Label?', *Scientific American*, May, p 86.

Homer, S. (1989) 'How Going Green Can Change Customer Perceptions', *Industrial Marketing Digest*, Vol 14(4), pp 67–74.

Hopfenbeck, W. (1993) *The Green Management Revolution: Lessons in Environmental Excellence*, Prentice Hall.

Houston, F.S. (1986) 'The Marketing Concept: What It Is and What It Is Not', *Journal of Marketing*, Vol 50(2), pp 81–7.

Hume, S. and Strand, P. (1989) 'Consumers Go Green', *Advertising Age*, Vol 60(41), p 3.

Hunkin, T. (1988) 'Things People Throw Away', *New Scientist*, 24 Dec, pp 38–40.

Hunt, C.B. and Auster, E.R. (1991) 'Proactive Environmental Management: Avoiding the Toxic Trap', *Sloan Management Review*, Winter, pp 7–18.

Hutchinson, C. (1992) 'Environmental Issues: The Challenge for the Chief Executive', *Long Range Planning*, Vol 25(3), pp 50–9.

Hutt, W.E. (1936), *Economists and the Public*, Jonathon Cape.

IBE (1988), *Company Philosophies and Codes of Business Ethics*, Institute of Business Ethics.

Illich, I. (1981) *Vernacular Values*, Marian Boyers.

Irvine, S. (1990) 'Green Camouflage', *Campaign*, 16 Feb, pp 42–3.

Irwin, A. and Hooper, P.D. (1992) 'Clean Technology, Successful Innovation and the Greening of Industry: A Case Study Analysis', *Business Strategy and the Environment*, Vol 1(2), pp 1–12.

Iyer, E. and Banerjee, B. (1993) 'Anatomy of Green Advertising', *Advertising Age*, Vol 20, pp 494–501.

Izatt, J. (1992) 'EC Forces Firms to Talk Rubbish', *Marketing Week*, 2 Oct, pp 35–8.

Jacobs, M. (1991) *The Green Economy: Environment, Sustainable Development and the Politics of the Future*, Pluto Press.

Jacoby, J., Berning, C.K. and Dietvorst, T.F. (1977) 'What About Disposition?', *Journal of Marketing*, Vol 41(3), p 23.

Jain, S.C. (1987) *International Marketing Management* (2nd edn.), Kent Publishing.

James, B.G. (1985) *Business Wargames*, Penguin.

James, P. (1994) 'Business Environmental Performance Measurement', *Business Strategy and the Environment*, Vol 3(2), pp 59–67.

Johnson, C. (1991) *The Green Dictionary*, Macdonald Optima.

Jolly, I. and Charter, M. (1992) 'Greener Logistics', *in* Charter, M. (ed) *Greener Marketing*, Greenleaf.

Jones, M. (1993) 'Going Green in the USA', *Certified Accountant*, Nov, pp 33–4.

Jones, R.R. (1987) 'Ozone Depletion and Cancer Risk', *The Lancet*, 22 Aug, p 443.

Kahn, R.L. *et al* (1976) *The Next 200 Years*, Associated Business Programmes.

Kamena, K.W. (1991) 'Plastics, Packaging and the Environment – A USA Perspective', paper presented to the conference organised by Papra Technology and Pira International 'Is Plastics Packaging Rubbish?', London, 30–1 Jan.

Kangun, N., Carlson, L. and Grove, S. (1991) 'Environmental Advertising Claims: A Preliminary Investigation', *Journal of Public Policy and Marketing*, Vol 10 (Fall), pp 47–58.

Kardash, W.J. (1974) 'Corporate Responsibility and the Quality of Life: Developing the Ecologically Concerned Consumer', *in* Henion, K.E. and Kinnear, T.C. (eds) *Ecological Marketing*, American Marketing Association.

Kellner, D. (1992) 'Popular Culture and the Construction of Post-Modern Identities', *in* Lash, S. and Friedman, J. (eds) *Modernity and Identity*, Basil Blackwell.

Kerby, J.K. (1972) 'The Marketing Concept: Suitable Guide to Product Strategy', *Business Quarterly*, Vol 37(3), pp 31–5.

Kiernan, M.J. (1992) 'The Eco-Industrial Revolution', *Business in the Contemporary World*, Vol 4(4), pp 133–43.

King, S. (1985) 'Has Marketing Failed, or Was It Never Really Tried?', *Journal of Marketing Management*, Vol 1(1), pp 1–19.

Kinnear, T.C., Taylor, J.R. and Sadrudin, A.A. (1974) 'Ecologically Concerned Consumers: Who Are They?', *Journal of Marketing*, Vol 38(2), pp 20–4.

Kleiner, A. (1991) 'What Does It Mean To Be Green?', *Harvard Business Review*, Vol 69(4), pp 38–47.

Koechlin, D. and Müller, K. (1992) *Green Business Opportunities: The Profit Potential*, Pitman.

Kordupleski, R.E., Rust, R.E., and Zahorik, A.J. (1993) 'Why Improving Quality Doesn't Improve Quality (or Whatever Happened to Marketing ?)', *California Management Review*, Vol. 35 (3), pp. 82–95.

Kotler, P. (1988) *Marketing Management: Analysis, Planning, Implementation and Control* (6th edn), Prentice Hall.

Kotler, P. (1994) *Marketing Management: Analysis, Planning, Implementation and Control* (7th edn), Prentice Hall.

Krause, D. (1993) *Environment and Behaviour*, Vol 25(1), pp 126–42.

Krusche, P. *et al* (1982) *Ökologisches Bauen*, Umweltbundesamt, Wiesbaden, Berlin.

Kulik, A. (1993), 'Differing Recycling Symbols Confuse German Consumers', *World Wastes*, Vol 36 (2), pp. 14–19.

LaBand, D.N. 'In Hugo's Path, A Man-Made Disaster', *Wall Street Journal*, 27 Sept 1989, p 22.

Laczniak, G.R. (1983) 'Business Ethics, A Manager's Primer', *Business*, Jan–Feb, pp 23–9.

Larson, M. (1990) 'Consumers Grapple With "Green" Packaging', *Packaging*, Vol 35(9), pp 8–10.

Laughlin B. and Varangu, L.K. (1991) 'Accounting for Waste or Garbage Accounting: Some Thoughts from Non-accountants', *Accountancy, Auditing and Accountability Journal*, Vol 4(3), pp 43–50.

Lawson, R. and Wall, S. (1993) 'Consumer Perception of Packaging Materials', *Proceedings of the 1993 Marketing Educators' Group Conference*.

Leaming, G.F. (1990) 'Capitalize Quickly on "Environment Increment" but Beware of Fads', *Marketing News*, Vol 24, 19 Mar, p 15.

Lean, G. and Hinrichsen, D. (1992), *Atlas of the Environment*, Helicon.

Ledgerwood, G., Street, E. and Therivel, R. (1992) *Environmental Audits and Business Strategy*, Pitman.

Ledgerwood G. and Street, E (1993) 'Corporate Strategy and Environmental Sustainability: Establishing an Environmental Market Ethos to Gain Competitive Advantage', *Greener Management International*, 3, pp. 41–9.

Lent, T. and Wells, R.P. (1992) 'Corporate Environmental Quality Study Shows Shift from Compliance to Strategy', *Total Quality Environmental Management*, Summer, pp 379–94.

Levin, G. (1990) 'Consumers Turning Green: JWT', *Advertising Age*, Vol 61.

Levitt, T. (1960) 'Marketing Myopia', *Harvard Business Review*, Vol 38(4), pp 45–56.

Levitt, T. (1970) 'The Morality (?) of Advertising', *Harvard Business Review*, Vol 48(4), pp 84–92.

Loudon, D.L. and Della Bitta, A.J. (1993) *Consumer Behaviour: Concepts and Applications*, McGraw-Hill.

Lovins, A.B. (1973) *Openpit Mining*, Earth Island.

Lovins, A.B. (1990) 'Utilities Conserve to Compete', *Best of Business International*, Vol 1 (3), p 56.

Lowe, P. and Goyder, J. (1983), *Environmental Groups in Politics*, George Allen and Unwin.

Luthans, F., Hodgetts, R.M., and Thompson, K.R. (1990) *Social Issues In Business*, (6th edn), Macmillan.

Lynn, M. (1991) 'Can The Environment Survive The Recession?', *Accountancy*, Sept, pp 76–7.

MacKenzie, D. (1990) 'Cheaper Alternatives to CFCs', *New Scientist*, 30 June, pp 13–14.

Mahon, J.F. and Kelly, P.C. (1987) 'Managing Toxic Wastes – After Bhopal and Sandoz', *Long Range Planning*, Vol 20(4), pp 50–9.

Marketing News (1990) 'Bonjour Tags Environment for PSA Campaign', *Marketing News*, Vol 24, 19 Mar, p 17.

Martin, B. and Simintiras, A.C. (1994) 'Determinants of Green Purchase Behaviour: A Review of the Literature and an Agenda for Future Research', *in Marketing: Unity and Diversity, Proceedings of the 1994 Marketing Educators Group Conference*, pp 628–37.

Maslow, A. (1954) *Motivation and Personality*, Harper and Row.

Mason, J. (1991) 'Direct Marketing: Promotion Without Pollution', *Sales and Marketing Manager Canada*, Vol 32(10), pp 9–11.

Mastrandonas, A. and Strife, P. (1992) 'Corporate Environmental Communications: Lessons from Investors', *Columbia Journal of World Business*, Vol 27(3/4), pp 234–40.

McBratney, K. (ed) (1990) *You and the Environment: Balanced Advice for Consumers on the Pros and Cons of Going Green*, Which? Books.

McCarthy, E.J. (1960) *Basic Marketing*, Irwin.

McCormick, J. (1989) *The Global Environmental Movement: Reclaiming Paradise*, Belhaven Press.

McDonagh, P. (1994) 'Towards an Understanding of What Constitutes Green Advertising as a Form of Sustainable Communication', Cardiff Business School Working Paper in Marketing and Strategy.

McDougall, G.H.G. (1994) 'The Green Movement in Canada: Implications for Marketing Strategy', *Journal of International Consumer Marketing*, Vol 5(3), pp 69–87.

McFate, K. (1991) *Poverty, Inequality and the Crisis of Social Policy*, Joint Centre for Political and Economic Studies, Washington DC.

McIntosh, A. (1990) 'The Impact of Environmental Issues on Marketing and Politics in the 1990s', *Journal of the Market Research Society*, Vol 33(3), pp 205–17.

McIntyre, R.P., Meloche, M.S. and Lewis, S.L.,(1992) 'National Culture as a Macro Tool For Environmental Sensitivity Segmentation', *in Allen, C.T. et al (eds), Marketing Theory and Applications, Proceedings of the 1992 AMA Winter Educators' Conference, Chicago*, pp 407–12.

McKenna, R. (1990) 'Marketing is Everything', *Harvard Business Review*, Vol 68(1), pp 65–79.

McMurdo, L. (1991) 'A New Discipline', *Marketing Week*, 6 Dec, pp 34–7.

Mead, M. (1970) 'Responsible Simplification of Consumption Patterns', *Ekistics*, Vol 30, Oct, pp 324–6.

Meadows, D.H., Meadows, D.L., Randers, J. and Behrens, W.W. (1972) *The Limits to Growth*, Universe Books.

Meadows, D.H., Meadows, D.L. and Randers, J. (1992), *Beyond the Limits*, Earthscan.

Medawar, C. (1978), *The Social Audit Consumer Handbook*, Macmillan.

Melchett, P. (1990) 'Time and Again the UK is Proved Wrong', *Public Relations special issue, The Greening of PR*, Vol 8(5), pp 32–4.

Midgely, M. (1992) *Science as Salvation*, Routledge.

Miller, C. (1993) 'Conflicting Studies Still Have Execs Wondering What Data to Believe', *Marketing News*, Vol 27(12), p 1.

Miller, J. and Szekely, F. (1994) 'Van Leer's Steel Drum Collection System', *Greener Management International*, 7, pp 74–94.

Mintzberg, H. (1988) 'Opening Up the Definition of Strategy, *in* Quinn, J.B. *et al* (eds) *The Strategy Process*, Prentice Hall.

Mintzberg, H. (1994) *The Rise and Fall of Strategic Planning*, Prentice Hall.

Miracle, G.E. (1969) 'Product Characteristics and Marketing Strategy', *Journal of Marketing*, Vol 33(1).

Mitchell, A. (1989) 'Milking The Greens', *Marketing*, 14 Sept, pp 34–5.

Mitchell, A. and Levy, L. (1989) 'Green About Greens', *Marketing*, 14 Sept, pp 28–33.

Morris D. (1991) 'As If Materials Mattered', *The Amicus Journal*, Fall, pp 17–18.

Morris, D. (1994) *The Human Animal*, BBC Publications.

Mulhall, D. (1992) 'Environmental Management: The Relationship Between Pressure Groups and Industry – a Radical Redesign', *in* Koechlin, D. and Müller, K. (eds) *Green Business Opportunities*, Pitman.

Mulhern, F.J. (1992) 'Consumer Wants and Consumer Welfare', *in* Allen, T.C. *et al* (eds) *Marketing Theory and Applications, Proceedings of the 1992 AMA Winter Educators' Conference*, pp 407–12.

Murphy, C. (1993) 'Thyme and Potion', *Marketing Week*, 11 June, pp. 30–3.

Myers, N. (1985) *The Gaia Atlas of Planet Management*, Pan Books.

Nash, T. (1990) 'Green About The Environment', *Director*, Vol 43(7), pp 40–4.

Neilssen, N. and Scheepers, P. (1992) 'Business Strategy and the Environment: The Need for Information About Environmental Consciousness and Behaviour', *Business Strategy and the Environment*, Vol 1(2), pp 13–23.

Neuman, K. (1986) 'Personal Values and Commitment to Energy Conservation', *Environment and Behaviour*, Vol 19(1), pp 53–74.

Nielsen, L.J. (1991) 'Measurement Techniques in Packaging Waste Management, *Proceedings of Corporate Quality/Environment Management Conference*, 9–10 Jan, Washington DC.

Nieuwenhuis, P. and Wells, P. (1992), *The Green Car Guide*, Green Print.

Nieuwenhuis, P. (1994) 'The Environmental Implications of Just-In-Time Supply in Japan – Lessons for Europe?', *Logistics Focus*, Vol 2(3), pp 2–4.

Nohrstead, S.A. (1993) 'Communicative Action in the Risk Society: Public Relations Strategies, the Media and Nuclear Power', *in* Hansen, A. (ed) *The Mass Media and Environmental Issues*, Leicester University Press, pp 81–104.

Nordic Environment (1991) *Nordic Environment*, 9, p 2.

Norman, P. 'A Cool Look At Global Warming', *Financial Times*, 26 Apr, 1993, p. 17.

North, K. (1992) *Environmental Business Management: An Introduction*, ILO.

OECD (1991) *The State of the Environment*, OECD.

Ohmae, K. (1982) *The Mind of the Strategist*, McGraw-Hill.

Opschoor, J.B. and Vos, H.B. (1989) *Economic Instruments for Environmental Protection*, OECD.

Otter, J. (1992) 'Some Aspects of Environmental Management Within a Chemical Corporation', *in* Koechlin, D. and Müller, K. (eds), *Green Business Opportunities: The Profit Potential*, Pitman.

Ottman, J.E. (1992a) 'Industry's Response to Green Consumerism', *Journal of Business Strategy*, Vol 13(4), pp 3–7.

Ottman, J.E. (1992b) 'The Four Es Make Going Green Your Competitive Edge', *Marketing News*, Vol 26(3), p 7.

Oxfam (1993) 'Which Way From Rio?', *Oxfam News – Environmental Issues Special*, Autumn.

Packard, V. (1957) *The Hidden Persuaders*, Penguin.

Palmer, A. and Worthington, I. (1992) *The Business and Marketing Environment*, McGraw-Hill.

Pearce, D. (1990) *Report on Sustainable Development*, UK Department of Energy.

Peat Marwick Mitchell (1990) *Business and the Environment*, Peat Marwick Mitchell.

Peattie, K.J. (1990) 'Painting Marketing Education Green: Or How to Recycle Old Ideas', *Journal of Marketing Management*, Vol 6(2), pp 105–27.

Peattie, K. (1992) *Green Marketing*, Pitman.

Peattie, K. and Charter, M. (1994), 'Green Marketing', *in* Baker, M. J. (ed) *The Marketing Book* (3rd edn), Butterworth Heinemann.

Peattie, K.J. and Notley, D.S. (1989) 'The Marketing and Strategic Planning Interface', *Journal of Marketing Management*, Vol 4(3), pp 330–49.

Peattie, K. and Ratnayaka, M. (1992) 'Greener Industrial Marketing', *Industrial Marketing Management*, Vol 21(2), pp 103–10.

Peattie, K. and Ringler, A. (1994) 'Management and the Environment: A Comparison Between the UK and Germany', *European Management Journal*, Vol 12(2), pp 216–25.

Peattie, K., Goode, M. and Moutinho, L. (1992) *Resolving the Tourism Paradox: The Marketing Challenge for Local Authorities*, Service Industries Management Research Unit Working Paper, p 11.

Peattie, S. and Peattie, K. (1994) 'Sales Promotion', *in* Baker, M.J. (ed) *The Marketing Book* (3rd ed), Butterworth-Heinemann.

Penman, I. (1994) 'Environmental Policy Development and Implementation: A Case Profile of Excel Logistics', *Greener Management International*, 6, pp 72–6.

Penzer, E. (1990) 'Turning Green', *Incentive Marketing*, Vol 167(7), pp 26–7 and 128.

Peters, T. (1992) *Liberation Management*, Macmillan.

Piercy, N.F. (1992) *Market Led Strategic Change*, Butterworth–Heinemann.

Piercy, N.F. and Morgan, N.A. (1993) 'Strategic and Operational Market Segmentation: a Managerial Analysis', *Journal of Strategic Marketing*, Vol 1(1), pp 123–40.

Polonsky, M., Zeffane, R. and Medley, P. (1992) 'Corporate Environmental Commitment in Australia: A Sectoral Comparison', *Business Strategy and the Environment*, Vol. 1(2), pp 25–39.

Popcorn, F. (1992) *The Popcorn Report: Revolutionary Trend Predictions for Marketing in the 1990s*, Century Business.

Popoff, F. (1990) 'Keeping Our Balance', *Business Horizons*, Vol 33(1), pp 113–17.

Porter, M.E. (1979) 'How Competitive Forces Shape Strategy', *Harvard Business Review*, Mar/Apr, pp 137–45

Porter, M.E (1985) *Competitive Advantage*, Free Press, New York.

Post, J.E. (1990) 'The Greening of Management', *Issues in Science and Technology*, Summer, pp 68–72.

Potter, J.F. (1993) 'A More Positive Outlook', *The Environmentalist*, Vol 14 (2), pp. 81–3.

Power, S.J. and Cox, C. (1994) 'Value-driven Organisations: A Look at the New Corporate Environmentalism', *Greener Management International*, 5, pp 29–35.

Prothero, A. (1990) 'Green Consumerism and the Societal Marketing Concept – Marketing Strategies for the 1990s', *Journal of Marketing Management*, Vol 6(2), pp 87–103.

Purchasing (1993) 'It's Not Easy Buying Green', *Purchasing*, Vol 115(9), pp 31–2.

Rawsthorn, A. and Zagor, K. 'Gunning for "Green Con" Commercials', *Financial Times*, 21 June 1990, p 13.

Reekie, W.D. (1979) *Advertising and Price*, The Advertising Association.

Rehak, R. (1993a) *Greener Marketing and Advertising*, Environmental Marketing and Advertising Council, Rodale Press.

Rehak, R. (1993b) 'Green Marketing Awash in Third Wave', *Advertising Age*, Vol 64(49), p 22.

Reich, R.B. (1991) *The Work of Nations: Preparing Ourselves for 21st Century Capitalism*, Alfred A. Knopf.

Research 2000 (1990) *Consumers and The Environment: The Impact of Environmental Change on Attitudes and Purchasing Behaviour*, Environmental Attitudes Survey No. 1.

Ries, A. and Trout, J. (1986) *Marketing Warfare*, McGraw-Hill.

Roberts, C.B. (1991) 'Environmental Disclosures: A Note on Reporting Practices in Mainland Europe', *Accounting, Auditing and Accountability Journal*, Vol 4(3), pp 62–71.

Robinson, S. (1990) *Healthier Profits: Business, Success and the Green Factor*, Environment Foundation.

Rock, S. (1989) 'Are Greens Good For You?', *Director*, Jan, pp 40–50.

Rolston C.P. and di Benedetto, C.A. (1994) 'Developing a Greenness Scale: An Exploration of Behaviour Versus Attitude', *in* Park, C.W. and Smith, D.C. (eds) *Marketing Theory and Applications, Proceedings of 1994, AMA Winter Educators' Conference*.

Roome, N. and Hinnells, M. (1992) *Managing Environmental Factors in Product Development*, paper presented to the 1992 Business Strategy and the Environment Conference, Leicester.

Rothenberg, S., Maxwell, J. and Marcus, A. (1992) 'Issues in the Implementation of Proactive Environmental Strategies', *Business Strategy and the Environment*, Vol 1(4), pp 1–12.

Rothschild, M.J. (1987) *Marketing Communications: From Fundamentals to Strategy*, D.C. Heath & Co.

Rothwell, R., Gardiner, P. and Schott, K. (1983) *Design and the Economy*, The Design Council.

Ruckelhaus, W.D. (1991) 'Quality in the Corporation: The Key to Sustainable Development', *Proceedings of the First Conference on Corporate Quality/Environmental Management*, Washington DC, pp 5–9.

Russell, C.B. (1976) 'Economical, Ecological Packaging', *in* Henion K.E. and Kinnear T.C. (eds) *Ecological Marketing*, AMA.

Sachs, W.S. and Benson, G. (1978) 'Is it not time to discard the marketing concept?', *Business Horizons*, Vol 21(4), pp 68–74.

Saemann, R. (1992) 'The Environment and the Need for New Technology, Empowerment and Ethical Values', *Columbia Journal of World Business*, Vol 27(3/4), pp 187–93.

Salzman, J. (1991) 'Green Labels for Consumers', *The OECD Observer*, No 169, pp 28–30.

Samdahl, D.M. and Robertson, R. (1989) 'Social Determinants of Environmental Concern', *Environment and Behaviour*, Vol 21(1), pp 57–81.

Sawyer, S. (1992) 'Conscience, Corporations and the "Green" Thing', *in How Green is Green*, IABC Communication World, Apr, pp 20–7.

Scerbinski, J. (1991) 'Consumers and the Environment: A Focus on Five Products', *The Journal of Business Strategy*, Vol 13(4).

Schaltegger, S. and Sturm, A. (1992) 'Eco-controlling', in Koechlin, D. and Muller, K. (eds) *Green Business Opportunities*, Pitman Publishing, London.

Schann, J. and Holzer, E. (1990) 'Studies of Individual Environmental Concern: The Role of Knowledge, Gender and Background Variables', *Environment and Behaviour*, Vol 22(6), pp 767–86.

Schlossberg, H. (1993a) 'Consumers More Aware, Still Want More Info.', *Marketing News*, Vol 25(25), p 6.

Schlossberg, H. (1993b), 'Hardware Industry Understands Importance of Going Green', *Marketing News*, Vol 25, 11 Oct, p 10.

Schmidheiny, S. (1992) 'The Business Logic of Sustainable Development', *Columbia Journal of World Business*, Vol 27(3/4), pp 19–26.

Schramm, W. (1954) 'How Communication Works', *in* Schramm, W. (ed) *The Process and Effects of Mass Communications*, University of Illinois Press.

Schumacher, E.F. (1973) *Small Is Beautiful: Economics as if People Mattered*, Harper and Row.

Schumacher, E.F. (1979) *Good Work*, Harper and Row.

Schwartz, W. and Schwartz, D. (1987) *Breaking Through*, Green Books.

Schwepker, C.H. and Cornwall, T.B. (1991) 'An Examination of Ecologically Concerned Consumers and Their Intention to Purchase Ecologically Packaged Goods', *Journal of Public Policy and Marketing*, Vol

10(2), pp 77–101.

Scitsovsky, T. (1976) *The Joyless Economy*, Oxford University Press.

Senge, P. (1990) *The Fifth Discipline: The Art and Practice of the Learning Organization*, Doubleday.

Seymour, J. and Giradet, H. (1987) *Blueprint for a Green Planet*, Dorling Kindersley.

Shultz, D.E. (1987), 'Above or Below the Line? Growth of Sales Promotion in the United States', *International Journal of Advertising*, 6, pp 17–27.

Simintiras, A.C., Schlegelmilch, B.B. and Diamantopolous, A. (1993), '"Greening" the Marketing Mix: A Review of the Literature and an Agenda for Future Research', *in* Chias, J. and Sureda, J. (eds) *Marketing for the New Europe: Dealing with Complexity, Proceedings of the 22nd European Marketing Academy Conference*.

Simms, C. (1992) 'Green Issues and Strategic Management in the Grocery Retail Sector', *International Journal of Retail and Distribution Management*, Vol 20(1), pp 32–42.

Simon, F. (1992) 'Marketing Green Products in the Triad', *The Columbia Journal of World Business*, Vol 27(3/4), pp 268–85.

Singer, S.F. (1992) 'Sustainable Development vs. Global Environment: Resolving the Conflict', *Columbia Journal of World Business*, Vol 27(3/4), pp 155–61.

Smith, A. (1776) *The Wealth of Nations*, Strahan and Cadell.

Smith, C.N. (1988) 'Consumer Boycotts and Consumer Sovereignty', *European Journal of Marketing*, Vol 21(5), pp 6–19.

Smith, G. (1990) 'How Green Is My Valley?', *Marketing and Research Today*, Vol 18(2), pp 76–82.

Smuts, J. (1920) *Holism and Evolution*, Macmillian.

Speirs, J. (1993) 'The Value of Environmental Reporting', *Greener Management International*, 1, pp 18–23.

Stacey, M. (1960) *Tradition and Change: A Study of Banbury*, Oxford University Press.

Stander, D.M. (1973) 'Testing New Product Ideas in an "Archie Bunker" World', *Marketing News*, Vol 7, 15 Nov, p 3.

Stead, W.E. and Stead, J.G. (1992) *Management for a Small Planet: Strategic Decision Making and the Environment*, Sage.

Stenross, M. and Sweet, G. (1992) 'Implementing an Integrated Supply Chain: The Xerox Example' *in* Christopher, M., *Logistics and Supply Chain Management*, Pitman Publishing, London.

Stevens, C. (1992) 'The Environment Industry', *The OECD Observer*, No 177, pp 26–8.

Stevens, C. (1993) 'Do Environmental Policies Affect Competitiveness?', *The OECD Observer*, No 183, pp 22–8.

Strid, S. and Cater, N. (1993) 'Eco-Ads', *Tomorrow*, 2, pp 45–50.

Strong, C. (1994) 'What Influences Grocery Retail Buyers To Select Environmentally Responsive Products', *in Proceedings of the 1994 Marketing Educators' Group Conference*.

Sutter, S. (1989) 'The Green Wars', *Marketing*, 9 July, p 9.

Swindley, D. (1991) 'The Role of the Buyer in UK Multiple Retailing', *in Proceedings of the 1991 SIMRU Conference Cardiff*.

Sykes, L. (1993) 'Changing your Tuna', *Green Magazine*, Jan, pp 44–5.

Szymankiewicz, J. (1993) 'Going Green: The Logistics Dilemma', *Focus on Logistics and Distribution Management*, Vol 12(5), pp 36–8.

Talwar, R. (1993) 'Business Re-engineering – a Strategy-Driven Approach', *Long Range Planning*, Vol 26(6), pp 22–40.

Tellis, G.J. (1986) 'Beyond The Many Faces of Price', *Journal of Marketing*, Vol 50(5), pp 146–60.

Tellis, G.J. and Crawford, M.C. (1981) 'An Evolutionary Approach to Growth Theory', *Journal of Marketing*, Vol 45(4), pp 125–32.

Tellis, G.J. and Gaeth, G.J. (1990) 'Best Value, Price-seeking and Price Aversion: The Impact of Learning and Information on Consumer Choices', *Journal of Marketing*, Vol. 54 (April), pp. 34–45.

Tennant, T. 'Time For Polluters to Come Clean', *The Independent on Sunday*, 14 Mar 1993.

Tennant, T. and Campanale, M. (1991) 'A Long Term Investment', *in Environment Strategy 1991*, Campden Publishing.

TEST (1991) *The Wrong Side of The Tracks?*, Transport and Environment Studies.

Toffler, A. (1970) *Future Shock*, Random House.

Tomlinson, A. (1990) 'Consumer Culture and the Aura of the Commodity', *in* Tomlinson, A. (ed) *Consumption, Identity and Style*, Routledge.

Toor, M. (1992) 'ISBA's Green Code Delays Government Legislation', *Marketing*, 30 Jan, p 8.

Toyne, P. (1993) *Environmental Responsibility: An Agenda for Further and Higher Education*, HMSO.

Troy, L.C. (1994) 'Consumer Environmental Consciousness: A Conceptual Framework and Exploratory Investigation', *in* Cravens, D.W. and Dickson, P.R. (eds) *Enhancing Knowledge Development in Marketing, Proceeding of the 1993 Summer AMA Educators' Conference*, pp 106–13.

Turner, R.K. (1992) 'An Economic Incentive Approach to Regulating the Throwaway Society', *European Environment*, Vol 3(2), pp 2–8.

Tyler, G. (1992) 'Buyers Show Their Colours', *Purchasing and Supply Management*, July, pp 36–7.

UNEP/IEO (1988) *APELL Handbook*, United Nations Environment Programme.

UN Population Fund (1990) *The State of World Population*, United Nations Population Fund, New York.

Unterman, I. (1974) 'American Finance: Three Views of Strategy', *Journal of General Management*, Vol 1(3).

Vallely, B., 'Bungled Chance to Help Shoppers Buy Green', *The Independent*, 1 June 1993.

Vandermerwe, S. and Oliff, M. (1990) 'Customers Drive Corporations Green', *Long Range Planning*, Vol 23(6), pp 10–16.

Van Liere, K.D. and Dunlap, R.E. (1981) 'Environmental Concern: Does It Make a Difference? How Is It Measured?', *Environment and Behaviour*, Vol 13(6), pp 651–76.

Varadarajan, P.R. and Thirunarayana, P.N. (1990) 'Consumers' Attitudes Towards Marketing Practices, Consumerism and Government Regulations: Cross National Perspectives', *European Journal of Marketing*, Vol 24(6), pp 6–23.

Veblen, T. (1899) *The Theory of the Leisure Class*, Macmillan.

Vidal, J., 'Shopping for a Paler Shade of Green', *The Guardian*, 7 April 1993, p 20.

Waddington, C.H. (1941) *The Scientific Attitude*, Penguin.

Wall, D. (1990) *Getting There: Steps Towards a Green Society*, Green Print, London.

Walley, N. and Whitehead, B. (1994) 'It's Not Easy Being Green', *Harvard Business Review*, Vol 72(3), pp 46–52.

Wasik, A. (1991) *Logistics Information Systems*.

Waterman, R.H., Peters, T.J. and Philips, J.R. (1980) 'Structure is not Strategy', *Business Horizons*.

Watts, R.L. and Zimmerman, J.L. (1986) *Positive Accounting Theory*, Prentice Hall.

WCED (1987) *Our Common Future*, UN World Commission on Environment and Development.

Webster, F.E. (1975) 'Determining the Characteristics of the Socially Conscious Consumer' *Journal of Consumer Research*, Vol 2 (Dec), pp 188–97.

Weissman, S.H. and Sekutowski, J.C. (1992) 'Environmentally Conscious Management: A Technology for the Nineties', *Total Quality Environmental Management*, Vol 1(4), pp 369–78.

Welford, R. and Gouldson, A. (1993) *Environmental Management and Business Strategy*, Pitman.

Wheeler, W.A. (1992) 'The Revival of Reverse Manufacturing', *The Journal of Business Strategy*, Vol 13(4), pp 8–13.

Williams, J. (1991) 'Cleaning The Air', *Investment Vision*, Feb/Mar, pp 76–8.

Wilson, D.C. and Rathje, W.L. (1990) 'Modern Middens', *Natural History*, May, pp 54–8.

Wind, Y. (1978) 'Issues and Advances in Segmentation Research', *Journal of Marketing Research*, Vol 15(3), pp 317–37.

Wind, Y. (1981) 'Marketing and the other Business Functions', *in* Sheth, J.N. (ed) *Research in Marketing*, 5, Jai Press.

Winters, L.C. (1990) 'The Greening of Marketing and Opinion Research', *Marketing Research*, Vol 1(4), pp 69–71.

Wong, J. (1988) 'Economic Incentives for the Voluntary Disclosure of Current Cost Financial Statements', *Journal of Accounting and Economics*, Vol 10(2), pp 151–67.

Wood, W. (1990) 'The End of The Product Lifecycle', *Journal of Marketing Management*, Vol 6(2), pp 145–55.

Woods, D.J. (1991) 'Toward Improving Corporate Social Performance', *Business Horizons*, Vol 34(4), pp 66–73.

Woodward, K.L. and Nordland, R. (1992) 'New Rules for an Old Faith', *Newsweek*, 30 Nov, p 71.

Worcester, R. (1993) 'Business and the Environment: The Weight of Public Opinion', *Admap*, 28 Jan, pp 71–5.

World Resources Institute (1992) *World Resources 1992–93: A Guide To The Global Environment*, Oxford University Press.

Yaranella, E.J. and Levine, R.S. (1992) 'Does Sustainable Development Lead to Sustainability?', *Futures*, Vol 24(8), pp 759–74.

Zeithaml, C.P. and Zeithaml, V. (1984) 'Environmental Marketing Management: Revising the Marketing Perspective', *Journal of Marketing*, Vol 48(2), pp 46–53.

INDEX